HULL–WHITE
ON DERIVATIVES

A COMPILATION OF ARTICLES
BY JOHN HULL AND ALAN WHITE
Faculty of Management
University of Toronto

Published by Risk Publications
104–112 Marylebone Lane, London W1M 5FU
Tel +44 (0)171 487 5326; Fax +44 (0)171 486 0879

This selection © Financial Engineering Ltd, London 1996

ISBN 1 899332 45 6

Designer: Judith Charlton
Typesetter: Eddie Mizzi

Printed and bound in Great Britain by Redwood Books, Trowbridge, Wiltshire

Contents

Part V. Term Structure Models: Implementation

Preface

This book brings together and sets in context important papers on derivatives written by John Hull and Alan White, two finance professors from the University of Toronto who have proved to be key theoreticians to the derivatives industry over the last decade. The papers discuss advanced techniques for hedging price exposures, valuing derivatives, and risk-managing derivative portfolios.

The first section of the book looks at the impact of stochastic volatility on the pricing and hedging of options. In effect, this section examines how to mitigate one of the key 'false' assumptions of the original Black–Scholes model for valuing options: that the volatility of the price of the underlying is constant. The second section of the book examines how trees and lattices provide an alternative to the more complicated implicit finite difference method when valuing derivative instruments; it includes applications of the control variate technique and computationally efficient procedures for valuing path-dependent options. The third section describes various approaches to one of the most important emerging topics in the derivatives industry today: how to value and manage the credit risk generated by derivative instruments.

The final two sections examine the area in which the research of Hull and White has perhaps had the greatest impact: the valuation of interest rate options, and the related problem of how to build a no-arbitrage model of the term structure of interest rates. The chapters focus on the properties and implementation of the standard 'Hull–White model', but also include detailed comparative discussions of some alternative approaches and models.

The authors have provided new introductions to each section. These offer a unique perspective—with the advantage of hindsight—on both the strengths and occasional weaknesses of the republished papers. The introductions to the final two sections clarify the essence of the

Hull–White approach to interest rate derivatives, pointing out the most important refinements to their model and defining how, and in which circumstances, the model should be applied. Many of these clarifications represent responses to the needs and empirical findings of derivatives industry practitioners—an interesting example of the 'virtuous' circle that now links together cutting-edge theoretical work, like that of Hull and White, and the applied and empirical research undertaken within the industry.

Risk Publications
April 1996

I
Stochastic Volatility

1. Introduction: Stochastic volatility

The Black–Scholes option pricing model, like most of the other models that have been developed to price derivatives in the last 25 years, assumes that the volatility of the price of the underlying is constant. This assumption is convenient, but it does not reflect reality. As all traders know, the volatilities of equity prices, exchange rates, futures prices, interest rates, and other market variables change significantly from day to day. Indeed, option trading is often referred to as "trading volatility". The first part of this book (Chapters 2–4) discusses the impact of stochastic volatility on the pricing and hedging of options.

1.1 BASIC PRICING RESULTS

Chapter 2 presents some key results on the impact of stochastic volatility on option pricing. It shows that if a stock price and its volatility are instantaneously uncorrelated then the price of a European option on the stock is equal to the Black–Scholes price integrated over the probability distribution of the average variance rate. This result can easily be generalized so that it applies to all European-style derivatives (that is, all derivatives that provide a payoff at one particular future time), provided that the underlying, S, follows a process of the form

$$dS = \mu S \, dt + \sqrt{V} S \, dw. \tag{1.1}$$

In this process, dw is a Wiener process and μ is the drift rate. The variance rate V is stochastic, but instantaneously uncorrelated with S. Expressed algebraically, the result is

$$c = \int C(\bar{V}) g(\bar{V}) \, d\bar{V}, \tag{1.2}$$

where c is the value of the derivative assuming a stochastic volatility, $\bar{V}$ is the average variance rate during the life of the derivative, $g(\bar{V})$ is the probability distribution of $\bar{V}$ in a risk-neutral setting, and $C(V)$ is the price of the derivative assuming that the variance rate is constant and equal to V.[1]

The shape of the function $C(V)$ depends on the terms of the derivative. Consider a European call option on a non-dividend-paying stock. When the option is at the money, so that the initial stock price is the present value of the strike price, the function is as shown in Figure 1.1(a). It is concave for all values of V. It follows from equation (1.2) that a stochastic variance rate always has the effect of reducing the option price when the price of the underlying and its variance rate are uncorrelated. This is a surprising result since we naturally tend to associate more uncertainty with higher option prices.

When the option is significantly in the money or out of the money, the function $C(V)$ has the form shown in Figure 1.1(b). It is predominantly convex and a stochastic variance rate tends to increase the option price.

When the correlation between the price of the underlying and its variance rate is non-zero, the result in equation (1.2) does not hold. The reason for this is explained in Chapter 2. When the volatility is positively correlated with the price of the underlying, an increase in the underlying's price tends to be accompanied by an increase in volatility. This means that subsequent large price increases are more likely. As a result, relatively high prices of the underlying are more likely to occur and the price of out-of-the-money calls will rise. Similarly, the prices of out-of-the-money puts fall. Put–call parity ensures that the prices of in-the-money puts rise and in-the-money calls fall. When volatility is significantly negatively correlated with the price of the underlying, the impact of stochastic volatility is the reverse. It decreases the prices of out-of-the-money call options and in-the-money put options. It increases the prices of out-of-the-money put options and in-the-money call options.

What, in practice, is the correlation between the price of the underlying and its volatility? For foreign exchange and commodity futures prices, the assumption of zero correlation may be reasonable. But it is not appropriate for equities. Most theoretical and empirical research suggests that a stock price and its variance rate are negatively correlated. The underlying reason for this is straightforward. As a company's stock price declines, the company's leverage (that is, the ratio of the market value of

---

[1] The result in equation (1.2) cannot be generalized to American-style options since the decision to exercise early depends on the volatility level.

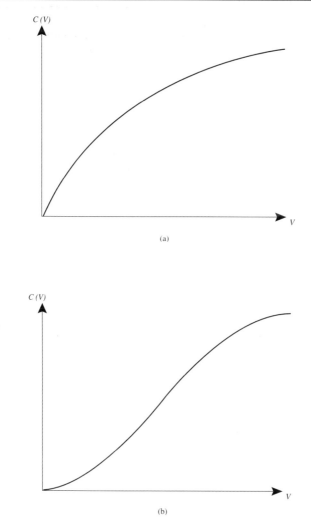

FIGURE 1.1. The Black–Scholes price as a function of its variance rate: (a) at-the-money option; (b) in-the-money or out-of-the-money option.

its debt to the market value of its equity) increases. This, in turn, leads to a higher volatility for the equity.

Figure 1.2 summarizes the main pricing results by showing the volatility smiles they imply. Figure 1.2(a, b, c) shows the expected volatility smile for the zero correlation, negative correlation, and positive correlation cases. Figure 1.2(a) corresponds to the type of volatility smile that is often observed in the market for foreign exchange options, while Figure 1.2(b) corresponds to that observed for equity options.

13

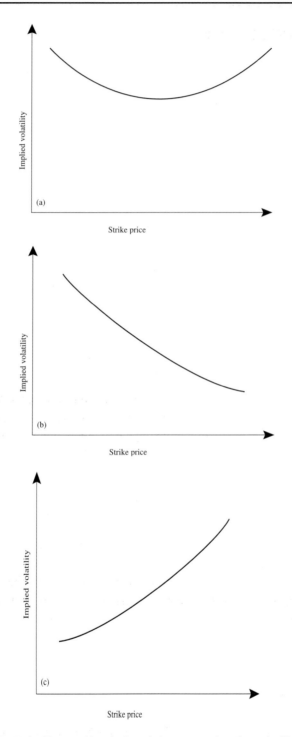

FIGURE 1.2. Volatility smiles induced by a stochastic volatility: (a) $\rho = 0$; (b) $\rho < 0$; (c) $\rho > 0$.

1.2 SERIES SOLUTIONS

There are very few analytic results for pricing derivatives when volatility is stochastic. Chapters 2 and 3 show that, when the volatility of volatility is not too large, option prices can be calculated in the form of a series. Chapter 2 considers a model where the variance rate V in equation (1.1) follows geometric Brownian motion:

$$dV = \mu V \, dt + \xi V \, dz. \tag{1.3}$$

Chapter 3 considers the model

$$dV = (a + bV) \, dt + \xi \sqrt{V} \, dz, \tag{1.4}$$

where $a > 0$ and $b < 0$. In this model, V follows a mean-reverting process, where the reversion rate is $-b$ and the reversion level is $-a/b$.

The model in Chapter 3 proves to be significantly more analytically tractable than the model in Chapter 2. Unlike the model in Chapter 2, it allows results to be produced for the situation where

(a) the correlation between dw and dz is non-zero; and
(b) the variance rate is mean-reverting.

Consider again a European-style derivative. Define Price 1 as the price assuming stochastic volatility and Price 2 as the price assuming that the variance is constant and equal to its expected average value during the life of the option. The excess of Price 1 over Price 2, which we will refer to as the pricing bias, is

$$f_1 \xi + f_2 \xi^2 + \cdots, \tag{1.5}$$

where f_1 and f_2 are given by equations (3.17) and (3.18). If ρ is significantly different from zero and ξ is small, the first term in equation (1.5) provides a reasonable estimate of the pricing bias. The sign of the pricing bias is then the same as the sign of $-\rho d_2$. When ρ is zero, f_1 is zero and the second term provides a reasonable estimate of the pricing bias. The bias is therefore negative when the condition in equation (3.20) is satisfied, and positive otherwise.

1.3 HEDGING

The impact of stochastic volatility on hedging strategies is considered in Chapters 3 and 4. Equation (3.21) shows how well traditional delta hedging works. W is a portfolio that is kept delta-neutral on the assumption that Black–Scholes holds. If the Black–Scholes model did in fact hold, the process for W would be deterministic. Under the stochastic volatility model, the process for W has two stochastic terms. The first term is

$$S\sqrt{V}\left(\frac{\partial C}{\partial S} - \frac{\partial c}{\partial S}\right) dz,$$

where, as before, C is the Black–Scholes price and c is the true stochastic volatility model price. This captures the effect of using the Black–Scholes model rather than a stochastic volatility model to calculate delta. The second term is

$$\xi\sqrt{V}\frac{\partial c}{\partial V} dw.$$

This captures the effect of failing to hedge against changes in the variance rate.

The absolute magnitude of the coefficient of dz in the first term is in general very small. This is reassuring. Practitioners are not making significant errors if they use Black–Scholes to calculate delta when the volatility is stochastic. The second term is significant and emphasizes the importance of doing vega as well as delta hedging. Chapter 3 shows that the vega risk is comparable to the risk of holding an unhedged position in the underlying asset.

Vega hedging involves taking a position in an option or other non-linear derivative. The same is true of gamma hedging. In practice, a trader usually has very few opportunities to introduce new options into a portfolio at competitive prices. When an opportunity does arise, it is important for the trader to know whether priority should be given to hedging gamma or vega. This question is addressed for foreign exchange options in Chapter 4.

Chapter 4 assumes the process for the variance rate is that shown in equation (1.3). A Taylor series expansion is used to calculate the variance of the change in the value of a portfolio. When delta plus vega hedging is employed, the variance of the value of the portfolio is given by equation (4.14). When delta plus gamma hedging is used, it is given by equation (4.15). Based on the assumption that true option prices are close to Black–Scholes prices, the criterion for delta plus vega hedging to be preferable to delta plus gamma hedging is surprisingly simple:

$$\xi > \frac{\sqrt{2\,\Delta t}}{T_1^*}. \tag{1.6}$$

In this equation Δt is the time between hedge rebalancing and T_1^* is the maturity of the option used for hedging. Interestingly, the composition of the portfolio is irrelevant provided that all options are assumed to be European. Making reasonable estimates for ξ, Chapter 4 shows that, with daily rebalancing, vega hedging is preferable to gamma hedging when the option being used has a maturity greater than about one month. The intuition behind the result in equation (1.6) is as follows. Long-term options tend to have small gammas and large vegas and are naturally more suited to hedging vega risk. Short-term options tend to have large gammas and small vegas and are naturally more suited to hedging gamma risk.

The final part of Chapter 4 tests the performance of the various hedging schemes considered using real data and compares different ways of implementing them. As expected, delta plus vega hedging performs better than delta hedging. Surprisingly, delta hedging performs better than delta plus gamma hedging. This is because the extra vega risk introduced into the portfolio by gamma hedging outweighs the reduction in the gamma risk. In the foreign exchange market, the theoretical and empirical evidence seems to indicate that vega hedging is significantly more important than gamma hedging. The best implementation procedure for all the hedging schemes appears to be to rebalance whenever the exchange rate has moved by a predetermined amount, rather than to rebalance at constant time intervals.

2. The pricing of options on assets with stochastic volatilities*

One option-pricing problem that has hitherto remained unsolved is the pricing of a European call on a stock that has a stochastic volatility. From the work of Merton (1973), Garman (1976), and Cox, Ingersoll, and Ross (1985), the differential equation that the option must satisfy is known. The solution of this differential equation is independent of risk preferences if (a) the volatility is a traded asset or (b) the volatility is uncorrelated with aggregate consumption. If either of these conditions holds, the risk-neutral valuation arguments of Cox and Ross (1976) can be used in a straightforward way. We can also use risk-neutral valuation arguments if we know the process for volatility in a risk-neutral world, rather than in the real world.

This paper produces a solution in series form for the situation in which the stock price is instantaneously uncorrelated with the volatility. We do not assume that volatility is a traded asset. Furthermore, a constant correlation between the instantaneous rate of change of the volatility and the rate of change of aggregate consumption can be accommodated. The option price is lower than the Black–Scholes price when the option is close to being at the money and higher when it is deep in or deep out of the money. The exercise prices for which overpricing by Black–Scholes takes place are within about ten percent of the security price. This is the range of exercise prices over which most option trading takes place, so we may, in general, expect the Black–Scholes price to overprice options. This effect is exaggerated as the time to maturity increases. One of the most surprising implications of this is that, if the Black–Scholes equation is used to determine the implied volatility of a near-the-money option, the longer the time to maturity the lower the implied volatility. Numerical solutions for

* This paper was first published in *Journal of Finance*, Vol. 42, No. 2 (June 1987). It is reprinted with permission of the *Journal of Finance*.

the case in which the volatility is correlated with the stock price are also examined.

The stochastic volatility problem has been examined by Merton (1976), Geske (1979), Johnson (1979), Johnson and Shanno (1985), Eisenberg (1985), Wiggins (1985), and Scott (1986). The Merton and Geske papers provide the solution to special types of stochastic volatility problems. Geske examines the case in which the volatility of the firm value is constant, so that volatility of the stock price changes in a systematic way as the stock price rises and falls. Merton examines the case in which the price follows a mixed jump–diffusion process. Johnson (1979) studies the general case in which the instantaneous variance of the stock price follows some stochastic process. However, in order to derive the differential equation that the option price must satisfy, he assumes the existence of an asset with a price that is instantaneously perfectly correlated with the stochastic variance. The existence of such an asset is sufficient to derive the differential equation, but Johnson was unable to solve it to determine the option price. Johnson and Shanno (1985) obtain some numerical results using simulation and produce an argument aimed at explaining the biases observed by Rubinstein (1985). Eisenberg (1985) examines how options should be priced relative to each other using pure arbitrage arguments. Numerical solutions are attempted by Wiggins (1985) and Scott (1986).

Section 2.1 of this paper provides a solution to the stochastic volatility option-pricing problem in series form. Section 2.2 discusses the numerical methods that can be used to examine pricing biases when the conditions necessary for the series solution are not satisfied. Section 2.3 investigates the biases that arise when the volatility is stochastic but when a constant volatility is assumed in determining option prices. Conclusions are in Section 2.4.

2.1 THE STOCHASTIC VOLATILITY PROBLEM

Consider a derivative asset f with a price that depends upon some security price S and its instantaneous variance $V = \sigma^2$, which are assumed to obey the following stochastic processes:

$$dS = \phi S\, dt + \sigma S\, dw, \qquad (2.1)$$

$$dV = \mu V\, dt + \xi V\, dz. \qquad (2.2)$$

The variable ϕ is a parameter that may depend on S, σ, and t. The variables μ and ξ may depend on σ and t, but, for the present, it is assumed that they do not depend on S. The Wiener processes dz and dw have correlation ρ. The process in equation (2.2) ensures that V is always positive. The risk-free rate, denoted by r, will be assumed to be constant or at least deterministic.

One reason why this problem has not previously been solved is that there is no asset that is clearly instantaneously perfectly correlated with the state variable σ^2. Thus, it does not seem possible to form a hedge portfolio that eliminates all the risk. However, as was shown by Garman (1976), a security f with a price that depends on state variables θ_i must satisfy the differential equation

$$\frac{\partial f}{\partial t} + \frac{1}{2}\sum_{i,j}\rho_{ij}\sigma_i\sigma_j\frac{\partial^2 f}{\partial\theta_i\partial\theta_j} - rf = \sum_i \theta_i\frac{\partial f}{\partial\theta_i}[-\mu_i + \beta_i(\mu^* - \mathbf{r})], \qquad (2.3)$$

where σ_i is the instantaneous standard deviation of θ_i, ρ_{ij} is the instantaneous correlation between θ_i and θ_j, μ_i is the drift rate of θ_i, β_i is the vector of multiple-regression betas for the regression of the state-variable "returns" $(d\theta/\theta)$ on the market portfolio and the portfolios most closely correlated with the state variables, μ^* is the vector of instantaneous expected returns on the market portfolio and the portfolios most closely correlated with the state variables, and $\mathbf{r}$ is the vector with elements that are the risk-free rate r. When variable i is traded, it satisfies the $(N+1)$-factor CAPM, and the ith element of the right-hand side of (2.3) is $-r\theta_i\,\partial f/\partial\theta_i$.

In the problem under consideration, there are two state variables, S and V, of which S is traded. The differential equation (2.3) thus becomes

$$\frac{\partial f}{\partial t} + \frac{1}{2}\left(\sigma^2 S^2\frac{\partial^2 f}{\partial S^2} + 2\rho\sigma^3\xi S\frac{\partial^2 f}{\partial S\partial V} + \xi^2 V^2\frac{\partial^2 f}{\partial V^2}\right) - rf$$

$$= -rs\frac{\partial f}{\partial S} - [\mu - \beta_V(\mu^* - \mathbf{r})]\sigma^2\frac{\partial f}{\partial V}, \qquad (2.4)$$

where ρ is the instantaneous correlation between S and V. The variable β_V is the vector of multiple-regression betas for the regression of the variance "returns" (dV/V) on the market portfolio and the portfolios most closely correlated with the state variables, and μ^* is as defined above. Note that, since these expected returns depend on investor risk preferences, this means that, in general, the option price will depend on investor risk preferences. For ease of exposition we shall assume that $\beta_V(\mu^* - r)$ is zero, or that volatility is uncorrelated with aggregate consumption. This assumption can easily be relaxed to $\beta_V(\mu^* - r)$ is constant by defining $\hat{\mu} = \mu - \beta_V(\mu^* - r)$ and then replacing μ by $\hat{\mu}$.

Alternatively, we can assume that equation (2.2) is the process for V in a risk-neutral world. The derivative asset must then satisfy

$$\frac{\partial f}{\partial t} + \frac{1}{2}\left(\sigma^2 S^2 \frac{\partial^2 f}{\partial S^2} + 2\rho\sigma^3 \xi S \frac{\partial^2 f}{\partial S \partial V} + \xi^2 V^2 \frac{\partial^2 f}{\partial V^2}\right) - rf$$

$$= -rs\frac{\partial f}{\partial S} - \mu\sigma^2 \frac{\partial f}{\partial V}. \qquad (2.5)$$

It will also be assumed at this point that $\rho = 0$, i.e., that the volatility is uncorrelated with the stock price. As the work of Geske (1979) shows, this is equivalent to assuming no leverage and a constant volatility of firm value.

An analytic solution to (2.5) for a European call option may be derived by using the risk-neutral valuation procedure. Since neither (2.5) nor the option boundary conditions depend upon risk preferences, we may assume in calculating the option value that risk neutrality prevails. Thus, $f(S, \sigma^2, t)$ must be the present value of the expected terminal value of f discounted at the risk-free rate. The price of the option is therefore

$$f(S_t, \sigma_t^2, t) = e^{-r(T-t)}\int f(S_T, \sigma_T^2, T)p(S_T \mid S_t, \sigma_t^2)\,dS_T, \qquad (2.6)$$

where

$$T = \text{time at which the option matures;}$$
$$S_t = \text{security price at time } t;$$
$$\sigma_t = \text{instantaneous standard deviation at time } t;$$
$$p(S_T \mid S_t, \sigma_t^2) = \text{the conditional probability distribution of } S_T \text{ in a risk-}$$
$$\text{neutral world given the security price and variance at}$$
$$\text{time } t; \text{ and}$$
$$f(S_T, \sigma_T^2, T) = \max\{0, S - X\}.$$

The conditional distribution of S_T depends on both the process driving S and the process driving σ^2. Making use of the fact that, for any three related random variables x, y, and z, the conditional density functions are related by

$$p(x \mid y) = \int g(x \mid z)h(z \mid y)\,dz,$$

equation (2.6) may be greatly simplified. Define $\bar{V}$ as the mean variance over the life of the derivative security defined by the stochastic integral

$$\bar{V} = \frac{1}{T-t}\int_t^T \sigma_\tau^2\,d\tau.$$

Using this, the distribution of S_T may be written as

$$p(S_T \mid \sigma_t^2) = \int g(S_T \mid \bar{V}) h(\bar{V} \mid \sigma_t^2) \, d\bar{V},$$

where the dependence upon S_t is suppressed to simplify the notation. Substituting this into (2.6) yields

$$f(S_t, \sigma_t^2, t) = e^{-r(T-t)} \iint f(S_T) g(S_T \mid \bar{V}) h(\bar{V} \mid \sigma_t^2) \, dS_T \, d\bar{V},$$

which can then be written as

$$f(S_t, \sigma_t^2, t) = \int \left(e^{-r(T-t)} \int f(S_T) g(S_T \mid \bar{V}) \, dS_T \right) h(\bar{V} \mid \sigma_t^2) \, d\bar{V}. \quad (2.7)$$

Under our current assumptions ($\rho = 0$; μ and ξ independent of S), the inner term in (2.7) is the Black–Scholes price for a call option on a security with a mean variance $\bar{V}$, which will be denoted $C(\bar{V})$. To see this, we need the following lemma:

LEMMA. *Suppose that, in a risk-neutral world, a stock price S and its instantaneous variance σ^2 follow the stochastic processes*

$$dS = rS \, dt + \sigma S \, d\tilde{z}, \qquad (a)$$

$$d\sigma^2 = \alpha \sigma^2 \, dt + \xi \sigma^2 \, d\tilde{w}, \qquad (b)$$

where r, the risk-free rate, is assumed constant, α and ξ are independent of S, and $d\tilde{z}$ and $d\tilde{w}$ are independent Wiener processes. Let $\bar{V}$ be the mean variance over some time interval $[0, T]$ defined by

$$\bar{V} = \frac{1}{T} \int_0^T \sigma^2(t) \, dt. \qquad (c)$$

Given (a), (b), and (c), the distribution of $\log\{S(T)/S(0)\}$ conditional upon $\bar{V}$ is normal with mean $rT - \frac{1}{2}\bar{V}T$ and variance $\bar{V}T$.

It is important to distinguish between the distributions of $\{S(T)/S(0) \mid \bar{V}\}$, $\{S(T)/S(0)\}$ and $\bar{V}$. The first is lognormal; the last two are not.

To see whether the lemma is true, first let us suppose that σ^2 is deterministic but not constant. In this case, the terminal distribution of $\log\{S(T)/S(0)\}$ is normal with mean $rT - \frac{1}{2}\bar{V}T$ and variance $\bar{V}T$. Note that the parameters of the lognormal distribution depend only on the risk-free rate, the initial stock price, the time elapsed, and the mean variance over the period. Thus, any path that σ^2 may follow and that has the same mean variance $\bar{V}$ will produce the same lognormal distribution. If σ^2 is

23

stochastic, there are an infinite number of paths that give the same mean variance $\bar{V}$, but all of these paths produce the same terminal distribution of stock price. From this we may conclude that, even if σ^2 is stochastic, the terminal distribution of the stock price given the mean variance $\bar{V}$ is lognormal.

An alternative way to consider this problem is to assume that the variance changes at only n equally spaced times in the interval from 0 to T. Define S_i as the stock price at the end of the ith period and V_{i-1} as the volatility during the ith period. Thus, $\log(S_i/S_{i-1})$ has a normal distribution with mean

$$\frac{rT}{n} - \frac{V_{i-1}T}{2n}$$

and variance

$$\frac{V_{i-1}T}{n}.$$

If S and V are instantaneously uncorrelated, this is also the probability distribution of $\log(S_i/S_{i-1})$ conditional on V_i. The probability distribution of $\log(S_T/S_0)$ conditional on the path followed by V is therefore normal with mean $rT - \frac{1}{2}\bar{V}T$ and variance $\bar{V}T$. This distribution depends only on $\bar{V}$. By letting $n \to \infty$, the lemma is seen to be true.

It is important to realize that the lemma does not hold when S and V are instantaneously correlated. In this case, $\log(S_i/S_{i-1})$ and $\log(V_i/V_{i-1})$ are normal distributions that in the limit have a correlation ρ. The density function of $\log(V_i/V_{i-1})$ is normal with mean

$$\frac{\mu T}{n} - \frac{\xi^2 T}{2n}$$

and variance

$$\frac{\xi^2 T}{n},$$

so that $\log(S_i/S_{i-1})$ conditional on V_i is normal with mean

$$\frac{rT}{n} - \frac{V_{i-1}T}{2n} + \frac{\rho\sqrt{V_{i-1}}}{\xi}\left[\log\left(\frac{V_i}{V_{i-1}}\right) - \frac{\mu T}{n} + \frac{\xi^2 T}{2n}\right]$$

and variance

$$\frac{V_{i-1}T}{n}(1 - \rho^2).$$

Thus, $\log(S_T/S_0)$ conditional on the path followed by V has a normal

24

distribution with mean

$$rT - \tfrac{1}{2}\bar{V}T + \sum_i \frac{\rho\sqrt{V_{i-1}}}{\xi}\left[\log\left(\frac{V_i}{V_{i-1}}\right) - \frac{\mu T}{n} + \frac{\xi^2 T}{2n}\right]$$

and variance

$$\bar{V}T(1 - \rho^2).$$

This distribution clearly depends on attributes of the path followed by V other than $\bar{V}$.

Although not relevant to the current analysis, it is also interesting to note that the lemma does not carry over to a world in which investors are risk-averse. In such a world, the drift rate of the stock price depends on σ^2 through the impact of σ^2 on the stock's β. This means that the mean of the terminal stock price distribution depends on the path that a non-constant σ^2 follows. Different paths for σ^2 that have the same mean variance produce distributions for the log of the terminal stock price that have the same variance but different means. In this case, it is not true that the terminal distribution of the stock price given the mean variance $\bar{V}$ is lognormal.

Since $\log(S_T/S_0)$ conditional on $\bar{V}$ is normally distributed with variance $\bar{V}T$ when S and T are instantaneously uncorrelated, the inner integral in equation (2.7) produces the Black–Scholes price $C(\bar{V})$, which is

$$C(\bar{V}) = S_t N(d_1) - X e^{-r(T-t)} N(d_2),$$

where

$$d_1 = \frac{\log(S_t/X) + (r + \tfrac{1}{2}\bar{V})(T - t)}{\sqrt{\bar{V}(T - t)}},$$

$$d_2 = d_1 - \sqrt{\bar{V}(T - t)}.$$

Thus, the option value is given by

$$f(S_t, \sigma_t^2) = \int C(\bar{V})h(\bar{V} \mid \sigma_t^2)\,d\bar{V}. \qquad (2.8)$$

Equation (2.8) is always true when the stock price and volatility are instantaneously uncorrelated and the process for V is the risk-adjusted or risk-neutral process. Equation (2.8) states that the option price is the Black–Scholes price integrated over the distribution of the mean volatility. It does not seem to be possible to obtain an analytic form for the distribution of $\bar{V}$ for any reasonable set of assumptions about the process driving V. It is, however, possible to calculate all the moments of $\bar{V}$ when

μ and ξ are constant. For example, when $\mu \neq 0$,

$$E(\bar{V}) = \frac{e^{\mu T} - 1}{\mu T} \dot{V}_0,$$

$$E(\bar{V}^2) = \left[\frac{2e^{(2\mu + \xi^2)T}}{(\mu + \xi^2)(2\mu + \xi^2)T^2} + \frac{2}{\mu T^2} \left(\frac{1}{2\mu + \xi^2} - \frac{e^{\mu T}}{\mu + \xi^2} \right) \right] V_0^2,$$

and, when $\mu = 0$,

$$E(\bar{V}) = V_0,$$

$$E(\bar{V}^2) = \frac{2(e^{\xi^2 T} - \xi^2 T - 1)}{\xi^4 T^2} V_0^2,$$

$$E(\bar{V}^3) = \frac{e^{3\xi^2 T} - 9e^{\xi^2 T} + 6\xi^2 T + 8}{3\xi^6 T^3} V_0^3.$$

These results, which are not difficult to derive, are also used by Boyle and Emanuel (1985).

Expanding $C(\bar{V})$ in a Taylor series about its expected value $\bar{\bar{V}}$ yields

$$f(S_t, \sigma_t^2) = C(\bar{\bar{V}}) + \frac{1}{2} \frac{\partial^2 C}{\partial \bar{V}^2} \bigg|_{\bar{\bar{V}}} \int (\bar{V} - \bar{\bar{V}})^2 h(\bar{V}) \, d\bar{V} + \cdots$$

$$= C(\bar{\bar{V}}) + \frac{1}{2} \frac{\partial^2 C}{\partial \bar{V}^2} \bigg|_{\bar{\bar{V}}} \mathrm{Var}(\bar{V}) + \frac{1}{6} \frac{\partial^3 C}{\partial \bar{V}^3} \bigg|_{\bar{\bar{V}}} \mathrm{Skew}(\bar{V}) + \cdots,$$

where $\mathrm{Var}(\bar{V})$ and $\mathrm{Skew}(\bar{V})$ are the second and third central moments of $\bar{V}$. For sufficiently small values of $\xi^2(T - t)$, this series converges very quickly. Using the moments for the distribution of $\bar{V}$ given above, this series becomes, when $\mu = 0$,

$$f(S, \sigma_t^2) = C(\sigma^2)$$

$$+ \frac{1}{2} \frac{S\sqrt{T - t}\, N'(d_1)(d_1 d_2 - 1)}{4\sigma^3} \times \left(\frac{2\sigma^4(e^k - k - 1)}{k^2} - \sigma^4 \right)$$

$$+ \frac{1}{6} \frac{S\sqrt{T - t}\, N'(d_1)[(d_1 d_2 - 3)(d_1 d_2 - 1) - (d_1^2 + d_2^2)]}{8\sigma^5}$$

$$\times \sigma^6 \left(\frac{e^{3k} - (9 + 18k)e^k + (8 + 24k + 18k^2 + 6k^3)}{3k^3} \right) + \cdots,$$

$$(2.9)$$

where

$$k = \xi^2(T - t)$$

and the t subscript has been dropped to simplify the notation. The choice of $\mu = 0$ is justified on the grounds that, for any non-zero μ, options of different maturities would exhibit markedly different implied volatilities. Since this is never observed empirically, we must conclude that μ is at least close to zero.

When the volatility is stochastic, the Black–Scholes price tends to overprice at-the-money options and underprice deep in-the-money and deep out-of-the-money options. (We define an at-the-money option as one for which $S = Xe^{-r(T-t)}$.) The easiest way to see this is to note that (2.8) is just the expected Black–Scholes price, the expectation being taken with respect to $\bar{V}$,

$$f = \mathrm{E}[C(\bar{V})].$$

When C is a concave function, $\mathrm{E}[C(\cdot)] < C(\mathrm{E}[\cdot])$, while, for a convex function, the reverse is true. The Black–Scholes option price $C(\bar{V})$ is convex for low values of $\bar{V}$ and concave for higher values. Thus, at least when ξ is small, we find that the Black–Scholes price tends to underprice for low values of $\bar{V}$ and overprice for high values of $\bar{V}$. It seems strange that a stochastic variance can lower the option price below the price it would have if the volatility were non-stochastic. However, this is consistent with the results Merton (1976) derived for the mixed jump–diffusion process. There he showed that, if the option is priced by the Black–Scholes results based on the expected variance (the expectation being formed over both jumps and continuous changes), then the price might be greater or less than the correct price.

To determine the circumstances under which the Black–Scholes price is too high or too low, examine the second derivative of $C(\bar{V})$:

$$C''(\bar{V}) = \frac{S\sqrt{T-t}}{4\bar{V}^{\frac{3}{2}}}\,\mathrm{N}'(d_1)(d_1 d_2 - 1),$$

where d_1 and d_2 are as defined above. The curvature of C is determined by the sign of C'', which depends on the sign of $d_1 d_2 - 1$. The point of inflection in $C(\bar{V})$ is given when $d_1 d_2 = 1$, that is, when

$$\bar{V} = \frac{2}{T-t}\left\{\sqrt{1 + [\log(S/X) + r(T-t)]^2} - 1\right\}.$$

Denote this value of $\bar{V}$ by I. When $\bar{V} < I$, $C'' > 0$ and C is a convex function of $\bar{V}$. When $\bar{V} > I$, $C'' < 0$ and C is a concave function of $\bar{V}$. If $S = Xe^{-r(T-t)}$, then $I = 0$; this means that C is always a concave function of $\bar{V}$, and, regardless of the distribution of $\bar{V}$, the actual option price will always be lower than the Black–Scholes price. As $\log(S/X) \to \pm\infty$, I becomes arbitrarily large, and C is always convex, so that the actual option price is always greater than the Black–Scholes price. Thus, we find

27

that the Black–Scholes price always overprices at-the-money options but underprices options that are sufficiently deeply in or out of the money.

It is clear from this argument that $\partial f / \partial \xi$ may be positive or negative. The comparative statics with respect to the remaining six parameters, S, $X, r, \sigma_t, T - t$, and μ, are consistent with Merton's (1973) distribution-free theorems. Since μ and ξ are presumed independent of S, the distribution $h(\bar{V})$ is independent of S, X, and r. Thus, with respect to these three parameters, the comparative statics of $f(\cdot)$ are the same as the comparative statics of $C(\cdot)$. This follows since $C(\cdot)$ is monotonic in these three parameters, and h is everywhere non-negative. Thus, we find, as one might expect,

$$\frac{\partial f}{\partial S} = E\left[\frac{\partial C(\bar{V})}{\partial S}\right] > 0,$$

$$\frac{\partial f}{\partial X} = E\left[\frac{\partial C(\bar{V})}{\partial X}\right] < 0,$$

$$\frac{\partial f}{\partial r} = E\left[\frac{\partial C(\bar{V})}{\partial r}\right] > 0.$$

The remaining three parameters $T - t$, μ, and σ_t affect both $C(\cdot)$ and $h(\cdot)$. The effect of increasing any of them is to increase the option price:

$$\frac{\partial f}{\partial \mu} > 0, \qquad \frac{\partial f}{\partial \sigma_t^2} > 0, \qquad \frac{\partial f}{\partial T} > 0.$$

To see this, note that $\partial f / \partial T$, $\partial f / \partial \mu$, and $\partial f / \partial \sigma_t^2$ are positive for every possible sample path of σ^2. Thus, they must also be positive when averaged across all possible sample paths.

In this section, it was shown that, if the stochastic volatility is independent of the stock price, the correct option price is the expected Black–Scholes price where the expectation is taken over the distribution of mean variances. This is given in equation (2.8). If the solution (2.8) is substituted into the differential equation (2.5), the equation is separable in h and C. The density function $h(\bar{V})$ is shown to satisfy the following differential equation:

$$\frac{\partial h}{\partial t} + \frac{\bar{V} - V_t}{T - t} \frac{\partial h}{\partial \bar{V}} + \tfrac{1}{2}\xi^2 \bar{V}_t^2 \frac{\partial h}{\partial V_t} + \mu V_t \frac{\partial h}{\partial V_t} = 0,$$

where $V_t = \sigma_t^2$. This can, in principle, be solved for the density function of the mean variance.

2.2 OTHER NUMERICAL PROCEDURES

We now consider efficient ways in which Monte Carlo simulation can be used to calculate the option price when some of the assumptions necessary for the series solution in (2.9) are relaxed. For our first result, we continue to assume that $\rho = 0$. However, we allow ξ and μ to depend on σ and t. This means that V can follow a mean-reverting process. One simple such process occurs when

$$\mu = a(\sigma^* - \sigma) \tag{2.10}$$

and ξ, a, and σ^* are constants.

The result in (2.8) still holds (i.e., the call price is the Black–Scholes price integrated over the distribution of $\bar{V}$). An efficient way of carrying out the Monte Carlo simulation involves dividing the time interval $T - t$ into n equal sub-intervals. Independent standard normal variates v_i ($1 \le i \le n$) are sampled and are used to generate the variance V_i at time $t + i(T - t)/n$ using the formula

$$V_i = V_{i-1} e^{(\mu - \frac{1}{2}\xi^2)\Delta t + v_i \xi \sqrt{\Delta t}},$$

where $\Delta t = (T - t)/n$ and, if μ and ξ depend on σ, their values are based on $\sigma = \sqrt{V_{i-1}}$. The Black–Scholes option price p_1 is calculated with the volatility set equal to the arithmetic mean of the V_i's ($0 \le i \le n$). The procedure is then repeated using the antithetic standard normal variables $-v_i$ ($0 \le i \le n$) to give a price p_2, and

$$y = \tfrac{1}{2}(p_1 + p_2)$$

is calculated. The mean value of y over a large number of simulations gives an excellent estimate of the option price. This can be compared with the Black–Scholes price based on V_0 to give the bias.

Note that is not necessary to simulate both V and S. Also, the antithetic variable technique described in Hammersley and Handscomb (1964) considerably improves the efficiency of the procedure. In the mean-reverting model in (2.10) when $S = X = 1$, $r = 0$, $T = 90$ days, $\sigma_0 = 0.15$, $\xi = 1.0$, $a = 10$, $\sigma^* = 0.15$, and $n = 90$, 1000 simulations gave a value for the option of 0.029 with a standard error of 0.000014. The bias is -0.00038 (with the same standard error). The method can be used to deal with the situation where the conditions for the series solution in (2.9) hold but where ξ is too large for the series to converge quickly. Table 2.1 compares the values given by this Monte Carlo procedure with the values given by (2.9) for particular cases.

For our second result, we allow ρ to be non-zero and allow μ and ξ to

TABLE 2.1. Comparison of Monte Carlo procedure and series solution; option parameters: $\sigma_0 = 10\%$, $\xi = 1$, $\mu = 0$, $T - t = 180$ days.

S/X	Price		B–S price bias		
	B–S	Equation (9)	Equation (9)	Monte Carlo	
			Percent bias	Percent bias	Standard error
0.75	0.0000	0.0000	—	—	237.85
0.76	0.0000	0.0000	—	—	139.41
0.77	0.0000	0.0000	—	970.57	153.57
0.78	0.0000	0.0000	786.47	787.43	133.70
0.79	0.0000	0.0000	588.78	383.43	44.22
0.80	0.0000	0.0001	436.12	336.43	39.21
0.81	0.0000	0.0001	354.37	330.68	46.90
0.82	0.0000	0.0001	232.00	173.55	21.21
0.83	0.0001	0.0002	164.02	134.14	14.91
0.84	0.0001	0.0003	114.54	102.17	10.67
0.85	0.0002	0.0004	78.32	69.55	8.41
0.86	0.0004	0.0006	52.14	54.55	6.74
0.87	0.0006	0.0008	33.53	37.95	5.43
0.88	0.0009	0.0011	20.55	23.50	3.02
0.89	0.0013	0.0015	11.70	16.46	2.74
0.90	0.0019	0.0021	5.83	10.07	2.19
0.91	0.0027	0.0028	2.07	5.53	1.45
0.92	0.0039	0.0039	−0.23	2.49	1.09
0.93	0.0053	0.0052	−1.53	0.22	0.90
0.94	0.0071	0.0069	−2.17	−1.45	0.78
0.95	0.0094	0.0091	−2.40	−2.36	0.58
0.96	0.0119	0.0117	−2.38	−2.53	0.38
0.97	0.0151	0.0148	−2.22	−2.61	0.29
0.98	0.0188	0.0185	−1.98	−2.52	0.25
0.99	0.0231	0.0228	−1.72	−2.32	0.21
0.01	0.0281	0.0276	−1.45	−2.16	0.19
1.01	0.0334	0.0330	−1.20	−1.61	0.16
1.02	0.0394	0.0390	−0.97	−1.24	0.12
1.03	0.0461	0.0456	−0.76	−1.09	0.13
1.04	0.0529	0.0526	−0.58	−0.65	0.10
1.05	0.0603	0.0601	−0.41	−0.35	0.08
1.06	0.0682	0.0681	−0.28	−0.19	0.08
1.07	0.0765	0.0764	−0.16	−0.05	0.07
1.08	0.0850	0.0850	−0.06	0.06	0.06
1.09	0.0939	0.0939	0.01	0.13	0.05
1.10	0.1030	0.1030	0.07	0.17	0.05
1.11	0.1122	0.1124	0.11	0.20	0.04
1.12	0.1216	0.1218	0.13	0.19	0.03
1.13	0.1312	0.1314	0.15	0.19	0.03
1.14	0.1409	0.1411	0.15	0.19	0.03
1.15	0.1506	0.1509	0.15	0.13	0.02
1.16	0.1605	0.1607	0.14	0.14	0.02
1.17	0.1703	0.1706	0.13	0.10	0.01
1.18	0.1802	0.1804	0.11	0.10	0.01
1.19	0.1902	0.1904	0.10	0.08	0.01
1.20	0.2001	0.2003	0.08	0.08	0.01
1.21	0.2101	0.2102	0.07	0.05	0.01
1.22	0.2201	0.2202	0.06	0.05	0.01
1.23	0.2300	0.2301	0.05	0.03	0.00
1.24	0.2400	0.2401	0.04	0.03	0.00

depend on S as well as σ and t. In this case, it is necessary to simulate both S and V. The time interval is divided up as before, and two independent normal variates u_i and v_i ($1 \leq i \leq n$) are sampled and used to generate the stock price S_i and variance V_i at time i in a risk-neutral world using the formulae

$$
S_i = S_{i-1}e^{(r-\frac{1}{2}V_{i-1})\Delta t + u_i\sqrt{V_{i-1}\Delta t}},
$$

$$
V_i = V_{i-1}e^{(\mu-\frac{1}{2}\xi^2)\Delta t + \rho u_i\xi\sqrt{\Delta t} + \sqrt{1-\rho^2}v_i\xi\sqrt{\Delta t}}. \tag{2.11}
$$

Again, the values of μ and ξ are based on $\sigma^2 = V_{i-1}$ and $S = S_{i-1}$. The value of

$$
e^{-r(T-t)}\max\{S_n - X, 0\}
$$

is calculated to give one "sample value" p_1 of the option price. A second price p_2 is calculated by replacing u_i with $-u_i$ ($1 \leq i \leq n$) and repeating the calculations; p_3 is calculated by replacing v_i with $-v_i$ ($1 \leq i \leq n$) and repeating the calculations; p_4 is calculated by replacing u_i with $-u_i$ and v_i with $-v_i$ ($1 \leq i \leq n$) and repeating the calculations. Finally, two sample values of the Black–Scholes price q_1 and q_2 are calculated by simulating S using $\{u_i\}$ and $\{-u_i\}$, respectively, with V kept constant at V_0. This provides the following two estimates of the pricing bias:

$$
\tfrac{1}{2}(p_1 + p_3 - 2q_1) \quad \text{and} \quad \tfrac{1}{2}(p_2 + p_4 - 2q_2).
$$

These estimates are averaged over a large number of simulations.

This procedure uses the antithetic variable technique (twice) and the control variate technique. Both are described in Hammersley and Handscomb (1964). The principle of the control variate technique is that the difference between the values of the two variables can often be obtained most accurately for a given number of simulations when both are calculated using the same random number streams. Furthermore, this is often true even when the value of one of the variables can be calculated analytically.

This procedure is applicable to a wider range of situations than the first one but is not as efficient. For the mean-reverting model example considered above, the standard error of the pricing bias using $n = 90$ and 1000 simulations was 0.000041 (compared with 0.000014 for the first procedure). Moreover, approximately three times as much computer time was used.

2.3 PROPERTIES OF THE OPTION PRICE

In this section, the properties of the option price given by the series solution in equation (2.9) and the numerical solutions of Section 2.2 are examined. The principal finding is that, when the volatility is uncorrelated with the stock price, the option price is depressed relative to the Black–Scholes price for near-the-money options. When the volatility is correlated with the stock price, this at-the-money price depression continues on into the money for positive correlation and out of the money for negative correlation. As might be expected, these effects are exaggerated as the volatility, σ, the volatility of the volatility, ξ, or the time to maturity, $T - t$ increases. The surprising result of this is that longer term options have lower implied volatilities, as calculated by the Black–Scholes equation, than do shorter term options whenever the Black–Scholes price overprices the option.

Consider first the case in which the volatility is uncorrelated with the stock price and μ and ξ are constant. Figure 2.1 shows the general relationship between the Black–Scholes price and the correct option price. The option being priced has 180 days to maturity; the volatility of the underlying asset is initially fifteen percent per annum; $\mu = 0$ and $\xi = 1$. The Black–Scholes price is too low deep in and out of the money and, surprisingly, too high at the money. The largest absolute price differences occur at or near the money. The actual magnitude of the pricing error is quite small and is magnified twenty-five-fold to make it visible in Figure 2.1.

The choice of a value of ξ is not obvious. It is possible to estimate ξ by

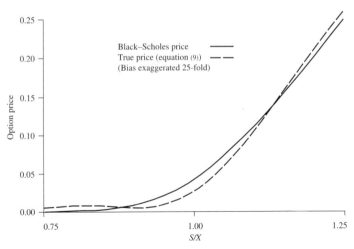

FIGURE 2.1. Pricing bias when $\mu = 0, r = 0, \sigma_t = 15\%, \xi = 1, T - t = 180$ days.

examining the changes in volatilities implied by option prices. Alternatively, ξ can be estimated from changes in the estimates of the actual variance. For currencies and currency options listed on the Philadelphia exchange, Hull and White (1987) found that the estimates of ξ using both methods ranged from 1 to 4. Both of the estimation methods have weaknesses. Using the implied volatilities is, at best, an indirect procedure for estimating ξ. It is also contaminated by the fact that the changes in implied volatility are, at least to some extent, a result of pricing errors in the options. The problem with using estimates of the actual variance is that it requires very large amounts of data. Because of these weaknesses, the low end of the range for ξ was chosen as a conservative estimate.

In Figure 2.2, the effect of changing σ_t is shown, and, in Figure 2.3, the effect of changing ξ is shown. While the absolute magnitude of the price bias is very small, as a percentage of the Black–Scholes price it is quite significant. The principal result of increasing σ_t^2 is to make the percentage price bias for out-of-the-money (in-the-money) options more positive (negative). When one looks sufficiently far out of the money, this effect is reversed, with higher σ_t^2 causing smaller biases. The effect on at- or in-the-money options is small. The main effect of increasing ξ is to lower the price of (i.e., to make the bias more negative for) near-the-money options. Although not evident from Figure 2.3, it is true that, for sufficiently deep out-of-the money options, the reverse is true; increasing ξ increases a positive bias.

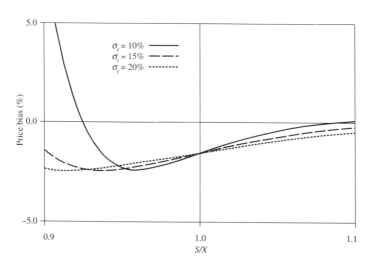

FIGURE 2.2. Effect of varying σ_t when $\mu = 0, r = 0, \xi = 1, T - t = 180$ days.

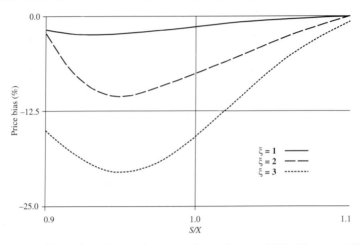

FIGURE 2.3. Effect of varying ξ when $\mu = 0, r = 0, \sigma_t = 15\%, T - t = 180$ days.

Figures 2.1 and 2.2 were produced using the series solution in equation (2.9). For Figure 2.3, when $\xi = 2$ and 3, it was found that series solution did not converge quickly, and the Monte Carlo simulation approach was used. This was also used to investigate the results for the mean-reverting process in (2.10). As might be expected, the results for this process show biases that are similar to but less pronounced than those for the case when μ and ξ are constant. The effect of moving to a mean-reverting process from a process where μ and ξ are constant is to reduce the variance of $\bar{V}$. It is similar to the effect of reducing ξ.

The effect of a non-zero ρ when both μ and ξ are constant was investigated using the Monte Carlo simulation approach in equation (2.11). The results are shown in Table 2.2. When the volatility is positively correlated with the stock price, the option price has a bias relative to the Black–Scholes price, which tends to decline as the stock price increases. Out-of-the-money options are priced well above the Black–Scholes price, while the price of in-the-money options is below the Black–Scholes price. The crossing point, the point at which the Black–Scholes price is correct, is slightly out of the money. When the volatility is negatively correlated with the stock price, the reverse is true. Out-of-the-money options are priced below the Black–Scholes price, while in-the-money options have prices above the Black–Scholes price. The crossing point is slightly in the money. When ρ is zero, the bias is a combination of these two effects. The price is above the Black–Scholes price for in- and out-of-the-money options and below the Black–Scholes price at the money. For all values of ρ, the absolute percentage bias tends to zero as S/X tends to infinity. These general observations appear to be true for all maturities.

TABLE 2.2. Price bias as a percentage of the Black–Scholes price for varying values of S/X and correlation ρ between the volatility and the stock price; option parameters: $\sigma_0 = 15\%, r = 0, \xi = 1,$ and $\mu = 0$.

T (days)	ρ	S/X				
		0.90	0.95	1.00	1.05	1.10
90	−1.0	−66.06	−22.68	−2.13	1.84	1.56
		(1.98)	(0.51)	(0.23)	(0.12)	(0.08)
	−0.5	−31.55	−10.89	−1.62	0.91	0.89
		(1.14)	(0.32)	(0.13)	(0.07)	(0.04)
	0.0	3.72	−0.98	−0.92	0.25	0.07
		(0.50)	(0.13)	(0.05)	(0.03)	(0.02)
	0.5	39.37	7.70	−0.53	−1.68	−0.85
		(1.12)	(0.28)	(0.12)	(0.07)	(0.04)
	1.0	72.24	15.62	−0.84	−3.12	−1.56
		(2.42)	(0.61)	(0.25)	(0.14)	(0.09)
180	−1.0	−56.22	−22.49	−4.77	0.94	1.79
		(1.23)	(0.55)	(0.31)	(0.21)	(0.15)
	−0.5	−25.96	−11.50	−2.93	0.27	1.29
		(0.80)	(0.35)	(0.20)	(0.13)	(0.09)
	0.0	0.63	−2.25	−1.87	−0.82	−0.09
		(0.42)	(0.17)	(0.09)	(0.06)	(0.04)
	0.5	24.04	5.30	−1.10	−2.57	−1.61
		(0.78)	(0.32)	(0.19)	(0.11)	(0.09)
	1.0	45.99	12.43	−1.11	−4.58	−4.05
		(1.69)	(0.77)	(0.40)	(0.27)	(0.18)
270	−1.0	−53.32	−23.12	−7.53	−0.20	2.01
		(1.11)	(0.58)	(0.39)	(0.28)	(0.21)
	−0.5	−25.33	−12.33	−5.29	−0.44	0.62
		(0.73)	(0.39)	(0.25)	(0.17)	(0.13)
	0.0	−1.88	−3.56	−2.45	−1.37	−0.52
		(0.04)	(0.21)	(0.14)	(0.09)	(0.07)
	0.5	17.87	4.36	−1.77	−2.81	−2.37
		(0.69)	(0.39)	(0.24)	(0.17)	(0.14)
	1.0	33.41	8.94	−1.09	−6.21	−5.07
		(1.64)	(0.87)	(0.55)	(0.34)	(0.26)

The intuition behind these effects can be explained by the impact that the correlation has on the terminal distribution of stock prices. First, consider the case in which the volatility is positively correlated with the stock price. High stock prices are associated with high volatilities; as stock prices rise, the probability of large positive changes increases. This means that very high stock prices become more probable than when the volatility is fixed. Low stock prices are associated with low volatilities; if stock prices fall, it becomes less likely that large changes take place. Low stock prices become like absorbing states, and it becomes more likely the terminal stock price will be low. The net effect is that the terminal stock price distribution is more positively skewed than the lognormal distribution arising from a fixed volatility. When volatility changes are negatively correlated with stock price changes, the reverse is true. Price increases reduce the volatility, so that it is unlikely that very high stock prices will result. Price decreases increase volatility, increasing the chance of large positive price changes; very low prices become less likely. The net effect is that the terminal stock price distribution is more peaked than the usual lognormal distribution.

One phenomenon arising from these results might be called the "time-to-maturity effect". If the time to maturity is increased with all else held constant, the effect is the same as increasing both σ_t and ξ. Thus, longer term near-the-money options have a price that is lower (relative to the Black–Scholes price) than that of shorter term options. Because the Black–Scholes price is approximately linear with respect to volatility, these proportional price differences map into equivalent differences in implied volatilities. If the Black–Scholes equation is used to calculate implied volatilities, longer term near-the-money options will exhibit lower implied volatilities than shorter term options. This effect occurs whenever the Black–Scholes formula overprices the option. Table 2.3 shows the effects of changing terms on the implied volatilities for an option with an expected volatility of fifteen percent, $\xi = 1$, $\mu = 0$, and $r = 0$ for different values of ρ and S/X. The time-to-maturity effect is clear. In the worst case, it changes the implied volatility by almost one-half of one percent. The effect increases as ξ increases and as the initial volatility increases.

This time-to-maturity effect is counterintuitive. One might expect that uncertainty about the volatility would increase uncertainty about the stock price, hence raising the option price, and that longer times to maturity would exacerbate this. The actual result is just the opposite. Wherever the Black–Scholes formula overprices the option, it is due to the local concavity of the Black–Scholes price with respect to σ. Because of the concavity of the option price with respect to volatility, increases in volatility do not increase the option price as much as decreases in volatility decrease the price. Thus, the average of the Black–Scholes prices for a stochastic volatility with a given mean lies below the Black–Scholes price for a fixed volatility with the same mean for all near-the-money options. As the time to maturity increases, the variance of the stochastic volatility increases, exacerbating the effect of the curvature of the option price with respect to volatility. Wherever the Black–Scholes price underprices the option, the reverse effect is observed.

The implications of these results for empirical tests of option pricing are interesting. Rubinstein (1985) compared implied volatilities of matched pairs of options differing only in exercise price. In the period 1976–77, he generally found that, as S/X increased, the implied volatility

TABLE 2.3. Implied volatility calculated by the Black–Scholes formula from the option prices given in Table 2; actual expected mean volatility 15%; option parameters: $\sigma_0 = 15\%$, $r = 0$, $\xi = 1$, and $\mu = 0$.

T (days)	ρ	S/X				
		0.90	0.95	1.00	1.05	1.10
90	−1.0	11.94	13.38	14.68	15.69	16.63
		(0.13)	(0.04)	(0.03)	(0.04)	(0.08)
	−0.5	13.75	14.23	14.76	15.34	15.97
		(0.05)	(0.02)	(0.02)	(0.03)	(0.04)
	0.0	15.13	14.93	14.86	14.91	15.08
		(0.02)	(0.01)	(0.01)	(0.01)	(0.02)
	0.5	16.32	15.53	14.92	14.36	13.98
		(0.03)	(0.02)	(0.02)	(0.03)	(0.05)
	1.0	17.29	16.07	14.87	13.80	13.00
		(0.07)	(0.04)	(0.04)	(0.05)	(0.13)
180	−1.0	11.66	13.04	14.28	15.26	15.99
		(0.09)	(0.05)	(0.05)	(0.06)	(0.08)
	−0.5	13.59	14.01	14.56	15.08	15.72
		(0.05)	(0.03)	(0.03)	(0.04)	(0.05)
	0.0	15.03	14.81	14.72	14.77	14.94
		(0.02)	(0.01)	(0.01)	(0.02)	(0.02)
	0.5	16.20	15.45	14.83	14.27	14.06
		(0.04)	(0.03)	(0.03)	(0.03)	(0.05)
	1.0	17.23	16.05	14.83	13.70	12.50
		(0.08)	(0.06)	(0.06)	(0.08)	(0.13)
270	−1.0	11.38	12.79	13.87	14.95	15.85
		(0.09)	(0.06)	(0.06)	(0.07)	(0.09)
	−0.5	13.38	13.83	14.20	14.89	15.27
		(0.05)	(0.04)	(0.04)	(0.04)	(0.06)
	0.0	14.88	14.66	14.63	14.66	14.77
		(0.02)	(0.02)	(0.02)	(0.02)	(0.02)
	0.5	16.07	15.41	14.73	14.30	13.96
		(0.04)	(0.04)	(0.04)	(0.04)	(0.06)
	1.0	16.97	15.84	14.84	13.44	12.70
		(0.09)	(0.08)	(0.08)	(0.09)	(0.13)

decreased. For the subsequent period 1977–78, the reverse was true. Rubinstein also compared matched pairs of options differing only in time to maturity. He found that, in the 1976–77 period, the shorter term options had higher implied volatilities for out-of-the-money options. For at-the-money and in-the-money options, the reverse is true. In the period 1977–78, almost all options exhibited the property that shorter term options had higher implied volatilities.

The observed implied volatility patterns in relation to S/X are consistent with a situation in which, during the 1976–77 period, the volatility was positively correlated with the stock price, while, in the 1977–78 period, the correlation was negative. However, the results from comparing implied volatilities across different times to maturity are not consistent with this. If the volatility were positively correlated with the stock price, we would expect out-of-the-money options to exhibit increasing implied volatility with increasing time to maturity.

It is difficult to draw direct comparisons between Rubinstein's results and our model. As suggested by equation (2.9), the key element is the relationship between the stock price and the present value of the exercise price. Thus, when Rubinstein chooses pairs matched on the basis of exercise price, they are not truly matched in the variable of interest, the present value of the exercise price. Figure 2.4 illustrates the price biases for different times to maturity for the case in which volatility is uncorrelated with the stock price and the risk-free rate is not zero. The net effect of the non-zero risk-free rate is to lower the effective exercise price of longer term options. Figure 2.4 shows that increasing the time to maturity raises the implied volatility for almost all options except the very deep in-the-money options, in which case the effect is very small. When the volatility is positively correlated with the stock price, the consequence is to enhance the time-to-maturity effect for all but very deep out-of-the-money options. When the correlation is negative, the result is a reduction of the time-to-maturity effect for out-of-the-money options and an enhancement of the tendency to observe higher implied volatilities in long-term in-the-money options. This latter effect is, however, very small. Thus, overall, we might expect the time-to-maturity effect to be strongest for out-of-the-money options and weakest for in-the-money options. This is exactly what Rubinstein found.

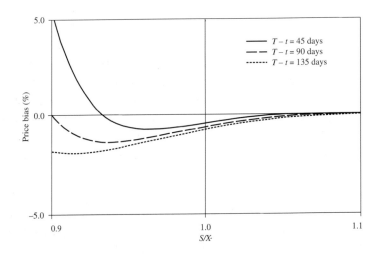

FIGURE 2.4. Effect of varying $T - t$ when $\mu = 0, r = 10\%, \sigma_t = 15\%, \xi = 1$.

The results of Rubinstein may not be inconsistent with the model presented in this paper, but neither do they seem to provide strong support. In order for them to support this model, it is necessary to posit that, from one year to the next, the correlation between stock prices and the associated volatility reversed sign. It is difficult to think of a convincing reason why this event should occur. It is tempting to suggest that the observed effect may be a sampling result that can occur if some stocks have positive correlations and some have negative correlations. In this case, by changing the relative numbers of each group in the sample from period to period, we could see the observed result. Unfortunately, Rubinstein found that the result also prevailed on a security-by-security basis.

2.4 CONCLUSIONS

The general differential equation of Garman (1976) is used to derive a series solution for the price of a call option on a security with a stochastic volatility that is uncorrelated with the security price. It is shown for such a security that the Black–Scholes price overvalues at-the-money options and undervalues deep in- and out-of-the-money options. The range over which overpricing by the Black–Scholes formula takes place is for stock prices within about ten percent of the exercise price. The magnitude of the pricing bias can be up to five percent of the Black–Scholes price.

The case in which the volatility is correlated with the stock price is examined using numerical methods. When there is a positive correlation between the stock price and its volatility, out-of-the-money options are underpriced by the Black–Scholes formula, while in-the-money options are overpriced. When the correlation is negative, the effect is reversed. These results can be used to explain the empirical observations of Rubinstein (1985), but require the questionable assumption that the correlation between volatilities and stock prices reverses from one year to the next.

This paper has concentrated on the pricing of a European call option on a stock subject to a stochastic volatility. The results are directly transferable to European puts through the use of put–call parity. They are also transferable to American calls on non-dividend-paying stocks. This follows from Merton's (1973) results. The pricing of American puts, however, cannot be easily determined.

References

Black, F., and M. Scholes. "The pricing of options and corporate liabilities." *Journal of Political Economy*, 81 (May 1973), pp. 637–659.

Boyle, P. P., and D. Emanuel. "Mean dependent options." Working Paper, Accounting Group, University is Waterloo, 1985.

Cox, J. C., J. E. Ingersoll, and S. A. Ross. "An intertemporal general equilibrium model of asset prices." *Econometrica*, 53 (March 1985), pp. 363–384.

Cox, J. C., and S. A. Ross. "The valuation of options for alternative stochastic processes." *Journal of Financial Economics*, 3 (January 1976), 145–166.

Eisenberg, L. "Relative pricing from no-arbitrage conditions: random variance option pricing." Working Paper, University of Illinois, Department of Finance, 1985.

Garman, M. "A general theory of asset valuation under diffusion state processes." Working Paper No. 50, University of California, Berkeley, 1976.

Geske, R. "The valuation of compound options." *Journal of Financial Economics*, 7 (March 1979), pp. 63–81.

Hammersley, J. M., and D. C. Handscomb. *Monte Carlo Methods*. Methuen, London, 1964.

Hull, J. C., and A. White. "Hedging the risks from writing foreign currency options." *Journal of International Money and Finance*, 6 (June 1987), pp. 131–152. Also Chapter 4 in this book.

Johnson, H. E. "Option pricing when the variance is changing." Graduate School of Management Working Paper 11-79, University of California, Los Angeles, 1979.

Johnson, H. E., and D. Shanno. "Option pricing when the variance is changing." Graduate School of Administration Working Paper 85-07, University of California, Davis, 1985.

Merton, R. C. "The theory of rational option pricing." *Bell Journal of Economics and Management Science*, 4 (Spring 1973), pp. 141–183.

Merton, R. C. "Options pricing when underlying stock returns are discontinuous." *Journal of Financial Economics*, 3 (January 1976), pp. 125–144.

Rubinstein, M. "Nonparametric tests of alternative option pricing models using all reported trades quotes on the 30 most active CBOE option classes from August 23, 1976, through August 31, 1978." *Journal of Finance*, 40 (June 1985), pp. 455–480.

Scott, L. O. "Option pricing when the variance changes randomly: theory and an application." Working Paper, University of Illinois, Department of Finance, 1986.

Wiggins, J. B. "Stochastic variance option pricing." Sloan School of Management, Massachusetts Institute of Technology, 1985.

3. An analysis of the bias in option pricing caused by a stochastic volatility*

In a major breakthrough, Black and Scholes (1973) produced a closed-form solution for the price of a European call option on a stock. In order to derive the option pricing formula, they assumed that markets are perfect, costless trading takes place continuously, the short-term interest rate is constant, the stock pays no dividends, and the stock price follows a geometric Brownian motion with a constant variance rate. These assumptions were subsequently relaxed by other authors.

Merton (1973) dropped the assumption of a fixed interest rate and showed how, in this case, an option can be priced in terms of a bond price. This solution methodology was later extended by Fischer (1978), Margrabe (1978), Stulz (1982), and Johnson (1983), who analyzed options to exchange one asset for another. The assumption of no dividends was addressed by Merton (1973), Roll (1977), and Geske (1978). Merton (1973) also showed how the Black–Scholes formula can be extended to cover the situation in which the variance rate is a deterministic function of time.

Solutions to European option pricing problems for a variety of different stock price processes have also been derived. Merton (1976), Cox and Ross (1976), and Jones (1984) determine the price of a call option if the stock price follows a discontinuous jump process or if it follows a mixed jump–diffusion process. Cox and Ross (1976) and Rubinstein (1983) solve option pricing problems for situations in which the variance of the instantaneous rate of return is a function of the stock price. Geske (1979) assumes that the variance rate of the firm value is fixed. Since the degree of financial leverage decreases as the firm value

* This paper was first published in *Advances in Futures and Options Research*, Vol. 3 (1988), pp. 29–61. It is reprinted with the permission of JAI Press.

increases, this leads to a model in which stock price volatility declines as the stock price increases.

There has been some empirical work on the distribution of stock returns. Christie (1982) finds that Geske's (1979) model is supported by the data. However, the unexplained portion of changes in the variance is very large. This may be due to errors in estimating the variance or due to other random changes in the variance. Kon (1984) finds that the observed distribution of stock returns is consistent with a randomly varying variance. Scott (1987), using 258 monthly estimates of the variance of daily stock returns, shows that the hypothesis that stock returns are distributed independently over time can be rejected. His results are consistent with a model in which the instantaneous variance of returns follows a mean-reverting stochastic process. Bodurtha and Courtadon (1984) and Hull and White (1987a) provide some evidence drawn from the prices of currencies and currency options that suggests that the variances of currency prices vary randomly. These empirical observations, coupled with fact that there is no particular reason to assume that the variance rate of a stock price or a firm value is either constant or deterministic, suggest that the volatility should be modeled as a separate state variable. The Black–Scholes option pricing formula is then no longer correct.

A number of authors have examined option pricing problems when the volatility is stochastic. Johnson (1979) was the first to consider this problem. He was able to derive the partial differential equation that such an option must satisfy. Although he was unable to solve this, he did infer some properties of the solution. More recent work has involved both analytic and numerical approaches. Johnson and Shanno (1987) and Wiggins (1987) produce numerical solutions to the problem. Scott (1987) tests the hypothesis that observed option prices are consistent with a stochastic volatility. Hull and White (1987b) produce analytic results for the special case in which the volatility is uncorrelated with the stock price.

This paper derives an expression in series form for the pricing bias caused by a stochastic volatility. Unlike Hull and White (1987b), it allows the volatility to be instantaneously correlated with the stock price. Furthermore, results are provided for the situation in which the volatility follows a mean-reverting process, as well as for the situation in which the volatility follows a stochastic process with no drift, a constant drift, or a constant proportional drift. The market price of the risk associated with the volatility is assumed constant. It might be guessed that the Black–Scholes price always underprices when the volatility is stochastic. This paper shows that this is not the case. The bias shows a rich pattern of behavior. Whether underpricing or overpricing takes place is found to depend primarily on (1) the drift rate of the volatility, (2) the sign of the correlation between the stock price and volatility, and (3) the extent to which the option is in- or out-of-the-money.

This paper is similar in spirit to Dothan (1987). However, the results here are more general than the results produced by Dothan in one important respect. Dothan assumes, in the mean-reverting case, that the rate at which the volatility is pulled toward its long-run average level is small. This paper does not make that assumption and goes on to investigate a problem not considered by Dothan: the implications of a stochastic volatility for option replication strategies.

The solution technique in this paper is a particular case of a more general procedure for pricing two-state-variable contingent claims. The procedure is applicable when the price of the contingent claim is known when one of the variables is deterministic. Other work involving two-state-variable contingent claims has been done by Brennan and Schwartz (1979, 1982), Boyle and Kirzner (1985), Stulz (1982), and Richard (1979).

The organization of this paper is as follows. Section 3.1 discusses the stochastic process that is assumed for the stock price. Section 3.2 provides a value for a European call option in series form. The results from using the series solution are compared with results from using Monte Carlo simulation in Section 3.3. Section 3.4 discusses the properties of the solution. Section 3.5 discusses the implications of a stochastic volatility for option replication strategies. Conclusions are in Section 3.6.

3.1 PRICE DYNAMICS

Define

$S(t)$:   stock price at time t;
$V(t)$:   variance of dS/S at time t;
$\phi(t)$:   drift rate of dS/S at time t;
$\eta(V)$:   drift rate of dV;
    ξ: instantaneous standard deviation of $dV/\sqrt{V}$;
    ρ: instantaneous correlation between dS/S and $dV/\sqrt{V}$.

The stock price S and volatility V are assumed to obey the following stochastic processes:

$$dS/S = \phi\, dt + \sqrt{V}\, dz, \tag{3.1}$$

$$dV = \eta\, dt + \xi\sqrt{V}\, dw, \tag{3.2}$$

where dz and dw are Wiener processes.

Roughly speaking, the implication of the model proposed in (3.1) and (3.2) is that over the next short instant of time the rate of return earned by the stock will be drawn from a normal distribution with mean $\phi\, dt$ and variance $V\, dt$. At the same time, the variance rate is itself changing to $V + dV$. Accordingly, in the following short instant of time, the rate of return earned by the stock will be drawn from a new normal distribution with mean $\phi\, dt$ and variance $(V + dV)\, dt$. The process for the unanticipated part of the stock price follows a martingale (as it must if markets are efficient), but it no longer follows a stationary process as has been traditionally assumed. Because the variance rate changes randomly, the probability density function of the stock price at some future time conditional on the current stock price is not lognormal.

The relation between V and S is captured by ρ, the instantaneous correlation between the Wiener processes dz and dw. Hull and White (1987b) analyze the case in which $\rho = 0$, while Cox and Ross (1976) and Geske (1979) examine the case in which $\rho = -1$. Dothan (1987) produces a series solution for the general case $-1 \leq \rho \leq 1$. The empirical data of Kon (1984) suggest that $-1 < \rho < 0$. This is in accord with casual observation. As stock prices rise, volatilities tend to decline, but the correlation appears to be less than perfect.

We shall assume that ξ is constant and that the drift rate η of V is given by

$$\eta = a + bV, \tag{3.3}$$

where a and b are constants. In order to ensure that V remains non-negative, we require $a \geq 0$. Equation (3.3) can give a constant drift $(b = 0)$, a constant proportional drift $(a = 0)$, or a mean-reverting process $(a > 0, b < 0)$. In this last case V tends to revert to a level $-a/b$ with a reversion rate $-b$.

Define $E[V(s, t)]$ as the expected volatility at time s $(s \geq t)$ conditional on the volatility $V(t)$ at time t. The mean-reverting model $(a > 0, b < 0)$ is analogous to the model considered by Cox, Ingersoll, and Ross (1985b) for the short-term rate of interest. The expected volatility at time s is given by

$$E[V(s, t)] = [V(t) - \hat{V}]e^{b(s-t)} + \hat{V}, \tag{3.4}$$

where $\hat{V}$ is the reversion level $-a/b$. The variance of $V(s)$ conditional on $V(t)$ is

$$V(t)\left(-\frac{\xi^2}{b}\right)[e^{b(s-t)} - e^{2b(s-t)}] + \hat{V}\left(-\frac{\xi^2}{2b}\right)[1 - e^{b(s-t)}]^2. \qquad (3.5)$$

Equations (3.4) and (3.5) allow us to infer some plausible parameters for the process for V. Equation (3.4) reveals that any deviations from the reversion value $V - \hat{V}$ are expected to die away at an exponential rate. The time required for the expected deviation to be halved, the half-life, is given by $-0.693/b$. Values of b in the range form -10 to -1 per year give half-lives of from a few days to about half a year. Reasonable values for the reversion level $\hat{V} = -a/b$ are in the range 0.05 to 0.10 per year.[1] Once a and b have been chosen, equation (3.5) allows us to determine whether the long-run variance of V for a give value of ξ is plausible. For example, if $a = 0.18$, $b = -2$, and $\xi = 0.10$, the long-run standard deviation of V is 0.015 and the two-standard-deviation range for V is from 0.06 to 0.12 per year.[2]

3.2 CALL OPTION PRICING WHEN THE VARIANCE RATE IS STOCHASTIC

In this section we consider a European call option on a stock with an exercise price X and a maturity time T. The stock price is assumed to follow the process given by (3.1). If the variance rate V is constant, then the option price C is the Black–Scholes price that satisfies the differential equation

$$\frac{\partial C}{\partial t} + \tfrac{1}{2}VS^2\frac{\partial^2 C}{\partial S^2} - rC = -rS\frac{\partial C}{\partial S}. \qquad (3.6)$$

If the variance rate V obeys the stochastic process given by (3.2), the call price c depends on two state variables S and V. Garman (1976) and Cox, Ingersoll, and Ross (1985a) show that a security f whose price

[1] This corresponds to an instantaneous standard deviation of 22–32% per annum.

[2] Hull and White (1987b) assumed that the volatility obeyed the process given by $dV = \hat{\xi}V\,dw$. The value of $\hat{\xi}$ which is comparable with the value of ξ used here is given by $\xi/\sqrt{V}$. If $\xi = 0.1$ and $V = 0.1$, the comparable $\hat{\xi}$ is about 0.3. Hull and White (1987a) provide some evidence indicating that for currencies $\hat{\xi}$ may be 1 or higher. However, it may be lower for stocks.

depends on state variables θ_i must satisfy the differential equation

$$\frac{\partial f}{\partial t} + \frac{1}{2} \sum_{i,j} \rho_{ij} \sigma_i \sigma_j \frac{\partial^2 f}{\partial \theta_i \partial \theta_j} - rf = \sum_i \theta_i \frac{\partial f}{\partial \theta_i} (-\mu_i + \lambda_i \sigma_i), \qquad (3.7)$$

where σ_i is the instantaneous standard deviation of the proportional change in θ_i, ρ_{ij} is the instantaneous correlation between θ_i and θ_j, μ_i is the proportional drift rate of θ_i, and λ_i is the market price of risk for variable θ_i. When variable i is traded, the ith element of the right-hand side of (3.7) is $-r\theta_i \, \partial f/\partial \theta_i$.

It follows that, for the two-state-variable case in question,

$$\frac{\partial c}{\partial t} + \frac{1}{2} \left(VS^2 \frac{\partial^2 c}{\partial S^2} + 2\rho V\xi S \frac{\partial^2 c}{\partial S \partial V} + \xi^2 V \frac{\partial^2 c}{\partial V^2} \right) - rc$$
$$= -rS \frac{\partial c}{\partial S} - (\eta - \lambda_V \xi \sqrt{V}) \frac{\partial c}{\partial V},$$

where λ_V is the market price of risk for variable V. Note that, since λ_V depends on investor risk preferences, the option price will, in general, depend on investor risk preferences. We assume initially that λ_V is zero, so that

$$\frac{\partial c}{\partial t} + \frac{1}{2} \left(VS^2 \frac{\partial^2 c}{\partial S^2} + 2\rho V\xi S \frac{\partial^2 c}{\partial S \partial V} + \xi^2 V \frac{\partial^2 c}{\partial V^2} \right) - rc = -rS \frac{\partial c}{\partial S} - \eta \frac{\partial c}{\partial V}.$$
$$(3.8)$$

Later it will be shown that the solution which is produced can be extended to accommodate the situation where λ_V is not zero, that is, where investors require compensation for bearing volatility risk.

Equation (3.8) is the differential equation that any security whose value is contingent on S and V must satisfy. If ξ and η are zero, (3.8) devolves into (3.6), the Black–Scholes equation. If ξ is zero but η is non-zero, then (3.8) becomes the differential equation that an option with a non-constant deterministic variance rate must satisfy. This was solved by Merton (1973).

In order to solve the option pricing problem when the volatility is stochastic, let us define the pricing bias

$$B = c - C.$$

This bias is the amount by which the actual option price when the variance rate is stochastic exceeds the Black–Scholes price when the variance is constant and equal to its initial value. Substituting $c = C + B$

in equation (3.8) and using equation (3.6), we obtain

$$\frac{\partial B}{\partial t} + \frac{1}{2}\left(VS^2\frac{\partial^2 B}{\partial S^2} + 2\rho V\xi S\frac{\partial^2 B}{\partial S\partial V} + \xi^2 V\frac{\partial^2 B}{\partial V^2}\right) - rB$$

$$+ \rho V\xi S\frac{\partial^2 C}{\partial S\partial V} + \tfrac{1}{2}\xi^2 V\frac{\partial^2 C}{\partial V^2} = -rS\frac{\partial B}{\partial S} - \eta\frac{\partial B}{\partial V} - \eta\frac{\partial C}{\partial V} \quad (3.9)$$

as the equation that the pricing bias must satisfy. The objective of this paper is to calculate B as a series in ξ,

$$B = f_0 + f_1\xi + f_2\xi^2 + \cdots, \quad (3.10)$$

where the f_i are functions of S, V, and t.

Define a differential operator D as follows:

$$Df = \frac{\partial f}{\partial t} + \tfrac{1}{2}VS^2\frac{\partial^2 f}{\partial S^2} - rf + rS\frac{\partial f}{\partial S}.$$

In terms of this operator, the Black–Scholes differential equation is $DC = 0$. If equation (3.10) is substituted into equation (3.9) and terms are collected by powers of ξ and if (3.9) is to be satisfied for arbitrary ξ, we obtain

$$Df_0 + \eta\frac{\partial f_0}{\partial V} + \eta\frac{\partial C}{\partial V} = 0, \quad (3.11)$$

$$Df_1 + \eta\frac{\partial f_1}{\partial V} + \rho VS\frac{\partial^2 f_0}{\partial S\partial V} + \rho VS\frac{\partial^2 C}{\partial S\partial V} = 0, \quad (3.12)$$

$$Df_2 + \eta\frac{\partial f_2}{\partial V} + \rho VS\frac{\partial^2 f_1}{\partial S\partial V} + \tfrac{1}{2}V\frac{\partial^2 C}{\partial V^2} + \tfrac{1}{2}V\frac{\partial^2 f_0}{\partial V^2} = 0, \quad (3.13)$$

and

$$Df_i + \eta\frac{\partial f_i}{\partial V} + \rho VS\frac{\partial^2 f_{i-1}}{\partial S\partial V} + \tfrac{1}{2}V\frac{\partial^2 f_{i-2}}{\partial V^2} = 0 \quad (i > 2). \quad (3.14)$$

Equations (3.11) to (3.14) define a family of differential equations that the coefficients of equation (3.10) must satisfy. Every function f_i must satisfy the boundary conditions

$$\left.\begin{array}{ll} f_i = 0 & \text{when } t = T, \\ f_i = 0 & \text{when } S = 0, \\ \partial f_i/\partial S \to 0 & \text{as } S \to \infty. \end{array}\right\} \quad (3.15)$$

The first of these follows from the fact that, at $t = T$,

$c = C = \max\{0, S - X\}$ regardless of the value of ξ. The second arises from $c = C = 0$ when $S = 0$. The third arises from the fact that both $\partial c/\partial S \rightarrow 1$ and $\partial C/\partial S \rightarrow 1$ as $S \rightarrow \infty$.[3]

The solutions to equations (3.11) to (3.13) for the process for V given by (3.2) and (3.3) are

$$f_0 = C(\bar{V}) - C(V), \tag{3.16}$$

$$f_1 = \frac{\rho}{b^2\delta}[(a + bV)(1 - e^\delta + \delta e^\delta) + a(1 + \delta - e^\delta)]S\frac{\partial^2 C(\bar{V})}{\partial S\partial \bar{V}}, \tag{3.17}$$

$$f_2 = \frac{\phi_1}{T - t}S\frac{\partial^2 C(\bar{V})}{\partial S\partial \bar{V}} + \frac{\phi_2}{(T - t)^2}\frac{\partial^2 C(\bar{V})}{\partial \bar{V}^2} + \frac{\phi_3}{(T - t)^2}S\frac{\partial^3 C(\bar{V})}{\partial S\partial \bar{V}^2}$$

$$+ \frac{\phi_4}{(T - t)^3}\frac{\partial^3 C(\bar{V})}{\partial \bar{V}^3}, \tag{3.18}$$

where

$$\phi_1 = \frac{\rho^2}{b^4}\{(a + bV)[e^\delta(\tfrac{1}{2}\delta^2 - \delta + 1) - 1] + a[e^\delta(2 - \delta) - (2 + \delta)]\},$$

$$\phi_2 = 2\phi_1 + \frac{1}{2b^4}\{(a + bV)(e^{2\delta} - 2\delta e^\delta - 1) - \tfrac{1}{2}a(e^{2\delta} - 4e^\delta + 2\delta + 3)\},$$

$$\phi_3 = \frac{\rho^2}{2b^6}\{(a + bV)(e^\delta - \delta e^\delta - 1) - a(1 + \delta - e^\delta)\}^2,$$

$$\phi_4 = 2\phi_3,$$

$$\delta = b(T - t),$$

and $\bar{V}$ is the average expected variance rate in the interval (t, T), that is,

$$\bar{V} = \frac{1}{T - t}\int_t^T E[V(s, t)]\,ds.$$

The proof that f_0, f_1, and f_2 satisfy the differential equations (3.11) to (3.13) is given in Appendix A, together with a procedure for calculating f_i for all values of i. It is not immediately obvious that f_0, f_1, and f_2 satisfy the boundary conditions in (3.15). A proof of this is given in Appendix C at the end of this chapter. The higher-order terms in the series are increasingly lengthy and complex, but are not difficult to derive.

When $\xi = 0$, the series gives

$$B = C(\bar{V}) - C(V)$$

---

[3] It should be noted that equations (3.11) to (3.15) are true for any contingent claim C that satisfies equation (3.6) and whose boundary conditions are independent of V. Thus, this solution technique can be used to determine the bias in the value of most one-state-variable contingent claims caused by a stochastic volatility.

or

$$c = C(\bar{V}).$$

This corresponds to the result in Merton (1973) for the situation where the volatility is a deterministic function of time. When the volatility is constant, $\bar{V} = V$ and the Black–Scholes result is obtained.

The special case $b = 0$ is found by taking the limits of (3.16) to (3.18). The value of f_0 is still given by (3.16),

$$f_1 = \rho[\tfrac{1}{3}a(T - t) + V] \cdot \tfrac{1}{2}(T - t)S\frac{\partial^2 C(\bar{V})}{\partial S \partial \bar{V}},$$

and f_2 is given by (3.18) with

$$\phi_1 = \rho^2[\tfrac{1}{4}a(T - t) + V] \cdot \tfrac{1}{6}(T - t)^3,$$
$$\phi_2 = (2 + 1/\rho^2)\phi_1,$$
$$\phi_3 = \rho^2[\tfrac{1}{3}a(T - t) + V]^2 \cdot \tfrac{1}{8}(T - t)^4,$$
$$\phi_4 = 2\phi_3.$$

Up to now we have assumed that λ_V is zero. We consider two cases in which λ_V is not zero. First, if $\lambda_V\xi\sqrt{V}$ is a constant, we can define a risk-adjusted drift rate η^* for V by

$$\eta^* = \eta - \lambda_V\xi\sqrt{V}.$$

If $a^* = a - \lambda_V\xi\sqrt{V}$, it follows that

$$\eta^* = a^* + bV.$$

Similarly, if $\lambda_V\xi\sqrt{V}$ is proportional to V, we define $b^* = b - \lambda_V\xi/\sqrt{V}$ and

$$\eta^* = a + b^*V.$$

The solution to the problem where λ_V is not zero and the drift rate of V is η is identical to the solution of the problem where $\lambda_V = 0$ and the drift rate in V is η^*. The results in equations (3.10) and (3.16) to (3.18) are therefore true with a replaced by a^* or b replaced by b^*.

3.3 THE ACCURACY OF THE SERIES SOLUTION

In this section the bias obtained by taking the first three terms of the series solution is compared with an estimate of the bias using a Monte Carlo simulation. The advantage of using a Monte Carlo estimate as a benchmark is that the standard error of the estimate is known. The range of parameter values tested were

S/X: 0.90, 0.95, 1.00, 1.05, 1.10;
ρ: $-1.0, -0.5, 0.0, 0.5, 1.0$;
ξ: 0.075, 0.150 per year;
(a, b): $(0, 0), (0.18, -2), (0.90, -10)$;
$V(0)$: 0.09 per year;
T: 180 days, or 0.493 years;
r: 0.

The argument at the end of Section 3.1 shows that the selected values for ξ are reasonable.

The results are shown in Tables 3.1, 3.2, and 3.3. Each table shows the series solution, the Monte Carlo estimate, and the standard error of this estimate. The patterns revealed in Tables 3.1 to 3.3 are the same as those found by Hull and White (1987b) and Johnson and Shanno (1987). When volatility is negatively correlated with the stock price, the Black–Scholes price is too high for out-of-the-money options and too low for in-the-money options. When the correlation is positive, the reverse is true.

Note that, for a sufficiently large sample size, the Monte Carlo result will differ from any imperfect estimate of the true value by more than two standard errors. If the Monte Carlo result differs from the series solution value by less than two standard errors, we can conclude only that the series solution is not significantly different from the Monte Carlo result. On this basis, inspection of Tables 3.1 to 3.3 reveals that the series solution is not significantly different from Monte Carlo estimates based on samples of size 40,000. These samples are chosen as 10,000 quadruplets using a two-dimensional antithetic variable approach. The Monte Carlo bias was calculated using a control variate approach (the Black–Scholes price and the stochastic volatility prices are estimated using the same random number streams). These procedures greatly increase the efficiency of the Monte Carlo estimate. (For a more detailed discussion of these approaches, see Hammersley and Handscomb (1964) and Hull and White (1987b).)

A more formal test of the accuracy of the series solution is based on the following t statistic:

$$t = \frac{B(\xi) - B(MC)}{SE(MC)},$$

where $B(\xi)$ is the bias determined by the series, and $B(MC)$ and $SE(MC)$ are the estimated bias and the standard error of the estimate from the

TABLE 3.1. The bias induced in the price of a call option when the variance rate is stochastic and reverts slowly to its long-run average level.[a]

ξ/year				S/X		
	ρ	0.90	0.95	1.00	1.05	1.10
0.15	−1.0	−7.57	−3.41	−0.95	0.39	1.03
		−7.39	−3.64	−0.92	0.51	0.94
		(0.29)	(0.22)	(0.16)	(0.13)	(0.11)
	−0.5	−3.90	−1.86	−0.60	0.11	0.48
		−3.87	−2.00	0.53	0.22	0.56
		(0.16)	(0.11)	(0.09)	(0.07)	(0.06)
	0.0	−0.35	−0.33	−0.26	−0.18	−0.11
		−0.36	−0.31	−0.24	−0.19	−0.13
		(0.02)	(0.02)	(0.01)	(0.01)	(0.01)
	0.5	3.07	1.17	0.08	−0.49	−0.73
		3.21	1.17	−0.07	−0.51	−0.68
		(0.15)	(0.10)	(0.08)	(0.06)	(0.06)
	1.0	6.37	2.64	0.41	−0.82	−1.39
		6.50	2.78	0.61	−0.79	−1.19
		(0.30)	(0.22)	(0.16)	(0.14)	(0.12)
0.075	−1.0	−3.63	−1.61	−0.41	0.25	0.56
		−3.83	−1.56	−0.38	0.26	0.65
		(0.15)	(0.10)	(0.07)	(0.06)	(0.05)
	−0.5	−1.85	−0.84	−0.24	0.10	0.27
		−1.85	−0.84	−0.20	0.09	0.25
		(0.07)	(0.05)	(0.04)	(0.04)	(0.03)
	0.0	−0.09	−0.08	−0.07	−0.05	−0.03
		−0.08	−0.09	−0.07	−0.04	−0.03
		(0.01)	(0.005)	(0.003)	(0.003)	(0.002)
	0.5	1.64	0.67	0.10	−0.20	−0.34
		1.57	0.65	0.12	−0.25	−0.37
		(0.06)	(0.06)	(0.04)	(0.03)	(0.03)
	1.0	3.33	1.41	0.27	−0.35	−0.65
		3.45	1.37	0.22	−0.36	−0.64
		(0.16)	(0.10)	(0.08)	(0.06)	(0.05)

a Bias is expressed as a percentage of the equivalent Black–Scholes price. The variance rate obeys the process $dV = (a + bV)\,dt + \xi\sqrt{V}\,dz$. The option parameters are $\sqrt{V(t)} = 0.30$ per year, $r = 0$, $a = 0.18$, $b = -2$, and time to maturity $T - t = 180$ days or 0.493 years. Every cell in the table contains three numbers: the bias calculated using equations (3.16) to (3.18), the Monte Carlo estimate of the bias based on a sample size of 40,000, and the standard error of the Monte Carlo estimate (in parentheses).

Monte Carlo calculation. Under the null hypothesis that the series solution is correct, this statistic should be distributed as a standard unit normal. The t statistic for all the observations in Tables 3.1 to 3.3 was tested to determine whether they were drawn from a standard unit

TABLE 3.2. The bias induced in the price of a call option when the variance rate is stochastic and has no drift.[a]

ξ/year		S/X				
	ρ	0.90	0.95	1.00	1.05	1.10
0.15	−1.0	−10.42	−4.66	−1.30	0.51	1.36
		−10.68	−4.27	−1.39	0.44	1.51
		(0.41)	(0.27)	(0.20)	(0.17)	(0.13)
	−0.5	−5.48	−2.68	−0.94	0.06	0.58
		−5.45	−2.62	−0.87	−0.07	0.67
		(0.19)	(0.17)	(0.11)	(0.11)	(0.08)
	0.0	−0.69	−0.65	−0.52	−0.36	−0.22
		−0.64	−0.68	−0.50	−0.35	−0.22
		(0.04)	(0.02)	(0.02)	(0.01)	(0.01)
	0.5	3.95	1.41	−0.02	−0.76	−1.06
		4.17	1.46	−0.11	−0.63	−0.97
		(0.20)	(0.14)	(0.10)	(0.09)	(0.07)
	1.0	8.46	3.52	0.54	−1.12	−1.92
		8.71	3.36	0.35	−1.18	−1.92
		(0.46)	(0.27)	(0.21)	(0.16)	(0.13)
0.075	−1.0	−4.96	−2.19	−0.56	0.33	0.75
		−4.73	−2.15	−0.55	0.47	0.70
		(0.18)	(0.11)	(0.12)	(0.08)	(0.07)
	−0.5	−2.55	−1.18	−0.35	0.12	0.35
		−2.54	−1.21	−0.39	0.17	0.29
		(0.10)	(0.07)	(0.06)	(0.04)	(0.04)
	0.0	−0.17	−0.16	−0.13	−0.09	−0.06
		−0.19	−0.16	−0.13	−0.09	−0.06
		(0.01)	(0.01)	(0.00)	(0.00)	(0.00)
	0.5	2.17	0.86	0.11	−0.29	−0.47
		2.15	0.83	0.17	−0.25	−0.47
		(0.09)	(0.07)	(0.06)	(0.05)	(0.03)
	1.0	4.47	1.90	0.37	−0.48	−0.89
		4.40	1.71	0.26	−0.53	−0.81
		(0.19)	(0.14)	(0.10)	(0.10)	(0.07)

[a] Bias is expressed as a percentage of the equivalent Black–Scholes price. The variance rate obeys the process $dV = (a + bV)\,dt + \xi\sqrt{V}\,dz$. The option parameters are $\sqrt{V(t)} = 0.30$ per year, $r = 0$, $a = b = 0$, and time to maturity $T - t = 180$ days or 0.493 years. Every cell in the table contains three numbers: the bias calculated using equations (3.16) to (3.18), the Monte Carlo estimate of the bias based on a sample size of 40,000, and the standard error of the Monte Carlo estimate (in parentheses).

normal (this gives a sample size of 150). The mean and variance of t were −0.08 and 0.93, respectively. The Kolmogorov D statistic was 0.06. Based on these results, we are unable to reject at the 5% level the hypothesis that the mean is zero, the variance is 1, or that the

TABLE 3.3. The bias induced in the price of a call option when the variance rate is stochastic and reverts quickly to its long-run average level.[a]

ξ/year	ρ	S/X				
		0.90	0.95	1.00	1.05	1.10
0.15	−1.0	−3.20	−1.43	−0.37	0.21	0.49
		−3.23	−1.50	−0.24	0.19	0.24
		(0.15)	(0.12)	(0.08)	(0.07)	(0.06)
	−0.5	−1.61	−0.73	−0.20	0.09	0.24
		−1.56	−0.66	−0.24	0.03	0.21
		(0.07)	(0.05)	(0.05)	(0.04)	(0.03)
	0.0	−0.06	−0.06	−0.04	−0.03	−0.02
		−0.05	−0.05	−0.03	−0.02	−0.02
		(0.01)	(0.01)	(0.01)	(0.01)	(0.00)
	0.5	1.45	0.59	0.10	−0.17	−0.29
		1.51	0.64	0.02	−0.12	−0.28
		(0.08)	(0.06)	(0.04)	(0.03)	(0.03)
	1.0	2.92	1.22	0.22	−0.32	−0.58
		2.79	1.10	0.32	−0.27	−0.57
		(0.13)	(0.10)	(0.09)	(0.08)	(0.06)
	−1.0	−1.56	−0.69	−0.17	0.12	0.25
		−1.57	−0.67	−0.12	0.15	0.24
		(0.08)	(0.05)	(0.04)	(0.04)	(0.03)
	−0.5	−0.78	−0.35	−0.09	0.06	0.13
		−0.79	−0.36	−0.12	0.09	0.13
		(0.05)	(0.03)	(0.02)	(0.02)	(0.02)
0.075	0.0	−0.02	−0.01	−0.01	−0.01	−0.00
		−0.01	−0.01	−0.01	−0.01	−0.00
		(0.00)	(0.00)	(0.00)	(0.00)	(0.00)
	0.5	0.74	0.31	0.06	−0.08	−0.14
		0.75	0.34	0.04	−0.06	−0.14
		(0.04)	(0.03)	(0.02)	(0.02)	(0.02)
	1.0	1.49	0.64	0.13	−0.15	−0.28
		1.48	0.60	0.14	−0.18	−0.29
		(0.08)	(0.06)	(0.04)	(0.04)	(0.03)

a Bias is expressed as a percentage of the equivalent Black–Scholes price. The variance rate obeys the process $dV = (a + bV)\,dt + \xi\sqrt{V}\,dz$. The option parameters are $\sqrt{V(t)} = 0.30$ per year, $r = 0$, $a = 0.90$, $b = -10$, and the time to maturity $T - t =$ 180 days or 0.493 years. Every cell in the table contains three numbers: the bias calculated using equations (3.16) to (3.18), the Monte Carlo estimate of the bias based on a sample size of 40,000, and the standard error of the Monte Carlo estimate (in parentheses).

distribution is normal. Thus, these Monte Carlo results do not permit us to distinguish between the series solution and the true value.

The solution given by equations (3.10) and (3.16) to (3.18) is equivalent to a Taylor series expansion of the bias caused a stochastic

TABLE 3.4. Comparison of bias with that produced by Dothan's model.[a]

(a, b)		S/X				
	ρ	0.90	0.95	1.00	1.05	1.10
(0,0)	−1.0	−10.42	−4.66	−1.30	0.51	1.36
		−10.87	−5.01	−1.56	0.32	1.22
		−10.68	−4.27	−1.39	0.44	1.51
	−0.5	−5.48	−2.68	−0.94	0.06	0.58
		−5.60	−2.76	−1.01	0.01	0.55
		−5.45	−2.62	−0.87	−0.07	0.67
	0.0	−0.69	−0.65	−0.52	−0.36	−0.22
		−0.69	−0.65	−0.52	−0.36	−0.22
		−0.64	−0.68	−0.50	−0.35	−0.22
	0.5	3.95	1.41	−0.02	−0.76	−1.06
		3.84	1.33	−0.09	−0.80	−1.09
		4.17	1.46	−0.11	−0.63	−0.97
	1.0	8.46	3.52	0.54	−1.12	−1.92
		8.00	3.17	0.29	−1.31	−2.06
		8.71	3.36	0.35	−1.18	−1.92
(0.9, −10)	−1.0	−3.20	−1.43	0.37	0.21	0.49
		4.64	1.72	−0.04	−1.02	−1.47
		−3.23	−1.50	−0.24	0.19	0.42
	−0.5	−1.61	−0.73	−0.20	0.09	0.24
		2.16	0.60	−0.25	−0.66	−0.80
		−1.56	−0.66	−0.24	0.03	0.21
	0.0	−0.06	−0.06	−0.04	−0.03	−0.02
		−0.69	−0.65	−0.52	−0.36	−0.22
		−0.05	−0.05	−0.03	−0.02	−0.02
	0.5	1.45	0.59	0.10	−0.17	−0.29
		−3.92	−2.04	−0.84	−0.13	0.26
		1.51	0.64	0.02	−0.12	−0.28
	1.0	2.92	1.22	0.22	−0.32	−0.58
		−7.51	−3.55	−1.23	0.03	0.64
		2.79	1.10	0.32	−0.27	−0.57

a Bias is expressed as percentage of the equivalent Black–Scholes price. Every cell in the table contains three numbers: the bias calculated using equations (3.16) to (3.18), the bias calculated using Dothan's [10] solution, and the Monte Carlo estimate of the bias based on a sample size of 40,000. The variance rate obeys the process $dV = (a + bV)\,dt + \xi\sqrt{V}\,dz$. The option parameters are $\sqrt{V(t)} = 0.30$ per year, $r = 0$, $\xi = 0.15$ per year, and time to maturity $T - t = 180$ days or 0.493 years.

volatility. Dothan (1987) also produces a Taylor series expansion for the solution to equation (3.8). The distinction between the two series solutions is that Dothan expands the series about the point $\eta = 0$ and $\xi = 0$. In this paper the expansion is about $\xi = 0$ with no approximation for η. This suggests that both solutions should be approximately the same for small η and differ most widely when η is large.

Table 3.4 shows the biases computed using equations (3.16) to (3.18) and those found using Dothan's solution for the cases $a = b = 0$ and $a = 0.9, b = -10$. As expected, when $\eta = 0$ the two solutions are very close, but when η is large they differ substantially. The values $a = 0.9$ and $b = -10$ are not extreme. They correspond to a variance rate that reverts to 0.09; perturbations from this reversion level die away with a half-life of about 25 days. Although not shown, we found that Dothan's approximation worked well when $b > -3$.

3.4 PROPERTIES OF THE SOLUTION

The impact of a stochastic volatility when ξ is small can be approximated by the first non-zero term in ξ in the series solution. If $\rho \neq 0$ and $V = -a/b$ (i.e., the variance rate is at the reversion value), then (3.17) approximates the bias as

$$B(\xi) \approx -\frac{\rho V}{b\delta}(1 + \delta - e^{\delta})S\frac{\partial^2 C(\bar{V})}{\partial S \partial \bar{V}}\xi,$$

where

$$\frac{\partial^2 C(\bar{V})}{\partial S \partial \bar{V}} = -\frac{N'(d_1)d_2}{2\bar{V}},$$

$$d_1 = \frac{\ln(S/X) + r(T - t) + \frac{1}{2}\bar{V}(T - t)}{\sqrt{\bar{V}(T - t)}}, \qquad d_2 = d_1 - \sqrt{\bar{V}(T - t)},$$

and $N(\cdot)$ is the cumulative normal distribution function. The sign of $B(\xi)$ is then the same as the sign of $-\rho d_2$. This means the bias is approximately zero when $d_2 = 0$ or when

$$\frac{S}{Xe^{-r(T-t)}} = e^{\frac{1}{2}\bar{V}(T-t)}, \tag{3.19}$$

that is, when the option is slightly in the money. For the parameters in Tables 3.1 to 3.3 ($V = 0.09$ per year, $T - t = 180$ days), the bias changes sign when $S/Xe^{(T-t)} \approx 1.022$. Inspection of Tables 3.1 to 3.3 reveals that (3.19) is a reasonable approximation of the crossing point of the bias in all of the cases considered.

When the volatility and the stock price are uncorrelated ($\rho = 0$) and $V = -a/b$, the first non-zero term in the series expansion (see equation (3.18)) gives

$$B(\xi) \approx \frac{V}{4b\delta^2}(e^{2\delta} - 4e^{\delta} + 2\delta + 3)\frac{\partial^2 C(\bar{V})}{\partial \bar{V}^2}\xi^2.$$

Since

$$\frac{\partial^2 C(\bar{V})}{\partial \bar{V}^2} = \frac{S\sqrt{T-t}}{4\bar{V}^{\frac{3}{2}}}N'(d_1)(d_1 d_2 - 1),$$

the sign of the bias is the same as the sign of $d_1 d_2 - 1$. Defining

$$k = \{[\tfrac{1}{2}\bar{V}(T - t)]^2 + \bar{V}(T - t)\}^{\frac{1}{2}},$$

we see that the bias is negative when

$$e^{-k} < \frac{S}{Xe^{-r(T-t)}} < e^k, \qquad (3.20)$$

and positive elsewhere. For the options in Tables 3.1 to 3.3, $e^k = 1.24$ and $e^{-k} = 0.81$. Thus, we see that in this case the Black–Scholes price is too high over a very wide range of stock prices around the exercise price. The properties in (3.19) and (3.20) have been derived under the assumption that $\bar{V} = V(t)$. When the current volatility differs from the average expected volatility ($\bar{V} \neq V(t)$), equations (3.19) and (3.20) give the crossing points for the bias with respect to $C(\bar{V})$, the Black–Scholes price based on the mean expected volatility.

The $\rho = 0$ result can be understood from Hull and White (1987b) and Scott (1987). These papers show that when $\rho = 0$ the option price is the Black–Scholes price, C, integrated over the distribution of the mean volatility during the life of the option. In general C is a convex (concave) function of V for small (large) values of V. It follows that both underpricing and overpricing by Black–Scholes are possible. In the particular case where the option is at the money,[4] C is always a concave function of V and overpricing always takes place.

The $\rho \neq 0$ results are consistent with the simulation results of Johnson and Shanno (1987) and Hull and White (1987b). They can be expressed in terms of the implied volatility, which is calculated using the Black–Scholes model. If $\rho > 0$, the implied volatility will tend to decrease as S/X increases. If $\rho < 0$, the implied volatility will tend to increase as S/X increases. It is interesting to compare these results with the empirical results of Rubinstein (1986), who compared the implied volatility of options that differed only in exercise price. In the period 1976–77, he found that as S/X increased there was a tendency for the

[4] At the money is defined as $S = Xe^{-r(T-t)}$.

implied volatility to decrease. For 1977–78 the reverse was observed. Under our model this is consistent with a situation where the volatility was positively correlated with stock price in 1976–77 and negatively correlated with stock price in 1977–78.

Rubinstein also compared matched pairs of options that only differed in time to maturity. He found that in the 1976–77 period shorter-term options had higher implied volatilities for out-of-the-money options. For at-the-money and in-the-money options the reverse was true. In the period 1977–78 almost all options exhibited the property that shorter-term options had higher implied volatilities. This is difficult to reconcile with equations (3.16) to (3.18), and the above hypothesis about the sign of the correlation in the two time periods. The effect of a longer time to maturity is to generally exaggerate the biases and the distortions in the implied volatility.

As was discussed in Section 3.2, when λ_V, which is a measure of the systematic risk of the variance rate V, is not zero, we can define a risk-adjusted drift rate η^* by

$$\eta^* = a^* + bV \quad \text{or} \quad \eta^* = a + b^* V,$$

where

$$a^* = a - \lambda_V \xi \sqrt{V} \quad \text{and} \quad b^* = b - \lambda_V \xi / \sqrt{V}.$$

The option price can then be determined in terms of the risk-adjusted parameters a^* and b^*. One of the results of this is that $\bar{V}$ is no longer the mean expected variance rate. It is now a risk-adjusted mean expected variance rate whose value is negatively related to λ_V. Thus, $\partial f_0 / \partial \lambda_V < 0$ and, at least for relatively small values of ξ, $\partial B / \partial \lambda_V < 0$. An intuitive explanation of this result is as follows. As λ_V increases, the systematic risk of the option increases and the return required on the option increases. Given the distribution of the terminal stock price, this means that the option price—the discounted value of the expected payoff—will have a lower value than if the variance rate had no systematic risk. Therefore, if the variance rate's systematic risk can be varied without affecting the correlation between V and S, increasing the systematic risk of V lowers the option price and vice versa. Note that this effect is proportional to the time to maturity of the option. Thus, to the extent that it exists, it will cause a marked trend in the implied volatilities of options of different maturities if these are computed using the Black–Scholes pricing equation.

3.5 IMPLICATIONS FOR OPTION REPLICATION STRATEGIES

Option replication strategies are of interest to investors who wish to buy portfolio insurance, market makers in options on an exchange, and financial institutions that write over-the-counter options. A stochastic volatility has serious implications for the effectiveness of option replication strategies that are based on the Black–Scholes model.

Suppose the stock price, variance rate, and time are S, V, and t, respectively, and the option price is $c(S, V, t)$. Applying Ito's lemma and using (3.1) and (3.2) gives

$$
dc = \left[\eta \frac{\partial c}{\partial V} + \phi S \frac{\partial c}{\partial S} + \frac{\partial c}{\partial t} \right.
$$
$$
\left. + \frac{1}{2} \left(\xi^2 V \frac{\partial^2 c}{\partial V^2} + V S^2 \frac{\partial^2 c}{\partial S^2} + 2\xi V S \rho \frac{\partial^2 c}{\partial S \partial V} \right) \right] dt
$$
$$
+ S\sqrt{V} \frac{\partial c}{\partial S} dz + \xi\sqrt{V} \frac{\partial c}{\partial V} dw.
$$

Consider the traditional Black–Scholes hedging portfolio that is short one call option and long $\partial C/\partial S$ shares. If the value of the portfolio is W, then

$$
dW = \frac{\partial C}{\partial S} dS - dc
$$
$$
= - \left[\eta \frac{\partial c}{\partial V} + \phi S \left(\frac{\partial c}{\partial S} - \frac{\partial C}{\partial S} \right) + \frac{\partial c}{\partial t} \right.
$$
$$
\left. + \frac{1}{2} \left(\xi^2 V \frac{\partial^2 c}{\partial V^2} + V S^2 \frac{\partial^2 c}{\partial S^2} + 2\xi V S \rho \frac{\partial^2 c}{\partial S \partial V} \right) \right] dt
$$
$$
+ S\sqrt{V} \left(\frac{\partial C}{\partial S} - \frac{\partial c}{\partial S} \right) dz + \xi\sqrt{V} \frac{\partial c}{\partial V} dw. \tag{3.21}
$$

This has two stochastic elements. The first of these is

$$
-S\sqrt{V} \frac{\partial B}{\partial S} dz
$$

and arises from the error $\partial B/\partial S$ in the hedge ratio which is calculated from the Black–Scholes price. The second is

$$
\xi\sqrt{V} \frac{\partial c}{\partial V} dw
$$

and arises from the fact that the volatility risk is not hedged at all.

Consider first the sign of $\partial B/\partial S$. From equation (3.10),

$$\frac{\partial B}{\partial S} = \frac{\partial f_0}{\partial S} + \frac{\partial f_1}{\partial S}\xi + \frac{\partial f_2}{\partial S}\xi^2 + \cdots.$$

When ξ is small, the first non-zero term in this expansion is a good approximation. If $\rho \neq 0$ and $V = -a/b$, then

$$\frac{\partial B}{\partial S} \approx \frac{\partial f_1}{\partial S}\xi.$$

It can be shown that the sign of this is the same as the sign of

$$\rho\left(-d_2 + \frac{d_1 d_2 - 1}{\sqrt{\bar{V}(T-t)}}\right).$$

Define

$$k_1 = \tfrac{1}{2}\bar{V}(T-t) - \sqrt{\bar{V}(T-t)}, \qquad k_2 = \tfrac{1}{2}\bar{V}(T-t) + \sqrt{\bar{V}(T-t)}.$$

If

$$e^{k_1} < \frac{S}{Xe^{-r(T-t)}} < e^{k_2},$$

then $\partial f_1/\partial S$ has the same sign as $-\rho$. Near-the-money options are less (more) sensitive to changes in the stock price than the Black–Scholes equation suggests if there is positive (negative) correlation between S and V. For the parameters used in Tables 3.1 to 3.3, the range over which this phenomenon is observed is

$$0.83Xe^{-r(T-t)} < S < 1.26Xe^{-r(T-t)}.$$

This result may seem paradoxical. If the stock price is positively correlated with the volatility, an increase in the stock price is likely to accompany an increase in the volatility. Both of these events raise the option value, so one might expect an abnormally large increase in the option price as a result of an increase in the stock price. However, the hedge ratio calculation is the change in the option price for some change in the stock price with all else (in particular, the volatility) held constant. It can be shown that in practice the absolute magnitude of $S\sqrt{V}\,\partial B/\partial S$ is very small. The degree of hedging error arising from the first stochastic term in equation (3.21) is therefore minimal.

The size of the second stochastic term in equation (3.21) can be assessed by approximating c and its derivatives with the corresponding Black–Scholes values. For an at-the-money option with $V = 0.09$ per year and $T - t = 0.493$ years (the parameters used in Tables 3.1 to 3.3), $\xi\sqrt{V}\,\partial c/\partial V$ is approximately $1.67\xi C$. For $\xi = 0.15$, this is about $0.25C$. In the situation where an option is being hedged using futures contracts, the actual wealth involved (ignoring margin requirements) is C, so that the instantaneous standard deviation of the rate of return would then be 0.25 or 25% per year. Thus, failing to hedge the stochastic volatility imposes a risk on the investor comparable to the risk of holding the stock alone.

The impact of a stochastic volatility on a hedged option position was first noted by Galai (1983). Hull and White (1987a) test a variety of hedging schemes designed to control this risk. Their results show that a significant improvement in hedge performance can be achieved in practice by using other options on the same stock to eliminate the second stochastic term in (3.21).

3.6 CONCLUSIONS

This paper uses a procedure to value two-state-variable contingent claims to derive a series solution for the price of a call option on a security with a stochastic volatility. The volatility may follow a mean-reverting process and is allowed to be instantaneously correlated with stock price. When this correlation is positive, it is shown that Black–Scholes tends to overprice out-of-the-money options and to underprice in-the-money options. When there is negative correlation, the reverse is true. For reasonable values of the parameters, the under- or overpricing is usually less than 1% of the Black–Scholes price for an at-the-money or in-the-money option. For an out-of-the-money option it can be considerably higher than this. It is possible that these pricing biases contribute to the results obtained by Rubinstein (1986).

The results in this paper apply to a European call option on a non-dividend-paying stock. They can be extended to European put options on the stock through the use of put–call parity, and, by using the results in Merton (1973), to American call options on the stock. The solution technique employed in this paper can be used to determine the bias in the value of most one-state-variable contingent claims caused by a stochastic volatility.

APPENDIX A: DERIVATION OF SERIES SOLUTION

In this appendix we prove that equations (3.16) to (3.18) are solutions to differential equations (3.11) to (3.13) and provide a general technique to find all higher-order terms. We start with a series of lemmas.

LEMMA 1.

$$D\left[\frac{\partial^n C(V)}{\partial V^n}\right] = -\frac{n}{T-t}\frac{\partial^n C(V)}{\partial V^n}.$$

Proof. Since $DC = 0$, the result is true for $n = 0$. Assume that it is true for $n = k$:

$$D\left[\frac{\partial^k C(V)}{\partial V^k}\right] = -\frac{k}{T-t}\frac{\partial^k C(V)}{\partial V^k}. \tag{A1}$$

From the structure of the D operator,

$$\frac{\partial}{\partial V}Dx = D\frac{\partial x}{\partial V} + \tfrac{1}{2}S^2\frac{\partial^2 x}{\partial S^2}$$

for any function x of S, V, and t. Putting $x = \partial^k C(V)/\partial V^k$ and using equation (A1), we obtain

$$D\left[\frac{\partial^{k+1} C(V)}{\partial V^{k+1}}\right] = -\frac{k}{T-t}\frac{\partial^{k+1} C(V)}{\partial V^{k+1}} - \tfrac{1}{2}S^2\frac{\partial^{k+2} C(V)}{\partial S^2 \partial V^k}. \tag{A2}$$

From the known functional forms for the derivative of C,

$$\tfrac{1}{2}S^2\frac{\partial^2 C(V)}{\partial S^2} = \frac{1}{T-t}\frac{\partial C(V)}{\partial V}.$$

Hence

$$\tfrac{1}{2}S^2\frac{\partial^{k+2} C(V)}{\partial S^2 \partial V^k} = \frac{1}{T-t}\frac{\partial^{k+1} C(V)}{\partial V^{k+1}} \tag{A3}$$

and equation (A2) becomes

$$D\left[\frac{\partial^{k+1} C(V)}{\partial V^{k+1}}\right] = -\frac{k+1}{T-t}\frac{\partial^{k+1} C(V)}{\partial V^{k+1}},$$

showing that the lemma is true for $n = k + 1$. It follows by mathematical induction that it is true for all n. $\square$

LEMMA 2.

$$\frac{\partial \bar{V}}{\partial t} + \eta\frac{\partial \bar{V}}{\partial V} = \frac{\bar{V} - V}{T - t}.$$

Proof. This result is generally true when η is a function of V and t. Here

61

we demonstrate that it is true for the model considered in this paper. Since

$$E[V(s, t)] = (V - \hat{V})e^{b(s-t)} + \hat{V},$$

it follows that

$$\bar{V} = \frac{1}{T - t}\int_t^T [(V - \hat{V})e^{b(s-t)} + \hat{V}]\,ds$$

$$= \hat{V} + \frac{1}{b(T - t)}(V - \hat{V})(e^{b(T-t)} - 1), \qquad (A4)$$

$$\frac{\partial \bar{V}}{\partial t} = \frac{1}{b(T - t)^2}(V - \hat{V})(e^{b(T-t)} - 1) - \frac{1}{T - t}(V - \hat{V})e^{b(T-t)},$$

and

$$\frac{\partial \bar{V}}{\partial V} = \frac{e^{b(T-t)} - 1}{b(T - t)}. \qquad (A5)$$

Since $\eta = b(V - \hat{V})$, we have

$$\frac{\partial \bar{V}}{\partial t} + \eta \frac{\partial \bar{V}}{\partial V} = \frac{V - \hat{V}}{T - t}\left(\frac{\partial \bar{V}}{\partial V} - 1\right).$$

From equation (A4),

$$V - \hat{V} = \frac{V - \bar{V}}{1 - \partial \bar{V}/\partial V}.$$

The lemma follows. □

LEMMA 3.

$$D\left[\frac{\partial^n C(\bar{V})}{\partial \bar{V}^n}\right] + \eta \frac{\partial}{\partial V}\left[\frac{\partial^n C(\bar{V})}{\partial \bar{V}^n}\right] = -\frac{n}{T - t}\frac{\partial^n C(\bar{V})}{\partial \bar{V}^n}.$$

Proof. Define $\theta(V) = \partial^n C(V)/\partial V^n$. Since $\bar{V}$ is a function of V and t, it follows from the structure of the D operator that

$$D[\theta(\bar{V})] = \frac{\partial \theta(\bar{V})}{\partial t} + \frac{\partial \theta(\bar{V})}{\partial \bar{V}}\frac{\partial \bar{V}}{\partial t} + \frac{1}{2}VS^2\frac{\partial^2 \theta(\bar{V})}{\partial S^2} - r\theta(\bar{V}) + rS\frac{\partial \theta(\bar{V})}{\partial S}$$

and

$$D[\theta(V)]\big|_{V=\bar{V}} = \frac{\partial \theta(\bar{V})}{\partial t} + \frac{1}{2}\bar{V}S^2\frac{\partial^2 \theta(\bar{V})}{\partial S^2} - r\theta(\bar{V}) + rS\frac{\partial \theta(\bar{V})}{\partial S}.$$

Hence

$$D[\theta(\bar{V})] = D[\theta(V)]\big|_{V=\bar{V}} + \frac{\partial\theta(\bar{V})}{\partial\bar{V}}\frac{\partial\bar{V}}{\partial t} + \tfrac{1}{2}(V - \bar{V})S^2\frac{\partial^2\theta(\bar{V})}{\partial S^2}.$$

Since

$$\frac{\partial\theta(\bar{V})}{\partial V} = \frac{\partial\theta(\bar{V})}{\partial\bar{V}}\frac{\partial\bar{V}}{\partial V},$$

it follows that

$$D[\theta(\bar{V})] + \eta\frac{\partial\theta(\bar{V})}{\partial V}$$

$$= D[\theta(V)]\big|_{V=\bar{V}} + \frac{\partial\theta(\bar{V})}{\partial\bar{V}}\left(\frac{\partial\bar{V}}{\partial t} + \eta\frac{\partial\bar{V}}{\partial V}\right) + \tfrac{1}{2}(V - \bar{V})S^2\frac{\partial^2\theta(\bar{V})}{\partial S^2}.$$

From Lemma 1,

$$D[\theta(V)]\big|_{V=\bar{V}} = -\frac{n}{T-t}\frac{\partial^n C(V)}{\partial V^n}\bigg|_{V=\bar{V}} = -\frac{n}{T-t}\frac{\partial^n C(\bar{V})}{\partial\bar{V}^n}.$$

From this and the result in Lemma 2,

$$D[\theta(\bar{V})] + \eta\frac{\partial\theta(\bar{V})}{\partial V} = -\frac{n}{T-t}\theta(\bar{V}) + (V-\bar{V})\left(\tfrac{1}{2}S^2\frac{\partial^2\theta(\bar{V})}{\partial S^2} - \frac{1}{T-t}\frac{\partial\theta(\bar{V})}{\partial\bar{V}}\right).$$

Equation (A3) shows that the last term in this equation vanishes. The lemma follows from the definition of θ. $\square$

LEMMA 4.

$$DC(\bar{V}) + \eta\frac{\partial C(\bar{V})}{\partial V} = 0.$$

Proof. This can be regarded as the particular case of Lemma 3 when $n = 0$. It is easily seen that the result is true by substituting $\theta(V) = C(V)$ and repeating the analysis in Lemma 3. $\square$

LEMMA 5.

$$D\left[S\frac{\partial^n C(\bar{V})}{\partial\bar{V}^{n-1}\partial S}\right] + \eta\frac{\partial}{\partial V}\left[S\frac{\partial^n C(\bar{V})}{\partial\bar{V}^{n-1}\partial S}\right] = -\frac{n-1}{T-t}S\frac{\partial^n C(\bar{V})}{\partial\bar{V}^{n-1}\partial S}.$$

Proof. From the definition of the D operator,

$$D\left[S\frac{\partial x}{\partial S}\right] = S\frac{\partial}{\partial S}[Dx]$$

for any function x of S, V, and t. By substituting

$$x = \frac{\partial^{n-1} C(\bar{V})}{\partial \bar{V}^{n-1}}$$

into this and using Lemma 3, the result follows. $\quad\square$

The results in Lemmas 3 to 5 enable equations (3.11) to (3.13) to be solved. Lemma 4 shows that

$$f_0 = C(\bar{V}) - C(V) \tag{A6}$$

is a solution to equation (3.11). Using this result, equation (3.12) becomes

$$Df_1 + \eta \frac{\partial f_1}{\partial V} + \rho V S \frac{\partial^2 C(\bar{V})}{\partial S \partial V} = 0,$$

or

$$Df_1 + \eta \frac{\partial f_1}{\partial V} + \rho V S \frac{\partial^2 C(\bar{V})}{\partial S \partial \bar{V}} \frac{\partial \bar{V}}{\partial V} = 0. \tag{A7}$$

Lemma 5 suggests that a solution to this is of the form

$$f_1 = \frac{\psi(V, t)}{T - t} S \frac{\partial^2 C(\bar{V})}{\partial S \partial \bar{V}}. \tag{A8}$$

To see why this is so, note first that, from the structure of the D operator,

$$D(xy) = \frac{\partial x}{\partial t} y + x D y$$

when x is a function of V and t, and y is a function of S, V, and t. Hence (A8) implies

$$Df_1 = \left(\frac{1}{T-t} \frac{\partial \psi}{\partial t} + \frac{1}{(T-t)^2} \psi \right) S \frac{\partial^2 C(\bar{V})}{\partial S \partial \bar{V}} + \frac{\psi}{T-t} D \left[S \frac{\partial^2 C(\bar{V})}{\partial S \partial \bar{V}} \right]. \tag{A9}$$

Also,

$$\eta \frac{\partial f_1}{\partial V} = \left(\frac{\eta}{T-t} \frac{\partial \psi}{\partial V} + \frac{\eta \psi}{T-t} \frac{\partial}{\partial V} \right) \left[S \frac{\partial^2 C(\bar{V})}{\partial S \partial \bar{V}} \right]. \tag{A10}$$

Using Lemma 5 with $n = 2$,

$$D \left[S \frac{\partial^2 C(\bar{V})}{\partial S \partial \bar{V}} \right] = -\eta \frac{\partial}{\partial V} \left[S \frac{\partial^2 C(\bar{V})}{\partial S \partial \bar{V}} \right] - \frac{1}{T-t} S \frac{\partial^2 C(\bar{V})}{\partial S \partial \bar{V}}. \tag{A11}$$

From (A9)–(A11) it follows that (A7) is satisfied by (A8) when

$$\frac{\partial \psi}{\partial t} + \eta \frac{\partial \psi}{\partial V} + \rho V (T - t) \frac{\partial \bar{V}}{\partial V} = 0. \tag{A12}$$

This has the condition that $\psi(V, T) = 0$. Using standard techniques, we obtain the solution as

$$\psi\big(\tau, V(\tau)\big) = -\int_{\tau}^{T} \rho\chi(s, k)(T - s)\frac{\partial \bar{V}(t)}{\partial V(t)}\bigg|_{t=s} ds,$$

where $V = \chi(t, k)$ is a solution to

$$\frac{dV}{\eta(V)} = dt$$

and k is the constant of integration. For the particular functional form of $\eta(V)$ given in equation (3.3), the solution is

$$\psi(t, V) = -\frac{\rho}{b^3}[(a + bV)(e^{\delta} - \delta e^{\delta} - 1) + a(e^{\delta} - \delta - 1)], \qquad \text{(A13)}$$

where $\delta = b(T - t)$. This means that the second term in the series is

$$f_1 = \frac{\rho}{b^2\delta}[(a + bV)(1 - e^{\delta} + \delta e^{\delta}) + a(1 + \delta - e^{\delta})]S\frac{\partial^2 C(\bar{V})}{\partial S \partial \bar{V}}. \qquad \text{(A14)}$$

Higher-order terms are calculated similarly. Substituting (A6) and (A8) into equation (3.13), we have

$$Df_2 + \eta\frac{\partial f_2}{\partial V} + \rho V S\frac{\partial^2}{\partial S \partial V}\left[\frac{\psi}{T - t}S\frac{\partial^2 C(\bar{V})}{\partial S \partial \bar{V}}\right] + \tfrac{1}{2}V\frac{\partial^2 C(\bar{V})}{\partial V^2} = 0,$$

which becomes

$$Df_2 + \eta\frac{\partial f_2}{\partial V} + \rho V S\frac{\partial}{\partial S}\left[\frac{\psi_V S}{T - t}\frac{\partial^2 C(\bar{V})}{\partial S \partial \bar{V}} + \frac{\psi}{T - t}S\frac{\partial^3 C(\bar{V})}{\partial S \partial \bar{V}^2}\frac{\partial \bar{V}}{\partial V}\right]$$
$$+ \tfrac{1}{2}V\frac{\partial^2 C(\bar{V})}{\partial V^2} = 0,$$

or

$$Df_2 + \eta\frac{\partial f_2}{\partial V} + \rho V S\frac{\psi_V}{T - t}\frac{\partial^2 C(\bar{V})}{\partial S \partial \bar{V}} + \rho V S\frac{\psi}{T - t}\frac{\partial^3 C(\bar{V})}{\partial S \partial \bar{V}^2}\frac{\partial \bar{V}}{\partial V}$$
$$+ \rho V S^2\frac{\psi_V}{T - t}\frac{\partial^3 C(\bar{V})}{\partial S^2 \partial \bar{V}} + \rho V S^2\frac{\psi}{T - t}\frac{\partial^4 C(\bar{V})}{\partial S^2 \partial \bar{V}^2}\frac{\partial \bar{V}}{\partial V} + \tfrac{1}{2}V\frac{\partial^2 C(\bar{V})}{\partial V^2} = 0,$$

where $\psi_V = \partial\psi/\partial V$. Since

$$S^2\frac{\partial^2 C(\bar{V})}{\partial S^2} = \frac{2}{T - t}\frac{\partial C(\bar{V})}{\partial V}$$

and, from (A5),

$$\frac{\partial^2 \bar{V}}{\partial V^2} = 0,$$

this becomes

$$Df_2 + \eta \frac{\partial f_2}{\partial V} + \frac{\rho V \psi_V}{T - t} S \frac{\partial^2 C(\bar{V})}{\partial S \partial \bar{V}} + \left[\frac{2\rho\psi_V}{(T - t)^2} + \frac{1}{2}\left(\frac{\partial \bar{V}}{\partial V}\right)^2 \right] V \frac{\partial^2 C(\bar{V})}{\partial \bar{V}^2}$$

$$+ \frac{\rho V \psi}{T - t} \frac{\partial \bar{V}}{\partial V} S \frac{\partial^3 C(\bar{V})}{\partial S \partial \bar{V}^2} + \frac{2\rho V \psi}{(T - t)^2} \frac{\partial \bar{V}}{\partial V} \frac{\partial^3 C(\bar{V})}{\partial \bar{V}^3} = 0. \quad \text{(A15)}$$

Lemmas 3 and 5 suggest

$$f_2 = \frac{\phi_1(V, t)}{T - t} S \frac{\partial^2 C(\bar{V})}{\partial S \partial \bar{V}} + \frac{\phi_2(V, t)}{(T - t)^2} \frac{\partial^2 C(\bar{V})}{\partial \bar{V}^2}$$

$$+ \frac{\phi_3(V, t)}{(T - t)^2} S \frac{\partial^3 C(\bar{V})}{\partial S \partial \bar{V}^2} + \frac{\phi_4(V, t)}{(T - t)^3} \frac{\partial^3 C(\bar{V})}{\partial \bar{V}^3}. \quad \text{(A16)}$$

When this is substituted into (A15) and the lemmas are used, a similar analysis to that for ψ gives the following first-order partial differential equations for the ϕ_i's:

$$\left.\begin{array}{l} \dfrac{\partial \phi_1}{\partial t} + \eta \dfrac{\partial \phi_1}{\partial V} + \rho V \psi_V = 0, \\[3mm] \dfrac{\partial \phi_2}{\partial t} + \eta \dfrac{\partial \phi_2}{\partial V} + V\left[2\rho\psi_V + \tfrac{1}{2}(T - t)^2 \left(\dfrac{\partial \bar{V}}{\partial V}\right)^2 \right] = 0, \\[3mm] \dfrac{\partial \phi_3}{\partial t} + \eta \dfrac{\partial \phi_3}{\partial V} + \rho V \psi \dfrac{\partial \bar{V}}{\partial V}(T - t) = 0, \\[3mm] \dfrac{\partial \phi_4}{\partial t} + \eta \dfrac{\partial \phi_4}{\partial V} + 2\rho V \psi \dfrac{\partial \bar{V}}{\partial V}(T - t) = 0. \end{array}\right\} \quad \text{(A17)}$$

For the particular form of η given in equation (3.3), these have solutions analogous to (A13),

$$\left.\begin{array}{l} \phi_1 = \dfrac{\rho^2}{b^4}\{(a + bV)[e^{\delta}(\tfrac{1}{2}\delta^2 - \delta + 1) - 1] + a[e^{\delta}(2 - \delta) - (2 + \delta)]\}, \\[3mm] \phi_2 = 2\phi_1 + \dfrac{1}{2b^4}\{(a + bV)(e^{2\delta} - 2\delta e^{\delta} - 1) - \tfrac{1}{2}a(e^{2\delta} - 4e^{\delta} + 2\delta + 3)\}, \\[3mm] \phi_3 = \tfrac{1}{2}\psi^2, \qquad \phi_4 = 2\phi_3. \end{array}\right\}$$

$$\text{(A18)}$$

Substituting these into (A16) gives f_2. Higher-order terms are derived in exactly the same way; however, the algebra becomes increasingly complex.

The full proofs that (A13) satisfies (A12) and (A18) satisfy (A17) are given in Appendix B.

APPENDIX B: A PROOF THAT (A13) AND (A18) SATISFY (A12) AND (A17)

Equation (A13) is

$$\psi(t, V) = -\frac{\rho}{b^3}[(a + bV)(e^\delta - \delta e^\delta - 1) + a(e^\delta - \delta - 1)],$$

where $\delta = b(T - t)$. So

$$\frac{\partial \psi}{\partial t} = -b\frac{\partial \psi}{\partial \delta} = \frac{\rho}{b^2}[(a + bV)(-\delta e^\delta) + a(e^\delta - 1)].$$

$$\frac{\partial \psi}{\partial V} = -\frac{\rho}{b^2}(e^\delta - \delta e^\delta - 1). \qquad (B1)$$

Since $\eta = a + bV$,

$$\frac{\partial \psi}{\partial t} + \eta\frac{\partial \psi}{\partial V} = \frac{\rho V}{b}(1 - e^\delta).$$

From equation (A5),

$$\rho V(T - t)\frac{\partial \bar{V}}{\partial V} = -\frac{\rho V}{b}(1 - e^\delta),$$

so it follows that equation (A12),

$$\frac{\partial \psi}{\partial t} + \eta\frac{\partial \psi}{\partial V} + \rho V(T - t)\frac{\partial \bar{V}}{\partial V} = 0,$$

is satisfied.

For equation (A18) first consider ϕ_1:

$$\phi_1 = \frac{\rho^2}{b^4}\{(a + bV)[e^\delta(\tfrac{1}{2}\delta^2 - \delta + 1) - 1] + a[e^\delta(2 - \delta) - (2 + \delta)]\},$$

$$\frac{\partial \phi_1}{\partial t} = -b\frac{\partial \phi_1}{\partial \delta} = -\frac{\rho^2}{b^3}[(a + bV)(\tfrac{1}{2}\delta^2 e^\delta) + a(e^\delta - \delta e^\delta - 1)],$$

$$\frac{\partial \phi_1}{\partial V} = \frac{\rho^2}{b^3}[e^\delta(\tfrac{1}{2}\delta^2 - \delta + 1) - 1].$$

Since $\eta = a + bV$,

$$\frac{\partial \phi_1}{\partial t} + \eta\frac{\partial \phi_1}{\partial V} = \frac{\rho^2}{b^3}[bV(e^\delta - \delta e^\delta - 1)] = \frac{\rho^2 V}{b^2}(e^\delta - \delta e^\delta - 1).$$

From equation (B1) the right-hand side of this is $-\rho V\psi_V$, so that

$$\frac{\partial \psi_1}{\partial t} + \eta\frac{\partial \phi_1}{\partial V} - \rho V\psi_V = 0, \qquad (B2)$$

showing that ϕ_1 satisfies the first equation in (A17).

Next consider ϕ_2:

$$\phi_2 = 2\phi_1 + \psi_2,$$

where

$$\psi_2 = \frac{1}{2b^4}[(a+bV)(e^{2\delta} - 2\delta e^\delta - 1) - \tfrac{1}{2}a(e^{2\delta} - 4e^\delta + 2\delta + 3)].$$

Substituting this into the second equation in (A17) gives

$$2\left(\frac{\partial \phi_1}{\partial t} + \eta \frac{\partial \phi_1}{\partial V} + \rho V \psi_V\right) + \frac{\partial \psi_2}{\partial t} + \eta \frac{\partial \psi_2}{\partial V} + \tfrac{1}{2}V(T-t)^2\left(\frac{\partial \bar{V}}{\partial V}\right)^2 = 0.$$

We see from the first equation in (A17) that the first term is zero. Thus, ψ_2 must satisfy

$$\frac{\partial \psi_2}{\partial t} + \eta \frac{\partial \psi_2}{\partial V} + \tfrac{1}{2}V(T-t)^2\left(\frac{\partial \bar{V}}{\partial V}\right)^2 = 0. \qquad \text{(B3)}$$

Differentiating, we get

$$\frac{\partial \psi_2}{\partial t} = -b\frac{\partial \psi_2}{\partial \delta} = -\frac{1}{2b^3}[(a+bV)(2e^{2\delta} - 2e^\delta - 2\delta e^\delta) - a(e^{2\delta} - 2e^\delta + 1)],$$

$$\frac{\partial \psi_2}{\partial V} = \frac{1}{2b^3}(e^{2\delta} - 2\delta e^\delta - 1).$$

Since $\eta = a + bV$,

$$\frac{\partial \psi_2}{\partial t} + \eta \frac{\partial \psi_2}{\partial V} = -\frac{1}{2b^3}[bV(e^{2\delta} - 2e^\delta + 1)] = -\frac{V}{2b^2}(e^{2\delta} - 2e^\delta + 1).$$

From (A5),

$$\frac{\partial \bar{V}}{\partial V} = \frac{e^\delta - 1}{b(T-t)},$$

so

$$\tfrac{1}{2}V(T-t)^2\left(\frac{\partial \bar{V}}{\partial V}\right)^2 = \frac{V}{2b^2}(e^{2\delta} - 2e^\delta + 1).$$

Thus,

$$\frac{\partial \psi_2}{\partial t} + \eta \frac{\partial \psi_2}{\partial V} + \tfrac{1}{2}V(T-t)^2\left(\frac{\partial \bar{V}}{\partial V}\right)^2 = 0,$$

which shows ψ_2 satisfies (B3) and ϕ_2 satisfies the second equation in (A17).

Now consider ϕ_3:

$$\phi_3 = \tfrac{1}{2}\psi^2, \qquad \frac{\partial \phi_3}{\partial t} = \psi \frac{\partial \psi}{\partial t}, \qquad \frac{\partial \phi_3}{\partial V} = \psi \frac{\partial \psi}{\partial V}.$$

Thus,

$$\frac{\partial \phi_3}{\partial t} + \eta \frac{\partial \phi_3}{\partial V} + \rho V \psi \frac{\partial \bar{V}}{\partial V}(T - t) = \psi \left(\frac{\partial \psi}{\partial t} + \eta \frac{\partial \psi}{\partial V} + \rho V \frac{\partial \bar{V}}{\partial V}(T - t) \right),$$

which (A12) shows to be zero. Thus, ϕ_3 satisfies the third equation in (A17). Given this, ϕ_4 trivially satisfies the fourth equation in (A17).

APPENDIX C: A PROOF THAT (3.16)–(3.18) SATISFY THE BOUNDARY CONDITIONS (3.15)

The boundary conditions are

$$f_i = 0 \quad \text{when } t = T, \qquad (C1)$$
$$f_i = 0 \quad \text{when } S = 0, \qquad (C2)$$
$$\partial f_i/\partial S \to 0 \quad \text{as } S \to \infty. \qquad (C3)$$

First consider f_0:

$$f_0 = C(\bar{V}) - C(V).$$

When $t = T$, $\bar{V} = V$, so (C1) is satisfied; when $S = 0$, $C(\bar{V}) = C(V) = 0$, so (C2) is satisfied; and

$$\lim_{S \to \infty} \frac{\partial f_0}{\partial S} = \lim_{S \to \infty} \frac{\partial C(\bar{V})}{\partial S} - \lim_{S \to \infty} \frac{\partial C(V)}{\partial S} = 0,$$

so (C3) is satisfied.

Now consider f_1. From (A8),

$$f_1 = \frac{\psi(V, t)}{T - t} S \frac{\partial^2 C(\bar{V})}{\partial S \partial \bar{V}},$$

where

$$\psi(V, t) = -\frac{\rho}{b^3} [(a + bV)(e^\delta - \delta e^\delta - 1) + a(e^\delta - \delta - 1)]$$

and

$$\delta = b(T - t).$$

To show that f_1 satisfies (C1), we must show

$$\lim_{t \to T} \frac{\psi(V, t)}{T - t} = 0.$$

Expanding ψ in a series in δ and dropping all but the lowest-order term gives

$$\lim_{t \to T} \psi(V, t) = -\frac{\rho}{b^3}[(a + bV)(-\tfrac{1}{2}\delta^2) + a(\tfrac{1}{3}\delta^2)] = \tfrac{1}{2}\rho V(T - t)^2.$$

Thus, $\lim_{t \to T}[\psi/(T - t)] = 0$. Since, from the properties of $C(\bar{V})$, we have $(\partial^2 C/\partial S \partial \bar{V})\big|_{t=T} = 0$, it follows that f_1 satisfies (C1).

To show that f_1 satisfies (C3), note that

$$\frac{\partial f_1}{\partial S} = \frac{\psi}{T - t}\left(\frac{\partial^2 C(\bar{V})}{\partial S \partial \bar{V}} + S\frac{\partial^3 C(\bar{V})}{\partial S^2 \partial \bar{V}}\right),$$

which, on making use of (A3), becomes

$$\frac{\partial f_1}{\partial S} = \frac{\psi}{T - t}\left(\frac{\partial^2 C(\bar{V})}{\partial S \partial \bar{V}} + \frac{2}{S(T - t)}\frac{\partial^2 C(\bar{V})}{\partial \bar{V}^2}\right).$$

From the properties of $C(\bar{V})$,

$$\lim_{S \to \infty}\frac{\partial C(\bar{V})}{\partial S} = 1 \quad \text{and} \quad \lim_{S \to \infty}\frac{\partial C(\bar{V})}{\partial \bar{V}} = 0,$$

so

$$\lim_{S \to \infty}\frac{\partial^2 C(\bar{V})}{\partial \bar{V} \partial S} = 0 \quad \text{and} \quad \lim_{S \to \infty}\frac{\partial^2 C(\bar{V})}{\partial \bar{V}^2} = 0.$$

It follows that f_1 satisfies (C3). Finally, f_1 trivially satisfies (C2).

Now consider f_2. From (3.18),

$$f_2 = \frac{\phi_1(V, t)}{T - t}S\frac{\partial^2 C(\bar{V})}{\partial S \partial \bar{V}} + \frac{\phi_2(V, t)}{(T - t)^2}\frac{\partial^2 C(\bar{V})}{\partial \bar{V}^2}$$

$$+ \frac{\phi_3(V, t)}{(T - t)^2}S\frac{\partial^3 C(\bar{V})}{\partial S \partial \bar{V}^2} + \frac{\phi_4(V, t)}{(T - t)^3}\frac{\partial^3 C(\bar{V})}{\partial \bar{V}^3},$$

where

$$\phi_1 = \frac{\rho^2}{b^4}\{(a + bV)[e^{\delta}(\tfrac{1}{2}\delta^2 - \delta + 1) - 1] + a[e^{\delta}(2 - \delta) - (2 + \delta)]\},$$

$$\phi_2 = 2\phi_1 + \frac{1}{2b^4}\{(a + bV)(e^{2\delta} - 2\delta e^{\delta} - 1) - \tfrac{1}{2}a(e^{2\delta} - 4e^{\delta} + 2\delta + 3)\},$$

$$\phi_3 = \tfrac{1}{2}\psi^2, \qquad \phi_4 = \psi^2.$$

To show that f_2 satisfies (C1), expand the ϕ's in a series in δ keeping only the lowest-order terms in δ and replacing δ with $b(T - t)$:

$$\lim_{t \to T} \phi_1 = \frac{\rho^2}{b^4}[(a + bV)(\tfrac{1}{6}\delta^3) + a(-\tfrac{1}{6}\delta^3)]$$

$$= \tfrac{1}{6}\rho^2 V(T - t)^3,$$

$$\lim_{t \to T} \phi_2 = 2 \lim_{t \to T} \phi_1 + \frac{1}{2b^4}[(a + bV)(\tfrac{1}{3}\delta^3) - \tfrac{1}{2}a(\tfrac{2}{3}\delta^3)]$$

$$= \tfrac{1}{3}\rho^2 V(T - t)^3 + \tfrac{1}{6}V(T - t)^3,$$

$$\lim_{t \to T} \phi_3 = \tfrac{1}{2}\left(\lim_{t \to T} \psi\right)^2$$

$$= \tfrac{1}{8}\rho^2 V^2(T - t)^4,$$

$$\lim_{t \to T} \phi_4 = 2 \lim_{t \to T} \phi_3$$

$$= \tfrac{1}{4}\rho^2 V^2(T - t)^4.$$

With these results, it is obvious that

$$\lim_{t \to T} f_2 = 0,$$

and f_2 satisfies (C1).

From the properties of $C(\bar{V})$, $\partial/\partial S$ of the second and fourth terms in f_2 vanish as $S \to \infty$. By analogy with the arguments used for f_1, $\partial/\partial S$ of the first and third terms also vanish as $S \to \infty$. Thus,

$$\lim_{S \to \infty} \frac{\partial f_2}{\partial S} = 0,$$

and f_2 satisfies (C3).

Finally, when $S = 0$, the first and third terms in f_2 vanish. Applying (A3) to the second and fourth terms shows that they also vanish when $S = 0$. Thus, when $S = 0$, $f_2 = 0$, so f_2 satisfies (C2).

REFERENCES

Black, F., and M. Scholes. "The pricing of options and corporate liabilities." *Journal of Political Economy*, 81 (May–June 1973), pp. 637–659.

Bodurtha, J. N., and G. Courtadon. "Empirical tests of the Philadelphia Stock Exchange foreign currency options market." Ohio State University Working Paper WPS 84-69, 1984.

Boyle, P. P., and E. Kirzner. "Pricing complex options: Echo-Bay Ltd. gold purchase warrants." *Canadian Journal of Administrative Studies*, 2 (1985), pp. 294-306.

Brennan, M. J., and E. S. Schwartz "A continuous time approach to the pricing of bonds." *Journal of Banking and Finance*, 3 (1979), pp. 133–155.

Brennan, M. J., and E. S. Schwartz. "An equilibrium model of bond pricing and a test of market efficiency." *Journal of Financial and Quantitative Analysis*, 17 (1982), pp. 301–329.

Christie, A. A., "The stochastic behaviour of common stock variances." *Journal of Financial Economics*, 10 (December 1982), pp. 407–432.

Cox, J. C., J. E. Ingersoll, and S. A. Ross. "An intertemporal general equilibrium model of asset prices." *Econometrica*, 53 (March 1985a), pp. 363–384.

Cox, J. C., J. E. Ingersoll, and S. A. Ross. "A theory of the term structure of interest rates." *Econometrica*, 53 (March 1985b), pp. 385–407.

Cox, J. C., and S. A. Ross. "The valuation of options for alternative stochastic processes." *Journal of Financial Economics*, 3 (March 1976), pp. 145–166.

Dothan, M. U. "A random volatility correction for the Black–Scholes option pricing formula." *Advances in Futures and Options Research*, 2 (1987), pp. 97–115.

Fischer, S. "Call option pricing when the exercise price is uncertain, and the valuation of index bonds." *Journal of Finance*, 33 (March 1978), pp. 169–176.

Galai, D. "The components of the return from hedging options against stocks." *Journal of Business*, 56 (January 1983), pp. 45–54.

Garman, M. "A general theory of asset valuation under diffusion state processes." Working Paper No. 50, University of California, Berkeley, 1976.

Geske, R. "The pricing of options with stochastic dividend yield." *Journal of Finance*, 33 (May 1978), pp. 617–625.

Geske, R. "The valuation of compound options." *Journal of Financial Economics*, 7 (March 1979), pp. 63–81.

Hammersley, J. M., and D. C. Handscomb. *Monte Carlo Methods*. Methuen, London, 1964.

Hull, J. C., and A. White. "Hedging the risks from writing foreign currency options." *Journal of International Money and Finance*, 6 (June 1987a), pp. 131–152. Also Chapter 4 in this book.

Hull, J. C., and A. White. "The pricing of options on assets with stochastic volatilities." *Journal of Finance*, 42 (June 1987b), pp. 281–300. Also Chapter 2 in this book.

Johnson, H. E. "Option pricing when the variance is changing." Graduate School of Management Working Paper 11-79, University of California, Los Angeles, 1979.

Johnson, H. E. "The pricing of complex options." Louisiana State University, Department of Finance, 1983.

Johnson, H. E., and D. Shanno. "Option pricing when the variance is changing." *Journal of Financial and Quantitative Analysis*, 22 (June 1987), pp. 143–151.

Jones, E. P. "Option arbitrage and strategy with large price changes." *Journal of Financial Economics*, 13 (1984), pp. 91–114.

Kon, S. J. "Models of stock returns—a comparison." *Journal of Finance*, 39 (March 1984), pp. 147–166.

Margrabe, W. "The value of an option to exchange one asset for another." *Journal of Finance*, 33 (March 1978), pp. 177–186.

Merton, R. C. "The theory of rational option pricing." *Bell Journal of Economics and Management Science*, 4 (Spring 1973), pp. 141–183.

Merton, R. C. "Option pricing when underlying stock returns are discontinuous." *Journal of Financial Economics*, 3 (March 1976), pp. 125–144.

Richard, S. F. "An arbitrage model of the term structure of interest rates." *Journal of Financial Economics*, 6 (1979), pp. 33–57.

Roll, R. "An analytic valuation formula for unprotected American call options on stocks with known dividends." *Journal of Financial Economics*, 5 (November 1977), pp. 251–258.

Rubinstein, M. "Displaced diffusion option pricing." *Journal of Finance*, 38 (March 1983), pp. 213–217.

Rubinstein, M. "Nonparametric tests of the alternative option pricing models using all reported trades and quotes on the 30 most active CBOE option classes from August 23, 1976, through August 31, 1978." *Journal of Finance,* 40 (June 1986), pp. 445–480.

Scott, L. O. "Option pricing when the variance changes randomly: theory, estimation, and an application." *Journal of Financial and Quantitative Analysis*, 22 (December 1987), pp. 419–438.

Stulz, R. "Options on the minimum or the maximum of two risky assets." *Journal of Financial Economics*, 10 (1982), pp. 161–185.

Wiggins, J. B. "Option values under stochastic volatility: theory and empirical evidence." *Journal of Finance Economics*, 19 (1987), pp. 351–372.

4. Hedging the risks from writing foreign currency options *

In the last few years the foreign currency options market has grown dramatically. A number of exchanges now trade standardized put and call options on the Canadian dollar, British pound, Japanese yen, German Deutschmark, and Swiss franc. In addition banks and other financial institutions write non-exchange-traded options which have exercise prices and maturities tailored to the needs of their clients. This paper discusses the hedging alternatives open to a financial institution when it writes non-exchange-traded currency options.

Delta hedging, which is based on an idea in Black and Scholes (1973), involves hedging a short position in a call option with a continuously varying long position in the underlying currency. At any given time the long position is adjusted so that it equals the rate of change of the call price with respect to the spot rate. The gain (loss) on the call option is then always balanced by the loss (gain) on the long position. Transactions costs normally present a major obstacle to the maintenance of a delta hedge for stock options. However, banks and other financial institutions trade the major currencies continually throughout each day. Their incremental transactions costs from maintaining the hedge for currency options are, therefore, close to zero.

For delta hedging to work perfectly, the following must be true:

1. The spot exchange rate follows a proportional Gauss–Wiener process.
2. The hedge is adjusted continuously.
3. The home and foreign risk-free rates are non-stochastic.

* This paper was first published in *Journal of International Money and Finance*, Vol. 6 (1987). pp. 131–152. It is reprinted with the permission of Butterworth-Heinemann Journals, Elsevier Science Ltd, The Boulevard, Langford Lane, Kidlington OX5 1GB, UK.

4. The instantaneous standard deviation of the proportional change in the spot exchange rate is non-stochastic.

In practice, none of these conditions is likely to be satisfied exactly and the performance of delta hedging is therefore less than perfect. In this paper we consider how hedging performance can be improved by introducing exchange-traded options into the hedge. One way of doing this is known by practitioners as 'gamma hedging' and is aimed at correcting for the fact that in practice the hedge can only be adjusted at discrete time intervals. Another approach aims to provide protection against a stochastic volatility and is referred to as 'vega hedging'.[1] We will show that in most situations vega hedging outperforms gamma hedging.

Previous work concerned with the performance of hedging schemes for stocks has been carried out by Boyle and Emanuel (1980) and Galai (1983). Boyle and Emanuel considered the effect of discrete hedge adjustments on the return from delta hedging assuming that all the above conditions except (2) hold. They showed that if options are priced correctly and there are no transactions costs then the expected return from a single hedging transaction is approximately zero while the distribution of the return is skewed. They question the reliability of statistical tests which fail to take this skewness into account. Galai decomposed the return from a discrete delta hedge into three components: the riskless rate of interest, the return arising from discrete adjustments to the hedge, and the return arising from the change in the deviation of the actual option price from the model price. He showed that in practice the third factor swamps the first two. This third factor is indistinguishable from price changes due to a stochastic volatility. His results suggest that in any hedging scheme it is likely to be more important to correct for a stochastic volatility than for discrete hedging. This is in accord with our findings for currency options.

The pricing of and calculation of hedge ratios for currency options had been investigated by Garman and Kohlhagen (1983), Grabbe (1983), and Biger and Hull (1983). These authors all show how European call and put options can be valued analytically under the assumptions that: the spot exchange rate follows geometric Brownian motion, markets are frictionless, interest rates in domestic and foreign markets are constant, and option prices are a function of only one stochastic variable, the spot

---

[1] Vega hedging has also been referred to as 'kappa hedging' and 'lambda hedging'. See Grabbe (1985). In the original version of this paper we referred to it as 'sigma hedging', but unfortunately this never caught on!

rate. The valuation problem is very similar to the problem considered by Merton (1973) of valuing an option on a stock paying a continuous dividend when the dividend yield is constant. Grabbe (1983) shows how the analysis can be extended to value European currency options when interest rates are stochastic.

One potential problem associated with hedging currency options is that most of the options traded on exchanges or by financial institutions are American. The early exercise of an American option can be optimal. In particular, early exercise is frequently optimal for deep in-the-money calls on currencies with negative forward premiums and deep in-the-money puts on currencies with positive forward premiums. It is rarely optimal to exercise early calls on currencies with positive forward premiums or puts on currencies with negative forward premiums. Hedge ratios for American currency options which are prone to early exercise can only be accurately calculated using numerical procedures such as those suggested by Cox, Ross, and Rubinstein (1979), Parkinson (1977), Geske and Johnson (1984), Shastri and Tandon (1984), and Courtadon (1982).

Section 4.1 of this paper defines a number of different hedging schemes that are extensions of the basic delta scheme. It then builds on the ideas in Boyle and Emanuel to produce estimates of the standard deviation of the hedger's gain/loss during the time interval between hedge rebalancing. The conclusions are reached on the circumstances under which certain schemes outperform other schemes. Section 4.2 presents results based on simulated data that show the performance of the hedging schemes over many hedging intervals. Section 4.3 discusses how the performance of the hedging scheme improves as the frequency of hedge rebalancing increased. In Section 4.4 the hedging schemes are tested using data on the currency options traded on the Philadelphia exchange between February 1983 and September 1984. The concluding remarks are in Section 4.5.

4.1 ANALYSIS OF HEDGING SCHEMES

In this section we consider how a portfolio of non-exchange-traded currency options can be hedged using the underlying currency and a portfolio of exchange-traded options. For simplicity of presentation we assume initially that all options are European calls and that there are only two sources of uncertainty: the spot exchange rate and the volatility of the spot exchange rate. Later in the section we discuss how the ideas can be extended to deal with American options, put options, and other sources of uncertainty.

We use notation as follows:

$S(t)$: spot exchange rate (i.e., value in the domestic currency of one unit of the foreign currency) at time t;

$v(t)$: the instantaneous variance of dS/S;

$\sigma(t) = \sqrt{v(t)}$: the instantaneous standard deviation of dS/S;

η: the drift rate of dv/v;

ξ: the instantaneous standard deviation of dv/v;

$C_j(S, v, t)$: the value of non-exchange-traded option j $(1 \leq j \leq m)$;

$w_j(t)$: the holding of non-exchange-traded option j at time t;

$C_i^*(S, v, t)$: the value of exchange-traded option i $(1 \leq i \leq n)$;

$w_i^*(t)$: the holding of exchange-traded option i at time t;

$h(t)$: the holding of the foreign currency at time t;

$P(t)$: the value of the hedge portfolio at time t;

T_j, X_j: time to maturity and exercise price of non-exchange-traded option j;

T_i^*, X_i^*: time to maturity and exercise price of exchange-traded option i;

r_D: domestic risk-free rate;

r_F: foreign risk-free rate;

$N(\cdot)$: cumulative normal distribution function.

The stochastic process for S and v will be assumed to be

$$dS/S = (r_D - r_F)\,dt + \sigma\,dz_1,$$
$$dv/v = \eta\,dt + \xi\,dz_2, \tag{4.1}$$

where dz_1 and dz_2 are possibly correlated Wiener processes and r_D, r_F, η, and ξ are constant.

The hedge portfolio contains non-exchange-traded options, exchange-traded options, and foreign currency. The cost of creating this portfolio is

$$P(t) = \sum_j w_j(t)C_j(t) + \sum_i w_i^*(t)C_i^*(t) + h(t)S(t). \tag{4.2}$$

Suppose that the hedge is not rebalanced between times t and $t + \Delta t$. This means that w_j, w_i^*, and h are constant during this period. Interest must be paid at rate r_D on $P(t)$ and interest is earned at rate r_F on $h(t)S(t)$. Hence

$$P(t + \Delta t) = \sum_j w_j(t)C_j(t + \Delta t) + \sum_i w_i^*(t)C_i^*(t + \Delta t) + h(t)S(t + \Delta t)$$

$$- P(t)(e^{r_D \Delta t} - 1) + h(t)S(t)(e^{r_F \Delta t} - 1). \quad (4.3)$$

If $\Delta S, \Delta C_j, \Delta C_i^*$, Δv, and ΔP are the changes in S, C_j, C_i^*, v, and P during Δt, it follows from equations (4.2) and (4.3) that

$$\Delta P =$$

$$\sum_j w_j \, \Delta C_j + \sum_i w_i^* \, \Delta C_i^* + h \, \Delta S - P(t)(e^{r_D \Delta t} - 1) + hS(t)(e^{r_F \Delta t} - 1).$$

For convenience we define

$$C_N = \sum_j w_j C_j, \qquad C_E = \sum_i w_i^* C_i^*, \qquad C_H = C_N + C_E,$$

so that

$$\Delta P = \Delta C_H + h \, \Delta S - P(t)(e^{r_D \Delta t} - 1) + hS(t)(e^{r_F \Delta t} - 1),$$

where ΔC_H is the change in C_H during Δt.

Since r_D and r_F are assumed to be constant, we can expand ΔC_H, $e^{r_D \Delta t}$, and $e^{r_F \Delta t}$ in a Taylor series about $S(t)$, $v(t)$, and t, to obtain

$$\Delta P = \left(\frac{\partial C_H}{\partial S} + h \right) \Delta S + \frac{\partial C_H}{\partial v} \Delta v + \left(\frac{\partial C_H}{\partial t} - P(t)r_D + hS(t)r_F \right) \Delta t$$

$$+ \frac{1}{2} \frac{\partial^2 C_H}{\partial S^2} (\Delta S)^2 + \frac{1}{2} \frac{\partial^2 C_H}{\partial v^2} (\Delta v)^2$$

$$+ \frac{1}{2} \left(\frac{\partial^2 C_H}{\partial t^2} - P(t)r_D^2 + hS(t)r_F^2 \right) (\Delta t)^2 + \frac{\partial^2 C_H}{\partial S \partial v} \Delta S \, \Delta v$$

$$+ \frac{\partial^2 C_H}{\partial S \partial t} \Delta S \, \Delta t + \frac{\partial^2 C_H}{\partial v \partial t} \Delta v \, \Delta t + \cdots. \quad (4.4)$$

The commonly used hedging schemes aim to minimize the variance of ΔP by setting key terms in equation (4.4) equal to zero. In the delta scheme, no exchange-traded options are included in the hedge, so that $C_H = C_N$, $w_i^* = 0$ for all i, and h is chosen so that the first term in equation (4.4) is equal to zero, i.e., so that

$$\frac{\partial C_N}{\partial S} + h = 0. \quad (4.5)$$

Practitioners refer to $\partial C_H / \partial S + h$ and $\partial^2 C_H / \partial S^2$ as the 'delta' and the 'gamma' of the hedge portfolio, respectively. It is sometimes recommended (see, for example, Dillman and Harding 1985) that a single exchange-traded option be included in the hedge portfolio so that both

79

gamma and delta are zero. This corresponds to choosing h and w_i^* so that

$$\frac{\partial C_N}{\partial S} + w_1^* \frac{\partial C_1^*}{\partial S} + h = 0,$$

$$\frac{\partial^2 C_N}{\partial S^2} + w_1^* \frac{\partial^2 C_1^*}{\partial S^2} = 0,$$

(4.6)

with all other w_i^* being zero. This ensures that the first and fourth terms in equation (4.4) are zero. Other hedging schemes aimed at setting other terms in equation (4.4) equal to zero can be developed similarly using the currency and a single exchange-traded option. If we define the 'vega' of the hedge portfolio as $\partial C_H / \partial v$, it is possible to set both delta and vega equal to zero by choosing h and w_i^* so that

$$\frac{\partial C_N}{\partial S} + w_1^* \frac{\partial C_1^*}{\partial S} + h = 0,$$

$$\frac{\partial C_N}{\partial v} + w_1^* \frac{\partial C_1^*}{\partial v} = 0,$$

(4.7)

with all other w_i^* being zero. The first and second terms in equation (4.4) will then be zero.

If the currency and two exchange-traded options are used in the hedge, delta, gamma, and vega can be set equal to zero by choosing h, w_1^*, and w_2^* so that

$$\left.\begin{array}{l} \dfrac{\partial C_N}{\partial S} + w_1^* \dfrac{\partial C_1^*}{\partial S} + w_2^* \dfrac{\partial C_2^*}{\partial S} + h = 0, \\[2mm] \dfrac{\partial^2 C_N}{\partial S^2} + w_1^* \dfrac{\partial^2 C_1^*}{\partial S^2} + w_2^* \dfrac{\partial^2 C_2^*}{\partial S^2} = 0, \\[2mm] \dfrac{\partial C_N}{\partial v} + w_1^* \dfrac{\partial C_1^*}{\partial v} + w_2^* \dfrac{\partial C_2^*}{\partial v} = 0. \end{array}\right\}$$

(4.8)

In general each additional exchange-traded option which is introduced into the hedge enables one additional term in equation (4.4) to be set equal to zero.

We now use equation (4.4) to derive approximate expressions for the variance of ΔP when different hedging schemes are used. Consider first delta hedging, which is a component of all hedging schemes. When this scheme is used, the first term in equation (4.4) vanishes. Furthermore the third and sixth terms are non-stochastic. It follows that

$$\text{var}(\Delta P) = \left(\frac{\partial C_H}{\partial v}\right)^2 \text{var}(\Delta v) + \frac{1}{4}\left(\frac{\partial^2 C_H}{\partial S^2}\right)^2 \text{var}(\Delta S^2)$$

$$+ \frac{1}{4}\left(\frac{\partial^2 C_H}{\partial v^2}\right)^2 \text{var}(\Delta v^2) + \left(\frac{\partial^2 C_H}{\partial S \partial v}\right)^2 \text{var}(\Delta S \, \Delta v)$$

$$+ \frac{\partial C_H}{\partial v}\frac{\partial^2 C_H}{\partial S^2}\text{cov}(\Delta v, \Delta S^2) + \frac{1}{2}\frac{\partial^2 C_H}{\partial S^2}\frac{\partial^2 C_H}{\partial v^2}\text{cov}(\Delta v^2, \Delta S^2)$$

$$+ \frac{\partial C_H}{\partial v}\frac{\partial^2 C_H}{\partial v^2}\text{cov}(\Delta v, \Delta v^2) + 2\frac{\partial C_H}{\partial v}\frac{\partial^2 C_H}{\partial S \partial v}\text{cov}(\Delta v, \Delta S \, \Delta v)$$

$$+ \frac{\partial^2 C_H}{\partial S^2}\frac{\partial^2 C_H}{\partial S \partial v}\text{cov}(\Delta S^2, \Delta S \, \Delta v)$$

$$+ \frac{\partial^2 C_H}{\partial v^2}\frac{\partial^2 C_H}{\partial S \partial v}\text{cov}(\Delta v^2, \Delta S \, \Delta v)$$

$$+ 2\frac{\partial C_H}{\partial v}\frac{\partial^2 C_H}{\partial v \partial t}\text{var}(\Delta v)\,\Delta t + \frac{\partial^2 C_H}{\partial v^2}\frac{\partial^2 C_H}{\partial S \partial t}\text{cov}(\Delta S, \Delta v^2)\,\Delta t$$

$$+ O(\Delta t^{\frac{5}{2}}). \qquad (4.9)$$

When r_D, r_F, and σ are constant, the price C of a European call with maturity T and exercise price X is given by

$$C = e^{-r_F T} S N(d_1) - e^{-r_D T} X N(d_2), \qquad (4.10)$$

where

$$d_1 = \frac{\log(S/X) + [r_D - r_F + \frac{1}{2}\sigma^2]T}{\sigma\sqrt{T}}, \qquad d_2 = d_1 - \sigma\sqrt{T}.$$

This is shown to be true by Garman and Kohlhagen (1983), Grabbe (1983), and Biger and Hull (1983) in the case of a currency option. It follows that

$$
\left.
\begin{aligned}
\frac{\partial C}{\partial S} &= e^{-r_F T} N(d_1), \\[4pt]
\frac{\partial C}{\partial v} &= \frac{S\sqrt{T}\, N'(d_1) e^{-r_F T}}{2\sigma}, \\[4pt]
\frac{\partial^2 C}{\partial S^2} &= \frac{N'(d_1) e^{-r_F T}}{S\sigma\sqrt{T}}, \\[4pt]
\frac{\partial^2 C}{\partial S \partial v} &= -\frac{N'(d_1) d_2 e^{-r_F T}}{2\sigma^2}, \\[4pt]
\frac{\partial^2 C}{\partial v^2} &= \frac{S\sqrt{T}\, N'(d_1)(d_1 d_2 - 1) e^{r_F T}}{4\sigma^3}, \\[4pt]
\frac{\partial^2 C}{\partial S \partial t} &= N'(d_1) e^{-r_F T}\left(-r_F \frac{N(d_1)}{N'(d_1)} + \frac{r_D - r_F}{\sigma\sqrt{T}} - \frac{d_2}{2T}\right), \\[4pt]
\frac{\partial^2 C}{\partial v \partial t} &= \frac{S N'(d_1) e^{-r_F T}}{4\sigma\sqrt{T}}\left(1 + d_1 d_2 + \frac{2\sqrt{T}}{\sigma}(r_F d_2 - r_D d_1)\right).
\end{aligned}
\right\} \qquad (4.11)
$$

We assume that the formulae in (4.10) and (4.11) are approximately correct when v is stochastic. This is reasonable in view of the work of Hull and White (1987), which shows that the pricing bias induced by a stochastic volatility is generally very small.[2]

Expressions for the variance and covariance terms in equation (4.9) are determined in Appendix A. These expressions, with equation (4.11), are used in Appendix B to investigate the relative magnitudes of the terms in equation (4.9). It is shown that in most circumstances a good approximation to var(ΔP) is given by

$$
\text{var}(\Delta P) \approx
$$

$$
\left(\frac{\partial C_H}{\partial v}\right)^2 \text{var}(\Delta v) + \frac{1}{4}\left(\frac{\partial^2 C_H}{\partial S^2}\right)^2 \text{var}(\Delta S^2) + \frac{\partial C_H}{\partial v}\frac{\partial^2 C_H}{\partial S^2}\text{cov}(\Delta v, \Delta S^2),
$$

$$(4.12)$$

where only the first terms in the expansions of each of var(Δv), var(ΔS^2) and cov($\Delta v, \Delta S^2$) need to be considered.

Under delta hedging,

$$
C_H = \sum_j w_j C_j.
$$

---

[2] The assumption may seem strange, since one of the things that we are investigating is the effect of a stochastic v on hedge performance. However, it is important to distinguish between (a) the effect of a stochastic v on the value of C and its partial derivatives at one point in time and (b) the effect of a stochastic v on the performance over time of a hedge which assumes v is constant. (a) is generally very small; (b) can be quite large.

Using (4.11) and the results in Appendix A, (4.12) becomes

$$\text{var}(\Delta P) \approx \tfrac{1}{4}\sigma^2 S^2 \xi^2 \, \Delta t \left(\sum_j w_j e^{-r_F T_j} N'(d_{1j}) T_j^{\frac{1}{2}} \right)^2$$

$$+ \tfrac{1}{2}\sqrt{2}\,\sigma^2 S^2 \xi \rho_3 \, \Delta t^{\frac{3}{2}} \left(\sum_j w_j e^{-r_F T_j} N'(d_{1j}) \right)^2$$

$$+ \tfrac{1}{2}\sigma^2 S^2 \, \Delta t^2 \left(\sum_j w_j e^{-r_F T_j} N'(d_{1j}) T_j^{-\frac{1}{2}} \right)^2, \qquad (4.13)$$

where d_{1j} is the value of d_1 for the jth non-exchange-traded option and ρ_3 is the correlation between Δv and ΔS^2. This shows that, when there is only one non-exchange-traded option and $\xi = 0$, $\text{var}(\Delta P)$ increases as T_1 decreases. (This was noted to be true in the case of stocks by Boyle and Emanuel, 1980.) It also shows that, when $\xi > 0$ and there is only one non-exchange-traded option, $\text{var}(\Delta P)$ is a U-shaped function of T_1. The reason for this is that when T_1 is small hedge performance is poor because of the discrete time between rebalancing, whereas when T_1 is large the stochastic volatility significantly reduces hedge effectiveness.

When delta + vega hedging is adopted, the first and third terms in equation (4.12) disappear, so that

$$\text{var}(\Delta P) \approx \frac{1}{4} \left(\frac{\partial^2 C_N}{\partial S^2} + w_1^* \frac{\partial^2 C_1^*}{\partial S^2} \right)^2 \text{var}(\Delta S^2),$$

where

$$w_1^* = -\frac{\partial C_N}{\partial v} \bigg/ \frac{\partial C_1^*}{\partial v}.$$

Using (4.11) and the results in Appendix A, this becomes

$$\text{var}(\Delta P) \approx \tfrac{1}{2}\sigma^2 S^2 \, \Delta t^2 \left(\sum_j \frac{w_j N'(d_{1j}) e^{-r_F T_j} (T_1^* - T_j)}{T_1^* \sqrt{T_j}} \right)^2. \qquad (4.14)$$

When delta + gamma hedging is adopted, the second and fifth terms in equation (4.9) disappear, so that

$$\text{var}(\Delta P) \approx \left(\frac{\partial C_N}{\partial v} + w_1^* \frac{\partial C_1^*}{\partial v} \right)^2 \text{var}(\Delta v),$$

where

$$w_1^* = -\frac{\partial^2 C_N}{\partial S^2} \bigg/ \frac{\partial^2 C_1^*}{\partial S^2}.$$

Using (4.11) and the results in Appendix A, this becomes

$$\text{var}(\Delta P) \approx \tfrac{1}{4}\sigma^2 S^2 \xi^2 \, \Delta t \left(\sum_j \frac{w_j N'(d_{1j}) e^{-r_F T_j}(T_1^* - T_j)}{\sqrt{T_j}} \right)^2. \qquad (4.15)$$

One might expect that delta + vega and delta + gamma hedging are necessarily superior to delta hedging. However, this is not the case. Equations (4.13) and (4.14) show that, for a sufficiently small value of T_1^*, delta + vega hedging is inferior to delta hedging. Similarly equations (4.13) and (4.15) show that, for a sufficiently large value of T_1^*, delta + gamma hedging is inferior to delta hedging when $\xi > 0$.

These results can be explained as follows. Both delta + gamma and delta + vega hedging involve adding to the delta hedge portfolio a position in an option and a position in the underlying currency necessary to hedge that option position. Delta + gamma hedging is aimed at correcting for discrete hedge rebalancing, whereas delta + vega hedging is aimed at correcting for a non-zero ξ. In the case of delta + gamma hedging, a non-zero ξ causes the variance of the return from the securities added to the portfolio to increase as T_1^* increases. Eventually a stage is reached where this effect swamps the advantages of correcting for discrete hedge rebalancing. In the case of delta + vega hedging, the variance of the return from the securities added to the portfolio increases as T_1^* decreases because of the discrete hedge rebalancing and eventually this swamps the advantages of correcting for a non-zero ξ.

A comparison of equations (4.13) and (4.14) shows that delta + vega hedging is more effective than delta hedging when $T_1^* > \tfrac{1}{2} T_j$ for all j. Similarly, a comparison of equations (4.13) and (4.15) shows that delta + gamma hedging is more effective than delta hedging when $T_1^* < \tfrac{1}{2} T_j$ for all j.

From equations (4.14) and (4.15) it can be concluded that delta + vega hedging is more effective than delta + gamma hedging if and only if[3]

$$\xi > \frac{\sqrt{2 \, \Delta t}}{T_1^*}. \qquad (4.16)$$

Table 4.1 presents some data on (a) the actual standard deviations calculated from the time series of the daily price changes of five major

---

[3] An exception to this occurs when $m = 1$ and $T_1 = T_1^*$. Delta + vega and delta + gamma hedging are then identical. Both the second and the fourth terms in equation (4.4) can be eliminated with a single exchange-traded option.

TABLE 4.1. Averages of actual and weighted implied standard deviations of spot rates (per US$) percent per annum.

Year	Qtr	Canadian dollar		Deutschmark		Swiss franc		Japanese yen		British pound	
		Actual	Implied	Actual	Implied	Actual	Implied	Actual	Implied	Actual	Implied
1983	2	2.61	3.95	6.12	13.96	6.08	13.06	8.42	14.02	10.27	*
	3	1.83	2.69	9.32	10.75	8.49	10.53	6.55	11.64	9.43	*
	4	1.59	2.05	7.38	10.84	7.38	9.76	7.47	11.15	6.37	*
1984	1	3.45	2.38	12.38	10.40	10.47	9.96	7.96	9.42	9.62	*
	2	2.31	4.12	9.04	11.59	7.38	10.15	5.30	9.09	7.06	*
	3	3.72	4.87	9.58	12.47	10.38	10.57	7.12	9.38	9.38	*

* Data not available.

currencies and (b) the average of daily weighted implied standard deviations calculated using the procedure suggested by Emanuel (1983) from option trades on the Philadelphia exchange. These data suggest that in practice ξ is not insignificant for currencies. The standard deviation of the log of the change in the average σ from one quarter to the next can be estimated from the actual standard deviations as 0.36. If we assume that $\eta = 0$ in the diffusion process for v, numerical methods can be used to show that this corresponds to a value of ξ of about 1.7 per year. The value of ξ calculated from the daily weighted implied standard deviations was about 1.15. If $\xi = 1.0$ and $\Delta t = 0.003$ (approximately 1 day), equation (4.16) shows that delta + vega hedging is more attractive than delta + gamma hedging when $T_1^* > 28$ days.

It will be noted that equations (4.14) and (4.15) do not involve X_1^*. This suggests that the performance of the delta + vega and delta + gamma schemes is independent of the exercise price of the exchange-traded option which is used. This is not completely true. If the exchange-traded option is deep in or deep out of the money, w_1^* is very large and the assumptions which have been made as to which terms in the expansion of the var(ΔP) are negligible may no longer be valid.

It is interesting to note that if only one exchange-traded option is to be used for hedging then neither delta + vega nor delta + gamma hedging minimizes the risk of the portfolio. From equation (4.4) we wish to choose h and w_1^* so that

$$\left(\frac{\partial C_N}{\partial S} + w_1^* \frac{\partial C_1^*}{\partial S} + h \right)^2 \text{var}(\Delta S)$$

$$+ \left(\frac{\partial C_N}{\partial v} + w_1^* \frac{\partial C_1^*}{\partial v} \right)^2 \text{var}(\Delta v) + \frac{1}{4} \left(\frac{\partial^2 C_N}{\partial S^2} + w_1^* \frac{\partial^2 C_1^*}{\partial S^2} \right)^2 \text{var}(\Delta S^2)$$

is minimized. This is achieved when h is defined as usual and

$$w_1^* = -\frac{\dfrac{\partial C_1^*}{\partial v} \dfrac{\partial C_N}{\partial v} \text{var}(\Delta v) + \dfrac{1}{4} \dfrac{\partial^2 C_1^*}{\partial S^2} \dfrac{\partial^2 C_N}{\partial S^2} \text{var}(\Delta S^2)}{\left(\dfrac{\partial C_1^*}{\partial v} \right)^2 \text{var}(\Delta v) + \dfrac{1}{4} \left(\dfrac{\partial^2 C_1^*}{\partial S^2} \right)^2 \text{var}(\Delta S^2)}. \tag{4.17}$$

The results in this section can easily be extended to deal with the situations where put options are included in the portfolios of exchange-traded and non-exchange-traded options. Since the formulae in equation (4.11) for $\partial C / \partial v$ and $\partial^2 C / \partial S^2$ are true when C is either a put option or a call option, equations (4.12) to (4.17) remain unchanged when some of the options are puts. The development of the hedging schemes for

American options is, in principle, no different from that for European options. In the case of American options, the formulae in equations (4.10) and (4.11) are at best approximations, and exact values of h and the w_i^*'s can only be calculated using appropriate numerical methods.

Finally the hedging schemes described here can be extended to deal with other sources of uncertainty. For example, interest rate uncertainty gives rise to extra terms of the form

$$\frac{\partial C_H}{\partial r_D} \Delta r_D \quad \text{and} \quad \frac{\partial C_H}{\partial r_F} \Delta r_F$$

in equation (4.4), and these can in theory be eliminated using additional exchange-traded options. In practice, however, the approach suggested by Grabbe (1983) involving a holding of foreign and domestic bonds is likely to be preferable.

4.2 RESULTS USING SIMULATED DATA

This section summarizes the results of a large number of simulations of the performance of different hedging schemes in different circumstances for European call options.[4] As a check, a smaller number of simulations of the performance of hedging schemes for American options were carried out in circumstances where there was a significant probability of early exercise.[5] The algorithms suggested by Cox, Ross, and Rubinstein (1979) were used to calculate option prices and partial derivatives of option prices with respect to S and v. It was found that there was no significant difference between the hedge performance for European and American options.

The simulations assume that a single call option with exercise price X and time to maturity T is sold for the price given by equation (4.10). The hedge portfolio is then set up. At the end of time periods of length Δt, new values are sampled for the stochastic variables and the hedge is rebalanced. All exchange-traded options are assumed to be priced

---

[4] There is no loss of generality in considering only call options. A call option to buy currency A for currency B at an exercise price of X is the same as a put option to sell B for A at $1/X$.

[5] As mentioned earlier, early exercise is frequently optimal for deep in-the-money calls on currencies with negative forward premiums and deep in-the-money puts on currencies with positive forward premiums. A considerable amount of computer time was saved by using European options in most of the simulations.

according to equation (4.10).[6] The initial wealth of the hedger is assumed to be zero. The interest rates r_D and r_F are applied to the positive or negative balances of the home and foreign currency in each time period. On each run the option either expires unexercised or is assumed to be exercised by the holder at maturity and W, the final wealth or cumulative cash flow of the hedger, is calculated. As would be expected, the mean value of W was not found to be significantly different from zero on any of the simulations. The performance of the hedge is measured by the ratio of the standard deviation of W to the initial option price C and will be denoted by q.[7] Except where otherwise stated:

1. $S(0) = 1.0$, $X = 1.0$, $r_D = r_F = 0$, $\sigma(0) = 4$ percent per annum, $\eta = 0, \xi = 1.0$ per annum, and $T = 30$ days.
2. The hedge is rebalanced daily.
3. $S(t)$ and $v(t)$ follow the diffusion processes in equation (4.1) with dz_1 and dz_2 being uncorrelated.[8]
4. Confidence intervals are reported on the assumption that W is normal.[9]

Consider first the situation where delta hedging is used. In this case, var(ΔP) is given by equation (4.13). However, successive ΔP's are dependent, so equation (4.13) cannot be used to obtain an estimate of q directly. Table 4.2 shows the variation of q with T and $S(0)/X$. For at-the-money options, q is a U-shaped function of T. This is a result of a

[6] As already mentioned, the Black–Scholes pricing formula usually gives a reasonable approximation to the true price when σ is stochastic.

[7] To provide an interpretation of q, suppose that the option is sold for $C + \alpha C$, where α is positive. The probability of a loss is the probability that $W < -\alpha C$, or that $W/C < -\alpha$. The chance of this is $N(-\alpha/q)$. If we require the probability of a loss to be some amount e, it follows that we require α to be uq, where $u = N^{-1}(e)$. Therefore q can be thought of as a measure of the percentage overpricing necessary to provide a certain level of protection against a loss.

[8] The diffusion processes were discretized for the purposes of the simulation. $\text{Log}[S(t+\Delta t)/S(t)]$ was approximated as a normal distribution with mean $[r_D - r_F - \frac{1}{2}\sigma(t)^2]\Delta t$ and standard deviation $\sigma(t)\sqrt{\Delta t}$. $\text{Log}[v(t+\Delta t)/v(t)]$ is normal with mean $(\eta - \frac{1}{2}\xi^2)\Delta t$ and standard deviation $\xi\sqrt{\Delta t}$. Note that since σ is stochastic the parameters of $\text{log}[S(t+\Delta t)/S(t)]$ change over time. For empirical evidence on the distribution of foreign exchange price changes, see McFarland, Pettit, and Sung (1982).

[9] Boyle and Emanuel (1980) show that for stock options the distribution of the hedger's wealth change in a single hedging period is non-normal. This is also true in the case of foreign currency options. Furthermore, as wealth changes in successive time periods are dependent, wealth changes over many hedging periods are liable to be non-normal. In practice only small departures from normality were observed.

TABLE 4.2. Variation of q with $S(0)/X$ and T when delta hedging with daily rebalancing is used. $\xi = 1.0$, $\eta = 0$, $\sigma = 0.04$, $r_D = r_F = 0$, and $X = 1$. Each result is based on 100 simulation runs and has a standard error of about 7 percent.

T	S(0)/X						
(days)	0.95	0.97	0.99	1.00	1.01	1.03	1.05
1	*	*	*	0.79	0.00	0.00	0.00
5	*	*	*	0.35	0.01	0.00	0.00
15	*	*	0.81	0.20	0.03	0.00	0.00
30	*	2.04	0.60	0.17	0.06	0.00	0.00
60	*	1.94	0.33	0.17	0.07	0.01	0.00
120	1.81	0.93	0.32	0.17	0.13	0.03	0.01
360	1.84	0.72	0.32	0.34	0.20	0.11	0.06

* Estimate of q is large but unreliable, as both standard deviation of W and option price C are very small.

number of factors. As T increases, C increases, the number of hedging intervals increases, and, as can be shown from equation (4.13), the value of $\text{var}(\Delta P)$ first decreases and then increases.

For a given value of T, the maximum value of the standard deviation of W occurs when the option is at the money. For deep in-the-money and deep out-of-the-money options, $\partial^2 C/\partial S\partial t$ is very small, so that the value of h can be expected to change very slowly and very little variance is introduced by rebalancing hedges discretely. Furthermore $\partial C/\partial \sigma$ is also very small, so that a stochastic σ has very little effect. The high values of q for deep out-of-the-money options is a reflection of their low price; similarly the low value of q for deep in-the-money options is a reflection of their high price.

Further simulations were carried out to test the variation of q with σ. Interestingly, the performance of delta hedging for an at-the-money option is relatively insensitive to σ. As σ increases, both the standard deviation of W and the option price increase by approximately the same proportion. (This result was also found to be true for the other hedging schemes tested.)

Table 4.3 shows the variation of q with ξ when a number of different hedging schemes were used. To assist in the interpretation of ξ values, the corresponding standard deviations of the log of the relative change in the average σ from one quarter to the next is shown in column 2. The first exchange-traded option available for hedging was assumed to have an exercise price of 1.005 and a maturity of 45 days; the second available

TABLE 4.3. Variation of q with hedging scheme and ξ when $S(0) = X = 1$, $r_D = r_F = 0$, $\sigma = 0.04$, $\eta = 0$, $T = 30$ days, $T_1^* = 45$ days, $T_2^* = 135$ days, and $X_1^* = X_2^* = 1.005$. Each result is based on 1000 simulation runs and has a standard error of about 2 percent.

ξ	SD of quarterly change in average σ	Hedging scheme				
		Delta	Delta + vega	Delta + gamma	Equation (4.17)	Delta + vega + gamma
0.0	0.00	0.15	0.10	0.03	0.03	0.03
0.5	0.10	0.15	0.10	0.05	0.05	0.03
1.0	0.21	0.17	0.09	0.09	0.07	0.03
1.5	0.31	0.20	0.11	0.14	0.09	0.04
2.0	0.43	0.23	0.11	0.18	0.09	0.04
2.5	0.53	0.24	0.10	0.20	0.10	0.05
3.0	0.61	0.31	0.11	0.25	0.10	0.06
3.5	0.74	0.32	0.12	0.30	0.11	0.07
4.0	0.83	0.39	0.12	0.35	0.11	0.08

exchange-traded option was assumed to have an exercise price of 1.005 and a maturity of 135 days.[10]

The third column of Table 4.3 shows that the impact of uncertainty in σ on the performance of delta hedging can be quite large.[11] The increase in q arises from the fact that, when the actual average volatility is different from the forecast volatility, the option has, *ex post*, been both priced incorrectly and hedged incorrectly. The effect of incorrect hedging alone was identified by assuming that the option was priced on the basis of the average value of σ sampled but hedged on the basis of $\sigma = 4$ percent per annum. It was found that, as ξ increases, approximately 25 percent of the increase in q arises from mishedging and 75 percent arises from mispricing.

The fourth and fifth columns of Table 4.3 show, as would be expected, that delta + vega hedging is more effective than delta + gamma hedging when ξ is large. These and other simulations show that, when many time periods are considered, the approximate condition for delta + vega hedging to be more attractive than

[10] For two-option hedging schemes, T_1^* and T_2^* should not be equal, as otherwise the equations in (4.8) do not form a consistent system. This is a restriction on the option series which can be used for two-option hedging schemes in practice.

[11] The results for delta hedging were found to be relatively insensitive to whether the hedger revised his estimate of σ over time. In other words using $\sigma(0)$ in all calculations and using $\sigma(t)$ in the calculations made at time t gave similar results.

TABLE 4.4. Variation of q with X_1^* and T_1^* for different hedging schemes when $S(0) = X = 1$, $r_D = r_F = 0$, $\sigma = 0.04$, $T = 30$ days, $\xi = 1.0$, $\eta = 0$, and $T_2^* = T_1^* + 90$. Each result is based on 100 simulation runs and has a standard error of about 7 percent. I, II, III, and IV refer to the delta + vega, delta + gamma, optimal single option, and delta + vega + gamma hedging schemes, respectively.

T_1^* (days)	X_1^* and hedging scheme											
	0.99				1.00				1.01			
	I	II	III	IV	I	II	III	IV	I	II	III	IV
30	0.08	0.08	0.08	0.08	0.00	0.00	0.00	0.00	0.09	0.09	0.09	0.09
35	0.08	0.06	0.06	0.06	0.06	0.04	0.03	0.02	0.08	0.05	0.05	0.05
40	0.10	0.07	0.06	0.05	0.09	0.06	0.06	0.02	0.09	0.07	0.06	0.05
50	0.09	0.10	0.07	0.04	0.12	0.11	0.09	0.03	0.11	0.12	0.08	0.05
60	0.13	0.20	0.12	0.04	0.11	0.21	0.11	0.03	0.12	0.17	0.08	0.04
90	0.12	0.38	0.13	0.05	0.13	0.33	0.13	0.03	0.13	0.34	0.13	0.04
120	0.15	0.45	0.14	0.05	0.14	0.54	0.13	0.05	0.13	0.47	0.12	0.03

delta + gamma hedging is given by equation (4.16) with T_1^* replaced by $T_1^* - \frac{1}{2}T$ (i.e., by the average value of T_1^* over the life of the option being hedged).

The results for the optimal single-option hedging scheme, as defined by equation (4.17), are shown in column 6. As expected the scheme is an improvement over the delta + vega and delta + gamma schemes. It is worth noting that, unlike the other schemes, it requires the hedger to make an explicit estimate of ξ. The final column of Table 4.3 shows the performance of the delta + vega + gamma hedging as defined by equation (4.8). As expected, the performance of this hedging scheme is significantly better than the performance of single-option hedging schemes.

The impact of the exercise price and time to maturity of the first exchange-traded option on the performance of the four hedging schemes is shown in Table 4.4. The exercise price of the second exchange-traded option is assumed to be equal to that of the first. The maturity of the second exchange-traded option is assumed to be 90 days later than that of the first. The table illustrates the fact that the performance of delta + gamma hedging declines rapidly as T_1^* increases. A point is quickly reached where delta + gamma hedging performs less well than delta hedging.[12] (For delta hedging $q = 0.17$.) However, the table

---

[12] Values of T_1^* less than T_1 were not tested. The analytic results in Section 4.1 clearly show that, for a sufficiently small value of T_1^*, delta + vega hedging would be worse than delta hedging.

illustrates that the other three hedging schemes are significantly better than delta hedging for a wide range of values of the parameters of the non-exchange-traded options.

4.3 HEDGING FREQUENCY

In this section we consider the variation of hedge performance with the frequency of hedge rebalancing. Initially we assume that the hedge is rebalanced at constant time intervals. We then move on to consider more complicated schemes where the frequency of hedge rebalancing is varied according to the option parameters.

Consider first delta + vega hedging. From equation (4.14), var(ΔP) is approximately $\lambda (\Delta t)^2$, where λ is a function of option parameters. In any short time interval ϵ, it can be assumed, as an approximation, that λ does not change. There are $\epsilon/\Delta t$ hedging intervals in time ϵ, so that the variance of the wealth change in time ϵ is approximately $\lambda \epsilon \Delta t$. Since the variance of the wealth change in any small time interval is approximately proportional to Δt, the variance of the total wealth change in any time interval T can also be expected to be approximately proportional to Δt. Hence, q can be expected to be proportional to $\sqrt{\Delta t}$.

For delta + gamma hedging var(ΔP) is approximately $\lambda \Delta t$, where λ is a (different) function of option parameters. A similar argument to the one above shows that q can be expected to be approximately constant. This is also to be expected from the fact that delta + gamma hedging is designed to ensure that hedging effectiveness is not affected by the time between hedges. Also, delta + gamma hedging, however frequently it is applied, does not provide protection against a non-zero ξ.

Table 4.5 shows the results of simulations of five different hedging schemes for a variety of Δt's. As in the previous section the portfolio of non-traded options consisted of a single call option and ξ was assumed to be 1.0. The predictions which would be made on the basis of the above arguments can be seen to be approximately correct. Under delta + gamma hedging q is relatively insensitive to Δt, while under delta + vega hedging q is approximately proportional to $\sqrt{\Delta t}$. Under delta hedging and under the optimal single-option hedging scheme var(ΔP) has the approximate form $\lambda_1 \Delta t + \lambda_2 (\Delta t)^2$, where λ_1 and λ_2 are functions of option parameters. As might be expected the sensitivity of q to Δt for these schemes is intermediate between its sensitivity to Δt for the delta + gamma and delta + vega schemes.

TABLE 4.5. Variation of q with the time between hedge rebalancing for different hedging schemes when $S(0) = X = 1$, $r_D = r_F = 0$, $T = 30$ days, $\sigma = 0.04$, $\xi = 1.0$, $\eta = 0$, $X_1^* = X_2^* = 1.005$, $T_1^* = 45$, and $T_2^* = 135$. Each result is based on 1000 simulations and has a standard error of approximately 2 percent.

Time between rebalancing (days)	Hedging scheme				
	Delta	Delta + vega	Delta + gamma	Equation (4.17)	Delta + vega + gamma
0.25	0.12	0.05	0.09	0.04	0.01
0.50	0.12	0.06	0.09	0.05	0.02
0.75	0.14	0.07	0.09	0.05	0.02
1.00	0.18	0.10	0.09	0.07	0.03
2.00	0.23	0.14	0.10	0.09	0.05
3.00	0.27	0.17	0.12	0.11	0.07
5.00	0.34	0.20	0.12	0.12	0.09

Finally, for the delta + vega + gamma scheme, arguments similar to those above suggest that q should be proportional to $\sqrt{\Delta t}$. Again, as a rough approximation, this appears to be true.

Table 4.5 demonstrates that, for a sufficiently small Δt, delta + vega hedging will always outperform delta + gamma hedging. However, if a hedge can only be rebalanced relatively infrequently, there will be a tendency for delta + gamma hedging to outperform delta + vega hedging. This is as would be expected from inequality (4.16).

Hedging at constant time intervals is not, in general, optimal. For example, it is usually best to hedge more frequently when an option is at the money than when it is deep out of or deep in the money. Suppose that a hedge is rebalanced at times t_i for $1 \leq i \leq n$. It is useful to distinguish two types of hedging schemes. In the first type t_i is chosen so that

$$t_i - t_{i-1} = k \, F[S(t_{i-1}), t_{i-1}, r_D, r_F, X, \sigma(t_{i-1})],$$

where F is the function and k is a constant chosen by the hedger. A simple example of such a hedging scheme occurs when $F = 1$ and the time between hedging rebalancing is constant and equal to k. This type of hedging scheme only requires the hedger's position to be evaluated at those times when the hedge is actually rebalanced. In the second type of hedging scheme, t_i is chosen as the first time (after t_{i-1}) for which

$$G[S(t_i), S(t_{i-1}), t_i, t_{i-1}, r_D, r_F, X, \sigma(t_i), \sigma(t_{i-1})] = k,$$

where G is a function and k is a constant chosen by the hedger. In

93

general this requires that the hedger's position be monitored on a continuous basis. An example is $G = |S(t_i) - S(t_{i-1})|$, which involves hedging every time the spot exchange rate changes by a certain amount.

Ideally we would like to determine for each hedging scheme a function F which minimizes q for a given average hedging frequency. Unfortunately, this problem appears to be totally intractable. A number of different functions were tested for the delta + vega scheme. The best of these had the form

$$F = \frac{\Delta t}{\sqrt{\text{var}(\Delta P)}},$$

where $\text{var}(\Delta P)$ is given by equation (4.14). This defines a plausible hedging scheme since it has the property that the *a priori* variance of the wealth change between hedge rebalancing is roughly constant. The use of this function produced an average improvement of 16 percent (standard error = 2.3 percent) in q over the $F = 1$ scheme for a given average hedging frequency.

The problem of determining the function G which minimizes q for a given average hedging frequency also appears intractable. In further tests of the delta + vega scheme, the function

$$G = |S(t_i) - S(t_{i-1})|$$

produced an average improvement of 35 percent (standard error = 2.3 percent) in q over the $F = 1$ scheme. A number of other functional forms for G were tested, but none was found to perform significantly better than this one.

4.4 TESTS USING REAL DATA

The simulations in Sections 4.2 and 4.3 assume that the hedger can monitor the instantaneous standard deviation of the underlying currency. In fact, instantaneous standard deviations are unobservable. However, as discussed by Latane and Rendleman (1976) and Whaley (1982), implied standard deviations can be calculated from traded options. In this section, the single-option hedging schemes which have been discussed are tested using real data and implied standard deviations. Unfortunately, it was not possible to test hedging schemes involving two options because synchronous prices for two exchange-traded options were frequently not available.

There are two alternatives for calculating the implied standard deviation. The first involves calculating a weighted implied standard deviation (WISD); the second involves using the implied standard deviation of the traded option which is used in the hedge. The first alternative has the disadvantage that the actual price of the exchange-traded option is typically different from its price, given the WISD measure. This induces some variation into the value of the hedge portfolio. The second alternative has the disadvantage that the standard deviation measure is noisier and therefore generates more trading in the exchange-traded option. This in turn induces variation into the value of the hedge portfolio. Our results show that using the implied standard deviation of the exchange-traded option gives slightly better results than using the WISD. Accordingly the WISD was used for delta hedging (where no exchange-traded option was involved) and the implied standard deviation of the exchange-traded option was used for the other schemes. The WISD was calculated using the scheme suggested by Emanuel (1983).

The primary data source for the tests was the transactions surveillance report compiled daily by the Philadelphia Stock Exchange during the period February 28, 1983, to September 27, 1984. This report contains the following information for each option trade: date of trade, currency, maturity date, exercise price, time of trade, number of contracts traded, option price, prevailing bid and ask prices at the time of the trade, and the actual spot bid and ask quotes reported by Telerate for the interbank market. February 28, 1983, is the beginning of the first week when all five currency options were trading.

To carry out the tests, 100 non-exchange-traded call options on each of the Deutschmark, Swiss franc, and Japanese yen were generated using a random procedure. The options had start dates between June 23, 1983, and May 9, 1984, and durations of between 5 weeks and 20 weeks.[13] The exercise prices were always chosen to be within the range of the exercise prices of traded options. The currencies chosen were all low interest rate currencies, so that it was reasonable to treat American options as European. The exchange-traded option used to

---

[13] The decrease in implied volatilities of all currencies during the first few months of the operation of the Philadelphia currency options market indicates that there may have been some market inefficiency in this period (see Table 4.1). For this reason the first 16 weeks of data were not used.

hedge each non-exchange-traded option was the one with the most similar exercise price and maturity.[14] The yields on US treasury bills were used to represent domestic interest rates.[15] The differences between domestic and foreign interest rates were estimated from published forward rates by assuming interest rate parity.

All hedges were balanced once each trading day at the time of the first trade in the exchange-traded option. The price at which this trade took place was the price used in calculating the hedger's gain or loss from rebalancing. (This assumes implicitly that the quoted price for an option is 'firm' regardless of the size of the trade.) The spot price used was the average bid and ask quotes at the time. If the exchange-traded option did not trade on a particular day, the hedge was not rebalanced on that day.

The results are shown in Table 4.6. The 'gain' from using a hedging scheme for a particular option is the final wealth position of the hedger when the option is sold for its Black–Scholes price and hedged using the scheme.[16] The 'normalized gain' is equal to the gain divided by the Black–Scholes price.[17]

The table shows that delta + vega hedging performs better on average than delta hedging and that delta hedging performs better on average than delta + gamma hedging. This is because the value of ξ is typically sufficiently high for the condition in equation (4.16) to hold and for equation (4.15) to give a higher value than equation (4.13). (Typical values of ξ for an individual option were in the range 1.0 to 4.0.) The 'optimal' single-option hedging scheme given by equation (4.17) performed badly. This is because it assumed a value of 1 for ξ and this was, *ex post*, found to be too low in most cases. The need to make a realistic estimate of ξ for an individual option is in practice a serious weakness of the optimal single-option scheme.

---

[14] The maturity date of the exchange-traded option was the earliest maturity date following the maturity of the non-exchange-traded option. The exercise price was the closest one to that of the non-exchange-traded option.

[15] These rates were used as Eurocurrency rates were not readily available. In fact results are not sensitive to the domestic rate when a good estimate of the spread between domestic and foreign rates is used.

[16] Transactions costs relating to the options trades were ignored. For an institution hedging a large portfolio of options it can be argued that the transactions costs associated with net trades on a particular day are relatively small.

[17] As illustrated by Table 4.2 the normalized gain can be very high for deep out-of-the-money options. This explains the high variability in the standard deviation of the normalized gain compared with the standard deviation of the gain.

TABLE 4.6. Results using different hedging schemes for 100 non-exchange-traded options on each of three currencies.

Currency	Standard deviation of gain				Standard deviation of normalized gain			
	Delta	Delta + vega	Delta + gamma	Equation (4.17) $\xi = 1$	Delta	Delta + vega	Delta + gamma	Equation (4.17) $\xi = 1$
Deutschmark	0.13	0.09	0.25	0.17	1.21	0.25	1.27	0.73
Swiss franc	0.11	0.07	0.35	0.33	0.12	0.10	0.20	0.19
Japanese yen	0.18	0.10	0.15	0.14	0.36	0.24	0.19	0.18
All	0.14	0.09	0.26	0.23	0.56	0.21	0.75	0.45

4.5 CONCLUSIONS

This paper has produced several interesting results concerning the relative performance of difference hedging schemes. Delta + gamma hedging performs well when the traded option being used has a fairly constant implied standard deviation and a short time to maturity. However, it can perform far worse than delta hedging in other situations. Delta + vega hedging outperforms other hedging schemes when the traded option being used has a non-constant implied standard deviation and long time to maturity.

Conditions for delta + vega hedging to outperform delta + gamma hedging have been satisfied. We conclude that if only one traded option is to be used in a hedging scheme then it should usually be for vega rather than gamma hedging.

APPENDIX A

In this appendix we produce expressions for the variance and covariance terms in equation (4.9). Define

$$x = \frac{v + \Delta v}{v}.$$

The function $\log x$ is normal with mean $(\eta - \frac{1}{2}\xi^2) \Delta t$ and variance $\xi^2 \Delta t$. From the properties of the lognormal distribution in Aitchison and Brown (1966), the jth moment of x is

$$e^{[j\eta + \frac{1}{2}(j^2 - j)\xi^2]\Delta t}.$$

97

Using this result for $j = 1, 2, 3, 4$, we obtain

$$v + E(\Delta v) = v e^{\eta \Delta t},$$
$$v^2 + 2vE(\Delta v) + E(\Delta v^2) = v^2 e^{(2\eta + \xi^2)\Delta t},$$
$$v^3 + 3v^2 E(\Delta v) + 3vE(\Delta v^2) + E(\Delta v^3) = v^3 e^{(3\eta + 3\xi^2)\Delta t},$$
$$v^4 + 4v^3 E(\Delta v) + 6v^2 E(\Delta v^2) + 4vE(\Delta v^3) + E(\Delta v^4) = v^4 e^{(4\eta + 6\xi^2)\Delta t}.$$

Solving these equations for $E(\Delta v)$, $E(\Delta v^2)$, $E(\Delta v^3)$, $E(\Delta v^4)$ and using Taylor series expansions yields

$$\left.\begin{aligned}
E(\Delta v) &= v\eta\,\Delta t + \tfrac{1}{2}v\eta^2\,\Delta t^2 + O(\Delta t^3), \\
E(\Delta v^2) &= v^2 \xi^2\,\Delta t + v^2(\eta^2 + 2\eta\xi^2 + \tfrac{1}{2}\xi^4)\,\Delta t^2 + O(\Delta t^3), \\
E(\Delta v^3) &= v^3(3\eta\xi^2 + 3\xi^4)\,\Delta t^2 + O(\Delta t^3), \\
E(\Delta v^4) &= 3v^4 \xi^4\,\Delta t^2 + O(\Delta t^3),
\end{aligned}\right\} \tag{A1}$$

from which it follows that

$$\begin{aligned}
\operatorname{var}(\Delta v) &= \xi^2 v^2\,\Delta t + (2\eta + \tfrac{1}{2}\xi^2)\xi^2 v^2\,\Delta t^2 + O(\Delta t^3), \\
\operatorname{var}(\Delta v^2) &= 2v^4 \xi^4\,\Delta t^2 + O(\Delta t^3).
\end{aligned} \tag{A2}$$

It is not possible to use precisely the same argument to obtain $\operatorname{var}(\Delta S)$ and $\operatorname{var}(\Delta S^2)$ since σ is stochastic and $(S + \Delta S)/S$ is not lognormal. However, the variation in σ during time Δt introduces only second-order effects, so that

$$\left.\begin{aligned}
E(\Delta S) &= S\mu\,\Delta t + O(\Delta t^2), \\
E(\Delta S^2) &= S^2 v\,\Delta t + O(\Delta t^2), \\
E(\Delta S^3) &= S^3(3\eta v + v^2)\,\Delta t^2 + O(\Delta t^3), \\
E(\Delta S^4) &= 3S^4 v^2\,\Delta t^2 + O(\Delta t^3),
\end{aligned}\right\} \tag{A3}$$

where $\mu = r_D - r_F$. It follows that

$$\begin{aligned}
\operatorname{var}(\Delta S) &= S^2 v\,\Delta t + O(\Delta t^2), \\
\operatorname{var}(\Delta S^2) &= 2S^4 v^2\,\Delta t^2 + O(\Delta t^3).
\end{aligned} \tag{A4}$$

Also, using (A1), we get

$$\begin{aligned}
\operatorname{cov}(\Delta v, \Delta v^2) &= E(\Delta v^3) - E(\Delta v)E(\Delta v^2) \\
&= v^3(3\xi^4 + 2\eta\xi^2)\,\Delta t^2 + O(\Delta t^3),
\end{aligned} \tag{A5}$$

and similarly, from (A3),

$$\operatorname{cov}(\Delta S, \Delta S^2) = S^2(3\sigma^4 + 2\mu\sigma^2)\,\Delta t^2 + O(\Delta t^3). \tag{A6}$$

Finally, we note that

$$
\begin{aligned}
\mathrm{var}(\Delta S\,\Delta v) &= E(\Delta v^2\,\Delta S^2) - [E(\Delta v\,\Delta S)]^2 \\
&= \{[E(\Delta v)]^2 + \mathrm{var}(\Delta v)\}\{[E(\Delta S)]^2 + \mathrm{var}(\Delta S)\} \\
&\quad + \mathrm{cov}(\Delta v^2,\,\Delta S^2) - [E(\Delta v)E(\Delta S) + \mathrm{cov}(\Delta v,\,\Delta S)]^2 \\
&= \mathrm{var}(\Delta v)\,\mathrm{var}(\Delta S) + \mathrm{cov}(\Delta v^2,\,\Delta S^2) \\
&\quad - [\mathrm{cov}(\Delta v,\,\Delta S)]^2 + O(\Delta t^3) \\
&= S^2\xi^2\sigma^6\,\Delta t^2(1 + 2\rho_2 - \rho_1^2) + O(\Delta t^3), \qquad (A7)
\end{aligned}
$$

where ρ_1 is the correlation between Δv and ΔS and ρ_2 is the correlation between Δv^2 and ΔS^2.

Equations (A2), (A4), (A5), (A6), and (A7) provide the required results.

APPENDIX B

In this appendix we investigate the relative size of the terms in equation (4.9). We assume first that C_H consists of a single option with exercise price X and time to maturity T. Using the results in Appendix A and equations (4.11), equation (4.9) gives

$$
\begin{aligned}
\mathrm{var}(\Delta P) = S^2[N'(d_1)]^2 e^{-2r_F T}\sigma^2 \Big[&\tfrac{1}{4}T\xi^2\,\Delta t + \tfrac{1}{4}T\xi^2(2\eta + \tfrac{1}{2}\xi^2)\,\Delta t^2 \\
&+ \frac{\Delta t}{2T} + \tfrac{1}{8}a^2 T\xi^4\,\Delta t^2 + \tfrac{1}{4}\xi^2 b^2 d_2^2\,\Delta t^2 + \frac{\xi\rho_3\,\Delta t^{\frac{3}{2}}}{\sqrt{2}} \\
&+ \tfrac{1}{4}\xi^2 a\rho_2\,\Delta t^2 + \tfrac{1}{8}Ta(3\xi^4 + 2\eta\xi^2)\,\Delta t^2 - \tfrac{1}{2}d_2\xi^2 b\sqrt{T}\,\rho_4\,\Delta t^{\frac{3}{2}} \\
&- \frac{d_2\xi b\rho_5\,\Delta t^2}{\sqrt{2T}} - \frac{\sqrt{T}\,abd_2\xi^3\rho_6\,\Delta t^2}{4\sqrt{2}} \\
&+ \tfrac{1}{4}\xi^2\Big(1 + d_1 d_2 + \frac{2r_F d_2\sqrt{T}}{\sigma} - \frac{2r_D d_1\sqrt{T}}{\sigma}\Big)\Delta t^2 \\
&+ \xi\sqrt{T}\,\rho_1\Big(-r_D\frac{N(d_1)}{N'(d_1)} + \frac{r_D - r_F}{\sigma\sqrt{T}} - \frac{d_2}{2T}\Big)\Delta t^2 \Big] \\
&+ O(\Delta t^{\frac{5}{2}}), \qquad\qquad\qquad (B1)
\end{aligned}
$$

where $a = d_1 d_2 - 1$, $b = (1 - \rho_1^2 + 2\rho_2)^{\frac{1}{2}}$, and $\rho_1, \rho_2, \rho_3, \rho_4, \rho_5, \rho_6$ are the correlations between Δv and ΔS, Δv^2 and ΔS^2, Δv and ΔS^2, Δv and $\Delta v\,\Delta S$, ΔS^2 and $\Delta v\,\Delta S$, Δv^2 and $\Delta S\,\Delta v$, respectively. The first two terms in this expression arise from the first term in equation (4.9); the remaining terms correspond in order to the remaining terms in (4.9).

When $S = X = 1$, $\sigma = 0.1$, $r_D = r_F = 0.1$, $\xi = 1$, $\eta = 0$, $T = 0.2$, $\Delta t = 0.01$, and $\rho_i = 0.5$ ($1 \leq i \leq 6$), we have

$$\tfrac{1}{4}T\xi^2 \, \Delta t = 5 \times 10^{-4}, \quad \Delta t^2/2T = 2.5 \times 10^{-4}, \quad \tfrac{1}{2}\sqrt{2}\,\xi\rho_3 \, \Delta t^{\frac{3}{2}} = 3.5 \times 10^{-4}.$$

In absolute value the next largest of the terms in parentheses on the right-hand side of (B1) is 2.4×10^{-5}. It follows that

$$\mathrm{var}(\Delta P) \approx S^2[\mathrm{N}'(d_1)]^2 e^{-2r_F T}\sigma^2(\tfrac{1}{4}T\xi^2 \, \Delta t + \Delta t^2/2T + \tfrac{1}{2}\sqrt{2}\,\xi\rho_3 \, \Delta t^{\frac{3}{2}}).$$
$$(B2)$$

Further numerical analysis shows that this is a good approximation for most of the values of the option parameters likely to be encountered in practice. When the option becomes deep in or deep out of the money, the absolute values or d_1, d_2, and a increase and other terms on the right-hand side of (B1) become relatively more important. However, $[\mathrm{N}'(d_1)]^2$ is then very small and $\mathrm{var}(\Delta P)$ is close to zero, so that even in this case (B2) provides a good approximation in absolute terms.

We deduce that, when only one option is being considered, the right-hand side of equation (4.9) can be approximated by the part of the first term which is $O(\Delta t)$, the second term, and the fifth term. These results can be generalized to the situation where several non-exchange-traded options are involved. We can therefore conclude that

$$\mathrm{var}(\Delta P) \approx$$

$$\left(\frac{\partial C_H}{\partial v}\right)^2 \mathrm{var}(\Delta v) + \frac{1}{4}\left(\frac{\partial^2 C_H}{\partial S^2}\right)^2 \mathrm{var}(\Delta S^2) + \frac{\partial C_H}{\partial v}\frac{\partial^2 C_H}{\partial S^2}\mathrm{cov}(\Delta v, \Delta S^2),$$

where only the first terms in the expansion of each of $\mathrm{var}(\Delta v)$, $\mathrm{var}(\Delta S^2)$, and $\mathrm{cov}(\Delta v, \Delta S^2)$ need to be considered.

References

Aitchison, J., and J. A. C. Brown. *The Lognormal Distribution.* Cambridge University Press, 1966.

Biger, N., and J. C. Hull. "The valuation of currency options." *Financial Management*, 12 (Spring 1983), pp. 24–28.

Black, F., and M. Scholes. "The pricing of options and corporate liabilities." *Journal of Political Economy*, 81 (May 1973), pp. 637–659.

Boyle, P. P., and D. Emanuel. "Discretely adjusted option hedges." *Journal of Financial Economics*, 8 (September 1980), pp. 259–282.

Courtadon, G. "A more accurate finite difference approximation for the valuation of options." *Journal of Financial and Quantitative Analysis*, 17 (December 1982), pp. 697–703.

Cox, J. C., S. A. Ross, and M. Rubinstein. "Option pricing: a simplified approach." *Journal of Financial Economics*, 7 (September 1979), pp. 229–263.

Dillman, S., and J. Harding. "Life after delta: the gamma factor." Supplement to *Euromoney*, February 1985, pp. 14–17.

Emanuel, D. "Optimal weighting of implied standard deviations." Working Paper, University of Texas at Dallas, 1983.

Galai, D. "The components of the return from hedging options against stocks." *Journal of Business*, 56 (January 1983), pp. 45–54.

Garman, M., and S. Kohlhagen. "Foreign currency option values." *Journal of International Money and Finance*, 2 (December 1983), pp. 231–237.

Geske, R., and H. Johnson. "The American put valued analytically." *Journal of Finance*, 39 (December 1984), pp. 1511–1524.

Grabbe, J. O. "The pricing of call and put options on foreign exchange." *Journal of International Money and Finance*, 2 (December 1983), pp. 239–253.

Grabbe, J. O. "A guide to FX options." Department of Finance, Wharton School, University of Pennsylvania, 1985.

Hull, J. C., and A. White. "The pricing of options on assets with stochastic volatilities." *Journal of Finance*, 42 (June 1987), pp. 281–300. Also Chapter 2 in this book.

Latane, H. A., and R. J. Rendleman. "Standard deviations of stock price ratios implied in option prices." *Journal of Finance*, 31 (May 1976), pp. 369–381.

McFarland, J., R. R. Pettit, and S. Sung. "The distribution of foreign exchange price changes: trading day effects and risk measurement." *Journal of Finance*, 37 (June 1982), pp. 693–715.

Merton, R. C. "The theory of rational optional pricing." *Bell Journal of Economics and Management Science*, 4 (Spring 1973), pp. 141–183.

Parkinson, M. "Option pricing: the American put." *Journal of Business*, 50 (January 1977), pp. 21–36.

Shastri, K., and K. Tandon, "The valuation of American options on foreign currency." University of Pittsburgh Working Paper, 1984.

Whaley, R. E. "Valuation of American call options on dividend-paying stocks." *Journal of Financial Economics*, 10 (March 1982), pp. 29–58.

II

Numerical Procedures

5. Introduction: Numerical procedures

This part of the book covers a number of topics concerned with the use of trees to value derivatives. Trees (sometimes referred to as lattices) are an alternative to the implicit finite difference method for valuing a wide range of derivatives. They are popular with practitioners because they are easy to understand and easy to use. It is usually simple to incorporate the boundary conditions of a complex derivative into a tree and it is easy to check that the calculations being carried out are correct for the particular derivative under consideration.[1]

5.1 THE EXPLICIT FINITE DIFFERENCE METHOD

Chapter 6 starts by comparing trees to finite difference methods. It shows that using the explicit finite difference method is equivalent to constructing a trinomial tree that matches the mean and standard deviation of the underlying's stochastic process in a risk-neutral world. One well-documented problem with the explicit finite difference method is that the solutions it provides do not always converge to the correct value. The corresponding problem with trinomial trees is that it is sometimes not possible to match the mean and standard deviation while keeping the branching probabilities positive.

Chapter 6 suggests a procedure for overcoming this problem. This involves

(1) using the tree to model a function of the variable of interest rather than the variable itself; and
(2) using a variety of branching patterns on the tree.

[1] As discussed in Chapter 6, another argument in favor of trees over implicit finite difference methods is that most of the differential equations that have to be solved to value derivatives are initial value problems rather than boundary value problems. When finite difference methods are used it is necessary to artificially introduce extra boundary conditions.

Suppose that the variable of interest, θ, follows the process

$$d\theta = \mu(\theta)\,dt + \sigma(\theta)\,dz,$$

where the drift rate μ and instantaneous standard deviation σ are functions of θ. The function we model is

$$\phi = \int \frac{d\theta}{\sigma(\theta)}.$$

This has a constant instantaneous standard deviation. The alternative branching patterns we use are shown in Figure 6.1. Loosely speaking, the central branch emanating from a node is always chosen so that it is as close as possible to the average direction in which ϕ moves from the node.

Section 6.4 shows how the approach can be extended to model two stochastic variables. The stochastic variables are first transformed into two new uncorrelated stochastic variables. These are then each modelled separately as just outlined and the trees are combined into a single three-dimensional tree. Chapter 6 illustrates the approach with the one-factor Cox–Ingersoll–Ross model and the two-factor Brennan–Schwartz model.

Chapter 6 is a forerunner of our more general trinomial tree approach described in Chapters 18 and 20. In the more general approach, the drift of θ is a function of time, and the center of the tree at a particular time is chosen to reflect the expected value of θ at that time.

5.2 THE CONTROL VARIATE TECHNIQUE

The control variate technique has been used for many years in conjunction with Monte Carlo simulation. It is applicable when there are two similar derivatives A and B: A is the derivative under consideration; B is a derivative that is similar to A and for which a known solution is available. Two similar simulations using the same random number streams are carried out in parallel. The first is used to obtain an estimate $\hat{C}_A$ of the value of A; the second is used to obtain an estimate $\hat{C}_B$ of the value of B. A better estimate C_A^* of the value of A is then obtained using the formula

$$C_A^* = C_B + \hat{C}_A - \hat{C}_B, \tag{5.1}$$

where C_B is the known true value of B. Chapter 2 provides an example of the use of the control variate technique to evaluate the effect of stochastic volatility on the price of a European call option. In this case, A is the value of the option assuming stochastic volatility and B is its value assuming constant volatility.

Chapter 7 shows that the control variate technique can also be used in conjunction with trees. Consider, for example, the use of a Cox–Ross–Rubinstein tree to value an American option. We use the same tree to calculate both the value $\hat{C}_A$ of the American option and the value $\hat{C}_B$ of the corresponding European option. We also calculate the Black–Scholes price C_B of the European option. The error given by the tree in the pricing of the European option is assumed to be equal to that given by the tree in the pricing of the American option. This gives the estimate of the price of the American option to be C_A^* as in equation (5.1). In essence, the tree is used to calculate the difference between the American and European prices rather than the American price alone.

Chapter 7 shows that, even after accounting for the extra time taken to compute $\hat{C}_B$, the control variate technique leads to a significant improvement in computational efficiency in most cases. A good rule of thumb is to use the control variate technique for all American options except those that are deep in the money. For these options, early exercise is so likely that they are not at all similar to European options.

Other issues discussed in Chapter 7 include the construction of trees when there are discrete dividends and the construction of three-dimensional trees to value American options using a stochastic volatility model.

5.3 PATH-DEPENDENT DERIVATIVES

Traditionally, the technique that has been used to value path-dependent options is Monte Carlo simulation. The main problem with it is that the computation time necessary to achieve the required level of accuracy can be unacceptably high. Also, American-style options cannot be handled. Chapter 8 shows how the binomial and trinomial tree methods can be extended to cope with some path-dependent derivatives. The procedure outlined in Chapter 8 can handle American-style path-dependent derivatives and is computationally more efficient than Monte Carlo simulation for European-style path-dependent derivatives. It has had a significant impact on the way in which instruments such as indexed-amortizing swaps are valued in practice.

For the procedure to work, two conditions must be satisfied:

1. The payoff from the derivative must depend on a single function F of the path followed by the underlying stochastic variable.
2. It must be possible to calculate the value of F at time $\tau + \Delta t$ from its value at time τ and the value of the underlying asset at time $\tau + \Delta t$.

The basic idea underlying the procedure is as follows. At a node we carry out calculations for a small number of representative values of the path function F. When the value of the derivative is required for other values of the path function, we calculate it from the known values using interpolation. There are a number of ways of choosing the values of F that are considered. The simplest is that described in Section 8.3. It involves first working forward through the tree establishing the maximum and minimum values of the path function at each node. (Since the value of the path function at time $\tau + \Delta t$ depends only on the value of the path function at time τ and the value of the underlying at time $\tau + \Delta t$, the maximum and minimum values of the path function for the nodes at time $\tau + \Delta t$ can be calculated in a straightforward way from those for the nodes at time τ.) The representative values of the path function that are considered are then the maximum value, the minimum value, and a number of other values that are equally spaced between the maximum and the minimum. As we roll back through the tree, we value the derivative for each of the representative values of the path function.

We illustrate the nature of the calculation by considering the problem of valuing a call option where the payoff is the excess (if any) of the arithmetic average stock price over the strike price. The initial stock price is 50, the strike price is 50, the risk-free interest rate is 10%, the stock price volatility is 40%, the time to maturity is one year, and the number of time steps on the tree is 20. In this case the binomial tree parameters are $\Delta t = 0.05$, $u = 1.0936$, $d = 0.9144$, $p = 0.5056$, and $1 - p = 0.4944$. The path function is the arithmetic average of the stock price.

Figure 5.1 shows the calculations that would be carried out in one small part of the tree. Node X is the central node at time 0.2 years (that is, at the end of the fourth time step). Nodes Y and Z are the two nodes at time 0.25 that can be reached from node X. The stock price at node X is 50. From the earlier part of the tree, which is not shown, the maximum average stock price that is achievable in reaching node X can be calculated as 53.83. The minimum is 46.65. (We include both the initial and final stock price when calculating the average, so these are based on five observations.) From node X we branch to one of the two nodes Y or Z.

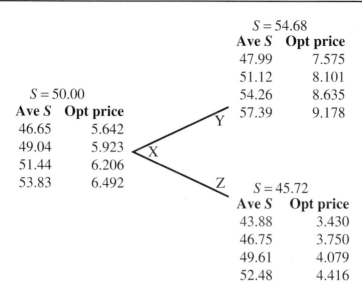

FIGURE 5.1. Part of tree for valuing option on the arithmetic average.

At node Y the stock price is 54.68 and the bounds for the average are 47.99 and 57.39. At node Z, the stock price is 45.72 and the bounds for the average stock price are 43.88 and 52.48.

We suppose that we have chosen the representative values of the average to be four equally spaced values at each node. This means that at node X we consider the averages 46.65, 49.04, 51.44, and 53.83. At node Y we consider the averages 47.99, 51.12, 54.26, and 57.39. At node Z we consider the averages 43.88, 46.75, 49.61, and 52.48. We assume that backwards induction has already been used to calculate the value of the option for each of the alternative values of the average at nodes Y and Z. The values are shown in Figure 5.1. For example, at node Y when the average is 51.12, the value of the option is 8.101.

Consider the calculations at node X for the case when the average is 51.44. If the stock price moves up to node Y, the new average will be

$$\frac{5 \times 51.44 + 54.68}{6} = 51.98.$$

The value of the derivative at node Y for this average can be found by interpolating between the values when the average is 51.12 and when it is 54.26. It is

$$\frac{(51.98 - 51.12) \times 8.635 + (54.26 - 51.98) \times 8.101}{54.26 - 51.12} = 8.247.$$

Similarly, if the stock price moves down to node Z, the new average will be

$$\frac{5 \times 51.44 + 45.72}{6} = 50.49,$$

and by interpolation the value of the derivative is 4.182.

The value of the derivative at node X when the average is 51.44 is therefore

$$(0.5056 \times 8.247 + 0.4944 \times 4.182)e^{-0.1 \times 0.05} = 6.206.$$

The other values at node X are calculated in a similar manner. Once the values at all nodes at time 0.2 years have been calculated in this way, we can move on to the nodes at time 0.15 years.

The value given by the full tree for the option at time zero is 7.17. As the number of time steps and the number of averages considered at each node is increased, the value of the option converges to the correct answer. With 60 time steps and 100 averages at each node, the value is 5.58. An advantage of this method is that it can handle American options. For example, the value of the American version of the average strike call calculated from a 20-step tree is 7.77. With 60 time steps and 100 averages, the value is 6.17.

In this example we used a piecewise linear approximation for the relationship between the value of the derivative and the value of F at each node. More accuracy can be obtained using a quadratic approximation. The number of F values that have to be considered at each node depends on the curvature of the relationship between the value of the derivative and F. Sometimes it is appropriate for the values of F to be unevenly spaced, with the spacing being least in the middle of the range between the maximum and minimum. Also, it may be desirable to increase the number of F values considered per node as we move through the tree.

6. Valuing derivative securities using the explicit finite difference method*

Two of the most popular procedures for valuing derivative securities are the lattice (or tree) approach and the finite difference approach. The lattice approach was suggested by Cox, Ross, and Rubinstein (1979), and has been extended by Rendleman and Bartter (1979), Boyle (1986, 1988), and Hull and White (1988). The finite difference approach was suggested by Schwartz (1977) and Brennan and Schwartz (1978), and has been extended by Courtadon (1982b). Both approaches involve discrete approximations to the processes followed by the underlying variables.

There are two alternative ways of implementing the finite difference approach. The first, known as the explicit finite difference method, relates the value of the derivative security at time t to three alternative values at time $t + \Delta t$. The second, known as the implicit finite difference method, relates the value of the derivative security at time $t + \Delta t$ to three alternative values at time t. Brennan and Schwartz (1978) show that the explicit finite difference method is equivalent to a trinomial lattice approach. They also show that the implicit finite difference method corresponds to a multinomial lattice approach where, in the limit, the underlying variable can move from its value at time t to an infinity of possible values at time $t + \Delta t$.

Geske and Shastri (1985) provide an interesting comparison of different lattice and finite difference approaches. They conclude that the explicit finite difference method, with logarithmic transformations, is the most efficient approach when large numbers of stock options are being evaluated. The explicit finite difference method is also attractive for a number of other reasons. It is computationally much simpler than the

* This paper was first published in *Journal of Financial and Quantitative Analysis*, Vol. 25 (1990), pp. 87–100. It is reprinted with the permission of the *Journal of Financial and Quantitative Analysis*.

implicit method since it does not require the inversion of matrices. It is conceptually simpler than the implicit method since it is, in effect, nothing more than an application of the trinomial lattice approach. Furthermore, as will be explained in Section 6.1, it can avoid the need to specify some boundary conditions. The method's only disadvantage is that the numerical solution does not necessarily converge to the solution of the differential equation as Δt tends to zero.

In Section 6.2, we modify the explicit finite difference method so that convergence of the calculated values to the correct solution is ensured. Brennan and Schwartz (1978) and Geske and Shastri (1985) show how a transformation of variables ensures convergence when stock options are being valued. The procedure in this paper involves both a transformation of variables and a new branching process. It can in principle be used for the valuation of any derivative security dependent on a single state variable and for the valuation of many derivative securities that are dependent on several state variables. In Section 6.3, we illustrate the procedure by valuing bonds and bond options when interest rates are governed by the Cox, Ingersoll, and Ross (1985b) model. Section 6.4 discusses the application of explicit finite difference methods to problems with two state variables. It values bonds and bond options using the Brennan and Schwartz (1982) model. Conclusions are in Section 6.5.

6.1 THE EXPLICIT FINITE DIFFERENCE METHOD

Consider a derivative security with price f that depends on a single stochastic variable θ. Suppose that the stochastic process followed by θ is

$$d\theta = \mu(\theta, t)\theta \, dt + \sigma(\theta, t)\theta \, dz,$$

where dz is a Wiener process. The variables μ and σ, which may be functions of θ and t, are the instantaneous proportional drift rate and volatility of θ.

If λ is the market price of risk of θ, then, as shown by Garman (1976) and Cox, Ingersoll, and Ross (1985a), f must satisfy the differential equation

$$\frac{\partial f}{\partial t} + \frac{\partial f}{\partial \theta}(\mu - \lambda\sigma)\theta + \tfrac{1}{2}\theta^2\sigma^2\frac{\partial^2 f}{\partial \theta^2} = rf, \tag{6.1}$$

where r the risk-free interest rate. Both r and λ may be functions of θ and t. When θ is the price of a non-dividend-paying stock, $\mu - \lambda\sigma = r$ and (6.1) reduces to the well-known Black and Scholes (1973) differential equation.

To implement the explicit finite difference method, a small time interval Δt and a small change $\Delta \theta$ in θ are chosen. A grid is then constructed for considering values of f when θ is equal to

$$\theta_0, \ \theta_0 + \Delta\theta, \ \theta_0 + 2\,\Delta\theta, \ \ldots, \ \theta_{max},$$

and time is equal to

$$t_0, \ t_0 + \Delta t, \ t_0 + 2\,\Delta t, \ \ldots, \ T.$$

The parameters θ_0 and θ_{max} are the smallest and largest values of θ considered by the model, t_0 is the current time, and T is the end of the life of the derivative security.

We will denote $t_0 + i\,\Delta t$ by t_i, $\theta_0 + j\,\Delta\theta$ by θ_j, and the value of the derivative security at the (i,j) point on the grid by f_{ij}. The partial derivatives of f with respect to θ at node $(i-1,j)$ are approximated as

$$\frac{\partial f}{\partial \theta} = \frac{f_{i,j+1} - f_{i,j-1}}{2\,\Delta\theta}, \tag{6.2}$$

$$\frac{\partial^2 f}{\partial \theta^2} = \frac{f_{i,j+1} + f_{i,j-1} - 2f_{ij}}{\Delta\theta^2}, \tag{6.3}$$

and the time derivative is approximated as

$$\frac{\partial f}{\partial t} = \frac{f_{ij} - f_{i-1,j}}{\Delta t}. \tag{6.4}$$

Substituting (6.2), (6.3), and (6.4) into (6.1) gives

$$f_{i-1,j} = a_{j-1} f_{i,j-1} + a_j f_{ij} + a_{j+1} f_{i,j+1}, \tag{6.5}$$

where

$$a_{j-1} = \frac{1}{1 + r\,\Delta t}\left(-\frac{(\mu - \lambda\sigma)\theta_j\,\Delta t}{2\,\Delta\theta} + \frac{1}{2}\frac{\theta_j^2\sigma^2\,\Delta t}{\Delta\theta^2} \right),$$

$$a_j = \frac{1}{1 + r\,\Delta t}\left(1 - \frac{\theta_j^2\sigma^2\,\Delta t}{\Delta\theta^2} \right),$$

$$a_{j+1} = \frac{1}{1 + r\,\Delta t}\left(\frac{(\mu - \lambda\sigma)\theta_j\,\Delta t}{2\,\Delta\theta} + \frac{1}{2}\frac{\theta_j^2\sigma^2\,\Delta t}{\Delta\theta^2} \right),$$

These equations form the basis of the explicit finite difference method.[1] They relate the value $f_{i-1,j}$ of the derivative security at time t_{i-1} to three alternative values of the derivative security at time t_i. The value of f at

---

[1] The equations for the implicit finite difference method are obtained in a similar way, with the approximation

$$\frac{\partial f}{\partial t} = \frac{f_{i+1,j} - f_{ij}}{\Delta t}$$

being used in place of (6.4) and the partial derivatives being assumed to apply to node (i,j). The implicit method relates $f_{i+1,j}$ to $f_{i,j-1}, f_{ij},$ and $f_{i,j+1}$.

time T is known. The value of f at time t can be obtained by using (6.5) repeatedly to work back from time T to time t in steps of Δt.[2]

Define

$$p_{j,j-1} = -\theta_j(\mu - \lambda\sigma)\frac{\Delta t}{2\Delta\theta} + \tfrac{1}{2}\theta_j^2\sigma^2\frac{\Delta t}{\Delta\theta^2},$$

$$p_{jj} = 1 - \theta_j^2\sigma^2\frac{\Delta t}{\Delta\theta^2},$$

$$p_{j,j+1} = \theta_j(\mu - \lambda\sigma)\frac{\Delta t}{2\Delta\theta} + \tfrac{1}{2}\theta_j^2\sigma^2\frac{\Delta t}{\Delta\theta^2},$$

so that equation (6.5) becomes

$$f_{i-1,j} = \frac{1}{1 + r\,\Delta t}(p_{j,j-1}f_{i,j-1} + p_{jj}f_{ij} + p_{j,j+1}f_{i,j+1}). \tag{6.6}$$

The variables $p_{j,j-1}$, p_{jj}, and $p_{j,j+1}$ can be interpreted as the probabilities of moving from θ_j to θ_{j-1}, θ_j, and θ_{j+1}, respectively, during time Δt, in a world where the proportional drift rate of θ is $\mu - \lambda\sigma$ and its volatility is σ. This is because

$$p_{j,j+1} + p_{jj} + p_{j,j-1} = 1,$$

$$p_{j,j+1}(\theta_j + \Delta\theta) + p_{jj}\theta_j + p_{j,j-1}(\theta_j - \Delta\theta) = \theta_j + (\mu - \lambda\sigma)\theta_j\,\Delta t,$$

and, when terms of $O(\Delta t^2)$ are ignored,

$$p_{j,j+1}(\theta_j + \Delta\theta)^2 + p_{jj}\theta_j^2 + p_{j,j-1}(\theta_j - \Delta\theta)^2$$
$$= [\theta_j + (\mu - \lambda\sigma)\theta_j\,\Delta t]^2 + \sigma^2\theta_j^2\,\Delta t.$$

When the p's are interpreted in this way, (6.6) gives the value of f at time t_i as its expected value at time t_{i+1}, in a world where the drift rate of θ is $\mu - \lambda\sigma$, discounted to time t_i at the risk-free rate of interest. This corresponds to the procedure suggested in Cox, Ingersoll, and Ross (1985: Lemma 4) for valuing derivative securities.

We can conclude from this that the explicit finite difference method is equivalent to a trinomial lattice approach. In Section 6.2, this equivalence is used to explain the conditions required to ensure convergence.

The explicit finite difference method has the advantage that it can require the specification of fewer boundary conditions than the implicit method. Consider, for example, the valuation of a derivative security dependent on a stock price S. The implicit method requires the user to specify boundary conditions for the derivative security as $S \to 0$ and

---

[2] The presentation here assumes that f is a European-style derivative security that pays no income. The arguments easily can be extended to other situations.

$S \to \infty$. The explicit method, when implemented as a trinomial lattice, does not require these boundary conditions.

Partial differential equations can be classified as either boundary value problems (where a full set of boundary conditions must be specified) or initial value problems (where only the value of the function at one particular time needs to be specified). Many derivative security pricing problems, including most option valuation problems, are initial value problems. Ames (1977: p. 62) makes the point that the explicit finite difference method is the best approach for initial value problems. This is because errors are introduced by the extra boundary conditions used in the implicit finite difference method. Consider, for example, the valuation of a derivative security dependent on a stock price S. Errors are introduced because the implicit method's boundary condition as $S \to \infty$ is applied to a finite value of S.

6.2 THE PROPOSED PROCEDURE

(a) The Transformation of Variables

As pointed out by Brennan and Schwartz (1978), Geski and Shastri (1985), and others, when θ is a stock price, it is efficient to use $\ln \theta$ rather than θ as the underlying variable when finite difference methods are applied. This is because, when σ is constant, the instantaneous standard deviation of $\ln \theta$ is constant, i.e., the standard deviation of changes in $\ln \theta$ in a time interval Δt is independent of θ and t.

Generalizing from this, it is always appropriate, when applying the explicit finite difference method, to define a new state variable $\phi(\theta, t)$ that has a constant instantaneous standard deviation. From Ito's lemma, the process followed by ϕ in a risk-neutral world is

$$d\phi = q(\theta, t)\, dt + \frac{\partial \phi}{\partial \theta} \sigma \theta \, dz, \tag{6.7}$$

where

$$q(\theta, t) = \frac{\partial \phi}{\partial t} + (\mu - \lambda\sigma)\theta \frac{\partial \phi}{\partial \theta} + \tfrac{1}{2}\sigma^2 \theta^2 \frac{\partial^2 \phi}{\partial \theta^2}. \tag{6.8}$$

We, therefore, wish to choose the variable ϕ so that

$$\sigma\theta \frac{\partial \phi}{\partial \theta} = v \tag{6.9}$$

for some constant v.

The state variable ϕ can be modeled in the same way as θ. A grid is constructed for values of ϕ equal to $\phi_0, \phi_1, \ldots, \phi_n$, where $\phi_j = \phi_0 + j\,\Delta\phi$, and the probabilities in (6.6) become

$$p_{j,j-1} = -q\frac{\Delta t}{2\,\Delta\phi} + \tfrac{1}{2}v^2\frac{\Delta t}{\Delta\phi^2}, \tag{6.10}$$

$$p_{jj} = 1 - v^2\frac{\Delta t}{\Delta\phi^2}, \tag{6.11}$$

$$p_{j,j+1} = q\frac{\Delta t}{2\,\Delta\phi} + \tfrac{1}{2}v^2\frac{\Delta t}{\Delta\phi^2}. \tag{6.12}$$

If θ is a non-dividend-paying stock with σ and r constant, $\phi = \ln\theta$, $v = \sigma$, $\mu - \lambda\sigma = r$, and $q = r - \tfrac{1}{2}\sigma^2$. The lattice then corresponds to Boyle's (1986) trinomial extension of the Cox, Ross, and Rubinstein (1979) binomial lattice. Since q is constant, it has the simplifying property that the probabilities are the same at all nodes (i.e., $p_{j,j-1}$, p_{jj}, and $p_{j,j+1}$ are independent of j). If the grid is selected so that $\Delta t/\Delta\phi^2 = 1/\sigma^2$, then a binomial lattice results.

(b) The Modification to the Branching Process

When using the explicit finite difference method, it is important to ensure that, as $\Delta t, \Delta\phi \to 0$, the estimated value of the derivative security converges to its true value.[3] From a theorem in Ames (1977: p. 45), a sufficient condition for convergence is that $p_{j,j-1}$, p_{jj}, and $p_{j,j+1}$ be positive as $\Delta t, \Delta\phi \to 0$. This can be seen intuitively from the equivalence of the explicit finite difference method and the trinomial lattice approach. From equations (6.10) to (6.12), this condition is satisfied if

$$v^2\frac{\Delta t}{\Delta\phi^2} < 1 \tag{6.13}$$

and

$$|q| < \frac{v^2}{\Delta\phi} \tag{6.14}$$

as $\Delta t, \Delta\phi \to 0$.[4]

---

[3] Strictly speaking, we are interested in both stability and convergence. A stable procedure is one where the results are relatively insensitive to round-off and other small computational errors (see Ames 1977: p. 28). In practice, the conditions for stability and convergence are the same in most derivative security pricing problems.

[4] When $\phi = \ln\theta$ and $\mu - \lambda\sigma = r$, these correspond to the conditions in Brennan and Schwartz (1978).

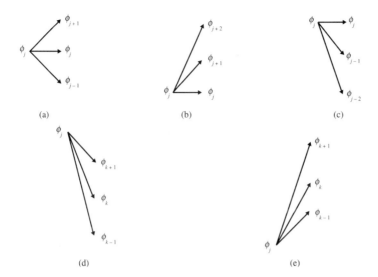

FIGURE 6.1. Alternative branching procedures in the explicit finite difference method designed to ensure that the probabilities associated with all three branches remain positive.

If q is bounded, (6.13) and (6.14) can be satisfied and convergence can be ensured. The simplest procedure is to let Δt and $\Delta \phi$ approach 0 in such a way that $\Delta t / \Delta \phi^2$ remains constant and less than $1/v^2$. The desirability of keeping the ratio of Δt to $\Delta \phi^2$ constant in order to ensure convergence also has been mentioned by Brennan and Schwartz (1978) and by Geske and Shastri (1985).

There are some situations where q is unbounded. As will be shown in Section 6.3, one such situation occurs when θ is an interest rate following a mean-reverting process. The explicit finite difference method, as it has been described so far, may not then converge. However, the method can be modified to overcome this problem. Instead of insisting that we move from ϕ_j to one of ϕ_{j-1}, ϕ_j, or ϕ_{j+1} in time Δt, we allow a movement from ϕ_j to one of ϕ_{k-1}, ϕ_k, and ϕ_{k+1}, where k is not necessarily equal to j. Figure 6.1(a–e) shows the situations where $k = j$, $k = j + 1$, $k = j - 1$, $k < j - 1$, and $k > j + 1$, respectively.

In all cases, we choose k so that ϕ_k is the value of ϕ on the grid closest to $\phi_j + q\Delta t$.[5] The probabilities of ϕ_j moving to ϕ_{k-1}, ϕ_k, and ϕ_{k+1} are chosen to make the first and second moments of the change in ϕ in the time interval Δt correct in the limit as $\Delta t \to 0$. The equations that must

---

[5] In most situations, $k = j - 1$, j, or $j + 1$. This means that the branching process corresponds to Figure 6.1(a), (b), or (c).

be satisfied are

$$p_{j,k-1}(k-1)\,\Delta\phi + p_{jk}k\,\Delta\phi + p_{j,k+1}(k+1)\,\Delta\phi = E(\phi),$$

$$p_{j,k-1}(k-1)^2\,\Delta\phi^2 + p_{jk}k^2\,\Delta\phi^2 + p_{j,k+1}(k+1)^2\,\Delta\phi^2 = v^2\,\Delta t + E(\phi)^2,$$

$$p_{j,k-1} + p_{jk} + p_{j,k+1} = 1,$$

where $E(\phi)$ is the expected value of $\phi - \phi_0$ at the end of the time interval Δt conditional on it being $j\,\Delta\phi$ at the beginning of the interval. The solution to these equations is

$$p_{j,k-1} = \frac{1}{2}\left(k^2 + k - (1+2k)\frac{E(\phi)}{\Delta\phi} + \frac{E(\phi)^2}{\Delta\phi^2} + \frac{v^2\,\Delta t}{\Delta\phi^2}\right), \qquad (6.15)$$

$$p_{jk} = 1 - k^2 + 2k\frac{E(\phi)}{\Delta\phi} - \frac{E(\phi)^2}{\Delta\phi^2} - \frac{v^2\,\Delta t}{\Delta\phi^2}, \qquad (6.16)$$

$$p_{j,k+1} = \frac{1}{2}\left(k^2 - k + (1-2k)\frac{E(\phi)}{\Delta\phi} + \frac{E(\phi)^2}{\Delta\phi^2} + \frac{v^2\,\Delta t}{\Delta\phi^2}\right). \qquad (6.17)$$

The procedure suggested in this section can be used to deal with jumps in θ. Suppose, for example, that θ is the price of a security, and a dividend at time τ is expected to cause θ to jump down by $\delta(\theta)$. For the time interval in which the dividend occurs, we can switch from Figure 6.1(a) to Figure 6.1(d). We define k in Figure 6.1(d) so that ϕ_k is the value of ϕ on the grid closest to $\phi(\theta_j - \delta(\theta_j), \tau)$.[6]

Finally, it is worth nothing that the explicit finite difference method provides one degree of freedom: the choice $v^2\,\Delta t/\Delta\phi^2$. We will denote this by w. One constraint on w is that it should always be possible to find a k such that $p_{j,k-1}$, p_{jk}, and $p_{j,k+1}$ are positive. It can shown that this constraint implies that $0.25 < w < 0.75$. If q is small, an examination of the errors in the way in which the differential equation is approximated suggests that a sensible value for w is $\frac{1}{3}$.[7] We find that this works well.

[6] Hull and White (1988) and Hull (1989) suggest that known dividends should be dealt with by defining θ as the security price less the present value of the known income. This has some theoretical appeal. If the dollar amount of future income is known, the price of the security logically should be divided into two components: a non-stochastic component that will be used to pay the known dividend, and a residual stochastic component. The approach suggested here may be more appropriate when long time periods are considered (e.g., in the valuation of warrants or convertible stock).

[7] If $q = 0$, the errors are $O(\Delta t^2)$ rather than $O(\Delta t)$ when $v^2\,\Delta t/\Delta\phi^2 = \frac{1}{3}$. If q is constant (as is the case when θ is a stock price), it is efficient to define a new "zero-q" variable ψ: $\psi = \phi - qt$. When this variable is modeled using $p_{j,j+1} = \frac{1}{6}$, $p_{jj} = \frac{2}{3}$, and $p_{j,j-1} = \frac{1}{6}$, the errors are $O(\Delta t^2)$.

6.3 APPLICATION TO A ONE-STATE-VARIABLE INTEREST RATE MODEL

A number of authors have suggested that an appropriate process for the short-term interest rate is

$$d\theta = a(b - \theta)\,dt + c\theta^\alpha\,dz,$$

where a, b, c, and α are constants, and θ is the short-term interest rate. In Vasicek (1977), $\alpha = 0$; in Cox, Ingersoll, and Ross (1985b), $\alpha = \frac{1}{2}$; in Courtadon (1982a), $\alpha = 1$. The modified version of the explicit finite difference method can be used for any value of α. We will illustrate its use for $\alpha = \frac{1}{2}$.

From (6.9), an appropriate transformation of θ is

$$\phi = \sqrt{\theta}.$$

In a risk-neutral world,

$$d\theta = [a(b - \theta) - uc\theta]\,dt + c\sqrt{\theta}\,dz,$$

where $u\sqrt{\theta}$ is the market price of risk. This means that

$$d\phi = q\,dt + v\,dz,$$

where $v = \frac{1}{2}c$, and

$$q = [a(b - \theta) - uc\theta]\frac{\partial\phi}{\partial\theta} + \frac{1}{2}c^2\theta\frac{\partial^2\phi}{\partial\theta^2}$$

$$= \frac{4ab - c^2}{8\phi} - \frac{1}{2}\phi(a + uc).$$

Since ϕ can take on any positive value, q is not bounded. It follows that the standard explicit finite difference method may not converge. However, the variation on the standard method described in Section 6.2 can be used.

Define

$$\alpha_1 = \frac{1}{8}(4ab - c^2), \qquad \alpha_2 = \frac{1}{2}(a + uc).$$

As suggested in Section 6.2, we choose $v^2\,\Delta t/\Delta\phi^2 = \frac{1}{3}$. It is easy to show

119

$k = j$ when

$$-\tfrac{1}{2} \le (\alpha_1/\phi - \alpha_2\phi)\frac{\Delta t}{\Delta \phi} \le \tfrac{1}{2}.$$

Assuming α_1 and α_2 are positive, this condition reduces to[8]

$$\phi_{min} \le \phi \le \phi_{max},$$

where

$$\phi_{min} = \frac{-\beta + \sqrt{\beta^2 + 4\alpha_1\alpha_2}}{2\alpha_2}, \qquad \phi_{max} = \frac{\beta + \sqrt{\beta^2 + 4\alpha_1\alpha_2}}{2\alpha_2},$$

with $\beta = \Delta\phi/2\,\Delta t$.

Using the approach outlined in Section 6.2, the values of ϕ considered on the grid for the explicit finite difference method are $\phi_0, \phi_1, \ldots, \phi_n$, where ϕ_0 is the largest multiple of $\Delta\phi$ less than ϕ_{min}, $\phi_j = \phi_0 + j\,\Delta\phi$, and n is the smallest integer such that $\phi_n \ge \phi_{max}$. (It is assumed that $\Delta\phi$ is also chosen so that some multiple of $\Delta\phi$ equals the current value of ϕ.) Note that, as Δt and $\Delta\phi$ tend to 0, ϕ_{min} approaches 0 and ϕ_{max} increases.

When $1 \le j \le n - 1$, the explicit finite difference method (trinomial lattice) approach operates in the usual way. The probabilities of moving from ϕ_j to ϕ_{j-1}, ϕ_j, and ϕ_{j+1} in time interval Δt are given by (6.15), (6.16), and (6.17). In this example, when the value ϕ_0 is reached, the three possible values that might be obtained after a time interval Δt are ϕ_0, ϕ_1, and ϕ_2. The probabilities p_{00}, p_{01}, and p_{02} are calculated from equations (6.15), (6.16), and (6.17), with $j = 0$ and $k = 1$. Similarly, when the value ϕ_n is reached, the three possible values of ϕ after a time interval of Δt has elapsed are ϕ_{n-2}, ϕ_{n-1}, and ϕ_n. The probabilities $p_{n,n-2}$, $p_{n,n-1}$, and p_{nn} of moving to these values are calculated from equations (6.15), (6.16), and (6.17), with $j = n$ and $k = n - 1$. Clearly, it is unnecessary to consider values of ϕ less than ϕ_0 or greater than ϕ_n, since these can never be reached.

The modified explicit finite difference method can be used to value any interest rate contingent claim. Table 6.1 shows the results of using the procedure to value a discount bond with face value of $100. Define B_{ij} as the value of the bond at the (i, j) node, and assume that the bond matures at time $t_0 + m\,\Delta t$. We know that $B_{mj} = 100$ for all j. Since the short-term interest rate is ϕ^2, the value of the bond prior to maturity can be

---

[8] Note that if $\alpha_2 < 0$ then the risk-adjusted drift rate of the short-term interest rate is always positive. This would imply infinite discount rates in a risk-neutral world. If $\alpha_1 < 0$, the effective ϕ_{min} is zero; if $\beta^2 + 4\alpha_1\alpha_2 < 0$, there is no effective ϕ_{max}.

calculated using

$$B_{ij} = \frac{1}{1 + \phi_j^2 \, \Delta t}(p_{j,j-1}B_{i+1,j-1} + p_{jj}B_{i+1,j} + p_{j,j+1}B_{i+1,j+1})$$

$$\text{for } j = 1, \ldots, n-1, \quad (6.18)$$

$$B_{i0} = \frac{1}{1 + \phi_0^2 \, \Delta t}(p_{00}B_{i+1,0} + p_{01}B_{i+1,1} + p_{02}B_{i+1,2}), \quad (6.19)$$

$$B_{in} = \frac{1}{1 + \phi_n^2 \, \Delta t}(p_{n,n-2}B_{i+1,n-2} + p_{n,n-1}B_{i+1,n-1} + p_{nn}B_{i+1,n}). \quad (6.20)$$

Table 6.1 compares the calculated bond price with the analytic solution given by Cox, Ingersoll, and Ross (1985b) for the interest rate process parameters

$$a = 0.4, \quad b = 0.1, \quad c = 0.06, \quad u = 0.$$

These parameters produce an interest rate model where the short-term interest rate reverts to 10 percent. The instantaneous volatility of the short rate is about 19 percent when the short-term rate is 10 percent. The parameter values choosen are, therefore, not unreasonable. Table 6.1 shows that the numerical solution is very close to the analytic solution.

Table 6.2 shows the results of using the method to value American call options on a bond paying a coupon at a continuous rate of $\gamma = \$10$ per unit time. First, the bond price at each node of the lattice was calculated

TABLE 6.1. Bond prices given by the explicit finite difference method for the Cox, Ingersoll, and Ross model in which the interest rate obeys the process $dr = a(b - r)\,dt + c\sqrt{r}\,dz$.

Bond maturity (years)	Current short-term interest rate				
	6%	8%	10%	12%	14%
5	66.31	63.53	60.86	58.30	55.85
	(66.24)	(63.45)	(60.78)	(58.23)	(55.78)
10	40.92	38.98	37.14	35.38	33.71
	(40.83)	(38.89)	(37.05)	(35.29)	(33.62)
15	25.02	23.82	22.68	21.59	20.55
	(24.94)	(23.74)	(22.59)	(21.51)	(20.47)
20	15.28	14.54	13.85	13.18	12.55
	(15.21)	(14.48)	(13.78)	(13.11)	(12.48)

Note: The market price of interest rate risk is $u\sqrt{r}$. True prices given by the analytic solution are shown in parentheses. Face value of bond = $100, Δt = 0.05 years, a = 0.4, b = 0.1, c = 0.06, and u = 0.

121

TABLE 6.2. Price of a 5-year American call option on a 10-year bond ($100 face value) using the Cox, Ingersoll, and Ross interest rate model in which the interest rate obeys the process $dr = a(b - r)\, dt + c\sqrt{r}\, dz$.

Δt	Exercise price				
(years)	90	95	100	105	110
0.500	10.34	6.09	2.69	0.47	0.02
0.250	10.36	6.21	2.46	0.44	0.01
0.100	10.47	6.13	2.54	0.45	0.01
0.050	10.51	6.15	2.54	0.46	0.01
0.025	10.52	6.14	2.53	0.45	0.01
0.010	10.52	6.14	2.53	0.45	0.01

Note: The market price of interest rate risk is $u\sqrt{r}$. The current short-term interest rate is 10 percent per annum and the bond pays a coupon at the rate of $10 per annum. The current price of the bonds is 100.39, $a = 0.4$, $b = 0.1$, $c = 0.06$, and $u = 0$.

using a similar approach to that described above.[9] The option price was then evaluated by working back through the lattice from the end of the option's life and applying the boundary conditions for an American call option.[10] From Table 6.2, we see that the procedure converges fairly rapidly.

6.4 DEALING WITH MORE THAN ONE STATE VARIABLE

To illustrate how the ideas presented above can be extended to deal with several state variables, consider the two-state-variable case. Suppose the variables are θ_1 and θ_2. These must first be transformed to two new variables ϕ_1 and ϕ_2 so that the instantaneous standard deviation of each is constant. Assume that the volatility of θ_i $(i = 1, 2)$ depends only on θ_i and t. The correct transformations can then be determined in the way indicated in Section 6.2. The processes for ϕ_1 and ϕ_2 have the form

$$d\phi_1 = q_1\, dt + k_1\, dz_1,$$
$$d\phi_2 = q_2\, dt + k_2\, dz_2,$$

where k_1 and k_2 are constants, and q_1 and q_2 are defined analogously to q in (6.8).

[9] To adjust for coupons, the expressions in parentheses in equations (6.18) to (6.20) were each increased by $\gamma\, \Delta t$.

[10] Suppose that C, B, and X are the call price, the bond price, and the exercise price, respectively. At the end of the option's life, $C = \max\{B - X, 0\}$. At each node, the boundary condition $C \geq B - X$ is imposed.

There is likely to be an instantaneous correlation ρ between the Wiener processes dz_1 and dz_2. Assume this to be constant. The next stage is to transform variables again to eliminate the correlation. This can be achieved by defining new variables ψ_1 and ψ_2 as follows:

$$\psi_1 = k_2\phi_1 + k_1\phi_2,$$
$$\psi_2 = k_2\phi_1 - k_1\phi_2.$$

These follow the processes

$$d\psi_1 = (k_2q_1 + k_1q_2)\,dt + k_1k_2\sqrt{2(1+\rho)}\,dz_3,$$
$$d\psi_2 = (k_2q_1 - k_1q_2)\,dt + k_1k_2\sqrt{2(1-\rho)}\,dz_4,$$

where the Wiener processes dz_3 and dz_4 are uncorrelated.

The possible unconditional movements of ψ_1 in the time interval Δt, together with their associated probabilities, are chosen in the same way as they are for ϕ in Section 6.2. The same is true for ψ_2. Unbounded drift rates are dealt with using the same approach as that described in Section 6.2. The variables ψ_1 and ψ_2 are, therefore, modeled using a two-dimensional lattice with nine branches emanating from each node. The probability of any given point being reached is the product of the unconditional probabilities associated with the corresponding movements in ψ_1 and ψ_2.

Tables 6.3 and 6.4 show results from the application of the explicit finite difference method to the Brennan–Schwartz two-state-variable

TABLE 6.3. Prices for a 3-year face value 8-percent continuous coupon bond using the Brennan–Schwartz model.

Δt (years)	Bond price Current short-term rate, r		
	6%	8%	10%
0.200	102.93	98.02	93.36
0.100	102.93	98.06	93.43
0.067	102.93	98.07	93.45
0.050	102.93	98.07	93.46
0.040	102.93	98.08	93.47

Note: The interest rates obey the processes $dr = a(l - r)\,dt + \sigma_1 r\,dz_1$ and $dl = \mu(r, l, t)\,dt + \sigma_2 l\,dz_2$, with $a = 0.1$, $\sigma_1 = 0.1$, and $\sigma_2 = 0.03$. The market price of short-term interest risk is -0.4, the correlation between dz_1 and dz_2 is 0.2, and the initial long-term rate $l = 10$ percent.

TABLE 6.4. Price of a European call option on a 3-year 8-percent coupon bond using the Brennan–Schwartz model.

Δt (years)	Call price Current short-term rate, r		
	6%	8%	10%
0.100	3.17	0.60	0.015
0.067	3.17	0.60	0.014
0.050	3.17	0.59	0.014
0.040	3.18	0.59	0.014

Note: The interest rates obey the processes $dr = a(l - r)\,dt + \sigma_1 r\,dz_1$ and $dl = \mu(r, l, t)\,dt + \sigma_2 l\,dz_2$, with $a = 0.1$, $\sigma_1 = 0.1$, and $\sigma_2 = 0.03$. The market price of short-term interest rate risk is -0.4, the correlation between dz_1 and dz_2 is 0.2, and the initial long-term rate $l = 10$ percent. The option has 1 year to maturity and an exercise price of 98. The corresponding bond prices are given in Table 6.3.

interest rate model. In this model,

$$dr = a(l - r)\,dt + \sigma_1 r\,dz_1,$$
$$dl = \mu(l, r, t)\,dt + \sigma_2 l\,dz_2,$$

where l is the yield on a consol bond, r is the instantaneous risk-free interest rate, and a, σ_1, and σ_2 are constants. The market price of short-term interest rate risk λ and the instantaneous correlation ρ between r and l also are assumed to be constant. Table 6.3 shows bond prices, while Table 6.4 shows European call prices. The rates of convergence are encouragingly fast.

6.5 SUMMARY AND CONCLUSIONS

The explicit finite difference method is both easier to implement and conceptually simpler than the implicit method. The explicit method's disadvantage is that it does not necessarily converge. This paper provides a systematic procedure for implementing a modified version of the method in such a way that convergence is ensured. This should make the method attractive to both practitioners and researchers.

Geske and Shastri (1985: Table 2) found that the explicit finite difference method, when implemented in the most efficient way for valuing stock options, uses about 60 percent as much CPU time as the implicit method. We have applied both the explicit and implicit methods to a variety of different problems using an IBM AT Personal Computer.

Our results are similar to those of Geske and Shastri. We find that the explicit method uses between 40 and 70 percent as much time as the implicit method to provide the same level of accuracy. One reason for the extra efficiency of the explicit method is that most derivative security pricing problems are initial value problems, not boundary value problems. Errors are introduced by the redundant boundary conditions in implicit methods.

REFERENCES

Ames, W. F. *Numerical Methods for Partial Differential Equations.* Academic Press, New York, 1977.

Black, F., and M. Scholes. "The pricing of options and corporate liabilities." *Journal of Political Economy*, 81 (May–June 1973), pp. 637–659.

Boyle, P. P. "Option valuation using a three-jump process." *International Options Journal*, 3 (1986), pp. 7–12.

Boyle, P. P. "A lattice framework for option pricing with two state variables." *Journal of Financial and Quantitative Analysis*, 23 (March 1988), pp. 1–12.

Brennan, M. J., and E. S. Schwartz. "Finite difference method and jump processes arising in the pricing of contingent claims." *Journal of Financial and Quantitative Analysis*, 13 (September 1978), pp. 461–474.

Brennan, M. J., and E. S. Schwartz. "An equilibrium model of bond pricing and a test of market efficiency." *Journal of Financial and Quantitative Analysis*, 17 (September 1982), pp. 301–330.

Courtadon, G. "The pricing of options on default-free bonds." *Journal of Financial and Quantitative Analysis*, 17 (March 1982a), pp. 75–100.

Courtadon, G. "A more accurate finite difference approximation for the valuation of options." *Journal of Financial and Quantitative Analysis*, 17 (December 1982b), pp. 697–705.

Cox, J. C., J. E. Ingersoll, and S. A. Ross. "An intertemporal general equilibrium model of asset prices." *Econometrica*, 53 (March 1985a), pp. 363–384.

Cox, J. C., J. E. Ingersoll, and S. A. Ross. "A theory of the term structure of interest rates." *Econometrica*, 53 (March 1985b), pp. 385–407.

Cox, J. C., S. Ross, and M. Rubinstein. "Option pricing: a simplified approach." *Journal of Financial Economics*, 7 (October 1979), pp. 229–264.

Garman, M. "A general theory of asset valuation under diffusion state processes." Working Paper No. 5, University of California, Berkeley, 1976.

Geske, R., and K. Shastri. "Valuation of approximation: a comparison of alternative approaches." *Journal of Financial and Quantitative Analysis*, 20 (March 1985), pp. 45–72.

Hull, J. C. *Options, Futures and Other Derivative Securities.* Prentice-Hall, Englewood Cliffs, NJ, 1989.

Hull, J. C., and A. White. "The use of control variate technique in option-pricing." *Journal of Financial and Quantitative Analysis*, 23 (September 1988), pp. 237–251. Also Chapter 7 in this book.

Rendleman, R., and B. Bartter. "The pricing options on debt securities." *Journal of Financial and Quantitative Analysis*, 15 (March 1980), pp. 11–24.

Schwartz, E. S. "The valuation of warrants: implementing a new approach." *Journal of Financial Economics*, 4 (January 1977), pp. 79–93.

Vasicek, O. A. "An equilibrium characterization of the term structure." *Journal of Financial Economics*, 5 (November 1977), pp. 177–188.

7. The use of the control variate technique in option pricing*

In spite of the theoretical advances made in recent years, many option pricing problems lack straightforward closed-form solutions.[1] For example, American put options on a stock, American currency options, American options on commodity futures, and options on a stock with a stochastic volatility all appear to present intractable pricing problems.

The various approaches that have been suggested for calculating option prices when there is no closed-form solution include analytic approximation, compound option methods, series solutions, Monte Carlo simulation, numerical integration, binomial models, and finite difference methods. Johnson (1983) and Macmillan (1986) show how analytic approximation can be used to value an American put on a non-dividend-paying stock. Blomeyer (1986) and Omberg (1987a) use analytic approximation to value American puts on dividend-paying stocks. Barone-Adesi and Whaley (1987) apply analytic approximation to other American options. Geske and Johnson (1984) present an ingenious compound option approach to valuing an American put on a dividend- or non-dividend-paying stock. Hull and White (1988) provide a series solution for valuing a European option on a stock when the volatility is stochastic. Monte Carlo simulation was suggested by Boyle (1977) and has

---

[1] As pointed out by Geske and Johnson (1984: p. 1513), describing a solution as closed form or analytical rather than numerical is tricky in the option context. In the end, all methods require numerical procedures. For example, the use of the Black–Scholes (1973) formula requires the numerical evaluation of the cumulative normal distribution function. This paper is concerned with option pricing problems in which existing numerical procedures are non-trivial, so that improvements in numerical efficiency are of interest.

* This paper was first published in *Journal of Financial and Quantitative Analysis*, Vol.23 (1988), pp. 237–251. It is reprinted with the permission of the *Journal of Financial and Quantitative Analysis*.

been used by both Johnson and Shanno (1985) and Hull and White (1987) to value options when the volatility is stochastic. Numerical integration has been used for American puts by Parkinson (1977). Both binomial models and finite difference methods have been used in a wide variety of situations. Binomial models are discussed by Cox, Ross, and Rubinstein (1979), while finite difference methods are discussed by Schwartz (1977), Brennan and Schwartz (1979), and Courtadon (1982).

All these numerical methods have a dual objective of accuracy and speed of computation. For any given method, greater accuracy can normally be achieved only by increasing the computation time. Geske and Shastri (1985) provide a careful comparison of binomial models and finite difference methods. They conclude that "researchers computing a smaller number of option values may prefer binomial approximation, while practitioners in the business of computing a larger number of option values will generally find that finite difference methods are more efficient" (p. 70).

The binomial model is a particular case of a more general set of multivariate multinomial models. For example, Boyle (1986) shows how stock options can be valued using a trinomial model, while Boyle (1988) shows how a bivariate multinomial model can be used to value options in which there are two underlying state variables. We shall refer to all multivariate multinomial models as lattice approaches. The main purpose of this paper is to show how a method known as the control variate technique can, in some circumstances, be used to improve the efficiency of lattice approaches.

The rest of the paper is organized as follows. Section 7.1 presents a generalized version of the lattice approach to option pricing. Section 7.2 discusses how dividends can be incorporated in lattice approaches. Section 7.3 describes the control variate technique and its application to lattice approaches. Section 7.4 applies the technique to the valuation of American puts. Section 7.5 discusses the application of the technique in other situations. Conclusions are in Section 7.6.

7.1 LATTICE APPROACHES

In this section, we present a generalized version of the lattice approach to option valuation. As already mentioned, this approach involves a multivariate multinomial extension of the Cox, Ross, and Rubinstein

(1979) (CRR) binomial model. The lattice approach can be viewed as an application of dynamic programming.[2]

A lattice approach requires the use of a risk-neutral argument.[3] If the underlying state variables are traded securities, risk-neutral arguments can be applied in a straightforward way. If one or more of the variables are non-traded, the basic risk-neutral valuation argument must be extended, as in Cox, Ingersoll, and Ross (1985).

In the generalized lattice approach, we consider a derivative security whose price depends on l underlying state variables. The life T of the security is divided into n subintervals of length Δt. At time $i \, \Delta t$, a finite number m_i of different possible states of the world is defined. We will denote these states of the world by x_{ij} $(1 \leq j \leq m_i)$. Each x_{ij} is an $l \times 1$ vector of values of the state variables. When $i = 0$, the state of the world is known and $m_i = 1$. Generally, as i increases, m_i also increases.

Transition probabilities q_{ijk} are defined as follows:

$$q_{ijk} = \text{probability of moving from state } x_{ij} \text{ at time } i \, \Delta t$$
$$\text{to state } x_{i+1,k} \text{ at time } (i+1) \, \Delta t.$$

The states of the world x_{ij}, together with the transition probabilities q_{ijk}, constitute the lattice that is used to model the underlying state variables. The q_{ijk} must be chosen so that they satisfy

$$\sum_k q_{ijk} = 1 \quad \text{for all } i, j \qquad \text{and} \qquad 0 \leq q_{ijk} \leq 1 \quad \text{for all } i, j, k.$$

Also, the transition probabilities and values of the state variables x_{ij} must be chosen so that the lattice accurately represents the actual state variables in a risk-neutral world. This is usually achieved by requiring that the lattice give the correct values for the means and standard deviations of, and the coefficients of correlation between, the changes in the state variables in each time interval Δt.

Once the lattice has been set up, the dynamic programming method can be used. The value of the derivative security at time T is known for all m_n states of the world possible at that time. Furthermore the value for all m_i states of the world at time $i \, \Delta t$ can be calculated using risk-neutral

---

[2] For a description of the dynamic programming technique, see Bellman and Dreyfus (1962). It should be emphasized that moving from a binomial model to, say, a trinomial model does not mean that a different underlying stochastic process is being assumed. Instead, it means that the same stochastic process is being approximated in a different way.

[3] The lattice approach calculates the option price as the discounted value of the expected option pay-off. In order to know the appropriate discount rate, risk-neutral valuation arguments are necessary.

valuation if the value is known for all m_{i+1} states of the world at time $(i+1)\,\Delta t$. By moving backwards through the lattice, the value at time 0 can be obtained.

In the CRR binomial model, there is one state variable, the stock price S. This is assumed to follow the stochastic process

$$dS = \mu S\,dt + \sigma S\,dz, \tag{7.1}$$

where σ is the constant instantaneous standard deviation of dS/S, μ is the instantaneous drift of dS/S, and dz is a Wiener process. In a risk-neutral world, equation (7.1) becomes

$$dS = r_f S\,dt + \sigma S\,dz, \tag{7.2}$$

where r_f is the risk-free interest rate.

If the initial stock price is S_0, then the stock prices corresponding to the $m_i = i+1$ states of the world x_{ij} $(1 \leq j \leq i+1)$ considered at time $i\,\Delta t$ in the CRR approach are

$$
\begin{aligned}
i &= 0: & &S_0, \\
i &= 1: & &dS_0,\, uS_0, \\
i &= 2: & &d^2 S_0,\, S_0,\, u^2 S_0, \\
i &= 3: & &d^3 S_0,\, dS_0,\, uS_0,\, u^3 S_0,
\end{aligned}
$$

and so on, where

$$u = \exp(\sigma\sqrt{\Delta t}), \tag{7.3}$$

and

$$d = 1/u. \tag{7.4}$$

The transition probabilities q_{ijk} are defined as

$$
q_{ijk} = \begin{cases}
p & \text{if } k = j+1, \\
1-p & \text{if } k = j, \\
0 & \text{otherwise,}
\end{cases}
$$

where

$$p = \frac{r-d}{u-d} \tag{7.5}$$

and

$$r = \exp(r_f\,\Delta t). \tag{7.6}$$

The definitions of p, u, and d in equations (7.3) to (7.5) provide a binomial approximation to the stochastic process in equation (7.2).[4]

Boyle (1986) has suggested an alternative to the CRR binomial pricing model, where $m_i = 2i + 1$ and there are three (rather than two) non-zero q_{ijk} for each i and j. He shows that a more efficient computational algorithm results. In another paper, Boyle (1987) has suggested using the lattice approach for the situation in which there are two independent variables. In this case, he finds it necessary to have five non-zero q_{ijk}'s for each i and j, and $m_i = 1 + 2i(i + 1)$.

For the lattice approach to work efficiently, the total number of nodes (unique values of x_{ij}) considered at any given time should not be allowed to become unnecessarily large. This is because computation time is proportional to the total number of nodes in the lattice. An efficient lattice also requires the x_{ij} to be representative of the possible future states of the world.[5] Generally, a satisfactory lattice is one in which the transition probabilities are not regularly close to either 0.0 or 1.0.

7.2 DIVIDENDS

There is an interesting issue concerned with the use of a CRR-type lattice (and lattices, in general) when there are known payouts, such as dividends. Suppose that it is known that a dividend of D will be paid and that the stock will go ex-dividend at τ $(0 \le \tau \le T)$. We can define a variable $S^*(t)$ as follows:

$$S^*(t) = \begin{cases} S(t) - De^{-r_f(\tau-t)} & \text{if } t \le \tau, \\ S(t) & \text{if } t > \tau. \end{cases}$$

---

[4] Actually, the CRR values for p, u, and d only give the correct mean and standard deviation of stock price changes in the limit as $\Delta t \to 0$. It is slightly more accurate to solve

$$pu + (1-p)d = m_1, \qquad pu^2 + (1-p)d^2 = m_2, \qquad u = 1/d,$$

where m_1 and m_2 are the first and second moments of the lognormal distribution of $S(t + \Delta t)/S(t)$. This gives

$$m_1 = \exp(r_f \Delta t), \qquad m_2 = \exp(2r_f \Delta t + \sigma^2 \Delta t),$$

$$u = \left((m_2 + 1) + \sqrt{(m_2 + 1)^2 - 4m_1^2}\right)/2m_1, \qquad d = 1/u, \qquad p = \frac{m_1 - d}{u - d}.$$

For all the calculations in this paper, the CRR binomial lattice was modified so that these values of u, d, and p were used.

[5] For example, a lattice in which all values considered for a state variable are within one-tenth of its standard deviation is not normally appropriate. Similarly, it is likely to be wasteful to consider values that are ten standard deviations from the mean.

When $t \leq \tau$, the stock price can be viewed as having two components: a part S^* that is stochastic and a part $De^{-r_f(\tau-t)}$ that is non-stochastic and will be used to pay a dividend D at time τ.[6] Define σ^* as the instantaneous standard deviation of dS^*/S^*. It is logical to assume that σ^* rather than σ is constant. If we make this assumption, the parameters p, u, and d can be calculated by replacing σ by σ^* in equations (7.3) to (7.5). At times $i\,\Delta t$, the values of the stock prices considered in the lattice are then

$$S^*(0)u^j d^{i-j} + De^{-r_f(\tau-i\Delta t)} \quad (j = 0, 1, \ldots, i),$$

when $i\,\Delta t < \tau$, and

$$S^*(0)u^j d^{i-j} \quad (j = 0, 1, \ldots, i),$$

when $i\,\Delta t > \tau$. For a European option on a stock with known dividends, the assumption that has been made here corresponds to the common practice of using the Black–Scholes price with the stock price reduced by the present value of the dividends.[7]

An alternative valuation approach (that does not have quite as much theoretical appeal) is to define a variable S' by

$$S'(t) = \begin{cases} S(t) & \text{if } t \leq \tau, \\ S(t) + De^{r_f(t-\tau)} & \text{if } t > \tau, \end{cases}$$

and to assume that the instantaneous standard deviation of dS'/S', say σ', is constant. (Since $S^*(t) = S'(t) - De^{-r_f(\tau-t)}$, this implies that the known dividend affects the volatility of the stochastic component of the stock price.) The parameters u, d, and p in equations (7.3) to (7.5) should then be calculated using σ' rather than σ. At time $i\,\Delta t$, the values considered in the lattice are then

$$S(0)u^j d^{i-j} \quad (j = 0, 1, \ldots, i),$$

when $i\,\Delta t \leq \tau$, and

$$S(0)u^j d^{i-j} - De^{r_f(i\Delta t-\tau)} \quad (j = 0, 1, \ldots, i),$$

when $i\,\Delta t > \tau$. For a European option on a stock with known dividends, this assumption corresponds to using the Black–Scholes formula with the exercise price increased by the value of the dividends compounded to time T at the risk-free rate.

The assumption frequently made for American options is that σ is constant. This implies that either the return from the known dividend is

---

[6] This corresponds to Rubinstein's (1983) displaced diffusion model.

[7] We have assumed that the stock price declines by D when it goes ex-dividend. This may not always be the case because of tax considerations. If the stock price is expected to decline by αD, the same conclusions apply with D replaced by αD.

uncertain, or the risk of the stock price declines after the dividend is paid. This is also the assumption for which it is most difficult to construct a lattice (see Cox and Rubinstein 1984: p. 241). A straightforward extension of CRR in which u, d, and p are held constant leads to a great increase in the number of nodes. This is because the branches of the binomial tree do not recombine. Suppose that $i \Delta t \leq \tau < (i + 1) \Delta t$. At time $(i + 1) \Delta t$, the nodes on the lattice correspond to stock prices

$$[S(0)u^j d^{i-j} - D]u \quad \text{and} \quad [S(0)u^j d^{i-j} - D]d,$$

for $j = 0, 1, \ldots, i$, so that there are, in general, $2(i + 1)$ rather than $i + 2$ nodes. At time $(i + q) \Delta t$, there are $(q + 1)(i + 1)$ rather than $i + q + 1$ nodes. If more than one dividend is expected, the number of terminal nodes is liable to be very large. It is possible to design lattices in which the number of nodes at time $i \Delta t$ is always $i + 1$. However, the transition probabilities vary from node to node.

If the dividend yield rather than the dividend itself is assumed to be known, Cox and Rubinstein (1984) show that a straightforward extension of the CRR lattice is possible. At times $i \Delta t$, the values of the stock price considered in the lattice are

$$S(0)u^j d^{i-j},$$

when $i \Delta t \leq \tau$, and

$$S(0)(1 - \delta)u^j d^{i-j},$$

when $i \Delta t > \tau$, where δ is the divided yield (i.e., the proportion of the stock price paid out as a dividend at time τ).

Finally, we note the observation of Cox, Ross, and Rubinstein (1979) that a slight modification of their lattice can be used to value an option on stock paying a continuous dividend when the instantaneous dividend yield γ is constant. It is necessary to replace r_f by $r_f - \gamma$ in the definition of r in equation (7.6). Currencies and commodities are analogous to stocks paying continuous dividends. In the case of a currency, the analogue to the dividend is the foreign risk-free rate; in the case of a commodity, it is the convenience yield net of storage costs. Options on currencies and commodities therefore can be valued using a suitably modified CRR lattice.

7.3 THE CONTROL VARIATE TECHNIQUE

The control variate technique can be used to improve the efficiency of numerical valuation procedures. It is applicable when we wish to value an option A and we have an accurate valuation for a similar option B. Boyle (1977) suggested the use of the control variate technique in conjunction with Monte Carlo simulation. Here, we show that it can also be applied in conjunction with lattice approaches.

The key element in the control variate technique is that the same numerical procedure is used to value both option A and option B. This may appear wasteful since an accurate value for B is already available. However, if the estimation errors from using the numerical procedure to value A and B are unbiased (or equally biased) and highly correlated, the technique enables a much better estimate of the value of A to be produced. Define

C_B: the accurate value of option B;
$\hat{C}_A$: the estimated value of option A using the numerical procedure;
$\hat{C}_B$: the estimated value of option B using the numerical procedure;
σ_A: the standard error of $\hat{C}_A$;
σ_B: the standard error of $\hat{C}_B$; and
ρ: the correlation between $\hat{C}_A$ and $\hat{C}_B$.

The control variate technique's estimate for the value $\hat{C}_A^*$ of A is given by

$$\hat{C}_A^* = C_B + (\hat{C}_A - \hat{C}_B). \tag{7.7}$$

This has a standard error of

$$(\sigma_A^2 + \sigma_B^2 - 2\rho\sigma_A\sigma_B)^{\frac{1}{2}},$$

which is less than σ_A if

$$\rho > \sigma_B/2\sigma_A. \tag{7.8}$$

When the control variate technique is used in conjunction with Monte Carlo simulation, the same random normal deviates are used to calculate $\hat{C}_A$ and $\hat{C}_B$. When it is used in conjunction with the lattice approach, the same lattice is used to calculate $\hat{C}_A$ and $\hat{C}_B$. In both cases, provided that an accurate value of option B is available, equation (7.7) can be used to calculate the control variate estimate $\hat{C}_A^*$.

The lattice approach and Monte Carlo simulation approach have some similarities.[8] Monte Carlo simulation considers a finite number of randomly selected paths for the state variables. Lattice approaches consider a finite number of representative paths for the state variables. In

[8] However, the two approaches are not direct substitutes for each other. Monte Carlo simulation can be used only for European options, whereas lattice approaches can be used for European or American options.

both cases, the paths considered will inevitably lead to less than perfectly accurate price estimates. However, in both approaches, there is a tendency for the errors in the price estimates of the two similar options to be highly correlated when the same set of paths is considered.

The control variate technique can also be used in conjunction with the lattice approach when derivatives of option prices are required. Suppose that we wish to evaluate $\partial C_A / \partial \phi$ at $\phi = \phi_0$, where ϕ is an option parameter and ϕ_0 is its current value. We assume that an accurate value of $\partial C_B / \partial \phi$ at $\phi = \phi_0$ is available, and we denote this value by D_B. First, $\hat{C}_A(\phi_0)$ and $\hat{C}_B(\phi_0)$ are calculated using the lattice in the usual way. Then a small change $\Delta \phi_0$ in ϕ_0 is chosen, and $\hat{C}_A(\phi_0 + \Delta \phi_0)$ and $\hat{C}_B(\phi_0 + \Delta \phi_0)$ are also calculated using the lattice. Define

$$\hat{D}_A = \frac{\hat{C}_A(\phi_0 + \Delta \phi_0) - \hat{C}_A(\phi_0)}{\Delta \phi_0},$$

$$\hat{D}_B = \frac{\hat{C}_B(\phi_0 + \Delta \phi_0) - \hat{C}_B(\phi_0)}{\Delta \phi_0}.$$

The control variate estimate $\hat{D}_A^*$ of $\partial C_A / \partial \phi$ is given by[9]

$$\hat{D}_A^* = D_B + (\hat{D}_A - \hat{D}_B).$$

This has a standard error of

$$\frac{1}{\Delta \phi_0} \hat{\sigma}_A^* \sqrt{2 - 2\rho_A(\phi_0, \Delta \phi_0)},$$

where $\hat{\sigma}_A^*$ is the standard error of $\hat{C}_A^*$, and $\rho_A(\phi_0, \Delta \phi_0)$ is the correlation between $\hat{C}_A^*(\phi_0 + \Delta \phi_0)$ and $\hat{C}_A^*(\phi_0)$. This is smaller than $\hat{\sigma}_A^*$ if

$$\rho_A(\phi_0, \Delta \phi_0) > 1 - \tfrac{1}{2}\Delta \phi_0^2.$$

7.4 AMERICAN PUT OPTIONS

In this section, we illustrate the control variate technique by considering American put options on a stock. The natural option to use as option B in this case is a European put option on the same stock with the same exercise price and maturity. Consider first the case in which there are no

---

[9] For greater accuracy, it may be desirable to calculate $\hat{D}_A$ and $\hat{D}_B$ using symmetrical rather than one-sided first differences.

TABLE 7.1. Use of the control variate technique for an American put option on a stock when $r_f = 0.0488$, $X = 35.0$, $T = 0.5833$, $\sigma = 0.2$, and $S_0 = 40.0$.[a]

n	C_B	$\hat{C}_B$	$\hat{C}_A$	$\hat{C}_A^*$
1	0.4170	0.3728	0.3728	0.4170
5	0.4170	0.4785	0.4884	0.4269
10	0.4170	0.4412	0.4530	0.4287
15	0.4170	0.4182	0.4319	0.4306
20	0.4170	0.4072	0.4276	0.4374
25	0.4170	0.4271	0.4437	0.4336
50	0.4170	0.4141	0.4302	0.4331
75	0.4170	0.4192	0.4348	0.4325
100	0.4170	0.4195	0.4351	0.4326

a C_B is the Black–Scholes price of the European put with the same parameters. $\hat{C}_B$ and $\hat{C}_A$ are the estimates of the European and American put prices using a binomial tree with n intervals. $\hat{C}_A^*$ is the control variate price calculated as $C_B + (\hat{C}_A - \hat{C}_B)$.

dividends. Define

S_0: initial stock price;

X: exercise price;

T: time to maturity in years;

σ: instantaneous proportional standard deviation per annum;

r_f: risk-free interest rate per annum;

Δt: length of time subinterval for lattice approach in years;

$n = T/\Delta t$: total number of subintervals; and

P: the American put price.

The control variate estimate $\hat{C}_A^*$ of P is calculated from equation (7.7). C_B is the European put price. $\hat{C}_A$ is the value obtained using the CRR lattice approach, as described in Section 7.1, and $\hat{C}_B$ is the value obtained for the European put using the same lattice (i.e., the same value of n).

In Table 7.1, the control variate technique is illustrated for the option defined by $r_f = 0.0488$, $X = 35.0$, $T = 0.5833$, $\sigma = 0.2$, and $S_0 = 40.0$. This is one of the options considered by Johnson (1983), Geske and Johnson (1984), Macmillan (1986), and Cox and Rubinstein (1984). The true value of the option, based on the use of the CRR lattice approach with $n = 500$, is 0.433. This is close to the value obtained by other authors. Table 7.1 shows that, as n increases, $\hat{C}_A$ oscillates about 0.433. $\hat{C}_B$ tends to oscillate about the true value of the European put option, 0.417, in a corresponding way.[10] This provides the basis for the control variate

[10] The convergence of binomial and other models to the true option value is discussed by Omberg (1987b). Whereas the Geske–Johnson compound option model converges uniformly, convergence for the binomial model is oscillatory.

technique. It will be noted that $\hat{C}_A^*$ converges to the true value far more quickly than $\hat{C}_A$.

The time taken to perform the calculations for the CRR lattice approach is approximately proportional to $n(n + 1)$. For a given value of n, the time taken to perform calculations for the control variate approach is approximately twice that for the CRR lattice approach. The relative efficiency of the CRR lattice approach and the control variate approach (measured by the relative computing time required to achieve a specified level of accuracy) therefore can be estimated by comparing the value of n required to achieve a specified level of accuracy in pricing. If n_{CRR} and n_{CV} are the values of n required to achieve the desired accuracy using the CRR lattice and the control variate approach, respectively, the relative efficiency is given by

$$\frac{n_{CRR}(n_{CRR} + 1)}{2n_{CV}(n_{CV} + 1)}.$$

Table 7.2 shows how the control variate technique with $n = 25$ performs on all the options considered by Geske and Johnson (1984). This set of options has been widely used to compare different numerical procedures. The results from using the CRR lattice approach with $n = 500$ are shown for the purposes of comparison. The table shows that the control variate approach is highly efficient when there is relatively small chance of early exercise. This is because ρ, the correlation between $\hat{C}_A$ and $\hat{C}_B$, is close to $+1$. For the nine out-of-the-money options in Table 7.2, the control variate approach was found to be highly efficient. The lowest relative efficiency measure was 4.8; the highest was over 2000. As the probability of early exercise increases, the control variate approach becomes relatively less efficient. Eventually, a stage is reached in which the control variate approach is actually less efficient than the CRR approach.[11] For the 21 at-the-money options in Table 7.2, the control variate technique was found to be, on average, 3.3 times more efficient than CRR approach, and, for the nine in-the-money options in Table 7.2, the control variate approach was found to be 1.2 times as efficient as the CRR approach, on average.

The control variate method can be used for American puts on stocks

---

[11] This is because ρ is so low that the condition in equation (7.9) is not satisfied. An example would be an option such as the nineteenth one in Table 7.2 that should be exercised immediately. The basic lattice approach recognizes this and assigns the option its correct value for any value of n. The control variate technique only estimates the correct value in the limit as $n \to \infty$.

TABLE 7.2. Comparison of control variate technique ($n = 25$), Geske–Johnson procedure, and CRR ($n = 500$) when used to calculate values for American put options on non-dividend-paying stocks.[a]

r_f	X	σ	T	S_0	P_{CV} ($n = 25$)	P_{GJ}	P_{CRR} ($n = 500$)	Relative efficiency
0.1250	1.0	0.5	1.0000	1.0	0.1475	0.1476	0.1480	2.2
0.0800	1.0	0.4	1.0000	1.0	0.1258	0.1258	0.1260	1.9
0.0450	1.0	0.3	1.0000	1.0	0.1004	0.1005	0.1005	2.5
0.0200	1.0	0.2	1.0000	1.0	0.0711	0.0712	0.0711	3.5
0.0050	1.0	0.1	1.0000	1.0	0.0377	0.0377	0.0377	7.3
0.0900	1.0	0.3	1.0000	1.0	0.0858	0.0859	0.0861	1.7
0.0400	1.0	0.2	1.0000	1.0	0.0639	0.0640	0.0640	1.3
0.0100	1.0	0.1	1.0000	1.0	0.0357	0.0357	0.0357	3.1
0.0800	1.0	0.2	1.0000	1.0	0.0525	0.0525	0.0527	1.2
0.0200	1.0	0.1	1.0000	1.0	0.0322	0.0322	0.0322	1.5
0.1200	1.0	0.2	1.0000	1.0	0.0439	0.0439	0.0442	0.4
0.0300	1.0	0.1	1.0000	1.0	0.0292	0.0292	0.0293	0.8
0.0488	35.0	0.2	0.0833	40.0	0.0062	0.0062	0.0062	>100.0
0.0488	35.0	0.2	0.3333	40.0	0.2000	0.1999	0.2002	8.5
0.0488	35.0	0.2	0.5833	40.0	0.4326	0.4321	0.4331	8.2
0.0488	40.0	0.2	0.0833	40.0	0.8527	0.8528	0.8519	3.9
0.0488	40.0	0.2	0.3333	40.0	1.5793	'1.5807	1.5794	2.2
0.0488	40.0	0.2	0.5833	40.0	1.9878	1.9905	1.9901	1.9
0.0488	45.0	0.2	0.0833	40.0	5.0007	4.9985	5.0000	0.5
0.0488	45.0	0.2	0.3333	40.0	5.0979	5.0951	5.0886	0.1
0.0488	45.0	0.2	0.5833	40.0	5.2626	5.2719	5.2674	0.2
0.0488	35.0	0.3	0.0833	40.0	0.0774	0.0744	0.0773	>100.0
0.0488	35.0	0.3	0.3333	40.0	0.6976	0.6969	0.6983	38.3
0.0488	35.0	0.3	0.5833	40.0	1.2273	1.2194	1.2212	4.8
0.0488	40.0	0.3	0.0833	40.0	1.3109	1.3100	1.3094	7.2
0.0488	40.0	0.3	0.3333	40.0	2.4833	2.4817	2.4819	3.1
0.0488	40.0	0.3	0.5833	40.0	3.1678	3.1733	3.1689	2.6
0.0488	45.0	0.3	0.0833	40.0	5.0626	5.0599	5.0597	1.1
0.0488	45.0	0.3	0.3333	40.0	5.7133	5.7012	5.7066	1.8
0.0488	45.0	0.3	0.5833	40.0	6.2421	6.2365	6.2446	1.9
0.0488	35.0	0.4	0.0833	40.0	0.2467	0.2466	0.2462	>100.0
0.0488	35.0	0.4	0.3333	40.0	1.3517	1.3450	1.3475	61.3
0.0488	35.0	0.4	0.5833	40.0	2.1571	2.1568	2.1552	36.7
0.0488	40.0	0.4	0.0833	40.0	1.7693	1.7679	1.7675	11.7
0.0488	40.0	0.4	0.3333	40.0	3.3891	3.3632	3.3865	5.2
0.0488	40.0	0.4	0.5833	40.0	4.3537	4.3556	4.3517	4.5
0.0488	45.0	0.4	0.0833	40.0	5.2927	5.2855	5.2872	1.7
0.0488	45.0	0.4	0.3333	40.0	6.5103	6.5093	6.5111	1.9
0.0488	45.0	0.4	0.5833	40.0	7.3839	7.3831	7.3851	1.3

a The variables n, r_f, X, σ, T, S_0, and P are the number of subintervals used, risk-free interest rate, exercise price, volatility per annum, time to maturity (years), initial stock price, and estimated option price, respectively. The relative efficiency measure shows the improvement in efficiency when the control variate method was used instead of CRR and 1 percent accuracy was required.

with known dividends. A European option that pays the same dividends as the American option is used as the control option B, and the appropriate lattice (see Section 7.2) is used to value both the American and the European option. Table 7.3 compares the results obtained from using the control variate technique with those of Geske and Johnson (1984) for options on stocks in which the dividend yield is assumed known. Again, the results from using the normal CRR approach with $n = 500$ are given for the purposes of comparison. The estimates $\hat{C}_A$ and $\hat{C}_B$ were calculated using the Cox and Rubinstein (1984) lattice for stocks that pay a known dividend yield (see Section 7.2) and $n = 25$. The relative efficiency measures are generally higher than those in Table 7.2. This is because put options are less likely to be exercised early when there are known dividends. For eight of the nine out-of-the-money options in Table 7.3, the control variate method was over 100 times more efficient than CRR. For the nine at-the-money options, the control variate method was, on the average, 39.3 times more efficient than CRR. For the nine in-the-money options, it was, on average, 16.2 times more efficient.

Geske and Johnson (1984) found their compound option approach to be ten times more efficient than standard numerical procedures. Our tests show that, overall, the control variate approach is also about ten times more efficient than the standard CRR approach when used to value American put options on stocks. Both the control variate technique and the compound option approach work best when there is a low chance of early exercise.[12] The control variate approach has the advantage that it is somewhat easier to implement.

As an additional test of the control variate technique, the procedure described in Section 7.3 was used to estimate the partial derivative of the option price with respect to the stock price for the options in Table 7.2 with $n = 25$.[13] The control variate technique produced an overall increase in efficiency. The absolute errors in the estimates relative to the values given by the normal CRR approach with $n = 500$ were, on average, about half those given by the Geske and Johnson (1984) approach using the same data. This provides additional evidence that the control variate method is an attractive alternative to the Geske–Johnson approach.

---

[12] In the limit, when there is no chance of early exercise, both methods work perfectly since the compound option collapses to a simple option and $\hat{C}_A = \hat{C}_B$, leaving $C_A^* = C_B$ in the control variate approach.

[13] The hedge ratio was calculated by slightly extending the lattice so that three values of the stock price, S_0, $S_0 u^2$, and $S_0 d^2$, were considered at time zero. For both the European and American options, the difference between the option prices at the $S_0 u^2$ and $S_0 d^2$ nodes was divided by $S_0(u^2 - d^2)$ to obtain the hedge ratio.

TABLE 7.3. Comparisons of control variate technique ($n = 25$), Geske–Johnson procedure, and CRR ($n = 500$) for American put options on dividend-paying stocks.[a]

X	σ	T	P_{CV} ($n = 25$)	P_{GJ}	P_{CRR} ($n = 500$)	Relative efficiency
35.0	0.2	0.0833	0.0116	0.0116	0.0116	>100.0
35.0	0.2	0.3333	0.3092	0.3071	0.3070	16.6
35.0	0.2	0.5833	0.6566	0.6580	0.6568	>100.0
40.0	0.2	0.0833	1.1113	1.1079	1.1087	15.8
40.0	0.2	0.3333	2.0224	2.0120	2.0135	2.9
40.0	0.2	0.5833	2.5781	2.5717	2.5762	3.4
45.0	0.2	0.0833	5.4119	5.4209	5.4139	0.5
45.0	0.2	0.3333	5.6736	5.6900	5.6710	3.8
45.0	0.2	0.5833	6.0203	6.0300	6.0208	1.3
35.0	0.3	0.0833	0.1078	0.1073	0.1074	>100.0
35.0	0.3	0.3333	0.8853	0.8837	0.8831	>100.0
35.0	0.3	0.5833	1.5456	1.5454	1.5457	>100.0
40.0	0.3	0.0833	1.5594	1.5590	1.5595	60.0
40.0	0.3	0.3333	2.9106	2.9072	2.9109	33.0
40.0	0.3	0.5833	3.7473	3.7435	3.7501	95.0
45.0	0.3	0.0833	5.4977	5.4996	5.4976	0.5
45.0	0.3	0.3333	6.3027	6.3089	6.2982	52.5
45.0	0.3	0.5833	6.9997	6.9977	6.9999	33.0
35.0	0.4	0.0833	0.3049	0.3049	0.3051	>100.0
35.0	0.4	0.3333	1.5834	1.5798	1.5794	>100.0
35.0	0.4	0.5833	2.5275	2.5277	2.5301	>100.0
40.0	0.4	0.0833	2.0127	2.0120	2.0127	52.5
40.0	0.4	0.3333	3.8087	3.8033	3.8072	52.2
40.0	0.4	0.5833	4.9187	4.9116	4.9229	39.0
45.0	0.4	0.0833	5.7033	5.7015	5.7018	7.5
45.0	0.4	0.3333	7.0834	7.0774	7.0700	33.0
45.0	0.4	0.5833	8.0973	8.0914	8.1014	14.0

a Dividends equal to 1.25 percent of the stock and paid in $\frac{1}{2}$, $3\frac{1}{2}$, and $6\frac{1}{2}$ months. Thus, one-, four-, and seven-month options ($T = 0.0833$, 0.3333, 0.5833) have one, two, and three scheduled dividend payments, respectively. The variables n, X, σ, T, and P are the number of subintervals used, exercise price, volatility per annum, time to maturity (years), and estimated option price, respectively. The initial stock price S_0 is 40, and the risk-free interest rate r_f is 0.0488. The relative efficiency measure shows the improvement in efficiency when the control variate method was used instead of CRR and 1 percent accuracy was required.

7.5 APPLICATION TO OTHER OPTIONS

The control variate approach can be used for American currency and commodity options. The natural option to use as option B is the European option with the same parameters. In the case of currency options, we find that the control variate technique generally works very efficiently for calls when the foreign interest rate is below the domestic interest rate, for puts when the foreign interest rate is above the domestic interest rate, and for all out-of-the-money options.

Consider next the pricing of an American put option on a non-dividend-paying stock when the volatility is stochastic. This presents an interesting problem in lattice design. Assume that

$$dS = \mu S \, dt + \sqrt{V} S \, dz_1, \qquad dV = \xi V \, dz_2,$$

where $V \, (= \sigma^2)$ is the instantaneous variance of dS/S, ξ^2 is the instantaneous variance of dV/V, and dz_1 and dz_2 are uncorrelated Wiener processes. This model is discussed by Hull and White (1987), who produce a series solution for the value of a Europe call. The value of the corresponding European put can be obtained using put–call parity. This option can be used as option B in the control variate approach.

Since there are two state variables, a two-dimensional lattice is necessary. The transition probabilities q_{ijk} must give correct values for the mean and standard deviation of changes in S, the mean and standard deviation of changes in V, and a zero coefficient of correlation between S and V. Experimentation shows that a tree with six non-zero q_{ijk} for each i and j works well. If, at time $i \, \Delta t$, the state of the world is $\{ S_i, V_i \}$ (i.e., the stock price is S_i and the volatility is V_i), the six possibilities at time $(i + 1) \Delta t$ are

$$
\begin{array}{ll}
\{ S_i u_1, V_i u_2 \}, & \{ S_i u_1, V_i d_2 \}, \\
\{ S_i, V_i u_2 \}, & \{ S_i, V_i d_2 \}, \\
\{ S_i d_1, V_i u_2 \}, & \{ S_i d_1, V_i d_2 \},
\end{array}
$$

where $u_1 = 1/d_1$ and $u_2 = 1/d_2$.

This problem is more complicated than the two-state-variable problem considered by Boyle (1988), because the variance of one of the state variables, the stock price, is different in different parts of the lattice. If u_1 and d_1 are constant throughout the lattice, they must be large enough to accommodate the maximum value of V in the lattice. The result is that the probability of a zero stock price change is liable to become close to 1.0 in other parts of the lattice where V is low, and the lattice may not be a good representation of possible states of the world at all times. Clearly, it is necessary to vary u_1 and d_1 according to the value of V. This must be done carefully so that the total number of nodes does not increase too fast. One solution that the authors have used successfully involves putting $u_1 = \alpha^m$ and $d_1 = 1/\alpha^m$, where α is a constant and m is an integer whose value depends on V.

7.6 CONCLUSIONS

This paper has considered the use of the lattice approach to option pricing. It has shown that, in principle, lattices can be constructed to deal with any number of state variables. It also has examined how a lattice can be used to deal efficiently with the situation in which there are known dividends (as opposed to known dividend yields) during the life of the option.

The main contribution of the paper has been to show how the control variate approach can be used in conjunction with the lattice approach. If the option under consideration is similar to another option for which an analytic solution is available, the same lattice can be used to evaluate both options, and a considerable improvement in numerical efficiency often results. The control variate approach also may be used to improve the efficiency of other numerical procedures such as the finite difference method.[14]

REFERENCES

Barone-Adesi, G., and R. E. Whaley. "Efficient analytic approximation of American option values." *Journal of Finance*, 42 (June 1987), pp. 301–320.

Bellman, R., and S. Dreyfus. *Applied Dynamic Programming*. Princeton University Press, 1962.

Black, F., and M. Scholes. "The pricing of options and corporate liabilities." *Journal of Political Economy*, 81 (May–June 1973), pp. 637–659.

Blomeyer, E. C. "An analytic approximation for the American put price for options on stocks with dividends." *Journal of Financial and Quantitative Analysis*, 21 (June 1986), pp. 229–233.

Boyle, P. P. "Options: a Monte Carlo approach." *Journal of Financial Economics*, 4 (May 1977), pp. 323–338.

Boyle, P. P. "Option valuation using a three jump process." *International Options Journal*, 3 (1986), pp. 7–12.

Boyle, P. P. "A lattice framework for option pricing with two state variables." *Journal of Financial and Quantitative Analysis*, 23 (March 1988), pp. 1–12.

Brennan, M. J., and E. S. Schwartz. "A continuous time approach to the pricing of bonds." *Journal of Banking and Finance*, 3 (April 1979), pp. 133–155.

Courtadon, G. "A more accurate finite difference approximation for the value of options." *Journal of Financial and Quantitative Analysis*, 17 (December 1982), pp. 697–703.

[14] Examples of its use in conjunction with the finite difference method are provided by Hull (1988).

Cox, J. C., J. E. Ingersoll, and S. A. Ross. "An intertemporal general equilibrium model of asset prices." *Econometrica*, 53 (March 1985), pp. 363–384.

Cox, J. C., S. A. Ross, and M. Rubinstein. "Option pricing: a simplified approach." *Journal of Financial Economics*, 7 (September 1979), pp. 229–263.

Cox, J. C., and M. Rubinstein. *Options Market*. Prentice-Hall, Englewood Cliffs, NJ, 1984.

Geske, R., and H. E. Johnson. "The American put option valued analytically." *Journal of Finance*, 39 (December 1984), pp. 1511–1524.

Geske, R., and K. Shastri. "Valuation by approximation: a comparison of alternative option valuation techniques." *Journal of Financial and Quantitative Analysis*, 20 (March 1985), pp. 45–71.

Hull, J. *Options, Futures and Other Derivative Securities*. Prentice-Hall, Englewood Cliffs, NJ, 1988.

Hull, J., and A. White. "The pricing of options on assets with stochastic volatilities." *Journal of Finance*, 42 (June 1987), pp. 281–300. Also Chapter 2 in this book.

Hull, J., and A. White. "An analysis of the bias caused by a stochastic volatility in option pricing." *Advances in Futures and Options Research*, 3 (1988), pp. 27–61. Also Chapter 3 in this book.

Johnson, H. E. "An analytic approximation to the American put price." *Journal of Financial and Quantitative Analysis*, 18 (March 1983), pp. 14]–148.

Johnson, H. E., and D. Shanno. "Option pricing when the variance is changing." *Journal of Financial and Quantitative Analysis*, 22 (June 1987), pp. 143–151.

Macmillan, L. "Analytic approximation for the American put option." *Advances in Futures and Options Research*, 1 (1986), pp. 119–139.

Omberg, E. "The valuation of American put options with exponential exercise policies." *Advances in Futures and Options Research*, 2 (1987a).

Omberg, E. "A note on the covergence of binomial pricing and compound option models." *Journal of Finance*, 42 (June 1987b), pp. 463–470.

Parkinson, M. "Option pricing: the American put." *Journal of Business*, 50 (January 1977), pp. 21–36. ·

Rubinstein, M. "Displaced diffusion option pricing." *Journal of Finance*, 38 (March 1983), pp. 213–217.

Schwartz, E. S. "The valuation of warrants: implementing a new approach." *Journal of Financial Economics*, 4 (August 1977), pp. 79–93.

8. Efficient procedures for valuing European and American path-dependent options *

Reseachers during the last 20 years have devoted considerable attention to the development of efficient numerical procedures for pricing options when analytic results are not available. A popular procedure suggested by Cox, Ross, and Rubinstein (1979) (CRR) involves representing movements in the asset price in the form of a binomial tree. Another proposed by Boyle (1977) involves using Monte Carlo simulation.

The CRR procedure involves working backward in time, evaluating the price of the option at each node of the tree. It can handle American-style options, but has not up to now been used in many situations where payoffs depend on the history of the asset price as well as its current value. This is because the history of the asset is not known when calculations are carried out at a node.

Monte Carlo simulation, by contrast, involves working forward, simulating paths for the asset price. It can handle options where the payoff is path-dependent, but it cannot easily handle American options, since there is no way of knowing whether early exercise is optimal when a particular stock price is reached at a particular time.

The purpose of this paper is to show how tree approaches such as CRR can be extended to value some types of path-dependent options. One interesting application is to European and American options on the arithmetic average price of an asset, the so-called "Asian" options. No numerical procedures have up to now been available for American options on the average price of an asset. For European average price options, the approach we describe is faster than Monte Carlo simulation and more accurate than the lognormal approximation suggested by Levy (1990) and Turnbull and Wakeman (1991). A second application is to the valuation of mortgage-backed securities and indexed-principal swaps.

8.1 THE FIRST EXTENSION OF CRR

We begin by assuming that the value of a derivative security at time t is a function of t and the price S of the underlying asset, and some function $F(t, S)$ of the path followed by the asset price between time zero and time t. The notation is as follows:

$S(t)$: price of the asset at time t;

$F(t, S)$: the function of the path followed by S between time zero and time t that underlies the price of the derivative security;

$v(S, F, t)$: the value of the derivative security at time t when the asset price is S and the path function has value F;

r: risk-free interest rate (assumed constant);

T: life of the derivative security.

The principle of risk-neutral valuation shows that the value of the derivative security is independent of the risk preferences of investors. This means that we may, with impunity, assume that the world is risk-neutral. We suppose that the process followed by S in a risk-neutral world is geometric Brownian motion:

$$dS = \mu S\, dt + \sigma S\, dz,$$

where μ, the drift rate, and σ, the volatility, are constant. (When the asset is a non-dividend-paying stock, $\mu = r$; if the stock pays a continuous proportional dividend at an annual rate δ, then $\mu = r - \delta$; when the asset is a foreign currency, μ is the excess of the domestic risk-free rate over the foreign risk-free rate; and so on.)

This process can be represented in the form of a Cox, Ross, and Rubinstein (1979) binomial tree, where the life of the option is divided into n time steps of length Δt ($\Delta t = T/n$). In time Δt the asset price moves up by a proportional amount u with probability p and down by a proportional amount d with probability $1 - p$, where

$$u = e^{\sigma\sqrt{\Delta t}}, \qquad d = \frac{1}{u}, \qquad a = e^{\mu \Delta t}, \qquad p = \frac{a - d}{u - d}.$$

For example, suppose that T is three months, $S(0)$ is 50, σ is 40% per annum, and r is 10% per annum. Figure 8.1 shows the tree obtained with only three time steps ($\Delta t = 0.0833$). In this case $u = 1.1224$, $d = 0.8909$, $a = 1.0084$, and $p = 0.5073$.

In general there are $i + 1$ nodes at time $i \, \Delta t$ in a tree such as Figure 8.1. We will denote the lowest node at time $i \, \Delta t$ by $(i, 0)$, the second lowest by $(i, 1)$, and so on. The value of S at node (i, j) is $S(0)u^j d^{i-j}$ ($j = 0, 1, \ldots, i$); at node B in Figure 8.1 (that is, node $(3, 2)$), the value of S is $50 \times 1.1224^2 \times 0.8909 = 56.12$.

If we were valuing a regular option, we would work back from the end of the tree in Figure 8.1 to the beginning, calculating a single option value at each node. To value a path-dependent option, one approach is to value

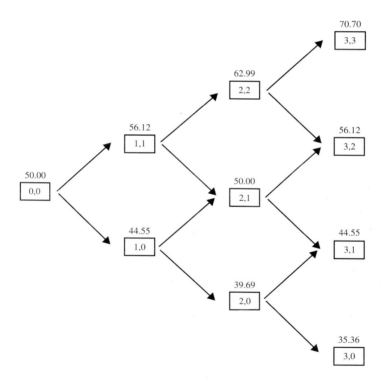

FIGURE 8.1. The CRR tree for stock price movements.

The initial stock price is 50; the time step is one month; the continuously compounded risk-free interest rate is 10% per annum; and the volatility is 40% per annum. The probability of an up movement at each node is 0.5073 and the probability of a down movement is 0.4927. At each node, the values of (i, j) are shown within the box. The stock price is shown above the box.

the option at each node for all alternative values of the path function $F(t, S)$ that can occur. There are two requirements for the method to be feasible:

1. It must be possible to compute $F(t + \Delta t, S)$ from $F(t, S)$ and $S(t + \Delta t)$. This means that the path function is Markov.
2. The number of alternative values of $F(t, S)$ must not grow too fast with the size of the tree.

We will denote the kth value of F at node (i, j) by $F_{i,j,k}$ and define $v_{i,j,k}$ as the value of the security at node (i, j) when F has this value. The value of the derivative security at its maturity, $v_{n,j,k}$, is known for all j and all k. To calculate its value at node (i, j) where $i < n$, we note that the stock price has a probability p of moving up to node $(i + 1, j + 1)$ and a probability $1 - p$ of moving down to node $(i + 1, j)$.

We suppose that the kth value of F at node (i, j) leads to the k_uth value of F at node $(i + 1, j + 1)$ when there is an up-movement in the stock price and to the k_dth value of F at node $(i + 1, j)$ when there is a down-movement in stock price.[1] For a European-style derivative security this means that

$$v_{i,j,k} = e^{-r\Delta t}\left[pv_{i+1,j+1,k_u} + (1 - p)v_{i+1,j,k_d}\right]. \tag{8.1}$$

If the derivative can be exercised at node (i, j), the value in equation (8.1) must be compared with the early exercise value and $v_{i,j,k}$ must be set equal to the greater of the two.

We illustrate the approach by considering a three-month American lookback put option on the non-dividend-paying stock portrayed in Figure 8.1. This pays off the amount by which the maximum stock price observed during the option's life exceeds the asset price at the time of exercise. We set $F(t, S)$ equal to the maximum stock price realized between time zero and time t. (This example is used to provide a simple first illustration of our approach. It is not the most efficient way of valuing a lookback option.)

Figure 8.2 shows the results of the rollback calculations. The top number at each node is the stock price. The next row of numbers shows the alternative values of F at the node. The final row of numbers shows the corresponding values of v.

Look at nodes A, B, and C to see the way the tree is used. At node A

---

[1] Note that we are assuming here that the first of the two conditions just given holds; that is, we are assuming that the value of F at time $(i + 1)\,\Delta t$ can be calculated from the value of F at time $i\,\Delta t$ and the value of S at time $(i + 1)\,\Delta t$.

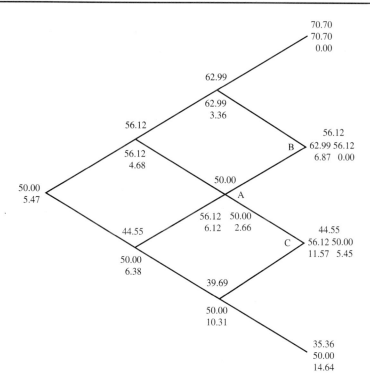

FIGURE 8.2. Tree for valuing an American lookback put option on a stock price.

The payoff from the option is the amount by which the maximum stock price achieved to date exceeds the current stock price. The tree has three time steps. The tree parameters are as in Figure 8.1. The upper number at each node is the stock price; the middle numbers are the alternative maximum stock prices to date; the lower numbers are the corresponding option prices.

Example of calculations: Consider node A when the maximum stock price is 50. There is a probability 0.5073 that the stock price will move up to 56.12. In this case the maximum stock price is 56.12, and the payoff is zero. There is a probability 0.4927 that the stock price will move down to 44.55. In this case the maximum stock price remains 50, and the payoff is 5.45. With an interest rate of 10% and a time step of 1 month, the value of being at node A when the maximum is 50 is therefore $(0.5073 \times 0 + 0.4927 \times 5.45)e^{-0.08333 \times 0.1} = 2.66$.

(that is, node (2, 1)), the value of F, the maximum stock price to date, is either 56.12 or 50.00. That is,

$$F_{2,1,1} = 56.12; \qquad F_{2,1,2} = 50.00.$$

Similarly, for node B (that is, node (3, 2)) and node C (that is, node (3, 1)) we obtain

$$F_{3,2,1} = 62.99, \quad F_{3,2,2} = 56.12, \quad F_{3,1,1} = 56.12, \quad F_{3,2,2} = 50.00.$$

149

The payoff at node B when $F = 62.99$ is the excess of 62.99 over the current stock price:

$$v_{3,2,1} = 62.99 - 56.12 = 6.87.$$

Similarly $v_{3,2,2} = 0$. At node C we obtain

$$v_{3,1,1} = 11.57, \quad v_{3,1,2} = 5.45.$$

Consider now the situation at node A when $F = 50.00$ (that is, $k = 2$). If there is an up-movement, so that we move from node A to node B, F changes from 50.00 to 56.12. In the notation of equation (8.1), this means that $k_u = 2$. If there is a down-movement, so that we move from node A to node C, F stays at 50.00. In the notation of equation (8.1), this means that $k_d = 2$.

According to equation (8.1), the value of being at node A when $F = 50$ is

$$[v_{3,2,2} \times 0.5073 + v_{3,1,2} \times 0.4927]e^{-0.1 \times 0.08333}$$
$$= (0 \times 0.5073 + 5.45 \times 0.4927)e^{-0.1 \times 0.08333}$$
$$= 2.66.$$

Clearly it is not worth exercising at node A when $F = 50$ since the payoff from doing so would be zero.

A similar calculation for the situation where the value of F at node A is 56.12 gives $k_u = 2$ and $k_d = 1$. The value of the derivative security at node A, without early exercise, is

$$[v_{3,2,2} \times 0.5073 + v_{3,1,1} \times 0.4927]e^{-0.1 \times 0.08333}$$
$$= (0 \times 0.5073 + 11.57 \times 0.4927)e^{-0.1 \times 0.08333}$$
$$= 5.65.$$

In this case, early exercise is optimal since it gives a value of 6.12.

Working back through the tree, repeating these types of calculations at each node, gives the value of the derivative security at time zero as $5.47.

8.2 THE SECOND EXTENSION OF CRR

The approach described in Section 8.1 is computationally feasible when the number of alternative F-values at each node does not grow too fast as n, the number of time steps, is increased. The example of the lookback option presents no problems, because the number of alternative values for the maximum or the minimum asset price at a node in a binomial tree with n time steps is never greater than n. An option on the arithmetic average would be very difficult to value using this approach, because the number of alternative arithmetic averages that can be realized at a node grows very fast with n.

An extension to the approach that places no constraints on the number of F-values involves computing $v(S, F, t)$ at a node only for certain predetermined values of F, not all of those that can occur. The value of $v(S, F, t)$ for other values of F is computed from the known values by interpolation as required.

We illustrate this approach by using it to calculate the prices of European and American options on the arithmetic average of the stock price. In this case, F at a node is defined as the arithmetic average of the asset prices from time zero to the node.

The first step is to choose the values of F for which the option will be calculated. Somewhat arbitrarily we choose to use values which have the form $S(0)e^{mh}$, where h is a constant and m is a positive or negative integer.[2]

The values of F that are considered at time $i \, \Delta t$ must span the full range of possible F's at that time. This is determined by inspection, using forward induction. To illustrate the approach, we return to the tree in Figure 8.1 and suppose that we choose $h = 0.1$.

The maximum and minimum averages achievable at time Δt are $\frac{1}{2}(50.00 + 56.12) = 53.06$ and $\frac{1}{2}(50.00 + 44.55) = 47.275$. To cover these, we should let m range from -1 to $+1$ at time Δt, so that the averages considered are 45.24, 50.00, and 55.26 . Given that averages of 45.24 and 55.26 are being considered at time Δt, the maximum and minimum average that are possible at time $2 \, \Delta t$ are

$$\tfrac{1}{3}(2 \times 55.26 + 62.99) = 57.84 \quad \text{and} \quad \tfrac{1}{3}(2 \times 45.24 + 39.69) = 43.39.$$

To cover these, we must let m range from -2 to $+2$ at time $2 \, \Delta t$, so that the averages considered are 40.94, 45.24, 50.00, 55.26, and 60.07. Similar calculations are carried out for later nodes.[3]

---

[2] This choice was made in the example we consider because S follows geometric Brownian motion. In other situations, other choices to span the range of possible values of F may be more appropriate, and some trial and error may be necessary to determine a good way of specifying the F's. In Section 8.3, we will refine the procedure used here.

[3] Formally the calculations are as follows. If $S(0)e^{m_1 h}$ is the highest value of F considered at time $i \, \Delta t$, the highest value considered at time $(i + 1) \, \Delta t$ is the smallest value of m for which

$$e^{mh} > \frac{(i + 1)e^{m_1 h} + u^i}{i + 2}.$$

Similarly if $S(0)e^{m_2 h}$ is the lowest value of F considered at time $i \, \Delta t$, the lowest value considered at time $(i + 1) \, \Delta t$ is the largest value of m for which

$$\frac{(i + 1)e^{m_1 h} + d^i}{i + 2} > e^{mh}.$$

151

Equation (8.1) still holds. The difference is that the values of $v_{i+1,j+1,k_u}$ and v_{i+1,j,k_d} are not necessarily calculated when the nodes at time $(i+1)\Delta t$ are considered. We determine $v_{i+1,j+1,k_u}$ by interpolating between $v_{i+1,j+1,k_1}$ and $v_{i+1,j+1,k_2}$, where k_1 and k_2 are chosen so that $F_{i+1,j+1,k_1}$ and $F_{i+1,j+1,k_2}$ are the closest values of F to $F_{i+1,j+1,k_u}$ that have the form $S_0 e^{mh}$ and are such that $F_{i+1,j+1,k_1} \le F_{i+1,j+1,k_u} \le F_{i+1,j+1,k_2}$. We determine v_{i+1,j,k_d} similarly.

Figure 8.3 illustrates the way calculations are carried out by supposing that a stock price has a 0.5 probability of moving from a node X where the stock price is 40 to node Y where it is 44, and a 0.5 chance of moving from node X to node Z where the stock price is 36.36. In this example $h = 0.08$; the values of F considered at node X are 36.92, 40.00, and 43.33; and the values of F considered at nodes Y and Z are 34.09, 36.92, 40.00, 43.33, and 46.94.

We suppose that the values of v corresponding to these values of F are 0.10, 0.90, 1.80, 3.00, and 4.60 at node Y, and 0.01, 0.50, 1.10, 1.80, and 2.80 at node Z. We also assume that the averages at node X are calculated over two time steps (using three values of the stock price), that each time step is three months, and that the risk-free interest rate is 10% per annum.

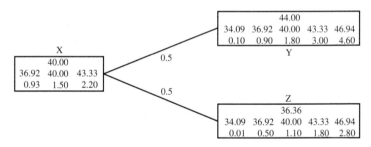

FIGURE 8.3. Part of a tree for valuing a call option on an average stock price.

At each node we consider certain predetermined values of the average. The upper number at each node shows the stock price; the middle numbers are the values of the average considered; the lower numbers are the values of the option. Node X is assumed to be at time $2\Delta t$; each time step is 3 months; and the probability of an up or down movement is 0.5.

Example of calculations: Consider node X when the average (calculated from three observations) is 43.33. There is a 0.5 probability of moving up to node Y, where the average becomes 43.50. Using linear interpolation, the value of the option is then 3.08. There is a 0.5 probability of moving down to node Z, where the average becomes 41.59, and using linear interpolation the value of the option is 1.43. The value of the option at node X when the average is 43.33 is therefore $(0.5 \times 3.08 + 0.5 \times 1.43)e^{-0.25 \times 0.1} = 2.20$.

Consider the calculation of v at node X when $F = 43.33$. There is a 0.5 probability that the stock price will move up to node Y, in which case the average stock price becomes $\frac{1}{4}(3 \times 43.33 + 44.00) = 43.50$. We interpolate to obtain the value of v for this value of F. Now 43.50 is 4.7% of the way between 43.33 and 46.94. Our estimate the value of v at node Y when $F = 43.50$ is therefore $3.0 + 0.047 \times 1.6 = 3.08$.

There is a 0.5 probability that the stock price will move down to node Z in which case the average stock price becomes 41.59. We interpolate between 1.1 and 1.8 to estimate the value of v at node Z when $F = 41.59$ to be 1.43. The value at node X when $F = 43.33$ is therefore $(3.08 \times 0.5 + 1.43 \times 0.5)e^{-0.25 \times 0.1} = 2.20$. (This assumes no early exercise.)

Table 8.1 shows the results of using the approach described in this section to value a variety of American and European options that pay off $\max[A(t) - X, 0]$, where X is the strike price, and $A(t)$ is the arithmetic average of the asset price between times 0 and t.

It also provides Monte Carlo estimates of the European option prices. The Monte Carlo simulations are based on 40 time steps and 100,000 simulation runs, and make use of the antithetic variable technique. This is a procedure for controlling sampling so as to reduce the standard error of the answer for a given number of runs. (The standard error is shown in parentheses.) The tree results are based on 40 time steps and a value for h of 0.005. In all cases the beginning and ending asset prices were included in the calculation of the average.

The European results for the tree approach and for Monte Carlo simulation are very close. The mean of the differences between the two is 0.003. Furthermore, 65%, 90%, and 100% of the Monte Carlo values are within one, two, and three standard deviations of the tree estimates respectively. These results do not allow rejection of the hypothesis that the tree value is the true value.

Table 8.1 also shows European option prices calculated using the analytic approximation recommended by Levy (1990) and by Turnbull and Wakeman (1991) (LTW), assuming that, for the purposes of calculating the average, the stock price is observed with the same frequency as for the Monte Carlo simulation and tree results.[4] This

---

[4] We did not incorporate the Edgeworth series adjustment suggested by Turnbull and Wakeman (1991). An alternative analytic approximation for calculating the prices of European options on the arithmetic average has recently been suggested by Curran (1992). This involves considering the probability distribution of the arithmetic average conditional on the geometric average. In the limit, our procedure will give more accurate European option prices than any analytic approximation.

TABLE 8.1. Value of options on the average price of a non-dividend-paying stock.

Life of option (years)		Strike price				
		40	45	50	55	60
0.5	Amer/Bin	12.115	7.261	3.275	1.152	0.322
	Euro/Bin	10.755	6.363	3.012	1.108	0.317
	Euro/LTW	10.764	6.379	3.012	1.094	0.307
	Euro/MC	10.759	6.359	2.998	1.112	0.324
		(0.003)	(0.005)	(0.007)	(0.005)	(0.003)
1.0	Amer/Bin	13.153	8.551	4.892	2.536	1.208
	Euro/Bin	11.545	7.616	4.522	2.420	1.176
	Euro/LTW	11.573	7.652	4.542	2.415	1.159
	Euro/MC	11.544	7.606	4.515	2.401	1.185
		(0.006)	(0.008)	(0.010)	(0.009)	(0.007)
1.5	Amer/Bin	13.988	9.652	6.199	3.771	2.194
	Euro/Bin	12.285	8.670	5.743	3.585	2.124
	Euro/LTW	12.332	8.728	5.786	3.601	2.116
	Euro/MC	12.289	8.671	5.734	3.577	2.135
		(0.008)	(0.010)	(0.012)	(0.012)	(0.010)
2.0	Amer/Bin	14.713	10.623	7.326	4.886	3.171
	Euro/Bin	12.953	9.582	6.792	4.633	3.057
	Euro/LTW	13.021	9.662	6.861	4.675	3.070
	Euro/MC	12.943	9.569	6.786	4.639	3.055
		(0.010)	(0.013)	(0.014)	(0.015)	(0.013)

Notes: Initial stock price is $50, the risk-free interest rate is 10% per annum, and the stock price volatility is 30% per annum. Averaging is between the beginning of the life of the option and the exercise date. Tree calculations are based on 40 time steps and a value for h equal to 0.005. The Monte Carlo simulations are based on 40 time steps and 100,000 trials using the antithetic variable technique. Amer/Bin = American option valued using a binomial tree; Euro/Bin = European option valued using a binomial tree; Euro/LTW = European option valued using Turnbull and Wakeman approach; Euro/MC = European option valued using Monte Carlo simulation. The standard errors of the Monte Carlo estimates are shown in parentheses.

procedure, which involves calculating the mean and standard deviation of the arithmetic average and then assuming that the distribution is lognormal, is faster but much less accurate than the procedure we propose. Some 60% of the Monte Carlo values are greater than three standard deviations from the LTW estimate. We can reject the hypothesis that the LTW values are the true values.

Table 8.2 investigates the convergence of the tree procedure by varying h and the number of time steps for the option in Table 8.1 where $X = 50$ and $T = 1$. We find our procedure to be at least twelve times as fast as

TABLE 8.2. Value of options on the average price of a non-dividend-paying stock as the number of time steps and the value of h change.

h	Option type	Number of time steps			
		20	40	60	80
0.100	American	5.197	5.311	5.360	5.377
	European	4.663	4.679	4.685	4.687
0.050	American	4.971	5.080	5.124	5.145
	European	4.588	4.605	4.612	4.614
0.010	American	4.823	4.906	4.941	4.962
	European	4.517	4.530	4.536	4.539
0.005	American	4.815	4.892	4.924	4.942
	European	4.513	4.522	4.526	4.529
0.003	American	4.814	4.890	4.920	4.936
	European	4.512	4.520	4.523	4.525

Notes: The initial stock price is $50, the strike price is $50, the risk-free interest rate is 10% per annum, the stock price volatility is 30% per annum, and the time to maturity is one year. Averaging is between the beginning of the life of the option and the exercise date. Calculations are carried out using the tree approach.

Monte Carlo simulation at the same level of accuracy. For a given number of time steps, a value of h equal to 0.005 gives penny accuracy.

The number of time steps determines the frequency with which the asset price is observed in calculating the average. This affects the option's fair value. An American option is more sensitive to the number of time steps than a European option, presumably because the number of time steps also determines the number of early exercise opportunities.

The decline in option prices with declining values of h can be attributed to the interpolation procedure. Because option prices are a convex function of the average, in this case the linear interpolation procedure leads to overpricing that disappears only asymptotically.

8.3 MORTGAGE-BACKED SECURITIES

Another application of the procedures described in Sections 8.1 and 8.2 is for the valuation of mortgage-backed securities (MBS) and indexed-principal swaps (IPS). An MBS is a fixed-rate debt security with a principal that may be paid off prior to maturity. The usual assumption is that prepayments at a particular time are a function of the prevailing level of interest rates. An IPS is a swap of fixed for floating interest rates for which the notional principal is reduced according to some contractually specified prepayment schedule dependent on the level of interest rates.

For both securities, the value at a particular time depends on the level of interest rates and the cumulative prepayments to date. Equivalently, it depends on the level of interest rates and the outstanding principal. The procedures outlined in the last two sections can be used with an interest rate tree replacing the stock price tree, with F defined as the outstanding principal. F satisfies the condition that its value at time $t + \Delta t$ can be calculated from the value at time t and interest rates at time $t + \Delta t$.

The first stage in the valuation of an MBS is to develop a prepayment function. This is the function that predicts how much of the principal will be prepaid under different circumstances. The function is estimated by observing the historic behavior of mortgage holders. In most cases, the prepayment function used for valuation purposes depends only on the current term structure.

To value the MBS, it is customary to model the evolution of the term structure using Monte Carlo simulation and to monitor the prepayments that are made on each run. Then the cashflows are discounted back down the interest rate path that has been simulated, in the manner

$$M_t = e^{-r_t \Delta t}[M_{t+\Delta t} + C_{t+\Delta t}] \quad (0 \le t \le T - \Delta t),$$

where T is the mortgage maturity, M_t is the value of the MBS, r_t is the short-term interest rate, and C_t is the cash flow (interest plus repayment of principal) at time t in the simulation.

As an alternative to Monte Carlo simulation, the technique described in Section 8.2 can be used to value an MBS, as an illustration will show. Consider a five-year 10% semi-annual pay mortgage which initially has a $100 principal prepaid according to the schedule

$$\text{Prepayment} = \begin{cases} 0 & R \ge 10\%, \\ \frac{100}{3}(10/R - 1) & 4\% \le R \le 10\%, \\ 50 & R \le 4\%, \end{cases}$$

where R is the six-month rate of interest (expressed as an annual percentage rate with continuous compounding). Prepayments are made only on the semi-annual interest payment dates, and the prepayment may not exceed the outstanding principal. When R is greater than 10%, there are no prepayments; as R decreases from 10% to 4%, the prepayments increases from zero to $50; when R is less than 4%, $50 of the outstanding principal is prepaid.

The term structure evolution is modeled using the interest rate model described in Hull and White (1993). In this model the short-term rate of interest r obeys

$$dr = (\theta(t) - ar)\, dt + \sigma\, dz.$$

This is an arithmetic process similar to the one assumed by Ho and Lee (1986), but with mean reversion.

The drift parameter $\theta(t)$ is chosen to replicate the initial term structure, and the parameters σ and a determine the volatility structure. The standard deviation of the short-term interest rate is σ and the standard deviations of longer-term rates decline exponentially from this value at rate a. For the purposes of our example, we will asume that the initial term structure is flat (at 10% per annum, quoted with semi-annual compounding), the short rate volatility is 20%, and the volatility of the five-year rate is about 12%.

An n-time-step trinomial tree in the short-term rate is constructed to replicate the initial term structure.[5] We let F be the value of the outstanding principal at each node in the tree and v be the value of the MBS.

First, the maximum and minimum possible values of F at each node in the interest rate tree are computed by forward induction through the tree. The set of possible F's is then approximated by m equally spaced representative values at each node.[6]

At time step $n - 1$, the value of the MBS is the discounted principal plus interest that will be paid at time n:

$$v_{n-1,j,k} = e^{-r_{n-1,j}\Delta t}\big[1.05\, F_{n-1,j,k}\big] \quad \text{for all } j, k.$$

At all earlier times t, the value of the MBS is the discounted expected value of coupon payments, prepayments, and the residual value of the MBS at $t + \Delta t$:

$$v_{i,j,k} = e^{-r_{i,j}\Delta t}\{Q_{i+1}\, F_{i,j,k} + [p_u(P_u + v_{i+1,j_u,k_u}) + p_m(P_m + v_{i+1,j_m,k_m}) + p_d(P_d + v_{i+1,j_d,k_d})]\}.$$

[5] See Chapters 18 and 20 for the details of the construction of the interest rate tree. An interest rate tree is analogous to a CRR tree for stock prices. The principal difference is that the discount rate varies from node to node.

[6] Here it proves appropriate to use equally spaced values of F. Note that we use a refinement of the procedure described in Section 8.2. The maximum and minimum F-values that are considered vary from node to node as well as from time to time.

In this equation Q_{i+1} is the coupon rate that will be paid at $t + \Delta t$, so that Q_{i+1} equals 0.05 if time $(i + 1) \Delta t$ corresponds to a coupon payment date, and zero otherwise. The variables p_u, p_m, and p_d are, respectively, the (risk-neutral) probabilitities that the short-term interest rate will move along the up (u), middle (m), and down (d) branch over the next time period Δt. P_x is the prepayment, if any, that takes place on branch x, and v_{i+1,j_x,k_x} is the value of the MBS on branch x given that the principal was $F_{i,j,k}$ and a prepayment P_x took place. This value is generally interpolated from known values of $v_{i+1,j_x,k}$.[7]

The procedure described in this section was implemented for 20-, 40-, 60-, and 80-step trees using 3, 6, 11, 16, and 21 different values of F at each node. Increasing the number of steps in the interest rate tree improves the accuracy of the replication of the distribution of possible future term structures. Increasing the number of F-values at each node improves the approximation of the function v at each node.

For comparison purposes a 10,000-sample Monte Carlo simulation was run through each interest rate tree to estimate the price of the MBS. For a tree of any particular size, a Monte Carlo simulation should in the limit perfectly replicate v.

The results are reported in Table 8.3. In general, the results are not very sensitive to the number of steps in the tree or to the number of F-values considered, as long as $m \geq 6$. In only one out of sixteen cases is the tree estimate more than two standard errors from the Monte Carlo estimate when $m \geq 6$. Even in that case, the discrepancy is only about 3 cents.

The results presented in Tables 8.1, 8.2, and 8.3 were produced using linear interpolation. In other words, v was assumed to be linear in F between any two computed values. In many instances, the derivative security price is a strongly non-linear function of F, so that linear interpolation leads to biased results.

In Table 8.4 we test the effect of using quadratic interpolation to value the mortgage-backed securities in Table 8.3. The evidence is that quadratic interpolation does produce significant improvements for small values of m.

The procedures suggested here can lead to significant improvements in

---

[7] At any time and interest rate, we are approximating the true value of the MBS, $v(F)$ for $F_{\min} \leq F \leq F_{\max}$, by interpolating between a limited number of estimates of the value, $\hat{v}(F_i)$ $(i = 1, 2, \ldots, m)$. For one type of MBS, the prepayment is defined as a proportion of the principal currently outstanding. In this case, $v(kF) = kv(F)$ and $v(F)$ can be approximated from a single point estimate $\hat{v}(F_1)$. All problems of path-dependence can be avoided for this type of MBS by using the tree to calculate at each node the value of an MBS with $1 of principal at the node.

TABLE 8.3. Value of a five-year, 10%, semi-annual pay mortgage-backed security with an initial principal of $100.

m	Number of time steps			
	20	40	60	80
3	98.3728	98.3818	98.3922	98.3935
6	98.3121	98.3065	98.3077	98.3065
11	98.3014	98.2862	98.2836	98.2816
16	98.2990	98.2814	98.2772	98.2747
21	98.2984	98.2795	98.2747	98.2718
Monte	98.2883	98.2934	98.2821	98.2715
Carlo	(0.0171)	(0.0171)	(0.0168)	(0.0170)

Notes: Prepayments are expected on interest payment dates according to the schedule:

$$\text{Prepayment} = \begin{cases} 0 & R \geq 10\%, \\ \frac{100}{3}(10/R - 1) & 4\% \leq R \leq 10\%, \\ 50 & R \leq 4\%, \end{cases}$$

where R is the six-month rate of interest. The term structure is initially flat at 10%, so in the absence of prepayments the MBS would be priced at $100. The difference between $100 and the value of the MBS is the value of the prepayment option. Monte Carlo estimates of the value based on 10,000 samples using the control variate technique are included for reference purposes. The standard error of the estimate is shown in parentheses.

TABLE 8.4. Value of a five-year, 10%, semi-annual pay mortgage-backed security with an initial principal of $100 when quadratic interpolation is used.

m	Number of time steps			
	20	40	60	80
3	98.2924	98.2722	98.2636	98.2599
6	98.2973	98.2794	98.2739	98.2704
11	98.2976	98.2775	98.2718	98.2685
16	98.2975	98.2774	98.2715	98.2681
21	98.2974	98.2773	98.2714	98.2679
Monte	98.2883	98.2934	98.2821	98.2715
Carlo	(0.0171)	(0.0171)	(0.0168)	(0.0170)

Notes: Parameter values are as in Table 8.3. The table shows that quadratic interpolation produces an improvement in accuracy for small values of m.

computer speed. They are at least ten times as fast as Monte Carlo simulation for the same level of accuracy. In some situations they are one hundred times as fast.

8.4 CONCLUSIONS

We have explored a method of using the CRR binomial tree to value a wide range of path-dependent options on stocks, currencies, indices, and futures contracts. The method can be extended to value path-dependent interest rate derivatives such as mortgage-backed securities if the evolution of the term structure is modeled using a binomial or trinomial tree.

One important application is for the pricing of a class of options that have not up to now been amenable to numerical analysis. These are American options where the payoff depends on the arithmetic average of an asset's price. Another important application is for mortgage-backed securities and indexed-principal swaps.

A key assumption in our analysis is that the value F of the path function at time $t + \Delta t$ can be calculated from its value at time t and the asset price at time $t + \Delta t$. Of course, this assumption does not hold for all path-dependent options. For example, it does not hold for American options where the payoff at time t depends on the average price of the asset over the previous six months. More generally, it does not hold when the average at time t is calculated between $t - \tau$ and t for a fixed τ. The pricing of these types of option present further challenges for analysts.

REFERENCES

Boyle, P. P. "Options: a Monte Carlo approach." *Journal of Financial Economics*, 4 (1977), pp. 323–338.

Cox, J., S. Ross, and M. Rubinstein. "Option pricing: a simplified approach." *Journal of Financial Economics*, 7 (1979), pp. 229–264.

Curran, M. "Beyond average intelligence." *RISK*, November 1992, p. 60.

Ho, T. S. Y., and S.-B. Lee. "Term structure movements and pricing interest rate contingent claims." *Journal of Finance*, 41 (December 1986), pp. 1011–1029.

Hull, J., and A. White. "One-factor interest rate models and the valuation of interest-rate derivative securities." *Journal of Financial and Quantitative Analysis*, 28 (June 1993), pp. 235–254. Also Chapter 17 in this book.

Levy, E. "Asian arithmetic." *RISK*, May 1990, pp. 7–8.

Turnbull, S., and L. Wakeman. "A quick algorithm for pricing European average options." *Journal of Financial and Quantitative Analysis*, 26 (September 1991), pp. 377–389.

III

Credit Risk

9. Introduction: Credit risk

As the over-the-counter derivatives market has grown, credit risk issues have become increasingly important both to financial institutions and to the bodies that regulate them. The traditional theory of the pricing of derivatives assumes that there is no chance that either of the two parties to a derivatives contract will default. The purpose of this part of the book is to extend the traditional theory so that default risk is explicitly considered.

9.1 THE BASIC ANALYSIS

The basic approach to adjusting the prices of derivatives for default risk is explained in Chapter 10. Consider a derivative transaction entered into by a financial institution. Suppose that $\beta(t) \Delta t$ is the risk-neutral probability of a bankruptcy by the counterparty between times t and $t + \Delta t$, and $U(t)$ is the value of the derivative to the financial institution at time t assuming no default risk. If the counterparty goes bankrupt at time t, and $U(t) \leq 0$, it is reasonable to assume that the financial institution makes neither a gain nor a loss. This is because the derivative is a liability to the financial institution and an asset to the counterparty. The liquidators of the counterparty can be expected to make decisions that preserve the value they have in the contract. However, if the counterparty goes bankrupt at time t and $U(t) > 0$ then, assuming no recovery, the loss to the financial institution is $U(t)$. In general, the loss is $\max[U(t), 0]$.

Define $v(t)$ as the value at time zero of a derivative that pays off $\max[U(t), 0]$ at time t. Assuming that the state variables affecting bankruptcy events are independent of the state variables affecting U, the possibility of a bankruptcy between times t and $t + \Delta t$ reduces the value of the derivative by $v(t)\beta(t) \Delta t$. The total reduction arising from a possible bankruptcy by the counterparty is therefore

$$\int_0^T v(t)\beta(t)\,dt, \tag{9.1}$$

where, assuming no defaults, the derivative lasts until time T. This (with different notation) is equation (10.1) in Chapter 10. Equation (10.2) states that the value $V(0)$ of the derivative when credit risk is taken into account is the value $U(0)$ assuming no default risk less the expression in equation (9.1).

If a partial recovery can be anticipated in the event of a bankruptcy, equation (9.1) becomes

$$\int_0^T v(t)[1 - \gamma(t)]\beta(t)\,dt,$$

where $\gamma(t)$ is the risk-neutral expected proportional recovery in the event of a default at time t.[1]

Chapter 10 applies the results to currency swaps, under the assumption that defaults are generated by a Poisson process. It shows that credit risk tends to be low when the financial institution pays a low interest rate currency and receives a high interest rate currency. It is high in the opposite situation: that is, when the financial institution pays a high interest rate currency and receives a low interest rate currency. The reason is as follows. When the low interest rate currency is paid, the expectation is that, as time passes, the pay side will become worth more than the receive side. In this case the swap becomes a liability to the financial institution and an asset to the counterparty, and the exposure is therefore zero. When a low interest rate currency is received, the expectation is that the receive side will become worth more than the pay side and that the credit exposure will be positive. Clearly a financial institution should be more concerned about the creditworthiness of a counterparty when it is receiving a low interest currency and paying a high interest currency than in the reverse situation.

9.2 USING BONDS TO IMPLY DEFAULT PROBABILITIES

Chapter 10 presents an analyst with the difficult task of estimating the

[1] This analysis assumes that if the counterparty goes bankrupt when $U(t) \le 0$ there can be no subsequent defaults. In practice, the liquidators of the counterparty may sell the contract to a new counterparty that itself has some probability of bankruptcy. This possibility is considered in Formulation 2 of Chapter 10.

risk-neutral probability $\beta(t)$ of bankruptcy and the recovery rate $\gamma(t)$. Chapter 11 shows how this problem can be finessed. It assumes that we know how to value bonds that are (or might be) issued by the counterparty and that rank equally with the derivative in the event of a default by the counterparty. This assumption is not unreasonable since bond traders in financial institutions regularly estimate zero-coupon yield curves for corporate bonds that have a variety of different credit ratings (AAA, AA, A, BBB, etc.) in order to identify those that are under- and overpriced.

Define[2]

$y^*(t)$: the t-year zero-coupon yield for Treasury instruments;

$y(t)$: the t-year zero-coupon yield calculated from the bonds issued by the counterparty;

$F^*(t)$: the instantaneous forward rate for a contract with maturity t calculated from the y^* zero curve;

$F(t)$: the instantaneous forward rate for a contract with maturity t calculated from the y zero curve;

$\alpha(t)$: $F(t) - F^*(t)$;

θ: vector of state variables determining the price of the derivative when there is no possibility of default;

ϕ: vector of state variables determining the occurrence of defaults and the proportional recovery made in the event of defaults.

The key result underlying the arguments in Chapter 11 is the following. If the θ variables are independent of the ϕ variables, the expected loss from defaults in a risk-neutral world between times t and $t + \Delta t$ is $\alpha(t)U(t)\,\Delta t$, where as above $U(t)$ is the no-default value at time t.[3] An alternative way of expressing this key result is as in Propositions 1 and 2 in Appendix A of Chapter 11. The value of a derivative is equal to the no-default value of a similar default-free derivative entered into by the financial institution, where the financial institution has to make payments at rate $\alpha(t)$ times the derivative's value at time t.

The result holds for all European-style options including those that are path-dependent. For instruments such as swaps, where the value of the derivative can be either positive or negative, the result must be modified to state that the expected loss is $\alpha(t)\max[U(t), 0]\,\Delta t$. With the notation

---

[2] The notation here is somewhat different from that in Chapter 11. For ease of exposition, we here assume that time t_0 in Chapter 11 is zero. Also, the variables f and f^* in Chapter 11 are V and U here.

[3] Note that this result does not depend on the assumption that there will be zero recovery.

introduced earlier, the result implies that

$$\alpha(t) = \beta(t)[1 - \gamma(t)].$$

The result does not apply to American-style options. This is because the decision on early exercise may be influenced by new information, received during the life of the option, on the fortunes of the counterparty. An example may help to illustrate the point here. Suppose that the financial institution buys a one-year American call option from a counterparty and that during the following six months the counterparty experiences financial difficulties. Assume that the option is somewhat in the money at the end of six months, but that it would not be optimal to exercise the default-free version of the option early. It might be optimal for the financial institution to exercise the default-exposed option at this time rather than to wait and risk the chance of the counterparty declaring bankruptcy prior to option expiration.

For ease of exposition, we will now drop the time argument and define V and U as the value of the derivative and the no-default value of the derivative at time zero. With the independence assumption mentioned above, the key results in Chapter 11 are:

1. If the derivative is a long position in a European-style option that promises a payoff at time T, then

$$V = Ue^{-[y(T)-y^*(T)]T}.$$

This means that the derivative is correctly valued using risk-neutral valuation provided that we use the counterparty's borrowing rate, not the Treasury rate, for discounting.

2. If the derivative can have either a positive or negative value to the financial institution, then

$$U - V = \int_0^T \alpha(t)e^{-[y(t)-y^*(t)]t}v(t)\, dt, \tag{9.2}$$

where, as earlier, $v(t)$ is the value today of a contingent claim that pays off the financial institution's exposure on the derivative at time t. If we assume that default can take place only at times $t_1, t_2, \ldots, t_n$ (for example, only on payment dates), this becomes

$$U - V = \sum_1^n [e^{-(y_{i-1}-y^*_{i-1})t_{i-1}} - e^{-(y_i-y^*_i)t_i}]v(t_i),$$

where $t_0 = 0$ and y_i denotes the zero rate for a maturity t_i.

3. A lower bound for the value of a long position in an American-style option is the value of a notional no-default American option which provides the same payoff as the option under consideration and is such that the financial institution is required to make payments at rate $\alpha(t)$ times the option's value at time t. This can be calculated using standard techniques.

Table 11.3 illustrates these results by calculating the basis points necessary to provide compensation for the credit risk on a currency swap. The assumed $\alpha(t)$ values approximate to those observed for a counterparty with a credit rating in the A to AA range. On a matched pair of five-year currency swaps, when the exchange rate volatility is 15%, a total of about 20 basis points is necessary to provide protection against defaults.[4] This compares with around 2 basis points on a matched pair of five-year interest rate swaps.

9.3 THE INDEPENDENCE ASSUMPTION

The above results are all based on the assumption that the variables determining defaults are independent of the variables determining the no-default value of the derivative.[5] How valid is this assumption?

One requirement for the assumption is that the value of the contract under consideration have a negligible bearing on the ability of the counterparty to meet its liabilities as they become due. This means that the contract must be a very small part of the counterparty's portfolio of assets and liabilities or that the contract's risk must entirely hedged by the counterparty. When the counterparty is a large financial institution, this requirement is likely to be met. Most large financial institutions have sizeable portfolios of derivatives and sophisticated systems for ensuring that they are not unduly exposed to movements in the values of any one underlying market variable.

The independence assumption can be criticized on the grounds that market variables (for example, interest rates) affect the performance of

[4] As indicated earlier, the spread required on each side of the swap depends on the interest rate differential. It turns out that the total spread required on a matched pair of swaps is relatively insensitive to this.

[5] Chapter 11 shows how bounds on a derivative's price can be calculated when the independence assumption is relaxed, and provides an example of one particular case where exact pricing is possible. Unfortunately, however, it is usually very difficult to implement models that do not assume independence.

particular sectors of the world economy and therefore the chance of defaults. However, this may not be as serious a problem for the independence assumption as it sounds. A great deal of time often elapses between a movement in market variables and the resultant defaults by companies. Defaults can therefore be expected to be only very weakly related to the values of market variables at the time when the default occurs. (An example may help to illustrate the point being made here. High interest rates in the early 1980s caused problems in many sectors, but most of the resulting defaults, bankruptcies, and loan losses by financial institutions occurred a few years later—when rates were much lower.)

Our view is that the independence assumption provides a good robust starting point for an evaluation of the impact of credit risk and provides a basis for incorporating credit risk into the systems used by financial institutions. In particular cases where the assumption is clearly inappropriate, a trader can use judgement to adjust the assessment of the credit risk upwards or downwards.

9.4 NETTING

We now move on to consider a situation in which a financial institution has entered into a portfolio of derivative transactions with the same counterparty. We can redefine V as the true value of the portfolio of derivatives and U as the value of the portfolio assuming no defaults. If there is no netting, equation (11.1) is correct with $v(t)$ equal to the value of a contingent claim that pays off the sum of the exposures on the derivatives at time t. The variable $v(t)$ then denotes the value of a portfolio of options rather than that of a single option. If there is netting, equation (11.1) is correct with $v(t)$ equal to the value of a contingent claim that pays off the net exposure on the derivatives at time t. The variable $v(t)$ is then the value of an option on a portfolio. Since the value of an option on a portfolio is never greater than, and is often considerably less than, the value of a portfolio of options, netting is beneficial to the financial institution.

9.5 TWO-SIDED DEFAULT RISK

Up to now we have assumed that when a financial institution enters into a derivative transaction with a counterparty, there is no chance that the counterparty will default. The analysis can be extended to relax this assumption. This is covered in footnote 13 of Chapter 11. We can extend the footnote and argue that a reasonable approximation for the two-sided default risk case is

$$U - V = a - b.$$

Here a is the right-hand side of equation (9.2), and b is a similar expression to the right-hand side of equation (9.2) but reflecting the impact of potential losses by the counterparty rather than the financial institution, that is,

$$b = \int_0^T \alpha_1(t) e^{-[y_1(t) - y_1^*(t)]t} v_1(t) \, dt,$$

where the variables α_1 and y_1 are calculated similarly to α and y but from a zero-coupon yield curve reflecting the prices of equivalent-ranking bonds issued by the financial institution rather than the counterparty, and the variable $v_1(t)$ is the value today of a contingent claim that pays off the counterparty's exposure on the derivative at time t.

10. Assessing credit risk in a financial institution's off-balance sheet commitments *

During the 1980s, there was a rapid increase in the off-balance sheet commitments of major banks. Among the contracts that led to this increase were swaps, forward rate agreements, currency options, interest rate caps, bankers' acceptances, note issuance facilities, and revolving underwriting facilities. Assessing the risks posed by these contracts has now become critically important to stock market analysts, to bank supervisory authorities, and to the banks themselves.

Two types of risk can be distinguished in off-balance sheet commitments: credit risk and market risk. Credit risk arises from the possibility of default by the counterparty. Market risk arises from the possibility of adverse movements in market variables such as interest rates and foreign exchange rates. Market risks can be hedged. Credit risks, by contrast, cannot usually be hedged. It is credit risks that are the main concern of this paper.

Traditionally, the capital adequacy of a bank has been measured using balance sheet ratios such as equity : total assets. The growth of off-balance sheet commitments has made these ratios less relevant. As a result, most bank supervisory authorities have moved towards a credit risk weighting scheme for monitoring capital adequacy.[1] This scheme involves assigning to each on- and off-balance sheet item a weight reflecting its relative credit

[1] See Bank for International Settlements (1988) and Federal Reserve Board and Bank of England (1987).

* This paper was first published in *Journal of Financial and Quantitative Analysis*, Vol. 24 (December 1989), pp. 489–501. It is reprinted with the permission of the *Journal of Financial and Quantitative Analysis*.

risk. Minimum levels are then set for the ratio of capital to total risk-weighted exposure.

The first part of this paper discusses how credit risk can be taken into account in the valuation of financial contracts. Other research has considered this question with reference to particular contracts. For example, Kane (1980) analyzes the effect of credit risk on forward and futures contracts; Johnson and Stulz (1987) show how options can be valued when there is credit risk; Whittaker (1987) considers the effect of credit risk on the valuation of interest rate swaps. The approach taken in this paper is more general and can, in principle, be applied to any off-balance sheet (or on-balance sheet) contract.

The second part of the paper discusses how capital requirements should be set so that they reflect the credit risk in off-balance sheet items. Santomero and Watson (1977) provide an excellent discussion on the objectives of bank regulators in setting capital requirements. They argue that regulators wish to reduce the probability of bankruptcy to an acceptable level and are faced with a trade-off between the costs associated with bank failure and the costs arising from forced over-capitalization. The discussion in the paper builds upon the work of these authors and upon the work of authors, such as Arak, Goodman, and Rones (1987), Belton (1987) Cooper and Watson (1987), and Wall and Fung (1987), who have considered the credit risk in swaps and other off-balance sheet contracts.

The rest of the paper is organized as follows. Section 10.1 shows how an off-balance sheet contract can be valued when there is credit risk. Section 10.2 applies the ideas in Section 10.1 to currency swaps. Section 10.3 presents a set of assumptions necessary to justify credit risk weighting. These assumptions are discussed in Section 10.4. Conclusions are in Section 10.5.

10.1 VALUATION OF CONTRACTS WHEN THERE IS CREDIT RISK

The option of a borrower to default on a debt contract has been widely discussed in the finance literature. It is generally assumed that, when the value of a company's liabilities exceeds the value of its assets, the company goes bankrupt and defaults on its liabilities.

Some off-balance sheet contracts, such as swaps and forward rate agreements, differ from debt contracts in that they can have either positive or negative values to the counterparty at any given time. In other words, they can be either assets or liabilities to the counterparty. We can reasonably assume that default will take place on these contracts only when the following two conditions are satisfied:

1. the counterparty is bankrupt; and

2. the value of the contract to the counterparty (assuming that it chooses not to default) is negative.

Note that condition 2 is not redundant. It is possible for a counterparty to experience financial distress even though it has positive value in one particular contract. Our assumption is that, if a counterparty goes bankrupt when the contract has a positive value to the counterparty, the counterparty is able to sell the contract to a third party, or rearrange its affairs in some way, so that its positive value in the contract is not lost.[2]

The default option in an off-balance sheet contract can be viewed as a contingent claim. There is now a well-established literature on the valuation of contingent claims. The risk-neutral valuation arguments of Cox and Ross (1976) show that claims contingent on the prices of traded securities can be valued on the assumption that the world is risk neutral. These arguments have been extended by Cox, Ingersoll, and Ross (1985), who show that any claim can be valued by reducing the proportional drift rate of each underlying variable by the product of its market price of risk and its volatility, and then assuming that the world is risk neutral.[3] This is true for history-dependent contingent claims as well as for contingent claims that are dependent only on the current value of the underlying variables.

Consider an off-balance sheet contract dependent on a number of state variables and time t. Define:

$V(t)$: value of off-balance sheet contract to bank at time t, if there has been no bankruptcy by the counterparty up to and including time t;

---

[2] Often, contracts can be sold, provided that the credit of the new counterparty is satisfactory. Clauses such as "consent to assignment to a third party will not reasonably be withheld" are common. Ideally, the bank would like to prohibit assignment to a third party whenever it feels that this is being done because of an impending bankruptcy. In practice, this is likely to be difficult. An issue related to the treatment of contracts in the event of bankruptcy is known as netting. Some banks have argued that, when they have several contracts with the same counterparty, only the net exposure is relevant for determining capital requirements, because a default on one contract will trigger defaults on the other contracts.

[3] For a discussion of this result, see Hull (1989).

$f(t) \Delta t$: probability of bankruptcy by the counterparty between times t and $t + \Delta t$ in a risk-neutral world;

$U(t)$: value of contract to bank at time t, assuming no default options;

$W(t)$: value of future default options to the counterparty at time t; and

T: life of the contract.

Both V and U can be positive or negative. The value of the contract to the counterparty is the reverse of its value to the bank. Thus, with no default possibilities, its value to the counterparty is $-U$ and, when default possibilities are taken into account, its value to the counterparty is $-V$. For ease of exposition, we assume no recoveries are made in the event of a default.[4] We also assume that the state variables affecting the probability of bankruptcy are independent of the state variables affecting U.

(a) Formulation 1

In our first formulation of the problem, we make the following assumptions:

1. there is no possibility of default by the bank; and

2. if the counterparty goes bankrupt, it has the option of selling the contract to another counterparty whose default risk is zero.

The second assumption implies that, if a counterparty goes bankrupt and sells the contract, there will be no further defaults and the contract is worth $-U$ to the new counterparty. It follows that, when bankruptcy occurs, the original counterparty can choose between (a) defaulting on the contract and (b) realizing an amount $-U$ for the contract. Hence, default will take place if $U > 0$. The loss to the bank arising from bankruptcy by the counterparty is, therefore, $\max(U, 0)$.[5] This loss can be regarded as the payoff from a contingent claim. Using the Cox–Ingersoll–Ross extension of the risk-neutral valuation argument, $W(0)$ is the discounted expected value of the default option in a world in which all state variables (i.e., those affecting U and those affecting bankruptcy probabilities) have risk-adjusted drift rates. Since the variables affecting U are independent of the variables affecting bankruptcy probabilities, we can integrate over the

---

[4] The analysis can easily be modified to allow for partial recoveries.

[5] Note that the loss is not $\max(V, 0)$. In essence, we are using U as our benchmark for determining the value of the contract to the bank, and we are considering different ways in which positive U's can be lost by the bank.

former first to obtain

$$W(0) = \int_0^T C(t)f(t)\,dt, \tag{10.1}$$

where $C(t)$ is the value of a contingent claim that pays off $\max(U, 0)$ at time t. (This contingent claim is a European call option on U with exercise price zero and maturity date t.) The value $V(0)$ of the contract at time zero can be calculated from (10.1) and the identity

$$V(0) = U(0) - W(0). \tag{10.2}$$

(b) Formulation 2

In our second formulation, we assume:
1. there is no possibility of default by the bank; and
2. if the counterparty goes bankrupt at time τ, it has the option of selling the contract to a new counterparty that has a probability $f(t)\,\Delta t$ of going bankrupt between times t and $t + \Delta t$ $(t \geq \tau)$.

In this case, if bankruptcy occurs and the contract is sold, it is worth $-V$ to the new counterparty. It follows that, in the event of bankruptcy, the counterparty can choose between (a) defaulting on the contract and (b) realizing an amount $-V$ for the contract. Hence, default will take place when $V > 0$. The default costs the bank U.[6] If $V < 0$, there is, in this formulation, a chance that there will be future defaults. Hence, when a bankruptcy occurs, $W = U$ if $V > 0$, and $W = U - V$ if $V < 0$, i.e.,

$$W = U + \max(-V, 0). \tag{10.3}$$

The value of $W(0)$ is given by equation (10.1) with $C(t)$ being defined as a contingent claim that pays off $U(t) + \max[-V(t), 0]$ at time t. Since $V(t) = U(t) - W(t)$, the situation is more complicated than before. As illustrated in the next section, the lattice approach of Cox, Ross, and Rubinstein (1979) (CRR) can be adapted to value the default option numerically.

10.2 APPLICATION TO CURRENCY SWAPS

Here, we show how the models developed in Section 10.1 can be used to value the default option in currency swaps.

A plain deal currency swap is a contract in which principal and fixed-rate interest payments on a loan in one currency are exchanged for

---

[6] Note that the cost of the default is U, not V (see footnote 5).

principal and fixed-rate interest payments on a similar loan in another currency. Suppose that a bank is making payments in US dollars and receiving payments in the foreign currency. The bank is long a foreign-denominated bond and short a US dollar-denominated bond. The value of the swap, assuming no defaults, is given by

$$U = SB_F - B_D, \tag{10.4}$$

where B_F is the default-free value, measured in the foreign currency, of the foreign-denominated bond; B_D is the default-free value, measured in US dollars, of the dollar-denominated bond; and S is the exchange rate (i.e., the value, measured in the domestic currency, of one unit of the foreign currency).

To simplify matters, we assume that the term structure of interest rates in both currencies is flat and that interest rates are constant. We also assume that payments are made under the swap every six months and that the payments made equal the risk-free rates of interest in the two currencies. We also assume that the probability of bankruptcy by the counterparty in time Δt, conditional on no earlier bankruptcy, is $\lambda \Delta t$, where λ is a constant.

Consider first Formulation 1, in which the probability of default by the bank is zero and, if the counterparty goes bankrupt when $U < 0$, the contract is sold to a new zero-risk counterparty.

Suppose that payment dates are at times $t_1, t_2, \ldots, t_n$, and that time zero is denoted by t_0. Under the assumptions made, the probability q_i of the counterparty going bankrupt between times t_{i-1} and t_i is given by

$$q_i = \exp(-\lambda t_{i-1}) - \exp(-\lambda t_i).$$

If $U(t_i) > 0$, a bankruptcy between times t_{i-1} and t_i leads to a default at time t_i.[7] Equation (10.1) therefore becomes

$$W = \sum_{i=1}^{n} q_i C(t_i). \tag{10.5}$$

Immediately prior to a payment date

$$B_F = A_F(1 + z_F), \tag{10.6}$$

$$B_D = A_D(1 + z_D), \tag{10.7}$$

where A_F is the face value of the foreign bond measured in the foreign currency, A_D is the face value of the domestic bond measured in the domestic currency, and z_F and z_D are the fixed interest payments in the

---

[7] This assumes that the bankrupt company is able to wait until time t_i before deciding whether to default.

two currencies. From the assumptions that have been made,

$$z_F = \exp(0.5r_F) - 1 \quad \text{and} \quad z_D = \exp(0.5r_D) - 1,$$

where r_F and r_D are the continuously compounded foreign and domestic risk-free rates of interest.

From equation (10.4),

$$\max(U, 0) = B_F \max(S - B_D/B_F, 0).$$

It follows from equations (10.6) and (10.7) that $C(t_i)$ is the value of $A_F(1 + z_F)$ European call options on a foreign currency with exercise price X equal to $A_D(1 + z_D)/A_F(1 + z_F)$. If we assume that S follows geometric Brownian motion with constant volatility σ, the price of each of these options is shown by Biger and Hull (1983), Garman and Kohlhagen (1983), and Grabbe (1983) to be

$$S \exp(-r_F t_i)N(d_1) - X \exp(-r_D t_i)N(d_2), \tag{10.8}$$

where

$$d_1 = \frac{\ln(S/X) + (r_D - r_F + \frac{1}{2}\sigma^2)t_i}{\sigma\sqrt{t_i}}, \qquad d_2 = d_1 - \sigma\sqrt{t_i},$$

and N is the cumulative normal distribution function.

In Table 10.1, equation (10.5) has been used to calculate the value of the default option when $\lambda = 0.01$, $\sigma = 0.06$, $A_D = 100$, $B_F = 100$, and the initial value of S is 1.0. As might be expected, the value of the default option increases with both σ and the life of the swap. Note that it is significantly higher when $r_F < r_D$ than when $r_F > r_D$. This is because, when $r_F < r_D$, the foreign currency is expected to appreciate over time and the bank's swap has a greater chance of becoming in the money than out of the money.[8] Similarly, when $r_F > r_D$, the swap has a greater chance of becoming out of the money than in the money.

When Formulation 2 is used, the default option can be valued using the binomial lattice approach of Cox, Ross, and Rubinstein (1979). In a small time interval $(t, t + \Delta t)$, S is assumed to move up to Su with probability p and down to Sd with probability $1 - p$, where

$$u = \exp(\sigma\sqrt{\Delta t}), \quad d = 1/u, \quad p = \frac{a - d}{u - d}, \quad a = \exp[(r_D - r_F)\Delta t].$$

---

[8] An alternative way of understanding this is as follows. When $r_F < r_D$, the bank can expect a net outflow on the early payment dates and a significant inflow when principals are exchanged at the end of the life of the swap. If bankruptcy occurs, the final exchange of principals never takes place.

TABLE 10.1. Value of default option on a currency swap using Formulation 1 when the principals A_D and A_F in the two currencies are both 100, the initial exchange rate S is 1.0, the domestic interest rate r_D is 6 percent per annum, and the parameter λ in the Poisson process generating defaults is 0.01.

Foreign risk-free interest rate r_F (% p.a.)	Volatility of exchange rate σ (% p.a.)	Life of swap (years)		
		5	10	15
	5	0.42	1.42	2.75
2	10	0.52	1.59	2.96
	15	0.64	1.84	3.31
	5	0.25	0.75	1.35
4	10	0.37	1.01	1.72
	15	0.50	1.30	2.15
	5	0.13	0.30	0.45
6	10	0.26	0.59	0.89
	15	0.39	0.89	1.33
	5	0.06	0.09	0.11
8	10	0.18	0.33	0.43
	15	0.30	0.59	0.80
	5	0.03	0.03	0.03
10	10	0.12	0.18	0.20
	15	0.23	0.39	0.47

The probability of default during the time interval is

$$\exp(-\lambda t) - \exp[-\lambda(t + \Delta t)].$$

Denoting this by $q(t)$, we have

$$V(S, t) = e^{-r_D \Delta t}[pX_u + (1 - p)X_d] + Q(S, t), \qquad (10.9)$$

where

$$X_u = V(Su, t + \Delta t) - q(t)\{U(Su, t + \Delta t) + \max[-V(Su, t + \Delta t), 0]\},$$

$$X_d = V(Sd, t + \Delta t) - q(t)\{U(Sd, t + \Delta t) + \max[-V(Sd, t + \Delta t), 0]\},$$

and $Q(S, t)$ is the financial institution's cash flow, if any, from the swap between times t and $t + \Delta t$, discounted to time t. The value of the swap immediately prior to time T is known to be $S_T A_F(1 + z_F) - A_D(1 + z_D)$, where S_T is the exchange rate at time T. Equation (10.9) can be used repeatedly to work back from time T to time zero.

TABLE 10.2. Value of default option on a currency swap using Formulation 2 when the principals A_D and A_F in the two currencies are both 100, the initial exchange rate S is 1.0, the domestic interest rate r_D, is 6 percent per annum, and the parameter λ in the Poisson process generating defaults is 0.01.

Foreign risk-free interest rate r_F (% p.a.)	Volatility of exchange rate σ (% p.a.)	Life of swap (years)		
		5	10	15
2	5	0.42	1.43	2.78
	10	0.52	1.60	2.99
	15	0.64	1.86	3.35
4	5	0.25	0.75	1.36
	10	0.38	1.02	1.74
	15	0.51	1.31	2.18
6	5	0.13	0.30	0.45
	10	0.26	0.60	0.91
	15	0.40	0.90	1.35
8	5	0.06	0.09	0.11
	10	0.18	0.33	0.43
	15	0.30	0.59	0.81
10	5	0.03	0.03	0.03
	10	0.12	0.18	0.20
	15	0.23	0.39	0.48

The results of using this approach for the same parameter values as before are shown in Table 10.2.[9] As might be expected, the values of the default option in Table 10.2 are very close to, but slightly higher than, the corresponding values in Table 10.1.

The analysis in this section can be used for plain vanilla interest rate swaps. A plain vanilla interest rate swap is an agreement to exchange fixed-rate interest payments on a certain notional principal for floating-rate interest payments on the same notional principal. Consider a bank that is receiving fixed and paying floating. Define

A: notional principal in the swap;

B_1: value of a bond with principal A, and coupons equal to the fixed payments underlying the swap; and

---

[9] To increase accuracy, the lattice was used to calculate the differences between the value of the default option under Formulation 2 and the value of the default option under Formulation 1. The number of time intervals used for each result was 60.

B_2: value of a bond with principal A, and coupons equal to the floating payments underlying the swap.

In this case,

$$U = B_1 - B_2.$$

Immediately prior to payout date t_i,

$$B_2 = A + y_i,$$

where y_i is the floating-rate payment required at time t_i. Hence,

$$\max(U, 0) = \max(B_1 - A - y_i, 0).$$

The value of the default option in Formulation 1 is therefore given by equation (10.5), with $C(t_i)$ being the value of a security paying

$$\max(B_1 - A - y_i, 0)$$

at time t_i. The security is a call option on a bond with exercise price $A + y_i$. Since y_i $(i > 1)$ is unknown at time zero, this option cannot be valued using standard analytic models. However, Monte Carlo simulation can be used.

10.3 ASSUMPTIONS TO JUSTIFY CREDIT RISK WEIGHTING

In July 1988, the Bank for International Settlements published a risk weighting scheme that had been approved by the Group of Ten central-bank governors. This scheme involves assigning to each asset and off-balance sheet contract a weight reflecting its risk per dollar of principal. Floating-rate loans to corporations are chosen as a benchmark and assigned a risk weight of 1.0. The total risk-weighted exposure is calculated as the sum of the products of the risk weights and principals for all assets and off-balance sheet contracts. Capital adequacy is monitored by setting minimum levels for the ratio of bank capital to total risk-weighted exposure.[10] Risk weights for off-balance sheet contracts are calculated using specified "credit conversion factors". A credit conversion factor is the ratio of the risk weight for an off-balance sheet contract to the risk weight for a floating-rate loan with the same maturity, counterparty, and principal as the off-balance sheet contract.

[10] Under the agreed international standard, two definitions for bank capital are used. The first is "equity less goodwill"; the second includes other items such as subordinated term debt. The standards require that, by 1992, the ratio of bank capital to total risk-weighted exposure be greater than 0.04 when the first definition is used, *and* greater than 0.08 when the second definition is used.

Kim and Santomero (1988) discuss risk weighting schemes in the context of the current fixed-rate deposit insurance system. In this section, we take a more general approach and consider the assumptions necessary to justify credit risk weighting. In Section 10.4, these assumptions will be critically reviewed.

Consider a bank supervisory authority that is setting a bank's capital requirements at time t. Following Santomero and Watson (1977), we assume that its objective is to ensure that the probability of the bank's capital dropping to zero between times t and $t + s$ is less than some level π for some s. We assume that no new capital issues are made between times t and $t + s$ and that, at time $t + s$, new capital requirements are specified by the supervisory authority.

We will show that credit risk weighting, as outlined above, can be justified when the following assumptions are made:

1. Banks have very large portfolios of commercial loans and off-balance sheet contracts.

2. The process generating bankruptcies is the same for all counterparties—both those with loans contracts and those with off-balance sheet contracts.

3. Average recoveries made in the event of a default are the same for all contracts.

4. The exposures on two different off-balance sheet contracts at any given time are independent.

5. The exposures on each off-balance sheet contract is independent of the variables underlying the process generating bankruptcies.

Consider one particular bank. The proportion of counterparties that go bankrupt between times t and $t + s$ is uncertain. However, assumptions 1 and 2 imply that it can, to a reasonable approximation, be assumed to be the same for both commercial loans and off-balance sheet contracts. Suppose that this proportion is b. The exposure on each defaulting loan can be assumed to be a random sample from the distribution of loan principals. Suppose that the number of loans is n and L_i ($1 \leq i \leq n$) is the principal amount of the ith loan. Since n is large, the central limit theorem can be used to show that the total exposure on all defaulting loans is approximately $b \sum_i L_i$ and the loss on the loan portfolio is approximately

$$b(1 - y) \sum_i L_i,$$

where y is the average proportion of a defaulting loan that is recovered.[11]

Suppose next that there are m off-balance contracts. The bank's exposure on the jth off-balance sheet contract is $\max(U_j, 0)$, where U_j $(1 \leq j \leq m)$ is the value of the contract to the bank, assuming no default possibilities. With assumptions 4 and 5, the central limit theorem can be used to show that the total loss on the off-balance sheet portfolio between times t and $t + s$ is approximately

$$b(1 - y) \sum_j E[\max(U_j, 0)],$$

where $E[\cdot]$ denotes expectations taken over all possible values of U_j and all times between t and $t + s$.

It follows from the above that the bank's total loss between times t and $t + s$ is approximately

$$b(1 - y)\left(\sum_i L_i + \sum_j E[\max(U_j, 0)] \right).$$

Let b^* be the value of b that has a probability π of being exceeded. It follows that the required capital H should be

$$H = b^*(1 - y)\left(\sum_i L_i + \sum_j E[\max(U_j, 0)] \right). \tag{10.10}$$

This equation shows that the capital requirement of loan i should be $b^*(1 - y)L_i$, and the capital requirement of off-balance sheet contract j should be $b^*(1 - y)E[\max(U_j, 0)]$. It implies that a credit risk weighting scheme is appropriate, with the credit conversion factor α for the jth off-balance sheet contract being

$$\alpha = \frac{E[\max(U_j, 0)]}{A_j}, \tag{10.11}$$

where A_j is the principal amount of the contract. This can be calculated using approaches similar to those discussed in Sections 10.1 and 10.2.

The above argument shows that the assumptions in 1 to 5 above are sufficient for a risk weighting scheme to be applicable. If any of the assumptions are relaxed, it is possible to provide an example of a situation

---

[11] The time value of money is assumed to affect the losses on all contracts equally.

where risk weighting is inappropriate. We can, therefore, conclude that the conditions are both necessary are sufficient.

The credit conversion factor, under the assumptions made, is the ratio of the expected payoff from the default option on the off-balance sheet item to the expected payoff from the default option on the loan. As is evident from the discussion in Section 10.1, this is only equal to the ratio of the values of the two options when the world is assumed to be risk neutral and the assumptions in Formulation 1 are made.

It is interesting to note that, as s approaches zero, equation (10.11) becomes

$$\alpha = \frac{\max(U_j, 0)}{A_j}. \qquad (10.12)$$

The credit conversion factor is then simply equal to the ratio of the current exposure on the contract to the principal amount of the contract.[12] If the contract is out of the money, the credit conversion factor is zero.

10.4 LIMITATIONS OF CREDIT RISK WEIGHTING

A number of the assumptions made in Section 10.3 are questionable. First, the bank's portfolio has to be sufficiently large that b and y are the only variables affecting the total losses experienced on all contracts. As the size of the portfolio decreases, the tails of the distribution of losses become fatter, and the capital requirement given by equation (10.10) becomes too low. Supervisory authorities have, in the past, recognized this and have set the capital : assets ratio higher for small banks than for large banks. In the case of many off-balance sheet contracts, there is not only uncertainty as to whether a default will take place but also uncertainty as to the size of the bank's exposure at the time of the default. It is therefore likely that, as the size of a bank decreases, the "fat tails" effect causes the capital requirements to increase proportionately more for off-balance sheet items than for on-balance sheet items. This means that the credit conversion factors given by equation (10.11) will tend to be too low for small banks.

[12] For swaps and similar contracts, the new international standard gives bank supervisory authorities a choice between two calculations. Under the first calculation, contracts are marked to market frequently and α is set slightly higher than its value in (10.12). This corresponds to using a very small value of s. Under the second calculation, α remains the same throughout the life of the contract. This corresponds to using a value of s equal to the life of the contract.

The second questionable assumption is that the exposures on two different off-balance sheet items at any future time are independent. In many situations, this is likely to be untrue, and a large movement in interest rates or exchange rates may have a significant effect on the average exposure per contract in a large portfolio of off-balance sheet contracts. The effect of a dependence between off-balance sheet items is to make the tails of the distribution of losses from them fatter and the credit conversion factors given by equation (10.11) too low. The credit risk weighting scheme is no longer valid because the incremental effect of a new contract on the loss experienced depends on the other contracts in the portfolio.

A final questionable assumption is that the exposure on each off-balance sheet contract is independent of the process generating bankruptcies. In general, bankruptcies can be expected to depend on macroeconomic variables such as the level of interest rates and exchange rates. These are the very variables that determine the exposures on many contracts. If it is argued that bankruptcies become more likely when interest rates are high, there is some comfort for banks as far as their interest rate swap portfolios are concerned. In a matched pair of plain vanilla interest rate swaps, the counterparty with the higher credit risk tends to be the one paying fixed and receiving floating. The bank has a positive exposure as far as this counterparty is concerned only when rates are low.

Even if, from a macroeconomic perspective, there is no relationship between interest rates and bankruptcy risk, there may be some relationship for any given counterparty. Consider an interest rate swap with a counterparty that is paying fixed and receiving floating. If the counterparty is a speculator, the probability of bankruptcy will, as a result of the swap, increase as rates decrease. If the counterparty is perfectly hedged, there should be no relationship between bankruptcy and interest rates. If the counterparty is using the swap as a partial hedge, the probability of bankruptcy will increase as rates increase.[13]

10.5 SUMMARY

This paper has presented a model for valuing financial contracts where there is credit risk. In some circumstances, the model can be evaluated

[13] This point was made by Belton (1987).

analytically. In other cases, an extension of the CRR lattice approach is appropriate.

The paper has also considered the credit risk weighting schemes now favored by bank supervisory authorities. It has presented a set of assumptions necessary to justify such schemes. The key assumptions are that every bank has a very large portfolio of loans and off-balance sheet contracts, that the future exposures on two different contracts are independent, and that the exposure on any given contract is independent of the probability of bankruptcy. The paper has argued that, in practice, these assumptions are questionable. The appropriate risk weight for an off-balance sheet contract is likely to depend on the size of the bank, the other contracts in the bank's portfolio, and the objectives of the counterparty when it entered into the contract.

REFERENCES

Arak, M., L. S. Goodman, and A. Rones. "Defining credit exposure for risk management products." *Review of Research in Banking and Finance*, 3 (Winter 1987), pp. 60–72.

Bank for International Settlements. "Proposals for international convergence of capital measurement and capital standards." July 1988.

Belton, T. M. "Credit risk in interest-rate swaps." Working Paper, Board of Governors of the Federal Reserve System, April 1987.

Biger, N., and J. Hull. "Valuation of currency options." *Financial Management*, 12 (Spring 1983), pp. 24–28.

Cooper, D. F., and I. R. Watson. "How to assess credit risks in swaps." *The Banker*, 137 (February 1987), pp. 28–31.

Cox, J. C., J. E. Ingersoll, and S. A. Ross. "An intertemporal general equilibrium model of asset prices." *Econometrica*, 53 (March 1985), pp. 363–384.

Cox, J. C., and S. A. Ross. "The valuation of options for alternative stochastic processes." *Journal of Financial Economics*, 3 (January–March 1976), pp. 145–166.

Cox, J. C., S. A. Ross, and M. Rubinstein. "Option pricing: a simplified approach." *Journal of Financial Economics*, 7 (September 1979), pp. 229–263.

Federal Reserve Board and Bank of England. "Agreed proposal of the United States Federal Banking Supervisory Authorities and the Bank of England on primary capital adequacy assessment." January 1987.

Garman, M. B., and S. W. Kohlhagen. "Foreign currency option values." *Journal of International Money and Finance*, 2 (December 1983), pp. 231–237.

Grabbe, J. O. "The pricing of call and put options on foreign exchange." *Journal of International Money and Finance*, 2 (December 1983), pp. 239–253.

Hull, J. *Options, Futures and Other Derivatives Securities.* Prentice-Hall, Englewood Cliffs, NJ, 1989.

Johnson, H., and R. Stulz. "The pricing of options under default risk." *Journal of Finance,* 42 (June 1987), pp. 267–280.

Kane, E. J. "Market incompleteness and divergences between forward and future interest rates." *Journal of Finance,* 35 (May 1980), pp. 221–234.

Kim, D., and A. M. Santomero. "Risk in banking and capital regulation." *Journal of Finance,* 43 (December 1988), pp. 1219–1233.

Santomero, A. M., and R. D. Watson. "Determining an optimal capital standard for the banking industry." *Journal of Finance,* 32 (September 1977), pp. 1267–1282.

Wall, L. D., and K.-W. Fung. "Evaluating the credit exposure of interest rate swap portfolios." Working Paper 87-8, Federal Reserve Bank of Atlanta, December 1987.

Whittaker, J. G. "Pricing interest rate swaps in an options pricing framework." Working Paper, Federal Reserve Bank of Kansas City and Northern Trust Company, Chicago, May 1987.

11. The impact of default risk on the valuation of options and other derivative securities*

When an option or other derivative security is valued, it is customary to assume that there is no risk that the counterparty will default. For an exchange-traded option or futures contract, this assumption is usually a reasonable one since most exchanges have been very successful in organizing themselves to ensure that their contracts are always honored. The no-default assumption is far less defensible in the non-exchange-traded (or over-the-counter) market. In recent years this market has become increasingly important. Many financial institutions actively trade a variety of forward contracts, swaps, and options with other financial institutions and with corporate clients.

This paper proposes a model for reflecting default risk in the calculated prices of over-the-counter options and other derivative securities in a way consistent with the prices of other securities that are subject to default risk. The importance of considering default risk in over-the-counter markets is recognized by bank capital adequacy standards. These standards require each over-the-counter derivative security purchased by a bank from a corporation or from another financial institution to be supported by an amount of capital related to the value of the security and the creditworthiness of the counterparty (see Bank for International Settlements, 1988).

Most previous research concerned with the default risk in derivative securities has focused on linear products such as forward contracts and swaps (see, for example, Kane 1980, Belton 1987, Wall and Fung 1987,

* This paper was first published in *Journal of Banking and Finance*, Vol. 19 (1995), pp. 299–322. It is reprinted with the permission of Elsevier Science.

Hull 1989, and Cooper and Mello 1991). An exception is Johnson and Stulz (1987). These authors examine the impact of default risk on option prices by assuming stochastic processes for the value of the assets of the option writer and the value of the asset underlying the option. They succeed in deriving closed-form solutions for the prices of European options in a number of different situations and show that the comparative statics for options subject to default risk are liable to be markedly different from those for default-free options. Following Johnson and Stulz, we will refer to a derivative security subject to default risk as a vulnerable derivative security.

Johnson and Stulz assume that, if the counterparty writing an option is unable to make a promised payment, the holder of a derivative security receives all the assets of the counterparty. This assumption is reasonable if there are no other claims on the assets of the counterparty that rank equally with the derivative security in the event of a default.[1] In this paper we extend the Johnson and Stulz model to cover situations where other equal ranking claims can exist. We assume that we know, or can estimate, the impact of default risk on bonds that have been (or could be) issued by the counterparty and rank equally with the derivative security. These are used to provide information on the impact of default risk on the derivative security itself. The rest of this paper is organized as follows. Section 11.1 outlines the model and applies it to European options and American options. Section 11.2 considers a special case of the model that is analytically very tractable. Section 11.3 applies the model to derivatives such as swaps that can become either assets or liabilities to a company. Conclusions are in Section 11.4.

11.1 THE MODEL

In this section we explain the model. For ease of exposition, it is initially assumed that we are interested in valuing a long position in a European option issued by a counterparty subject to credit risk. Later we show how the model can be extended to value other types of vulnerable derivative securities.

We define two securities as ranking equally in the event of a default if both pay off the same proportion of their no-default values when a

---

[1] The Johnson and Stulz model can be extended to cover the situation where there are claims senior to the one under consideration by defining defining "assets" as total assets net of the senior claims.

default occurs.[2] We assume that we know the prices of bonds that are issued by the counterparty and rank equally with the option. It is not necessary for these bonds to exist. All that is required is that we be able to estimate what the prices of the bonds would be if they did exist. The bonds relevant to our analysis are zero-coupon bonds. It may be necessary for analysts to estimate yields on a number of different coupon-bearing bonds that could be issued by the counterparty and then to use approaches such as that of Fong and Vasicek (1982) to estimate a zero-coupon yield curve for the counterparty. This is not as onerous as it sounds. Bond traders in financial institutions regularly estimate zero-coupon yield curves for corporate bonds that have a variety of different credit ratings in order to identify those that are under- or overpriced.

Define

f: current value of vulnerable option under consideration;

f^*: current value of the option assuming no defaults;[3]

B: current value of a vulnerable zero-coupon bond issued by the option writer that pays off $1 at time T and ranks equally with the option in the event of a default;

B^*: current value of a similar default-free zero-coupon bond;

t_0: current time;

T: time of promised payoff;

f_T^*: value of f^* at time T;

r: the short-term risk-free interest rate;

p: proportion of no-default value received when there is a default for the option under consideration and for other securities that rank equally with it in the event of a default;

---

[2] Our definition of equal ranking securities implicitly assumes that the claim made by a security holder against the assets of a defaulting counterparty equals the no-default value of the security. This is an approximation and does not reflect all the details of the bankruptcy law. For example, in some jurisdictions, the claim made against the assets of a corporation for a risky coupon-bearing bond issued by the corporation is equal to the tax basis for the bond. Depending on how interest rates have moved since the bond was purchased, this may be greater than or less than the bond's default-free market value. But, since the bond is worth less than its default-free value at the time of issue, our assumption can be expected to overstate the claim on average. It is worth noting that proportional recovery cannot be based on the market value of a security at the time of default, since the latter is by definition equal to the amount recovered.

[3] Strictly speaking f^* is not the value the security would have in a default-free world since, when we move from the vulnerable world to a default-free world, the stochastic processes followed by the underlying state variables may change. The variable f^* is the value the security has when state variables follow their vulnerable-world processes and promised payments are always made.

θ: vector of state variables determining the f^* and r variables;

ϕ: vector of state variables determining the occurrence of defaults and p.

The θ and ϕ variables are assumed to follow continuous-time diffusion processes. In the most general version of the model, some of the θ variables may also be ϕ variables.

It is assumed that defaults occur at the first time t when $G(\phi, t) = 0$ for some function G.[4] This defines what will be termed the "default boundary" in $\{\phi, t\}$ space. The "payoff boundary" is the earlier of $t = T$ and the default boundary. The payoff is pf^* if the default boundary is reached first, and f^* if the $t = T$ boundary is reached first. For ease of exposition, we generalize the definition of p so that it equals unity on the $t = T$ boundary. This means that the payoff is pf^* at all points on the payoff boundary. The variable p is a function of ϕ and t.

We assume that θ and ϕ are sufficiently well behaved for us to be able to use the risk-neutrality approach initially developed by Cox and Ross (1976) and formalized by Harrison and Pliska (1981). This means that

$$f = \hat{E}_{\theta,\phi}\left[e^{-\int_{t_0}^{t_b} r\,dt} p_b f_b^*\right], \tag{11.1}$$

where $\hat{E}$ denotes expectations under an equivalent martingale measure over all first-passage paths to the payoff boundary, the subscripts to $\hat{E}$ indicate the vectors of variables over which expectations are taken, b denotes the payoff boundary point reached, t_b is the time at point b, f_b^* is the value of f^* at point b, and p_b is the value of p at point b. Equation (11.1) gives the value of a vulnerable option at time t_0 in terms of its no-default value on the payoff boundary. It can be simplified by noting that the no-default value at a payoff boundary point b equals the expected discounted no-default value at time T; that is,

$$f_b^* = \hat{E}_\theta\left[e^{-\int_{t_b}^{T} r\,dt} f_T^*\right], \tag{11.2}$$

where $\hat{E}$ denotes expectations under the equivalent martingale measure over all paths for θ between times t_b and T that start at point b. Combining (11.1) and (11.2),

$$f = \hat{E}_{\theta,\phi}\left[e^{-\int_{t_0}^{T} r\,dt} p_b f_T^*\right], \tag{11.3}$$

---

[4] We assume that all market participants know G and the current values of the ϕ variables. Some of the results can be extended to cover the situation where there is some probability measure that encodes the beliefs of market participants about G and ϕ.

where the expectations operator $\hat{E}$ is taken over all paths for θ and ϕ between times t_0 and T, and b denotes the first payoff boundary point crossed by the path. Equation (11.3) can be written

$$f = \hat{E}_\theta \left[e^{-\int_{t_0}^{T} r\, dt} \hat{E}_{\phi|\theta}(p_b) f_T^* \right].$$

Defining

$$w(\theta, T) = \hat{E}_{\phi|\theta}(p_b),$$

this becomes

$$f = \hat{E}_\theta \left[e^{-\int_{t_0}^{T} r\, dt} w(\theta, T) f_T^* \right]. \tag{11.4}$$

This can be compared with the equation

$$f^* = \hat{E}_\theta \left[e^{-\int_{t_0}^{T} r\, dt} f_T^* \right],$$

which is the value of the security when there is no possibility of defaults.

The variable $1 - w(\theta, T)$ is the expected loss proportion on the option between time zero and time T for a particular realization of θ. Equation (11.4) has a great deal of intuitive appeal. It states that a derivative security promising a payoff at time T can be valued in the usual way if the promised payoff from a particular θ outcome is multiplied by $w(\theta, T)$.[5] It is relatively easy to see that this result holds if defaults can occur only at the maturity of the option. Our analysis shows that the result is also true when defaults can occur at any time during the life of the option.

Equation (11.4) is true for all derivative securities that promise a non-negative payoff at time T and rank equally with f in the event of a default. In particular, it is true for a zero-coupon bond. From (11.4),

$$B = \hat{E}_\theta \left[e^{-\int_{t_0}^{T} r\, dt} w(\theta, T) \right]. \tag{11.5}$$

---

[5] For an immediate application of equation (11.4), consider a warrant issued by a company on its own stock. It is reasonable to assume that, in circumstances where the company has defaulted on its liabilities, the stock price is so low that that the warrant has no value. With this assumption, $w(\theta, T) = 1$ whenever $f_T^* \neq 0$ so that $f = f^*$. As indicated by footnote 3, this result must be interpreted carefully. It does not mean that the warrant has the same value in a no-default world as it has in the real world. This means that, once we have correctly identified the true terminal stock price distribution, we can assume that the promised payoff is always made.

Also,

$$B^* = \hat{E}_\theta \left[e^{-\int_{t_0}^{T} r \, dt} \right].$$ (11.6)

Equations (11.5) and (11.6) define conditions that must be satisfied by the function $w(\theta, T)$ in (11.4).

(a) Upper and Lower Bounds for Vulnerable European Option Prices

Without any further assumptions, it is possible to derive upper and lower bounds for the price of a European option. The lower bound is calculated by assuming that the relationship between the θ's and ϕ's is such that defaults take place in the worst possible states of the world, that is, in those where the default-free value of the option is as high as possible. The upper bound is similarly calculated by assuming that defaults take place in states where the default-free value of the option is as low as possible.

We illustrate the approach by considering the valuation of a call option on a stock paying a continuous dividend yield in a Black–Scholes world. In this case there is one θ variable: the stock price S.

Define

S_T: terminal stock price;
X: strike price;
q: dividend yield;
σ: volatility of the stock price;
$g(S_T)$: probability density function for S_T in a risk-neutral world.

The vector of state variables determining the probability of defaults and proportional losses in the event of a default are, as before, denoted by ϕ. Consistent with the previous notation, we define

$$w(\theta, T) = \hat{E}_{\phi|\theta}(p_b),$$

where θ represents a path for the stock price S. Since the payoff is dependent only on the terminal stock price S_T, it is convenient to define $u(S_T)$ as the expected value of $w(\theta, T)$ over all stock price paths ending at S_T. The function $1 - u(S_T)$ is the expected loss proportion on the option for all stock price paths that end at S_T.

Since the short-term interest rate r is constant in the Black–Scholes model, equation (11.5) gives the value f of the call option as

$$f = B^* \int_0^\infty u(S_T) \max(S_T - X, \, 0) g(S_T) \, dS_T.$$ (11.7)

Similarly,

$$B = B^* \int_0^\infty u(S_T)g(S_T)\,dS_T. \tag{11.8}$$

Equation (11.8) defines one condition that must be satisfied by u. Another is

$$0 \le u(S_T) \le 1. \tag{11.9}$$

Since the payoff from a call option is a monotonic increasing function of S_T, the maximum value of f in (11.7), subject to the constraints in (11.8) and (11.9), is obtained by setting $u(S_T) = 1$ for as many high values of S_T as possible. Specifically, the maximum is obtained by setting

$$u(S_T) = \begin{cases} 1 & \text{if } S_T \ge S_1, \\ 0 & \text{if } S_T < S_1, \end{cases}$$

where S_1 is chosen so that $u(S_T)$ satisfies (11.8), that is, so that

$$B = B^* \int_{S_1}^\infty g(S_T)\,dS_T. \tag{11.10}$$

Similarly the values of $u(S_T)$ that minimize f are

$$u(S_T) = \begin{cases} 0 & \text{if } S_T \ge S_2, \\ 1 & \text{if } S_T < S_2, \end{cases}$$

where S_2 is chosen to satisfy (11.8), that is, so that

$$B = B^* \int_0^{S_2} g(S_T)\,dS_T. \tag{11.11}$$

Under the Black–Scholes assumptions, the function $\log S_T$ is normally distributed in a risk-neutral world with mean m and standard deviation s given by

$$m = \log S + (r - q - \tfrac{1}{2}\sigma^2)(T - t_0), \qquad s = \sigma\sqrt{T - t_0}.$$

It follows from (11.10) and (11.11) that

$$S_1 = \exp\left[m - N^{-1}\left(\frac{B}{B^*}\right)s\right], \qquad S_2 = \exp\left[m + N^{-1}\left(\frac{B}{B^*}\right)s\right],$$

where N^{-1} is the inverse cumulative normal distribution function.

Denote by $C(Z)$ the Black–Scholes call price when the strike price is Z and define

$$\pi(Z) = N\left[\frac{\ln(S/Z) + (r - q - \tfrac{1}{2}\sigma^2)(T - t_0)}{\sigma\sqrt{T - t_0}}\right].$$

From the above analysis and equation (11.7), the maximum value of a vulnerable call option with strike price X is given by

$$C_{max} = B^* \int_{S_1}^{\infty} \max\,(S_T - X,\, 0)g(S_T)\,dS_T,$$

or

$$C_{max} = \begin{cases} C(X) & \text{if } S_1 \leq X, \\ C(S_1) + B^*(S_1 - X)\pi(S_1) & \text{if } S_1 > X. \end{cases}$$

To understand this result, recall that, in order to obtain the maximum option price, we have considered a scenario where defaults are associated with the lowest possible values of S_T. When $S_1 < X$, this scenario has all defaults occurring when $S_T < X$, that is, when the option closes out of the money. The maximum vulnerable option price is therefore the same as its no-default price $C(X)$. When $S_1 > X$, some defaults must occur when the option closes in the money and the maximum vulnerable option price is therefore less than the no-default price in this case.

The minimum value of a vulnerable call is given by

$$C_{min} = B^* \int_{X}^{S_2} \max\,(S_T - X,\, 0)g(S_T)\,dS_T,$$

or

$$C_{min} = \begin{cases} 0 & \text{if } S_2 \leq X, \\ C(X) - C(S_2) - B^*(S_2 - X)\pi(S_2) & \text{if } S_2 > X. \end{cases}$$

To obtain these results, we have looked for worst-case scenarios. When $S_2 \leq X$, the probability of default is sufficiently high that all circumstances where $S_T > X$ can be associated with defaults where there is zero recovery. Hence the minimum value of the option is zero in this case. When $S_2 > X$, defaults cannot wipe out all positive payoffs and the minimum value of the call is positive.

A similar analysis gives the maximum and minimum values, P_{max} and P_{min}, of a vulnerable put option:

$$P_{max} = \begin{cases} P(S_2) + B^*(X - S_2)[1 - \pi(S_2)] & \text{if } S_2 \leq X, \\ P(X) & \text{if } S_2 > X, \end{cases}$$

$$P_{min} = \begin{cases} P(X) - P(S_1) - B^*(X - S_1)[1 - \pi(S_1)] & \text{if } S_1 \leq X, \\ 0 & \text{if } S_1 > X. \end{cases}$$

Options on foreign exchange, stock indices, and futures contracts are analogous to options on a stock paying a continuous dividend yield (see Hull 1993: Chap. 11) The results in this section can therefore be extended to cover these types of options.

(b) American Options

Vulnerable American-style derivative securities are more complicated to value than their European counterparts. This is because the holder can use the latest information about the ϕ variables, as well as the θ variables, when deciding whether to exercise early.

A general result is that a vulnerable American option should not be exercised later than its no-default counterpart. To prove this, suppose that option U is the American-style option under consideration and option U* is the no-default version of U. Define

h: the value of U;
h^*: the value of U*;
Q: the promised payoff.

Option U should not be exercised when $h > Q$, and option V should not be exercised when $h^* > Q$. Since $h^* \geq h$, the second condition is satisfied whenever the first condition is satisfied. This proves the general result.

(c) An Example

We now illustrate these results by considering a particular situation where a bank has written a call option on a foreign currency. We first assume that we have a full knowledge of the model, so that the prices of both bonds and options can be computed. We then assume that we only know bond prices and use the results in Section 11.1(a) to calculate bounds on the option prices. Define

S: foreign currency exchange rate;
A: assets of the bank;
X: strike price;
r: domestic risk-free interest rate (assumed constant);
r_f: foreign risk-free interest rate (assumed constant);
T: time to maturity of the option;
C: option price;
p: proportional recovery made in the event of a default (assumed constant in this example).

We assume that whenever A falls to a level D, the bank defaults. In this situation, A is the only ϕ variable and S is the only θ variable. The default boundary is $A - D = 0$.

We suppose that the risk-neutral processes for S and A are

$$dS = (r - r_f)S\,dt + \sigma_S S\,dz_S, \qquad dA = rA\,dt + \sigma_A A\,dz_A,$$

where σ_S and σ_A, the volatilities of S and A, are constant and dz_S and dz_A are Wiener processes. We suppose that the instantaneous correlation between S and A is ρ.

The variables S and A can be modeled in the form of a three-dimensional tree using an approach suggested by Hull and White (1990). Define two new orthogonal variables:

$$x_1 = \sigma_A \log S + \sigma_S \log A, \qquad (11.12)$$

$$x_2 = \sigma_A \log S - \sigma_S \log A, \qquad (11.13)$$

These variables follow the processes

$$dx_1 = [\sigma_A(r - r_f - \sigma_S^2/2) + \sigma_S(r - \sigma_A^2/2)]\,dt + \sigma_S\sigma_A\sqrt{2(1 + \rho)}\,dz_1,$$

$$dx_2 = [\sigma_A(r - r_f - \sigma_S^2/2) - \sigma_S(r - \sigma_A^2/2)]\,dt + \sigma_S\sigma_A\sqrt{2(1 - \rho)}\,dz_2,$$

where dz_1 and dz_2 are uncorrelated Wiener processes. The variables can be modeled using two separate binomial trees where, in time Δt, x_i has a probability q_i of increasing by h_i and a probability $1 - q_i$ of decreasing by h_i. The variables h_i and q_i are chosen so that the tree gives correct values for the first two moments of the distribution of x_1 and x_2. Since the variables are uncorrelated, the two binomial trees can be combined together to form a three-dimensional tree where the probabilities of movements in x_1 and x_2 in time Δt are as follows:

$q_1 q_2$: x_1 increases by h_1 and x_2 increases by h_2;
$q_1(1 - q_2)$: x_1 increases by h_1 and x_2 decreases by h_2;
$(1 - q_1)q_2$: x_1 decreases by h_1 and x_2 increases by h_2;
$(1 - q_1)(1 - q_2)$: x_1 decreases by h_1 and x_2 decreases by h_2.

At each node of the tree, S and A can be calculated from x_1 and x_2 using the inverse of the relationships in (11.12) and (11.13):

$$S = \exp\left[\frac{x_1 + x_2}{2\sigma_A}\right], \qquad A = \exp\left[\frac{x_1 - x_2}{2\sigma_S}\right].$$

At the final nodes of the tree,

$$C = \begin{cases} \max(S - X, 0) & \text{if } A > D, \\ 0 & \text{if } A \leq D. \end{cases}$$

For a European option, we apply the following boundary condition as we roll back through the tree:

$$C = pC^* \quad \text{when } A \leq D.$$

In the case of an American option, the additional boundary condition

$$C \geq S - X \quad \text{when } A > D$$

is applied.

The price B of a discount bond ranking equally with the option in the event of default and maturing at time T can be obtained from the same tree by setting

$$B = \begin{cases} 1 & \text{if } A \geq D, \\ 0 & \text{if } A \leq D \end{cases}$$

at the final nodes, and applying the boundary condition

$$B = pB^* \quad \text{when } A \leq D$$

at earlier nodes as we roll back through the tree where B^* is the default-free value of the bond.

Table 11.1 considers the case where $S = X = 1$, $A = 100$, $r = r_f = 0.05$, $T = 1$, $\sigma_A = 0.05$, $\sigma_S = 0.15$, and $p = 0$. It provides results based on 100 time steps for the percentage reduction in the prices of European and American call options for a variety of different values of ρ and D. The no-default prices of the European and American options are 0.0569 and 0.0575 respectively. The table shows that the impact of default risk on the prices of American options is significantly less than its impact on the prices of European options. This is because, as discussed above, the holder of an American option can alleviate the impact of defaults by exercising when A is just above D.[6] The advantage of being able to do this is greatest for situations when the correlation between S and A is highly negative. Regardless of what subsequently happens the owner of the option is then likely to have few regrets about the early exercise decision. If A declines, the bank defaults and the gain from early exercise is significant; if A increases, there is a tendency for S to decrease and for the value of the call option to decline. This explains why the difference between the percentage price reduction from default risk for American and European call options increases as the correlation between S and A decreases. For put options the reverse is true: the difference between the

[6] Our model may overstate the difference between the impact of default risk on the values of American and European options because it assumes that the option holder has full knowledge of the default boundary and that all obligations related to option transactions are honored right up until the time when the default boundary is reached.

TABLE 11.1. Percentage reduction arising from default risk in the price of one-year foreign currency call options. The strike price and current exchange rate are both 1.0000. The foreign and domestic interest rates are both 5% per annum. The volatility of the exchange rate is 15% per annum. The assets of the option writer have an initial value of 100 and a volatility of 5%. The writer defaults when the value of the assets reach D. The coefficient of correlation between the value of the assets and the exchange rate is ρ. The option holder makes no recovery in the event of a default. The no-default prices of the European and American options are 0.0569 and 0.0575 respectively.

ρ		D			
		90	92	94	96
−0.80	European	1.72	6.18	17.86	40.87
	American	0.00	0.00	0.11	1.78
−0.40	European	0.86	3.21	9.48	23.88
	American	0.02	0.11	0.72	3.72
0.00	European	0.30	1.24	4.44	13.95
	American	0.04	0.22	1.10	4.93
0.40	European	0.03	0.20	1.21	5.69
	American	0.01	0.10	0.68	3.61
0.80	European	0.00	0.01	0.13	1.81
	American	0.00	0.01	0.12	1.78
One-year bond yield (%)		5.30	6.25	9.55	20.05
Minimum percent reduction implied by bond yield		0.00	0.00	0.00	0.00
Maximum percent reduction implied by bond yield		2.83	9.56	26.73	60.31

percentage reduction increases as the correlation between S and A increases.

Table 11.2 shows how the results in Table 11.1 change when the proportional recovery changes from 0 to 50%. The percentage reductions in the prices of all European options are halved as might be expected. The percentage reductions in the prices of American options also decrease, but in most cases by less than 50%. This is because the incentive to exercise early in order to reduce default risk is less than before.

Tables 11.1 and 11.2 show the yields on one-year vulnerable bonds implied by the different values of D considered. As explained in Section 11.1(a), the yields on vulnerable bonds can be used to produce maximum and minimum values for vulnerable European option prices. Tables 11.1 and 11.2 also show the minimum and maximum percentage

TABLE 11.2. Percentage reduction arising from default risk in the price of one-year foreign currency call options. The strike price and the current exchange rate are both 1.0000. The foreign and domestic interest rates are both 5% per annum. The volatility of the exchange rate is 15% per annum. The assets of the option writer have an initial value of 100 and a volatility of 5%. The writer defaults when the value of the assets reach D. The coefficient of correlation between the value of the assets and the exchange rate is ρ. The option holder makes a 50% recovery in the event of a default. The no-default European and American option prices are 0.0569 and 0.0575 respectively.

ρ		D			
		90	92	94	96
−0.80	European	0.86	3.09	8.93	20.43
	American	0.00	0.00	0.10	1.73
−0.40	European	0.43	1.61	4.74	11.94
	American	0.01	0.09	0.59	3.03
0.00	European	0.15	0.62	2.22	6.97
	American	0.03	0.15	0.73	3.24
0.40	European	0.01	0.10	0.61	2.84
	American	0.01	0.06	0.40	2.07
0.80	European	0.00	0.00	0.06	0.91
	American	0.00	0.00	0.06	0.89
One-year bond yield (%)		5.15	5.62	7.25	12.24
Minimum percent reduction implied by bond yield		0.00	0.00	0.00	0.00
Maximum percent reduction implied by bond yield		1.53	5.29	15.45	37.50

reductions in the option price implied by the calculated bond yields.[7] These are independent of the model and depend only on the prices of bonds that rank equally with the option. It can be seen that the actual percentage reduction in each table is always between the minimum and maximum.

11.2 A SPECIAL CASE

The most general version of the model that has been presented requires data on the ϕ variables, the default boundary, and the way in which p depends on the ϕ variables. In practice this data is unlikely to be available.

---

[7] The minimum percentage reduction is not always zero. In this example it exceeds zero when the one-year yield is greater than 80%.

This means that the model can usually produce only fairly wide bounds for the price of a derivative security. In this section we consider a special case of the model where the adjustments for credit risk depend only on the prices of bonds.

We suppose the state variables comprising θ are independent of the state variables comprising ϕ. In this case

$$w(\theta, T) = \hat{E}_{\phi|\theta}(p_b) = \hat{E}_{\phi}(p_b).$$

The function $w(\theta, T)$ is independent of θ and can be written as $w(T)$. Equation (11.5) becomes

$$B = w(T)\hat{E}_{\theta}\left[e^{-\int_{t_0}^{T} r\, dt}\right], \qquad (11.14)$$

and, combining this with (11.6), we get

$$w(T) = B/B^*. \qquad (11.15)$$

Equation (11.4) becomes

$$f = w(T)\hat{E}_{\theta}\left[e^{-\int_{t_0}^{T} r\, dt} f_T^*\right].$$

Since the current value the derivative security equals its expected discounted value at time T, this reduces to

$$f = w(T)f^*, \qquad (11.16)$$

so that, from (11.15),

$$f = (B/B^*)f^*,$$

or

$$f/f^* = B/B^*. \qquad (11.17)$$

The intuition behind equation (11.17) is as follows. For any path followed by the ϕ variables, the proportional loss on the bond and the derivative security is the same. Since the θ and ϕ variables are independent, the expected no-default values of the bond and the derivative security are independent of the path followed by the ϕ variables. Integrating across all such paths must therefore lead to the result in equation (11.17).

Defining y and y^* as the yields on B and B^*, respectively, (11.17) reduces to

$$f = e^{-(y-y^*)(T-t_0)}f^*. \qquad (11.18)$$

Equation (11.18) has a great deal of intuitive appeal. It suggests that the discount rates used when a vulnerable European-style derivative security is valued should be higher that those used when a similar default-free security is valued by an amount $y - y^*$.[8]

For an example of the application of this result, we consider the data in Table 11.1. When $D = 90, 92, 94$, and 96, $y - y^*$ is 0.30%, 1.25%, 4.55%, and 15.05%, respectively. The percentage reductions in the European option price in these four cases can be calculated from equation (11.18) as 0.30, 1.24, 4.44, and 13.97. These agree very closely with the $\rho = 0$ results calculated numerically in Table 11.1.

Although the independence assumption does not hold perfectly true, it may not in practice be too unreasonable for many of the over-the-counter derivative securities written by large financial institutions. One reason for this is that any particular security is usually only a very small part of the portfolio of the financial institution. As such, its influence on the fortunes of the financial institution is minimal. Another reason is that the variables underlying the securities traded over the counter by financial institutions are typically interest rates, exchange rates, and commodity prices. Most financial institutions try to ensure that they are at all times reasonably well hedged against the impact of these market variables.

Equation (11.18) leads to the following modifications to the Black–Scholes formulas for the prices C and P of European calls and puts on non-dividend-paying stocks:

$$C = e^{-(y-y^*)(T-t_0)} S N(d_1) - e^{-y(T-t_0)} X N(d_2),$$

$$P = e^{-y(T-t_0)} X N(-d_2) - e^{-(y-y^*)(T-t_0)} S N(-d_1),$$

where

$$d_1 = \frac{\ln(S/X) + (y^* + \sigma^2/2)(T - t_0)}{\sigma\sqrt{T - t_0}}, \qquad d_2 = d_1 - \sigma\sqrt{T - t_0},$$

S is the current stock price, X is the strike price, σ is the volatility, and N is the cumulative normal distribution function.[9] It is interesting to note that the normal put–call parity relationship between C and P does not apply when there is default risk. A relationship which does hold is

$$C + X e^{-y(T-t_0)} = P + S e^{-(y-y^*)(T-t_0)}.$$

Unlike the usual put–call parity relationships, this relies on the

[8] For a discussion of the relationship between yield spreads and maturity, see Cook and Hendershott (1978), Jonkhart (1979), Rodriguez (1988), and Yawitz et al. (1985).

[9] For a sufficiently large yield differential, a call option price decreases as the time to maturity increases. Johnson and Stulz (1987) show that this is also a feature of some of the models they consider.

independence assumption and cannot be proved using simple arbitrage arguments.

(a) American Options

When the θ and ϕ variables are assumed to be independent, it is possible to produce lower bounds for the prices of American options. Define

$F^*(t_0, t)$: the instantaneous forward rate at time t as seen at time t_0 calculated from the risk-free yield curve;

$F(t_0, t)$: the instantaneous forward rate at time t as seen at time t_0 calculated from the yield curve corresponding to bonds that rank equally with the option (or category of options) under consideration in the event of a default;

$\alpha(t_0, t)$: the forward rate differential, $F(t_0, t) - F^*(t_0, t)$.

Appendix A proves a series of propositions that lead to two general results:

1. The percentage reduction in the price of an American option caused by default risk is always less than that for the corresponding European option.
2. A lower bound to the price of a vulnerable American option is the price of a notional no-default option X which is such that the holder is required to make continuous payments at rate $\alpha(t_0, t)$ times the options value at time t until the option either expires or is exercised.

The first result can be used to provide a lower bound for the price of the American option:

$$h > h^*f/f^*,$$

where h and f are the values of the vulnerable American option and its European counterpart, and h^* and f^* are the values of the corresponding no-default options. The second result produces a tighter lower bound than this. Option X is the value the American option would have if the market does not change its view of the probability of the counterparty defaulting during particular time intervals. It can be valued using a Cox, Ross, and Rubinstein (1979) binomial tree in which the discount rate at time t is increased by $\alpha(t_0, t)$.[10]

---

[10] The use of a higher discount rate on the tree tends to cause the option to be exercised earlier. This is consistent with Section 11.1(b).

11.3 EXTENSION TO SWAPS AND SIMILAR CONTRACTS

The results in Sections 11.1 and 11.2 apply to contracts that are always positively valued. One of the attractive features of the analysis is that it can be extended to cover contracts such as swaps and forward contracts that can be either assets or liabilities to a company. In this section we first present the general model and then show the effect of making the independence assumption of Section 11.2.

We suppose that the company for which the valuation is being carried out is company A and that its counterparty is company B. We make the simplifying assumption that there is no chance of a default by company A.[11] We assume that if company B defaults when the no-default value of the security to company A is positive, company A is able to make a claim equal to the no-default value of the security against the assets of company B. If company B defaults on its liabilities when the no-default value of the security is negative, we assume that there is no effect on the position of company A.[12]

Using the same notation as in Section 11.1, the company's exposure when payoff boundary point b is reached is $\max(f_b^*, 0)$ and the credit loss at this point is

$$(1 - p_b) \max(f_b^*, 0).$$

The difference between the vulnerable and no-default value of the security is therefore given by

$$f^* - f = \hat{E}_{\theta, \phi}\left[e^{-\int_{t_0}^{t_b} r\, dt} (1 - p_b) \max(f_b^*, 0) \right]. \tag{11.19}$$

This can also be termed the value of company B's default option. In principle it can be calculated numerically once the ϕ variables and the default boundary have been specified.

---

[11] The model can be extended to cover two-sided default risk, but it becomes considerably more complicated. Company A makes a gain at time t if (a) it defaults, (b) the no-default value of the contract is positive to A, and (c) company B has not already defaulted at an earlier time when the no-default value of the contract to B was positive. Company A makes a loss at time t if (a) B defaults, (b) the no-default value of the contract is positive to B, and (c) company A has not already defaulted at an earlier time when the no-default value of the contract to A was positive.

[12] As noted in footnote 2, we are not reflecting all the details of bankrupcy law in our analysis. Many issues associated with swap defaults are being decided on a case by case basis. Litzenberger (1992) has shown that the legal position of company A in the event of a default by company B may in some circumstances be slightly better than that assumed here. The assumptions made here are a reasonable approximation to reality and are the same as those made by most researchers and bank regulators.

When the θ variables and ϕ variables are assumed to be independent equation (19) can be simplified. Suppose that the security under consideration lasts until time T. Equation (11.19) can be written

$$f^* - f = \int_{t_0}^{T} \hat{E}_\theta \left[e^{-\int_{t_0}^{t} r \, dt} \max(f_t^*, 0) \right] \pi(t) \, dt, \tag{11.20}$$

where f_t^* is the value of f^* at time t, $\pi(t)$ is the rate at which losses are experienced as a proportion of the no-default value of contracts at time t, and expectations are taken at time t_0.

Define

B_t: price at time t_0 of a discount bond ranking equally with the security and maturing at time t;

B_t^*: price at time t_0 of a riskless bond maturing at time t;

y_t: yield on B_t;

y_t^*: yield on B_t^*.

When the derivative security is a discount bond maturing at time t, equation (11.20) becomes

$$B_t^* - B_t = B_t^* \int_{t_0}^{t} \pi(s) \, ds,$$

or

$$1 - e^{-(y_t - y_t^*)(t - t_0)} = \int_{t_0}^{t} \pi(s) \, ds.$$

Differentiating with respect to t, we get

$$\pi(t) = \alpha(t_0, t) e^{-(y_t - y_t^*)(t - t_0)}, \tag{11.21}$$

where as before $\alpha(t_0, t)$ is the instantaneous forward rate differential as seen at time t_0 for a contract maturing at time t. Substituting (11.21) into (11.20), we obtain

$$f^* - f = \int_{t_0}^{T} \alpha(t_0, t) e^{-(y_t - y_t^*)(t - t_0)} v(t) \, dt, \tag{11.22}$$

where

$$v(t) = \hat{E} \left[e^{-\int_{t_0}^{t} r \, dt} \max(f_t^*, 0) \right] dt. \tag{11.23}$$

The variable $v(t)$ is the value of a contingent claim that pays off the exposure at time t.

The structure of equation (11.22) can be understood by considering the situation where no recoveries are made. The term $\alpha(t_0, t)\,\Delta t$ is the probability of a default between times t and $t + \Delta t$ conditional on no earlier default; the term $e^{-(y_t - y_t^*)(t - t_0)}$ is the probability of no default between time t_0 and t; the term $v(t)$ is the expected present value of the loss incurred by a default at time t.

In some circumstances $v(t)$ can be calculated analytically; in other circumstances a tree or Monte Carlo simulation must be used to estimate it. Once $v(t)$ has been obtained, numerical integration can be used to evaluate the expression in (11.22).

As as illustration of equation (11.22), consider a currency swap where a fixed rate of interest in the domestic currency is received and a fixed rate of interest in a foreign currency is paid. Principals are exchanged at the end of the life of the swap and interest payments are exchanged periodically. At time t, the value of the swap is $B_d(t) - S(t)B_f(t)$, where $B_d(t)$ is the value in the domestic currency of the domestic bond underlying the swap at time t, $B_f(t)$ is the value in the foreign currency of the foreign bond underlying the swap at time t, and $S(t)$ is the exchange rate at time t.

In this case, $v(t)$ is the value of an option that pays off $\max[B_d(t) - S(t)B_f(t),\ 0]$ at time t. Assuming interest rates are constant, the values of $B_d(t)$ and $B_f(t)$ are known and $v(t)$ is the value of a currency option.

Table 11.3 shows the impact of defaults on the value of the swap for different exchange rate volatilities and swap lives. Both domestic and foreign interest rates are assumed to be 5% per annum with annual compounding. The principal in each currency is assumed to be 100 and interest at the rate of 5% in each currency is assumed to be exchanged annually. The values of $y_t - y_t^*$ for t equal to 1, 2, 3, 4, 5, and 10 years were assumed to be 25, 50, 70, 85, 95, and 120 basis points with intermediate values of t being calculated using linear interpolation. The Garman and Kohlhagen (1983) model was used to calculate $v(t)$ and Simpson's rule was used to evaluate the integral in equation (11.22) numerically.

Table 11.3 shows the payments on an annuity which lasts for the same length of time as the swap and which (using the domestic risk-free interest rate as the discount rate) has the same value as $f^* - f$. These payments are expressed in basis points on the principal and provide a guide to the spread required on the currency swap to compensate for credit risk. (For example, the 10.2 basis points shown for a volatility of

TABLE 11.3. Cost of defaults expressed in basis points per year on a currency swap where interest and principal in the domestic currency is received and interest and principal in the foreign currency is paid. The initial exchange rate is 1.0000 and principals in the two currencies are both 100. Interest is paid at 5% once a year in both currencies. The risk-free interest rate is assumed to be constant at 5% per annum (with annual compounding) in both currencies. The spread over the risk-free rate for zero-coupon bonds of maturities 1, 2, 3, 4, 5, and 10 years issued by the counterparty is 25, 50, 70, 85, 95, and 120 basis points respectively.

Swap life (yrs)	Exchange rate volatility (% per annum)			
	5.0	10.0	15.0	20.0
2	1.2	2.3	3.5	4.6
4	2.6	5.3	7.9	10.5
6	3.6	7.2	10.7	14.3
8	4.4	8.7	13.0	17.3
10	5.1	10.2	15.3	20.3

10% per annum and a swap life of 10 years was calculated from a value for $f^* - f$ of 0.79.) The table indicates that the required spread increases with both the volatility and the life of the swap.[13]

11.4 CONCLUSIONS

This paper has proposed a model for incorporating default risk into the prices of derivative securities. It shows how the value of a vulnerable security can be related in a consistent way to the no-default value of the security, the values of default-free zero-coupon bonds, and the values of vulnerable zero-coupon bonds that would be issued by the writer of the derivative security. The latter can be estimated from the yields on actively traded corporate bonds.

Upper and lower bounds for the prices of European options subject to

[13] Since a swap spread is not riskless, Table 11.3 slightly understates the required swap spread. Note that Table 11.3 is indicative of the spread required on a single currency swap. For this particular example, the spread on a matched pair of swaps would be twice as great. If the foreign interest rate is higher than the domestic rate, the swap in which we receive domestic is worth more than the corresponding swap where we pay domestic. The reverse is true when the domestic rate is higher than the foreign rate. However, the total spread required on a matched pair of swaps is fairly insensitive to differences between the two rates.

default risk can be calculated analytically. The model can also be implemented numerically when full information about the variables affecting defaults is available. We have produced results for the situation where a bank writes a foreign currency option and the assets of the bank are correlated with the foreign exchange rate. The impact of default risk on the price of an American option is less than that on the price of a European option. In the case of call options the difference between the two is greatest when the correlation between the foreign exchange rate and the value of the assets of the financial institution is negative. For put options the difference is greatest when this correlation is positive.

The model leads to analytic pricing formulas for European warrants issued by a company on its own stock and for some types of convertibles. It also leads to procedures for calculating the impact of default risk on contracts such as forwards and swaps that can become either assets or liabilities to a company.

A simplifying assumption likely to have a great deal of appeal to practitioners is that variables concerned with defaults are independent of the variables underlying the value of the derivative security in a no-default world. This avoids the need for assumptions to be made about the variables concerned with defaults. Vulnerable European option prices can then be determined analytically. Lower bounds can be calculated for the prices of vulnerable American options. The impact of default risk on contracts such as swaps and forwards can be calculated using numerical integration.

In this analysis, a vulnerable derivative security is regarded as a claim partially contingent on a similar vulnerable bond. An important issue is therefore whether vulnerable bonds are correctly priced by the market. Altman's (1989, 1990) research shows that the excess yields on corporate bonds over treasury bonds are higher than can be justified by their default experience. This may be because of market inefficiency, illiquidity, or some other factor that we do not wish to reflect in the prices of derivative securities. If so, the market prices of vulnerable bonds in the analysis in this paper should be replaced by notional bond prices calculated to reflect the actual default experience on bonds with a similar credit rating.

APPENDIX A

In this appendix we prove a number of propositions which lead to results for American options in the situation where the θ variables are assumed to be independent of the ϕ variables.

PROPOSITION A1. *When the θ variables are independent of the ϕ variables, the value of a vulnerable derivative security that promises a non-negative payment only at time T is equal to the value of a similar no-default security where the holder is required to make continuous payments at rate $\alpha(t_0, t)$ times the security's value at time τ $(t_0 \leq t \leq T)$, where $\alpha(t_0, t)$ is the forward rate differential defined in Section 11.2(a).*

Proof. As usual we define f as the price of the vulnerable derivative security and f^* as the price it would have in a no-default world. In addition, we define

g^*: price of security which is the same as the no-default security under consideration except that the holder is required to make payments at rate $\alpha(t_0, t)$ times its value at time τ $(t_0 \leq t \leq T)$.

If f_T^* and g_T^* are the values of f^* and g^* at time T, then

$$f^* = \hat{E}_\theta \left[e^{-\int_{t_0}^{T} r\, dt} f_T^* \right] \quad \text{and} \quad g^* = \hat{E}_\theta \left[e^{-\int_{t_0}^{T} [r + \alpha(t_0,\, t)]\, dt} g_T^* \right].$$

Since $f_T^* = g_T^*$,

$$g^* = f^* e^{-\int_{t_0}^{T} \alpha(t_0,\, t)\, dt}.$$

Since

$$\int_{t_0}^{T} \alpha(t, s)\, ds = (y - y^*)(T - t_0), \tag{A1}$$

it follows that

$$g^* = f^* e^{-(y - y^*)(T - t_0)}.$$

From equation (11.18) this in turn means that $f = g^*$, which is the desired result. $\square$

This result applies to all European-style derivative securities including those where the promised payoff depends on the path followed by θ variables. It should be emphasized that f and g^* have equal values only at time t_0. When we move to a new time t^* $(t^* > t_0)$, the value of the vulnerable security is equated to the value of a new no-default security where the continuous payments at time t are at a rate $\alpha(t^*, t)$ times the security value. In general $\alpha(t_0, t)$ and $\alpha(t^*, t)$ are not equal.

The next proposition extends the result in Proposition A1 to securities with a general payoff boundary in a no-default world.

PROPOSITION A2. *The result in Proposition A1 is true for any derivative security that has a no-default payoff boundary that is a function of θ and t.*

Proof. The derivative security can be regarded as the sum of Arrow–Debreu securities each promising a payoff if one particular path in $\{\theta, t\}$ space is followed, but promising zero payoff if any other path is followed. Suppose that the path used to define a particular Arrow–Debreu security first crosses the payoff boundary at time τ. The security can be regarded as a European-style security promising a (path-dependent) payoff at the time τ. As shown in Proposition A1, it is equal in value to a similar no-default Arrow–Debreu security where the option holder is required to make a continuous payment at rate $\alpha(t_0, t)$ times the option's value at time t until time τ. The sum of these no-default Arrow–Debreu securities is option X. The result follows. □

We now move on to consider the effect of relative effects of default risk on European and American options.

PROPOSITION A3. *In the situation where the θ variables are independent of the ϕ variables, the proportional effect of default risk on the price of an American option is always less than the proportional effect of default risk on its European counterpart.*

Proof. Define

h, h^*: the values of a vulnerable American option and its no-default counterpart;
f, f^*: the values of the vulnerable and no-default European versions of the option;
Option W: a notional option that is the same as the vulnerable American option except that the option holder is constrained to exercise the option on the early exercise boundary that is optimal for the no-default American option.

Denote the value of option W by h'. As with (11.16),

$$h' = \hat{E}_\phi(p_c)h^*, \tag{A2}$$

where the expectations operator is taken over all paths followed by ϕ, c is the first point reached on the payoff boundary for W and p_c is the value of p at point c. For any path followed by the ϕ variables, when the default boundary is reached before the early exercise boundary, the proportional payoff on W is the same as the proportional payoff on the corresponding European option, that is, $p_c = p_b$. In other circumstances, $p_c = 1$. Consequently, it is always true that

$$p_c \geq p_b,$$

so that

$$\hat{E}_\phi(p_c) \geq \hat{E}_\phi(p_b).$$

From (11.16) and (A2), we have

$$h'/h^* \geq f/f^*. \tag{A3}$$

Option W is the same as the American option under consideration except that the holder is constrained to use a possibly suboptimal early exercise boundary. By definition the optimal early exercise boundary is the one that maximizes the value of an option. It follows that $h \geq h'$, so that, from (A3),

$$\frac{h}{h^*} \geq \frac{f}{f^*},$$

which is the required result. □

For the next proposition, define

Option X: a notional no-default American option which provides the same payoff as the option under consideration and is such that the option holder is required to make continuous payments at rate $\alpha(t_0, t)$ times the option's value at time t until the option either expires or is exercised (recall that $\alpha(t_0, t)$ is the spread between the risky and riskless forward rates at time t as seen at time t_0);

Option Y: a notional vulnerable option which is the same as the option under consideration except that the holder is constrained to use the optimal early exercise boundary for option X.

PROPOSITION A4. *In the situation where the θ variables are independent of the ϕ variables, a lower bound for an American option is the value of option X.*

Proof. Since the optimal early exercise boundary is the one that maximizes the value of an option, the American option under consideration is worth no less than option Y. From Proposition A2 the values of options X and Y are the same. The result follows. □

REFERENCES

Altman, E. I. "Measuring corporate bond mortality and performance." *Journal of Finance*, 44 (1989), pp. 902–922.

Altman, E. I. "Setting the record straight on junk bonds: a review of the research on default rates and returns." *Journal of Applied Corporate Finance*, 3 (1990), pp. 82–95.

Bank for International Settlements. "Proposals for international convergence of capital adequacy standards," 1988.

Belton, T. M. "Credit risk in interest rate swaps." Working Paper, Board of Governors of Federal Reserve System, 1987.

Black, F., and M. Scholes. "The pricing of options and corporate liabilities." *Journal of Political Economy*, 81 (1973), pp. 637–659.

Cook, T. Q., and P. H. Hendershott. "The impact of taxes, risk and relative security supplies on interest rate differentials." *Journal of Finance*, 33 (1978), pp. 1173–1186.

Cooper, I. A., and A. S. Mello. "The default risk of swaps." *Journal of Finance*, 46 (1991), pp. 597–620.

Cox, J. C., and S. A. Ross. "The valuation of options for alternative stochastic processes." *Journal of Financial Economics*, 3 (1976), pp. 145–166.

Cox, J. C., S. A. Ross, and M. Rubinstein. "Option pricing: a simplified approach." *Journal of Financial Economics*, 7 (1979), pp. 229–264.

Fong, H. G., and O. A. Vasicek. "Term structure modeling using exponential splines." *Journal of Finance*, 37 (1982), pp. 339–348.

Garman, M. B., and S. W. Kohlhagen. "Foreign currency option value." *Journal of International Money and Finance*, 2 (1983), pp. 231–237.

Harrison, J. M., and S. R. Pliska. "Martingales and stochastic integrals in the theory of continuous trading." *Stochastic Processes and their Applications*, 11 (1981), pp. 215–260.

Hull, J. "Assessing credit risk in a financial institution's off-balance sheet commitments." *Journal of Financial and Quantitative Analysis*, 24 (1989), pp. 489–501. Also Chapter 10 in this book.

Hull, J. *Options, Futures, and Other Derivative Securities*, Second Edition. Prentice-Hall, Englewood Cliffs, NJ, 1993.

Hull, J., and A. White. "The use of the control variate technique in option pricing." *Journal of Financial and Quantitative Analysis*, 23 (1988), pp. 237–251. Also Chapter 7 in this book.

Hull, J., and A. White. "Valuing derivative securities using the explicit finite difference method." *Journal of Financial and Quantitative Analysis*, 25 (1990), pp. 87–100. Also Chapter 6 in this book.

Johnson, H., and R. Stulz. "The pricing of options under default risk." *Journal of Finance*, 42 (1987), pp. 267–280.

Jonkhart, M. J. L. "On the term structure of interest rates and the risk of default: an analytical approach." *Journal of Banking and Finance*, 3 (1979), pp. 253–262.

Kane, E. J. "Market incompleteness and divergences between forward and future interest rates." *Journal of Finance*, 35 (1980), pp. 221–234.

Litzenberger, R. H. "Swaps: Plain and Fanciful." *Journal of Finance*, 47, 3 (1992), pp. 831–850.

Rodriguez, R. J. "Default risk, yield spreads, and time to maturity." *Journal of Financial and Quantitative Analysis*, 23 (1988), pp. 111–117.

Wall, L. D., and K.-W. Fung. "Evaluating the credit exposure of interest rate swap portfolios." Working Paper 87-8, Federal Reserve Board of Atlanta, 1987.

Yawitz, J. B., K. J. Maloney, and L. H. Ederington. "Taxes, default risk, and yield spreads." *Journal of Finance*, 4 (1985), pp. 1127–1140.

IV

Term Structure Models: Theory

12. Introduction: Term structure theory

The most popular model for valuing European-style interest rate options is Black's (1976) model. This model assumes that, at the maturity of the option, the variable underlying the option (typically an interest rate or a bond price) is lognormally distributed. Define V as the forward value of the variable, X as the strike price of the option, t_1 as the time when the variable is observed for the purposes of determining the payoff, t_2 as the time when the payoff is made, and R as the zero-coupon risk-free rate for maturity t_2. The price c of a European call and the price p of a European put are, respectively,

$$c = [VN(d_1) - XN(d_2)]e^{-Rt_2}, \tag{12.1}$$

$$p = [XN(-d_2) - VN(-d_1)]e^{-Rt_2}, \tag{12.2}$$

where

$$d_1 = \frac{\ln V/X + \frac{1}{2}\sigma_V^2 t_1}{\sigma_V}, \qquad d_2 = \frac{\ln V/X - \frac{1}{2}\sigma_V^2 t_1}{\sigma_V},$$

and σ_V is defined so that $\sigma_V\sqrt{t_1}$ is the standard deviation of logarithm of the variable at time t_1.

Black's model is very versatile. When a caplet is valued, the underlying variable that is assumed to be lognormal is the interest rate that is being capped. When a bond option is valued, it is the bond price at the maturity of the option. When a swap option is valued, it is the swap rate at the maturity of the option. The main disadvantage of Black's model and its extensions is that it can be used only when a derivative depends on a single interest rate observed at a single time. The model provides no linkages between different interest rates and their volatilities. The appropriate value to use for σ_V depends on the option being considered. The model cannot be used for valuing American options and other more complex interest rate derivatives. For these types of instruments, a no-arbitrage model of the term structure is essential.

12.1 APPROACHES TO CONSTRUCTING MODELS OF THE TERM STRUCTURE

There are several different approaches to building a no-arbitrage model of the term structure. Perhaps the simplest is to specify the process followed by zero-coupon bond prices in a risk-neutral world. This is the approach we follow in Chapter 14. Since a zero-coupon bond is a traded security that provides no income, its expected return in a risk-neutral world must be the risk-free interest rate. When there is one factor, we can therefore write the process followed by zero-coupon bonds as[1]

$$dP(t, T) = r(t)P(t, T)\,dt + v(t, T)P(t, T)\,dz, \qquad (12.3)$$

where $P(t, T)$ is the price at time t of a zero-coupon bond maturing at time T, $r(t)$ is the short-term risk-free rate at time t, $v(t, T)$ is the bond price volatility, and dz is a Wiener process. The variable $v(t, T)$ can be a function of past and present bond prices as well as t and T. However, it must satisfy the condition $v(t, t) = 0$ for all t. In other words, a bond's price volatility must decline to zero as the bond approaches maturity.

A second approach to modeling the term structure is to specify the process followed by instantaneous forward rates in a risk-neutral world. When there is one factor, we can write this as

$$dF(t, T) = m(t, T)\,dt + s(t, T)\,dz, \qquad (12.4)$$

where $F(t, T)$ is the instantaneous forward rate at time t for a contract maturing at time T, and $m(t, T)$ and $s(t, T)$ are the drift and instantaneous standard deviation of $F(t, T)$. The variables m and s can be functions of past and present forward rates. But, for an internally consistent model, they must satisfy the condition

$$m(t, T) = s(t, T) \int_t^T s(t, \tau)\,d\tau. \qquad (12.5)$$

This result was first derived by Heath, Jarrow, and Morton (1992). It is shown in Section 14.1 to follow in a straightforward way from the $v(t, t) = 0$ condition on bond price volatilities. A forward rate process is structurally simpler than a bond price process in that it does not usually depend on the short rate r.

The advantage of specifying a model in terms of the processes followed by either bond prices or forward rates is that the model is automatically consistent with the initial term structure. This is because the initial term

---

[1] We make the assumption of one factor for ease of exposition. Our arguments can be extended to accommodate several factors.

218

structure determines the initial values of the variables being modelled. The disadvantage is that the model is usually non-Markov. This makes the model very slow computationally. In a non-Markov model the term at time t depends on the history of the underlying stochastic variables between time zero and time t as well as on their values at time t. Section 14.3 shows that, if the bond price volatility $v(t, T)$ is a function only of t and T, a necessary and sufficient condition for a Markov model is that $v(t, T)$ have the form[2]

$$v(t, T) = x(t)[y(T) - y(t)].$$

A third approach to constructing a term structure model is designed to ensure that a Markov, computationally tractable, model results. It involves defining the model in terms of the process followed by the short rate r in a risk-neutral world. Provided that the drift and volatility of r depend only on the current value of r, the model is always Markov.[3] This model is, by construction, consistent with the initial value of r. However, it is not automatically consistent with the rest of the initial term structure. Some extra work is necessary to ensure consistency. The usual approach is to include in the drift of the process for r a function of time, $\theta(t)$, and then estimate $\theta(t)$ so that the model prices bonds of all maturities correctly at time zero. This may seem *ad hoc*, but it is a reasonable approach. In all no-arbitrage models of the term structure, the average drift of r is a function of t.[4]

12.2 THE EXTENDED VASICEK OR HULL–WHITE MODEL

Chapter 13 describes the properties of the extended Vasicek or Hull–White model. The most general version of the model is

$$dr = [\theta(t) - a(t)r] \, dt + \sigma(t) \, dz. \tag{12.6}$$

There are three functions of time: $\theta(t)$, $a(t)$, and $\sigma(t)$. Each plays a separate role in this model. The function $\theta(t)$ is chosen so that the model exactly matches the initial term structure; the function $\sigma(t)$ defines the volatility of

---

[2] As discussed in Chapter 14, it is of interest to consider models where a bond's price volatility is a function only of t and T, because they lead to analytic valuations of European bond options.

[3] A similar statement does not apply to the models in equations (12.3) and (12.4). For example, even when m and s in equation (12.4) are functions only of t and T, the term structure model is in general still non-Markov.

[4] The average drift rate in r at time t is, to a first approximation, $\partial F(0, t)/\partial t$. For most of the term structures that are encountered in practice, this has a significant dependence on t.

the short rate at future times; the function $a(t)$ defines the relative volatilities of long and short rates.

Equation (12.6) is superficially attractive because the a and σ functions can be chosen so that the prices of a set of caps or swap options (or both) observed in the market at time zero are exactly matched. Unfortunately this has side effects. The pattern of volatilities assumed for rates in the future is liable to be quite different from that assumed today. As a result, non-standard interest rate options can be badly mispriced. This point is discussed further in Chapter 20. This problem with the general extended Vasicek model (which we realized shortly after Chapter 13 was first published) has led us to recommend keeping a and σ constant, so that the model becomes

$$dr = [\theta(t) - ar]\,dt + \sigma\,dz. \tag{12.7}$$

This model can match the prices of caps and swaptions in the market only approximately. However, it does lead to a stationary volatility structure and robust pricing for non-standard interest rate options.

The attractive feature of the models in equations (12.6) and (12.7) is their analytic tractability. The prices of discount bonds have the form

$$P(t, T) = A(t, T)e^{-B(t, T)r(t)}.$$

In the case of the model in equation (12.6), the A and B functions are given by equations (13.13) and (13.14). In the case of the model in equation (12.7), A and B are given by equations (14.21) and (14.22).

It is interesting to note that when it comes to pricing European options on discount bonds the model is consistent with Black's model. The formulas in equations (12.1) and (12.2) apply where V is the forward bond price. For the model in equation (12.6) when $t_1 = t_2 = T$,

$$\sigma_V^2 = \frac{[B(0, s) - B(0, T)]^2}{T} \int_0^T \left[\frac{\sigma(\tau)}{\partial B(0, \tau)/\partial \tau}\right]^2 d\tau,$$

where s is the maturity of the bond underlying the option. For the model in equation (12.7) where a and σ are constant,

$$\sigma_V^2 = \frac{\sigma^2}{2a^3 T}[1 - e^{-a(s-T)}]^2[1 - e^{-2aT}].$$

The model in equation (12.7) becomes the Ho and Lee (1986) model when the reversion rate parameter is set equal to zero. The A and B functions are then given by equations (14.17) and (14.18) and

$$\sigma_V = \sigma(s - T).$$

European options on coupon-bearing bonds can be handled using the approach, originally suggested by Jamshidian (1989), outlined at the end of Section 13.2. A decrease in r at any given time leads to an increase in all discount bond prices, and an increase in r leads to an decrease in all discount bond prices. As a result, an option on a coupon-bearing bond can be decomposed into options on the discount bonds that make up the coupon-bearing bond. The first step is to calculate r^*, the "at-the-money value of r" at the maturity of the option. This is the value of r for which the coupon-bearing bond price equals the strike price. Let X_i be the value at option maturity of the ith discount bond underlying the coupon-bearing bond when $r = r^*$. The option on the coupon-bearing bond is the sum of options on the underlying discount bonds, with the strike price of the option on the ith discount bond being X_i.

12.3 OPTIONS ON CAPS AND FLOORS

A caplet is an option on an interest rate with the payment being one period in arrears. As shown in Section 13.5, it can be expressed as an option on a discount bond and valued using the Hull–White model in a straightforward way. Since a cap is a portfolio of caplets, it can also be valued without difficulty.

Chapter 15 discusses the pricing of options on caps and floors using the Hull–White model. Consider, for example, the pricing of a call option on a cap. This is an option on a portfolio of caplets. We have just discussed how an option on a coupon-bearing bond can be decomposed into a portfolio of options on discount bonds. In the same way, an option on a cap can be decomposed into a portfolio of options on caplets. We first calculate r^*, the value of r that has the property that the value of the cap equals the strike price at the maturity of the option. The strike price for each caplet is then set equal to the value it will have at the maturity of the option if $r = r^*$.

To finish the analysis, it is necessary to derive a formula for an option on a caplet. This is an option on an option on a lognormally distributed asset. The valuation formula is very similar to that derived by Geske (1979) for a compound stock option. It is given by equation (15.8).

12.4 THE EXTENDED COX–INGERSOLL–ROSS MODEL

Chapter 13 analyzes the extended Cox–Ingersoll–Ross model. This model is

$$dr = [\theta(t) - a(t)r]\,dt + \sigma(t)\sqrt{r}\,dz. \tag{12.8}$$

It has some analytic tractability. As in the case of the extended Vasicek model, discount bond prices have the form

$$P(t, T) = A(t, T)e^{-B(t,T)r}.$$

The A and B functions are given by equations (13.26) and (13.27). Equation (13.26) is a partial differential equation that must be solved numerically. There are no analytic expressions for option prices except in the particular case when $\theta(t)$, $a(t)$, and $\sigma(t)$ are all constant.

An unfortunate feature of the extended Cox–Ingersoll–Ross model (which we did not realize until a few months after the first publication of Chapter 13) is that it cannot accommodate situations where $\partial F(0, t)/\partial t$ is significantly negative at some time $t = \tau$ (that is, situations where the term structure of forward rates is significantly downward-sloping at time τ). This is because in this case $\theta(\tau)$ is negative. This makes it possible for the short rate r to become negative and the instantaneous standard deviation of r to be undefined.

An essential property of any model that is selected is that it should be possible to fit it to any initial term structure. It is for this reason that we recommend in Chapter 18 models of the form

$$df(r) = [\theta(t) - af(r)]\,dt + \sigma\,dz,$$

where $f(r)$ is some function of r. When $f(r) = \log r$, the model becomes a version of the Black and Karasinski (1991) model. When $f(r) = \sqrt{r}$, it is a model considered by Pelsser (1996).

References

Black, F. "The pricing of commodity contracts." *Journal of Financial Economics*, 3 (1976), pp. 167–179.

Black, F., and P. Karasinski. "Bond and option pricing when short rates are lognormal." *Financial Analysts Journal*, July–August, 1991, pp. 52–59.

Geske, R. "The valuation of compound options." *Journal of Financial Economics*, 7 (1979), pp. 63–81.

Heath, D., R. Jarrow, and A. Morton. "Bond pricing and the term structure of interest rates: a new methodology for contingent claims evaluation." *Econometrica*, 60 (1992), pp. 77–105.

Ho, T. S. Y., and S.-B. Lee. "Term structure movements and pricing interest rate contingent claims." *Journal of Finance*, 41 (1986), pp. 1011–1029.

Jamshidian, F. "An exact bond option formula." *Journal of Finance*, 44 (1989), pp. 205–209.

Pellser, A. A. J. "Efficient methods for valuing and managing interest rate and other derivative securities." Ph.D. thesis, Erasmus University, Rotterdam.

13. Pricing interest rate derivative securities*

In recent years, interest rate contingent claims such as caps, swaptions, bond options, captions, and mortgage-backed securities have become increasingly popular. The valuation of these instruments is now a major concern of both practitioners and academics.

Practitioners have tended to use different models for valuing different interest rate derivative securities. For example, when valuing caps, they frequently assume that interest rates are lognormal and use Black's (1976) model for valuing options on commodity futures. When valuing European bond options, practitioners often also use Black's (1976) model. However, in this case, bond prices rather than interest rates are assumed to be lognormal. Using different models in different situations has a number of disadvantages. First, there is no easy way of making the volatility parameters in one model consistent with those in another model. Second, it is difficult to aggregate exposures across different interest rate dependent securities. For example, it is difficult to determine the extent to which the volatility exposure of a swaption can be offset by a position in caps. Finally, it is difficult to value non-standard derivatives.

Several models of the term structure have been proposed in the academic literature. Examples are Brennan and Schwartz (1979, 1982), Courtadon (1982), Cox, Ingersoll, and Ross (1985b), Dothan (1978), Langetieg (1980), Longstaff (1989), Richard (1979), and Vasicek (1977). All these models have the advantage that they can be used to value all interest rate contingent claims in a consistent way. Their major disadvantages are that they involve several unobservable parameters and do not provide a perfect fit to the initial term structure of interest rates.

* This paper was first published in *The Review of Financial Studies*, Vol. 3 (1990), pp. 573–592. It is reprinted with the permission of Oxford University Press.

Ho and Lee (1986) pioneered a new approach by showing how an interest rate model can be designed so that it is automatically consistent with any specified initial term structure. Their work has been extended by a number of researchers including Black, Derman, and Toy (1990), Dybvig (1988), and Milne and Turnbull (1989). Heath, Jarrow, and Morton (1987) present a general multi-factor interest rate model that is consistent with the existing term structure of interest rates and any specified volatility structure. Their model provides important theoretical insights, but in its most general form has the disadvantage of being computationally quite time-consuming.

In this paper, we present two one-state-variable models of the short-term interest rate. Both are consistent with both the current term structure of interest rates and the current volatilities of all interest rates. In addition, the volatility of the short-term interest rate can be a function of time. The user of the models can specify either the current volatilities of spot interest rates (which will be referred to as the term structure of spot rate volatilities) or the current volatilities of forward interest rates (which will be referred to as the term structure of forward rate volatilities). The first model is an extension of Vasicek (1977). The second model is an extension of Cox, Ingersoll, and Ross (1985b).

The main contribution of this paper is to show how the process followed by the short-term interest rate in the two models can be deduced from the term structure of interest rates and the term structure of spot or forward interest rate volatilities. The parameters of the process can be determined analytically in the case of the extended Vasicek model and numerically in the case of the extended Cox, Ingersoll, and Ross model. Once the short-term interest rate process has been obtained, either model can be used to value any interest rate contingent claim. European bond options can be valued analytically when the extended Vasicek model is used.

The analytic tractability of the extended Vasicek model makes it very appealing as a practical tool. It is therefore of interest to test whether the option prices given by this model are similar to those given by other models. In this paper we compare the extended Vasicek model with the one-factor Cox–Ingersoll–Ross model and with two different two-factor models. The results are encouraging. They suggest that, if two models are fitted to the same term structure of interest rates and the same term structure of interest rate volatilities, the differences between the option prices produced by the models are small.

The rest of this paper is organized as follows. Section 13.1 outlines the properties of the Vasicek and Cox–Ingersoll–Ross models. Sections 13.2 and 13.3 develop extensions of the two models. Section 13.4 discusses how market data can be used to estimate the unknown functions in the models. Section 13.5 compares the bond option and cap prices calculated using the extended Vasicek model with their true values when interest rates are assumed to follow the one-factor Cox–Ingersoll–Ross model. Section 13.6 compares bond option prices calculated using the extended Vasicek model with the true prices when interest rates are assumed to follow two different two-factor models. Conclusions are in Section 13.7.

13.1 THE VASICEK AND COX–INGERSOLL–ROSS MODELS

A number of authors have proposed one-state-variable models of the term structure in which the short-term interest rate r follows a mean-reverting process of the form

$$dr = a(b - r)\, dt + \sigma r^\beta\, dz, \qquad (13.1)$$

where a, b, σ, and β are positive constants and dz is a Wiener process. In these models, the interest rate r is pulled towards a level b at rate a. Superimposed upon this "pull" is a random term with variance $\sigma^2 r^{2\beta}$ per unit time.

The situations where $\beta = 0$ and $\beta = 0.5$ are of particular interest because they lead to models that are analytically tractable. The $\beta = 0$ case was first considered by Vasicek (1977), who derived an analytic solution for the price of a discount bond. Jamshidian (1989) showed that, for this value of β, it is also possible to derive relatively simple analytic solutions for the prices of European call and put options on both discount bonds and coupon-bearing bonds. One drawback of assuming $\beta = 0$ is that the short-term interest rate r can become negative. Cox, Ingersoll, and Ross consider the alternative $\beta = 0.5$. In this case, r can, in some circumstances, become zero, but it can never become negative. Cox, Ingersoll, and Ross derive analytic solutions for the prices of both discount bonds and European call options on discount bonds.

It is reasonable to conjecture that in some situations the market's expectations about future interest rates involve time-dependent parameters. In other words, the drift rate and volatility of r may be functions of time as well being functions of r and other state variables. The time dependence can arise from the cyclical nature of the economy, expectations concerning the future impact of monetary policies, and expected trends in other macroeconomic variables.

In this paper we extend the model in (13.1) to reflect this time dependence. We add a time-dependent drift $\theta(t)$ to the process for r, and allow both the reversion rate a and the volatility factor σ to be functions of time. This leads to the following model for r:

$$dr = [\theta(t) + a(t)(b - r)] \, dt + \sigma(t)r^\beta \, dz. \qquad (13.2)$$

This can be regarded as a model in which a drift rate $\theta(t)$ is imposed on a variable that would otherwise tend to revert to a constant level b. Since (13.2) can be written

$$dr = a(t)\left[\frac{\theta(t)}{a(t)} + b - r\right] dt + \sigma(t)r^\beta \, dz,$$

it can also be regarded as a model in which the reversion level is a function $\theta(t)/a(t) + b$ of time. We will examine the situations where $\beta = 0$ and $\beta = 0.5$. The $\beta = 0$ case is an extension of Vasicek's model; the $\beta = 0.5$ case is an extension of the Cox–Ingersoll–Ross model. We will show that, when appropriate assumptions are made about the market price of interest rate risk, the model can be fitted to the term structure of interest rates and the term structure of spot or forward rate volatilities.

As shown by Dybvig (1988) and Jamshidian (1988), the continuous time equivalent of the Ho and Lee (1986) model is

$$dr = \theta(t) \, dt + \sigma \, dz.$$

This is the particular case of (13.2) where $\beta = 0$, $a(t) = 0$, and $\sigma(t)$ is constant. If the market price of interest rate risk is a function of time, $\theta(t)$ can chosen so that the model fits the initial term structure of interest rates. The model has the disadvantage that it incorporates no mean reversion; the instantaneous standard deviations of all spot and forward rates are the same.

The continuous-time equivalent of the Black, Derman, and Toy (1990) model can be shown to be

$$d(\log r) = \left[\theta(t) + \frac{\sigma'(t)}{\sigma(t)}\log r\right] dt + \sigma(t) \, dz.$$

In this model $\log r$ is mean reverting. The function $\sigma(t)$ is chosen to make the model consistent with the term structure of spot rate volatilities and may not give reasonable values for the future short rate volatility. The model has the disadvantage that neither bond prices nor European bond option prices can be determined analytically.

13.2 THE EXTENDED VASICEK MODEL

Our proposed extension of Vasicek's model is given by (13.2) with $\beta = 0$:

$$dr = [\theta(t) + a(t)(b - r)]\,dt + \sigma(t)\,dz. \tag{13.3}$$

We will assume that the market price of interest rate risk is a function $\lambda(t)$ of time that is bounded in any interval $(0, \tau)$.[1] From Cox, Ingersoll, and Ross (1985a), this means that the price f of any contingent claim dependent on r must satisfy

$$f_t + [\phi(t) - a(t)r]f_r + \tfrac{1}{2}\sigma(t)^2 f_{rr} - rf = 0, \tag{13.4}$$

where

$$\phi(t) = a(t)b + \theta(t) - \lambda(t)\sigma(t).$$

The price of a discount bond that pays off \$1 at time T is the solution to (13.4) that satisfies the boundary condition $f = 1$ when $t = T$. Consider the function

$$f = A(t, T)e^{-B(t,T)r}. \tag{13.5}$$

This satisfies (13.4) and the boundary condition when

$$A_t - \phi(t)AB + \tfrac{1}{2}\sigma(t)^2 AB^2 = 0 \tag{13.6}$$

and

$$B_t - a(t)B + 1 = 0, \tag{13.7}$$

with

$$A(T, T) = 1, \qquad B(T, T) = 0. \tag{13.8}$$

It follows that if (13.6) and (13.7) are solved subject to the boundary conditions in (13.8) then equation (13.5) provides the price of a discount bond maturing at time T. Solving (13.6) and (13.7) for the situation where $a(t)$, $\phi(t)$, and $\sigma(t)$ are constant leads to the Vasicek bond-pricing formula:

$$B(t, T) = \frac{1 - e^{-a(T-t)}}{a},$$

$$A(t, T) = \exp\left[\frac{(B(t, T) - T + t)(a\phi - \sigma^2/2)}{a^2} - \frac{\sigma^2 B(t, T)^2}{4a}\right].$$

[1] This corresponds to the assumption made by Vasicek. In fact, the same final model is obtained if the market price of interest rate risk is set equal to $\lambda(t)r$ or even if it is set equal to $\lambda_1(t) + \lambda_2(t)r$. If $\chi(r, t)$ is the market price of risk, Girsanov's theorem shows that, for no arbitrage, the condition $E[\exp(\tfrac{1}{2}\int_0^T \chi^2\,ds)] < \infty$ must hold. Duffie (1988: p. 229) provides a discussion of this. The function $\chi(r, t) = \lambda_1(t) + \lambda_2(t)r$ presents no problems as far as this condition is concerned if we assume $\lambda_1(t)$ and $\lambda_2(t)$ are always bounded in any interval $(0, \tau)$.

The function $\sigma(t)$ in the extended model should be chosen to reflect the current and future volatilities of the short-term interest rate r. As shown below, $A(0, T)$ and $B(0, T)$ are defined by $\sigma(0)$, the current term structure of interest rates, and the current term structure of spot or forward interest rate volatilities. The first step in the analysis is therefore to determine $a(t)$, $\phi(t)$, $A(t, T)$, and $B(t, T)$ in terms of $A(0, T)$, $B(0, T)$, and $\sigma(t)$.

Differentiating (13.6) and (13.7) with respect to T, we obtain

$$A_{tT} - \phi(t)[A_T B + AB_T] + \tfrac{1}{2}\sigma(t)^2[A_T B^2 + 2ABB_T] = 0, \qquad (13.9)$$

$$B_{tT} - a(t)B_T = 0. \qquad (13.10)$$

Eliminating $a(t)$ from (13.7) and (13.10) gives

$$B_t B_T - BB_{tT} + B_T = 0. \qquad (13.11)$$

Eliminating $\phi(t)$ from (13.6) and (13.9) yields

$$ABA_{tT} - BA_t A_T - AA_t B_T + \tfrac{1}{2}\sigma(t)^2 A^2 B^2 B_T = 0. \qquad (13.12)$$

The boundary conditions for (13.11) and (13.12) are the known values of $A(0, T)$ and $B(0, T)$, $A(T, T) = 1$, and $B(T, T) = 0$. The solutions to (13.11) and (13.12) that satisfy these boundary conditions are

$$B(t, T) = \frac{B(0, T) - B(0, t)}{\partial B(0, t)/\partial t}, \qquad (13.13)$$

$$\hat{A}(t, T) = \hat{A}(0, T) - \hat{A}(0, t) - B(t, T)\frac{\partial \hat{A}(0, t)}{\partial t}$$

$$- \frac{1}{2}\left[B(t, T)\frac{\partial B(0, t)}{\partial t}\right]^2 \int_0^t \left[\frac{\sigma(\tau)}{\partial B(0, \tau)/\partial \tau}\right]^2 d\tau, \qquad (13.14)$$

where $\hat{A}(t, T) = \log[A(t, T)]$. Substituting into (13.6) and (13.7), we obtain

$$a(t) = -\frac{\partial^2 B(0, t)/\partial t^2}{\partial B(0, t)/\partial t}, \qquad (13.15)$$

$$\phi(t) = -a(t)\frac{\partial \hat{A}(0, t)}{\partial t} - \frac{\partial^2 \hat{A}(0, t)}{\partial t^2} + \left[\frac{\partial B(0, t)}{\partial t}\right]^2 \int_0^t \left[\frac{\sigma(\tau)}{\partial B(0, \tau)/\partial \tau}\right]^2 d\tau.$$

$$(13.16)$$

We now move on to discuss option valuation under the extended Vasicek model. Define $P(r, t_1, t_2)$ as the price at time t_1 of a discount bond maturing at time t_2. From the above analysis,

$$P(r, t_1, t_2) = A(t_1, t_2)e^{-B(t_1, t_2)r}.$$

Using Ito's lemma, the volatility of $P(r, t_1, t_2)$ is $\sigma(t_1)B(t_1, t_2)$. Since this is independent of r, the distribution of a bond price at any given time conditional on its price at an earlier time must be lognormal.

Consider a European call option on a discount bond with exercise price X. Suppose that the current time is t, the option expires at time T, and the bond expires at time s ($s \geq T \geq t$). The call option can be regarded as an option to exchange X units of a discount bond maturing at time T for one unit of a discount bond maturing at time s. Define $\alpha_1(\tau)$ and $\alpha_2(\tau)$ as the volatilities at time τ of the prices of discount bonds maturing at times T and s, respectively, and $\rho(\tau)$ as the instantaneous correlation between the two bond prices. From the lognormal property mentioned above and the results in Merton (1973), it follows that the option price C is given by

$$C = P(r, t, s)N(h) - XP(r, t, T)N(h - \sigma_P), \qquad (13.17)$$

where

$$h = \frac{1}{\sigma_P} \log \frac{P(r, t, s)}{P(r, t, T)X} + \frac{\sigma_P}{2},$$

$$\sigma_P^2 = \int_t^T [\alpha_1(\tau)^2 - 2\rho(\tau)\alpha_1(\tau)\alpha_2(\tau) + \alpha_2(\tau)^2] \, d\tau, \qquad (13.18)$$

and $N(\cdot)$ is the cumulative normal distribution function. Since we are using a one-factor model, $\rho = 1$. Furthermore,

$$\alpha_1(\tau) = \sigma(\tau)B(\tau, s), \qquad \alpha_2(\tau) = \sigma(\tau)B(\tau, T).$$

Hence,

$$\sigma_P^2 = \int_t^T \sigma(\tau)^2 [B(\tau, s) - B(\tau, T)]^2 \, d\tau.$$

From (13.13) this becomes

$$\sigma_P^2 = [B(0, s) - B(0, T)]^2 \int_t^T \left[\frac{\sigma(\tau)}{\partial B(0, \tau)/\partial \tau} \right]^2 d\tau. \qquad (13.19)$$

Equations (13.17) and (13.19), provide a simple analytic solution for European call option prices. European put option prices can be obtained using put–call parity. In the case where a and σ are constant,

$$B(\tau, s) = \frac{1 - e^{-a(s-\tau)}}{a}, \qquad B(\tau, T) = \frac{1 - e^{-a(T-\tau)}}{a},$$

and (13.19) becomes

$$\sigma_P = v(t, T) \frac{1 - e^{-a(s-T)}}{a},$$

where

$$v(t, T)^2 = \frac{\sigma^2(1 - e^{-2a(T-t)})}{2a}.$$

This is the result in Jamshidian (1989). It is interesting to note that Jamshidian's result does not depend on $\theta(t)$ and $\lambda(t)$ being constant.

To value European options on coupon-bearing bonds, we note (similarly to Jamshidian (1989)) that, since all bond prices are decreasing functions of r, an option on a portfolio of discount bonds is equivalent to a portfolio of options on the discount bonds with appropriate exercise prices.[2] Consider a European call option with exercise price X and maturity T on a coupon-bearing bond that pays off c_i at a time $s_i > T$ ($1 \leq i \leq n$). The option will be exercised when $r(T) < r^*$, where r^* is the solution to

$$\sum_{i=1}^{n} c_i P(r^*, T, s_i) = X.$$

The payoff from the option is

$$\max\left[0, \sum_{i=1}^{n} c_i P(r, T, s_i) - X\right].$$

This is the same as

$$\sum_{i=1}^{n} c_i \max[0, P(r, T, s_i) - X_i],$$

where

$$X_i = P(r^*, T, s_i).$$

The option on the coupon-bearing bond is therefore the sum of n options on discount bonds with the exercise price of the ith option being X_i.

American bond options and other interest rate contingent claims can be valued by first calculating $a(t)$ and $\phi(t)$ from (13.15) and (13.16) and then using numerical procedures to solve the differential equation in (13.4) subject to the appropriate boundary conditions. One approach that can be used is described in Hull and White (1990).

13.3 THE EXTENDED COX–INGERSOLL–ROSS MODEL

Our proposed extension of the Cox–Ingersoll–Ross model is given by

---

[2] This argument can be used to value options on coupon-bearing bonds in other one-state-variable models. Later in this paper we will use it in conjunction with the Cox–Ingersoll–Ross model.

(13.2) with $\beta = 0.5$:

$$dr = [\theta(t) + a(t)(b - r)]\, dt + \sigma(t)\sqrt{r}\, dz.$$

We assume that the market price of interest rate risk is $\lambda(t)\sqrt{r}$ for some function λ of time that is bounded in any interval $(0, \tau)$.[3]

The differential equation that must be satisfied by the price f of any claim contingent on r is

$$f_t + [\phi(t) - \psi(t)r]f_r + \tfrac{1}{2}\sigma(t)^2 r f_{rr} - rf = 0, \tag{13.20}$$

where

$$\phi(t) = a(t)b + \theta(t) \quad \text{and} \quad \psi(t) = a(t) + \lambda(t)\sigma(t).$$

Again, we consider the function

$$f = A(t, T)e^{-B(t,T)r}. \tag{13.21}$$

This satisfies (13.20) when

$$A_t - \phi(t)AB = 0 \tag{13.22}$$

and

$$B_t - \psi(t)B - \tfrac{1}{2}\sigma(t)^2 B^2 + 1 = 0. \tag{13.23}$$

If A and B are the solutions to the ordinary differential equations (13.22) and (13.23) subject to the boundary conditions $A(T, T) = 1$ and $B(T, T) = 0$, equation (13.21) gives the price at time t of a discount bond maturing at time T. Solving (13.22) and (13.23) for the situation where $\phi(t)$, $\psi(t)$, and $\sigma(t)$ are constants leads to the Cox–Ingersoll–Ross bond-pricing formula:

$$B(t, T) = \frac{2(e^{\gamma(T-t)} - 1)}{(\gamma + \psi)(e^{\gamma(T-t)} - 1) + 2\gamma}, \tag{13.24}$$

$$A(t, T) = \left[\frac{2\gamma e^{(\gamma+\psi)(T-t)/2}}{(\gamma + \psi)(e^{\gamma(T-t)} - 1) + 2\gamma}\right]^{2\phi/\sigma^2}, \tag{13.25}$$

where

$$\gamma = \sqrt{(\psi^2 + 2\sigma^2)}.$$

The function $\sigma(t)$ in the extended model should be chosen to reflect the current and future volatilities of the short-term interest rate. As in the case of the extended Vasicek model, $A(0, T)$ and $B(0, T)$ can be

[3] This corresponds to the assumption made by the Cox–Ingersoll–Ross model. It is interesting to note that a market price of risk equal to $\lambda(t)/\sqrt{r}$ appears to give rise to the same final model as $\lambda(t)\sqrt{r}$. However, it violates the no-arbitrage condition referred to in footnote 1.

determined from $\sigma(0)$, the current term structure of interest rates, and the current term structure of interest rate volatilities. These, together with the conditions $A(T, T) = 1$ and $B(T, T) = 0$, are the boundary conditions for determining $A(t, T)$ and $B(t, T)$ from (13.22) and (13.23).

Differentiating (13.23) with respect to T and eliminating $\psi(t)$, we obtain

$$B_t B_T - B B_{tT} + B_T + \tfrac{1}{2}\sigma(t)^2 B^2 B_T = 0. \tag{13.26}$$

This equation can be solved using finite difference methods. The function $\psi(t)$ can then be obtained from (13.23). The solution to (13.22) is

$$A(t, T) = A(0, T) \exp\left[\int_0^t \phi(s) B(s, T)\, ds\right]. \tag{13.27}$$

Since $A(T, T) = 1$, $\phi(t)$ can be obtained iteratively from

$$\int_0^T \phi(s) B(s, T)\, ds = -\log A(0, T).$$

It does not appear to be possible to obtain European option prices analytically except when ϕ, ψ, and σ are constant. All option prices must therefore be computed using numerical procedures such as those in Hull and White (1990).

13.4 FITTING THE MODELS TO MARKET DATA

In order to apply the models, it is necessary to estimate the functions $A(0, T)$ and $B(0, T)$. The appendix derives results showing how the $B(0, T)$ function is related to the term structure of spot and forward rate volatilities. Historical data can be used in conjunction with these results to estimate this function. We can calculate $A(0, T)$ from $B(0, T)$ and the current term structure of interest rates using the bond-pricing equation

$$P\big(r(0), 0, T\big) = A(0, T) e^{-B(0, T) r(0)},$$

where $r(0)$ is the short-term interest rate at time zero.

An alternative approach to using historical data is to imply $A(0, T)$ and $B(0, T)$ from the term structure of interest rates and the prices of options. Caps are actively traded options that are particularly convenient for this purpose. In the case of the extended Vasicek model they allow $B(0, T)$ to be implied directly in a relatively straightforward way.[4]

---

[4] As will be explained later, a cap is a portfolio of European put options on discount bonds. A matrix of cap prices can be used in conjunction equations (13.17) and (13.19) and put–call parity to obtain best-fit values for points on the $B(0, T)$ function.

An interesting question is whether the functions $A(t, T)$ and $B(t, T)$ estimated at some time τ_1 are the same as those estimated at another time τ_2 ($\tau_1, \tau_2 < t < T$). In other words, does the same model describe the term structure of interest rates and the term structure of interest rate volatilities at two different times? If it is found that the functions $A(t, T)$ and $B(t, T)$ change significantly over time, it would be tempting to dismiss the model as being a "throw-away" of no practical value. However, this would be a mistake. It is important to distinguish between the goal of developing a model that adequately describes term structure movements and the goal of developing a model that adequately values most of the interest rate contingent claims that are encountered in practice. It is quite possible that a two- or three-state-variable model is necessary to achieve the first goal.[5] Later in this paper we will present evidence supporting the argument that the extended Vasicek one-state-variable model achieves the second goal.

In this context it is useful to draw an analogy between the models used to describe stock price behavior and our proposed model for interest rates. The usual model of stock price behavior is the one-factor geometric Brownian motion model. This leads to the Black and Scholes (1973) stock option pricing model, which has stood the test of time and appears to be adequate for most purposes. Since stock price volatilities are in practice stochastic, we cannot claim that a one-factor model perfectly represents stock price behavior. Indeed, practitioners, when they use the Black–Scholes model, frequently adjust the value of the volatility parameter to reflect current market conditions. The justification for the Black–Scholes model is that, when fitted as well as possible to current market data, it gives similar option prices to more complicated two-state-variable models.[6] Our justification of the one-factor models we have presented here will be similar.[7]

Another interesting issue is whether the choice of the $\sigma(t)$ function affects the shape of the current term structure of interest rate volatilities. Suppose that $R(r, t, T)$ is the yield at time t on a discount bond maturing

[5] In fact, empirical research in Dybvig (1988) shows that a one-factor Vasicek-type model provides a surprisingly good fit to observed term structure movements.

[6] See Hull and White (1987) for a comparison of Black–Scholes with a two-factor stock option pricing model that incorporates stochastic volatility.

[7] When using Black–Scholes, practitioners monitor their exposure to changes in the volatility parameter even though the model assumes that the parameter is constant. Similarly, when using the models suggested here, practitioners should monitor their exposure to (a) all possible shifts in the term structure of interest rates (not just those that are consistent with the model) and (b) all possible shifts in the term structure of volatilities.

at time T. Ito's lemma shows that the instantaneous standard deviation of R in the general model of equation (13.2) is $\sigma(t)r^{\beta}\,\partial R/\partial r$. In the extended Vasicek model ($\beta = 0$), $\partial R/\partial r$ is independent of $\sigma(t)$. The function $\sigma(t)$ therefore affects the instantaneous standard deviations of all discount yields equally and has no effect on the shape of the term structure of instantaneous standard deviations. When $\beta \neq 0$, the shape of the term structure of instantaneous standard deviations is affected by $\sigma(t)$ to the extent that $\partial R/\partial r$ is affected by the path followed by σ between t and T.[8]

13.5 COMPARISONS OF ONE-FACTOR MODELS

Of the two models proposed in this paper, the extended Vasicek model is particularly attractive because of its analytic tractability. A key question is whether it gives similar prices to other models when $A(0, T)$ and $B(0, T)$ are fitted to the initial term structure of interest rates and the initial term structure of interest rate volatilities, and $\sigma(t)$ is chosen to match the expected future instantaneous standard deviation of the short rate. In this section, we compare the bond option prices and cap prices produced by the extended Vasicek model with those produced by the original one-factor Cox–Ingersoll–Ross model. We also calculate volatilities implied by these prices when Black's model is used.

Assume that ϕ, ψ, and σ are the parameters of the Cox–Ingersoll–Ross model and that this model describes the true evolution of the term structure. This means that the $A(0, T)$ and $B(0, T)$ functions that would be estimated for the extended Vasicek model from historical data are

$$A(0, T) = \left[\frac{2\gamma e^{(\gamma+\psi)T/2}}{(\gamma + \psi)(e^{\gamma T} - 1) + 2\gamma}\right]^{2\phi/\sigma^2}, \qquad (13.28)$$

$$B(0, T) = \frac{2(e^{\gamma T} - 1)}{(\gamma + \psi)(e^{\gamma T} - 1) + 2\gamma}, \qquad (13.29)$$

where $\gamma = \sqrt{(\psi^2 + 2\sigma^2)}$. The complete A and B functions for the extended Vasicek model can be calculated from $A(0, T)$ and $B(0, T)$ using (13.13) and (13.14). Equations (13.17) and (13.19) can be used to value European options on discount bonds. The analytic results in Cox, Ingersoll, and Ross (1985b) can be used to obtain the true European option prices.

The parameter values chosen were $\sigma = 0.06$, $\phi = 0.02$, and $\psi = 0.2$. The initial short-term interest rate was assumed to be 10% per annum.

---

[8] In most circumstances we can expect $\partial R/\partial r$ to be relatively insensitive to the path followed by $\sigma(t)$.

TABLE 13.1. Prices of call options on a five-year bond with a face value of $100 and a coupon of 10% per annum paid semi-annually.

Option maturity (years)	Model	Exercise price				
		95.0	97.5	100.0	102.5	105.0
0.5	Ext Vas	4.27 (4.50)	2.30 (4.51)	0.94 (4.51)	0.27 (4.52)	0.05 (4.52)
	CIR	4.30 (4.73)	2.32 (4.63)	0.94 (4.52)	0.25 (4.40)	0.04 (4.28)
1.0	Ext Vas	4.28 (4.05)	2.51 (4.05)	1.23 (4.05)	0.50 (4.06)	0.16 (4.06)
	CIR	4.32 (4.27)	2.54 (4.17)	1.24 (4.06)	0.46 (3.94)	0.13 (3.82)
1.5	Ext Vas	4.20 (3.59)	2.54 (3.59)	1.33 (3.60)	0.59 (3.60)	0.22 (3.60)
	CIR	4.25 (3.81)	2.59 (3.71)	1.33 (3.60)	0.55 (3.49)	0.17 (3.37)
2.0	Ext Vas	4.06 (3.13)	2.48 (3.13)	1.31 (3.14)	0.58 (3.14)	0.22 (3.14)
	CIR	4.12 (3.35)	2.52 (3.25)	1.31 (3.14)	0.54 (3.03)	0.17 (2.91)
3.0	Ext Vas	3.68 (2.18)	2.16 (2.19)	1.05 (2.19)	0.40 (2.19)	0.12 (2.19)
	CIR	3.73 (2.39)	2.21 (2.20)	1.05 (2.19)	0.36 (2.08)	0.08 (1.96)
4.0	Ext Vas	3.31 (1.16)	1.74 (1.16)	0.59 (1.16)	0.11 (1.16)	0.01 (1.16)
	CIR	3.32 (1.34)	1.77 (1.26)	0.60 (1.16)	0.08 (1.05)	0.00 (0.89)

The current short-term interest rate is 10% per annum. Interest rates are assumed to follow the original Cox–Ingersoll–Ross model with $\sigma = 0.06$, $\phi = 0.02$, and $\psi = 0.2$. The extended Vasicek (Ext Vas) model is chosen to fit the initial term structure of interest rates and the initial term structure of interest rate volatilities. Numbers in parentheses are the forward bond price volatilities (% per annum) implied from the option prices when Black's model is used.

For the extended Vasicek model, $\sigma(t)$ was set equal to the constant $0.06\sqrt{0.1}$. This ensured that the initial short-term interest rate volatility equaled that in the Cox–Ingersoll–Ross model.

(a) Bond Options

Table 13.1 shows the prices given by the two models for European call options on a five-year bond that has a face value of $100 and pays a coupon of 10% per annum semi-annually.[9] It can be seen that the models give very similar prices for a range of different exercise prices and maturity dates. The biggest percentage differences are for deep-out-of-the-money options. The extended Vasicek model gives higher prices than Cox–Ingersoll–Ross for these options. This is because very low interest rates (and, therefore, very high bond prices) have a greater chance of occurring in the extended Vasicek model.

Since Black's model is frequently used by practitioners to value bond

[9] For both models, the bond option was decomposed into discount bond options using the approach described in Section 13.2.

options, it is interesting to compare it with the two models.[10] The numbers in parentheses in Table 13.1 are the forward bond price volatilities implied by the option prices when Black's model is used. It will be noted that the implied volatilities decline dramatically as the time to expiration of the option increases. In the limit, when the expiration date of the option equals the maturity date of the bond, the implied volatility is zero. For the extended Vasicek model, implied volatilities are roughly constant across different exercise prices. This is because the bond price distributions are approximately lognormal.[11] Under the Cox–Ingersoll–Ross model, the implied volatilities are a decreasing function of the exercise price. If the same volatility is used in Black's model for all bond options with a certain expiration date, there will be a tendency under a Cox–Ingersoll–Ross type economy for in-the-money options to be underpriced and out-of-the-money options to be overpriced.

(b) Interest Rate Caps

Consider an option that caps the interest rate on $1 at R_X between times t_1 and t_2. The payoff from the option at time t_2 is

$$\Delta t \max(R - R_X, 0),$$

where $\Delta t = t_2 - t_1$ and R is the actual interest rate at time t_1 for the time period (t_1, t_2). (Both R and R_X are assumed to be compounded once during the time period.)

The discounted value of this payoff is equivalent to

$$(1 + R_X \Delta t) \max\left[\frac{1}{1 + R_X \Delta t} - \frac{1}{1 + R \Delta t}, 0\right]$$

at time t_1. Since $1/(1 + R \Delta t)$ is the value at time t_1 of a bond maturing at time t_2, this expression shows that the option can be regarded as $1 + R_X \Delta t$ European puts with exercise price $1/(1 + R_X \Delta t)$ and expiration date t_1 on a $1 face value discount bond maturing at time t_2. More generally, an interest rate cap is a portfolio of European puts on discount bonds.

Table 13.2 shows the prices given by the two models for caps on the risk-free interest rate when the principal is $100. Again we see that the

[10] Black's model assumes that forward bond prices are lognormal. In the case of options on discount bonds, it is equivalent to the extended Vasicek model, but does not provide a framework within which the volatilities of different forward bond prices can be related to each other.

[11] For a discount bond, the bond price distribution is exactly lognormal. For a coupon-bearing bond, it is the sum of lognormal distributions.

238

TABLE 13.2. Prices of caps on the risk-free interest rate when the principal is $100, interest payments are made every 6 months, and the cap rate is compounded semi-annually.

Life of cap (years)	Model	Cap rate (% per annum)				
		8.0	9.0	10.0	11.0	12.0
1.0	Ext Vas	2.10 (19.68)	1.21 (18.63)	0.41 (17.73)	0.10 (16.94)	0.02 (16.24)
	CIR	2.09 (18.56)	1.20 (18.11)	0.41 (17.72)	0.10 (17.36)	0.03 (17.04)
2.0	Ext Vas	4.05 (18.42)	2.47 (17.59)	1.13 (16.81)	0.45 (16.04)	0.16 (15.27)
	CIR	4.03 (17.30)	2.45 (17.08)	1.13 (16.80)	0.47 (16.46)	0.19 (16.07)
3.0	Ext Vas	5.86 (17.42)	3.70 (16.70)	1.89 (15.99)	0.87 (15.25)	0.37 (14.48)
	CIR	5.82 (16.32)	3.66 (16.20)	1.89 (16.00)	0.91 (15.66)	0.43 (15.26)
4.0	Ext Vas	7.52 (16.57)	4.85 (15.92)	2.62 (15.28)	1.30 (14.56)	0.61 (13.79)
	CIR	7.44 (15.49)	4.79 (15.44)	2.63 (15.28)	1.36 (14.97)	0.69 (14.56)
5.0	Ext Vas	9.03 (15.82)	5.90 (15.24)	3.31 (14.64)	1.72 (13.95)	0.84 (13.19)
	CIR	8.92 (14.76)	5.83 (14.77)	3.32 (14.65)	1.80 (14.36)	0.95 (13.95)

The current short-term interest rate is 10% per annum. Interest rates are assumed to follow the original Cox–Ingersoll–Ross model with $\sigma = 0.06$, $\phi = 0.02$, and $\psi = 0.2$. The extended Vasicek (Ext Vas) model is chosen to fit the initial term structure of interest rates and the initial term structure of interest rate volatilities. The numbers in parentheses are the forward rate volatilities implied by the cap prices when Black's model is used. The same volatility is applied to all forward interest rates for the purposes of the calculations underlying this table.

prices are very close for a range of different cap rates and maturities. The percentage differences between the prices are greatest for deep-out-of-the-money caps. The Cox–Ingersoll–Ross model gives higher prices than extended Vasicek for these caps. This is because very high interest rates have a greater chance of occurring under the Cox–Ingersoll–Ross model.

Practitioners frequently use Black's (1976) model for valuing caps. The numbers in parentheses in Table 13.2 show the forward rate volatilities implied by the cap prices when Black's model is used. It can be seen that the implied volatilities decrease as the life of the cap increases for both the extended Vasicek and Cox–Ingersoll–Ross models. This is a reflection of the fact that the mean reversion of interest rates causes the volatility of a forward rate to decrease as the maturity of the forward contract increases. Implied volatilities also decrease as the cap rate increases for both models. This means that, if the same volatility is used for all caps with a certain life, there will be a tendency for Black's model to underprice in-the-money caps and overprice out-of-the-money caps.

13.6 COMPARISON WITH TWO-FACTOR MODELS

In this section we test how well the extended Vasicek model can duplicate the bond option prices given by a two-factor model. We consider two different models. The first is a two-factor Vasicek model where the risk-neutral process for r is

$$r = x_1 + x_2, \qquad dx_i = (\phi_i - a_i x_i)\,dt + \sigma_i\,dz_i \quad (i = 1, 2). \qquad (13.30)$$

We choose $\phi_2 = a_2 = 0$. This means that σ_2 equals the long-term rate's instantaneous standard deviation. The second model is a two-factor Cox–Ingersoll–Ross model where the risk-neutral process for r is

$$r = x_1 + x_2, \qquad dx_i = (\phi_i - \psi_i x_i)\,dt + \sigma_i\sqrt{x_i}\,dz_i \quad (i = 1, 2). \quad (13.31)$$

These types of models were analyzed by Langetieg (1980). In both cases we assume zero correlation between dz_1 and dz_2.

Discount bond prices for both models are given by

$$P(r, t, T) = P_1(x_1, t, T)P_2(x_2, t, T),$$

where

$$P_i(x_i, t, T) = A_i(t, T)e^{-B_i(t,T)x_i}$$

denotes the price of a bond under the corresponding constant parameter one-factor model when the short-term rate is x_i. When the extended Vasicek model is fitted to the two-factor Vasicek model,

$$\sigma(0) = \sqrt{(\sigma_1^2 + \sigma_2^2)}$$

and

$$\sigma(0)B(0, T) = \sqrt{[\sigma_1^2 B_1(0, T)^2 + \sigma_2^2 B_2(0, T)^2]}.$$

When it is fitted to the two-factor Cox–Ingersoll–Ross model,

$$\sigma(0) = \sqrt{(\sigma_1^2 x_1 + \sigma_2^2 x_2)}$$

and

$$\sigma(0)B(0, T) = \sqrt{[\sigma_1^2 x_1 B_1(0, T)^2 + \sigma_2^2 x_2 B_2(0, T)^2]}.$$

In both cases the prices of European call options on discount bonds can be calculated using (13.17) and (13.19). We assume that $\sigma(t)$ is constant.

For the two-factor Vasicek model the prices of a European call options

TABLE 13.3. Values of European call options on a five-year discount bond with a face value of $100.

Option maturity (years)	Model	Exercise price				
		0.96	0.98	1.00	1.02	1.04
1.0	Ext Vas	2.80	1.93	1.24	0.74	0.40
	Two-factor Vas	2.80	1.93	1.24	0.73	0.40
2.0	Ext Vas	2.86	2.00	1.32	0.81	0.46
	Two-factor Vas	2.85	1.99	1.31	0.80	0.46
3.0	Ext Vas	2.69	1.79	1.08	0.59	0.29
	Two-factor Vas	2.69	1.78	1.07	0.58	0.28
4.0	Ext Vas	2.47	1.41	0.63	0.20	0.04
	Two-factor Vas	2.47	1.40	0.62	0.20	0.04

Interest rates are assumed to follow the two-factor Vasicek model described by equation (13.30). The parameter values are $\phi_1 = 0.005$, $a_1 = 0.1$, $\sigma_1 = 0.01$, $\sigma_2 = 0.01$, $\phi_2 = 0$, $a_2 = 0$, and the initial values of both x_1 and x_2 are 0.05. The extended Vasicek (Ext Vas) model is chosen to fit the initial term structure of interest rates and the initial term structure of interest rate volatilities. The exercise price is expressed as a proportion of the forward bond price.

TABLE 13.4. Values of European call options on a five-year discount bond with a face value of $100.

Option maturity (years)	Model	Exercise price				
		0.96	0.98	1.00	1.02	1.04
1.0	Ext Vas	2.54	1.55	0.81	0.35	0.12
	Two-factor CIR	2.55	1.56	0.81	0.34	0.11
2.0	Ext Vas	2.56	1.60	0.87	0.40	0.15
	Two-factor CIR	2.58	1.61	0.86	0.38	0.13
3.0	Ext Vas	2.49	1.47	0.71	0.27	0.08
	Two-factor CIR	2.51	1.48	0.70	0.24	0.06
4.0	Ext Vas	2.43	1.27	0.41	0.06	0.00
	Two-factor CIR	2.44	1.28	0.40	0.05	0.00

Interest rates are assumed to follow the two-factor Cox–Ingersoll–Ross model described by equation (13.31). The parameter values are $\phi_1 = 0.05$, $\phi_2 = 0.05$, $\sigma_1 = 0.03$, $\sigma_2 = 0.03$, $\psi_1 = 0.1$, $\psi_2 = 0.001$, and the initial values of both x_1 and x_2 are 0.05. The extended Vasicek (Ext Vas) model is chosen to fit the initial term structure of interest rates and the initial term structure of interest rate volatilities. The exercise price is expressed as a proportion of the forward bond price.

on discount bonds are given by (13.17) with[12]

$$\sigma_P^2 = \left[v_1(t, T) \frac{1 - e^{-a_1(s-T)}}{a_1} \right]^2 + \left[v_2(t, T) \frac{1 - e^{-a_2(s-T)}}{a_2} \right]^2,$$

where

$$v_i(t, T)^2 = \frac{\sigma_i^2(1 - e^{-2a_i(T-t)})}{2a_i} \quad (i = 1, 2).$$

To compute option prices under the two-factor Cox–Ingersoll–Ross model, we used Monte Carlo simulation in conjunction with the antithetic variable technique. Each price was based on a total of 40,000 runs and the maximum standard error was 0.0043.

The results are shown in Tables 13.3 and 13.4. The extended Vasicek model produces prices that are very close to those of the other models. Other tests similar to those reported here have been carried out. In all cases we find that the extended Vasicek model provides a good analytic approximation to other more complicated models.

13.7 CONCLUSIONS

This paper has shown that the Vasicek and Cox–Ingersoll–Ross interest rate models can be extended so that they are consistent with both the current term structure of spot or forward interest rates and the current term structure of interest rate volatilities. In the case of the extension to Vasicek's model, the parameters of the process followed by the short-term interest rate and European bond option prices can be determined analytically. This makes the model very attractive as a practical tool.

The extended Vasicek model can be compared to another interest rate model by fitting it to the initial term structure of interest rates, the initial term structure of interest rate volatilities, and the expected future instantaneous standard deviation of short rate volatilities given by the other model, and then testing to see whether the interest rate option prices it gives are significantly different from those of the other model. We have tested it against a variety of different one- and two-factor models in this way. Our conclusion is that it provides a good analytic approximation to the European option prices given by these other models.

[12] Note that an option on a coupon-bearing bond cannot be decomposed into a portfolio of options on discount bonds in the case of the two-factor models considered here.

APPENDIX

In this appendix we derive the relationship between $B(t, T)$ and the current term structure of spot rate and forward rate volatilities. As is the usual convention, the term "volatility" will be used to refer to the standard deviation of proportional changes, not actual changes, in the value of a variable.

Define

$P(r, t, T)$: price at time t of a discount bond maturing at time T;

$R(r, t, T)$: continuously compounded interest rate at time t applicable to period (t, T);

$F(r, t, T_1, T_2)$: instantaneous forward rate at time t corresponding to the time period (T_1, T_2);

$\sigma_r(r, t)$: volatility of r at time t;

$\sigma_R(r, t, T)$: volatility of $R(r, t, T)$;

$\sigma_F(r, t, T_1, T_2)$: volatility of $F(r, t, T_1, T_2)$.

In both models, P has the functional form

$$P(r, t, T) = A(t, T)e^{-B(t, T)r}. \tag{A1}$$

Since

$$R(r, t, T) = -\frac{1}{T - t} \ln P(r, t, T),$$

it follows that

$$R(r, t, T) = -\frac{1}{T - t}[\ln A(t, T) - rB(t, T)]$$

and

$$\frac{\partial R(r, t, T)}{\partial r} = \frac{B(t, T)}{T - t}.$$

From Ito's lemma,

$$R(r, t, T)\sigma_R(r, t, T) = r\sigma_r(r, t)\frac{\partial R(r, t, T)}{\partial r}.$$

Hence,

$$B(t, T) = \frac{R(r, t, T)\sigma_R(r, t, T)(T - t)}{r\sigma_r(r, t)}. \tag{A2}$$

The forward rate F is related to spot rates by

$$F(r, t, T_1, T_2) = \frac{R(r, t, T_2)(T_2 - t) - R(r, t, T_1)(T_1 - t)}{T_2 - T_1}.$$

Since $R(r, t, T_1)$ and $R(r, t, T_2)$ are instantaneously perfectly correlated in a one-state-variable model, it follows from (A2) that

$$F(r, t, T_1, T_2)\sigma_F(r, t, T_1, T_2) = \frac{B(t, T_2) - B(t, T_1)}{T_2 - T_1}r\sigma_r(r, t),$$

or

$$B(t, T_2) - B(t, T_1) = \frac{F(r, t, T_1, T_2)\sigma_F(r, t, T_1, T_2)(T_2 - T_1)}{r\sigma_r(r, t)}. \qquad (A3)$$

Equation (A2) enables $B(0, T)$ to be determined for all T from the current term structure of spot rate volatilities. Equation (A3) enables $B(0, T)$ to be determined from the current term structure of forward rate volatilities. $A(0, T)$ can be determined from $B(0, T)$ and the current term structure of interest rates using (A1). Thus, $A(0, T)$ and $B(0, T)$ can be determined for all T from the current term structure of interest rates and the current term structure of spot rate or forward rate volatilities.

REFERENCES

Black, F. "The pricing of commodity contracts." *Journal of Financial Economics*, 3 (1976), pp. 167–179.

Black, F., E. Derman, and W. Toy. "A one-factor model of interest rates and its application to Treasury bond options." *Financial Analysts Journal*, Jan–Feb 1990, pp. 33–39.

Black, F., and M. Scholes. "The pricing of options and corporate liabilities." *Journal of Political Economy*, 81 (1973), pp. 637–659.

Brennan, M. J., and E. S. Schwartz. "A continuous time approach to the pricing of bonds." *Journal of Banking and Finance*, 3 (1979), pp. 133–155.

Brennan, M. J., and E. S. Schwartz. "An equilibrium model of bond pricing and a test of market efficiency." *Journal of Financial and Quantitative Analysis*, 17 (1982), pp. 301–329.

Courtadon, G. "The pricing of options on default-free bonds." *Journal of Financial and Quantitative Analysis*, 17 (1982), pp. 75–100.

Cox, J. C., J. E. Ingersoll, and S. A. Ross. "An intertemporal general equilibrium model of asset prices." *Econometrica*, 53 (1985a), pp. 363–384.

Cox, J. C., J. E. Ingersoll, and S. A. Ross. "A theory of the term structure of interest rates." *Econometrica*, 53 (1985b), pp. 385–467.

Dothan, L. U. "On the term structure of interest rates." *Journal of Financial Economics*, 6 (1978), pp. 59–69.

Duffie, D. *Security Markets: Stochastic Models.* Boston: Academic Press, 1988.

Dybvig, P. H. "Bond and bond option pricing based on the current term structure." Working Paper, Olin School of Business, University of Washington, 1988.

Heath, D., R. Jarrow, and A. Morton. "Bond pricing and the term structure of interest rates: a new methodology for contingent claims evaluation." Working paper, Cornell University, Ithaca, New York, 1987.

Ho, T .S. Y., and S.-B. Lee. "Term structure movements and pricing of interest rate claims." *Journal of Finance*, 41 (1986), pp. 1011–1029.

Hull, J., and A. White. "The pricing of options on assets with stochastic volatilities." *Journal of Finance*, 42 (1987), pp. 281–300. Also Chapter 2 in this book.

Hull, J., and A. White. "Valuing derivative securities using the explicit finite difference method." *Journal of Financial and Quantitative Analysis*, 25 (1990), pp. 87–100. Also Chapter 6 in this book.

Jamshidian, F. "The one-factor Gaussian interest rate model: theory and implementation." Working Paper, Financial Strategies Group, Merrill Lynch Capital Markets, New York, 1988.

Jamshidian, F. "An exact bond option formula." *Journal of Finance*, 44 (1989), pp. 205–209.

Langetieg, T. C. "A multivariate model of the term structure." *Journal of Finance*, 35 (1980), pp. 71–97.

Longstaff, F. A. "A nonlinear general equilibrium model of the term structure of interest rates." *Journal of Financial Economics*, 23 (1989), pp. 195–224.

Merton, R. C. "Theory of rational option pricing." *Bell Journal of Economics and Management Science*, 4 (1973), pp. 141–183.

Milne, F., and S. Turnbull. "A simple approach to interest rate option pricing." Working Paper, Australian National University, 1989.

Richard, S. "An arbitrage model of the term structure of interest rates." *Journal of Financial Economics*, 6 (1979), pp. 33–57.

Vasicek, O. A. "An equilibrium characterization of the term structure." *Journal of Financial Economics*, 5 (1977), pp. 177–188.

14. Bond option pricing based on a model for the evolution of bond prices*

This paper develops a general theory of bond option pricing based on assumptions about the process followed by discount bond prices. The theory provides an alternative to the Heath, Jarrow, and Morton (1992) approach for characterizing arbitrage-free yield curve models in terms of the processes followed by instantaneous forward rates. Any model of discount bond prices can be converted into an equivalent model of instantaneous forward rates and vice versa.

When discount bond price volatilities are non-stochastic, discount bond prices are lognormal. A European option on a discount bond can then be viewed as the right to exchange one lognormal asset (the bond underlying the option) for another lognormal asset (a discount bond maturing at the same time as the option with face value equal to the strike price). This characterization of the option enables its price to be obtained analytically using the results in Merton (1973) and Margrabe (1978). Furthermore, when there is only one factor and an analytic relation between the discount bond prices can be derived, the approach suggested in Jamshidian (1989) can be used to value options on coupon-bearing bonds in terms of options on discount bonds.

For the valuation of American bond options, it is highly desirable that the yield curve model give rise to a Markov process for the short rate.[1] This is because a Markov process can always be represented by a recombining tree where the number of nodes considered at time $i \Delta t$ grows linearly with i (see Nelson and Ramaswamy 1990 and Hull and

---

[1] The process for the short rate defines the current yield curve and its evolution. It follows that when the short rate follows a Markov process, all rates do so.

* This paper was first published in *Advances in Futures and Options Research*, Vol. 6 (1993), pp. 1–13. It is reprinted with the permission of JAI Press.

White 1990b, 1993). For a non-Markov process, the trees that are constructed are in general non-recombining and the number of nodes at time $i \Delta t$ grows exponentially with i so that accurate pricing is computationally extremely time-consuming. This paper identifies a necessary and sufficient condition for discount bond price volatilities to be consistent with a Markov interest rate process when bond prices are lognormal.

The rest of this paper is organized as follows. Section 14.1 explains three different but equivalent ways of characterizing a yield curve model. Section 14.2 presents standard results concerned with the valuation of options when discount bond price volatilities are non-stochastic. Section 14.3 derives the functional form that a discount bond price volatility must have if it is to be non-stochastic and lead to a Markov short rate process. Section 14.4 examines two volatility functions that are of practical interest and derives the properties of the underlying models. Section 14.5 provides comparisons of European and American option prices. Section 14.6 indicates how the results can be extended to the situation where there is more than one factor. The conclusions are in Section 14.7.

14.1 ALTERNATIVE CHARACTERIZATIONS OF A YIELD CURVE MODEL

Define

$P(t, T)$: price at time t of a discount bond maturing at time T;[2]
$F(t, T)$: instantaneous forward rate as seen at time t for a contract maturing at time T;
$r(t)$: short-term interest rate at time t.

In this paper we define a yield curve model in terms of the processes followed by the $P(t, T)$. Heath, Jarrow, and Morton (1992) use as their starting point the process followed by $F(t, T)$. A common third approach, adopted for example by Black, Derman, and Toy (1990) and Hull and White (1990a), is to express the model in terms of a process for $r(t)$. In this section we explore the relationship between these three different approaches to characterizing the evolution of the yield curve. For ease of exposition we assume that a single factor drives the whole term structure. The analysis can be extended to cover the situation where there are several factors.

---

[2] A discount bond maturing at time T is a zero coupon bond worth $1 at time T.

Suppose that the risk-neutral process for $P(t, T)$ is

$$dP(t, T) = r(t)P(t, T)\,dt + v(t, T)P(t, T)\,dz, \qquad (14.1)$$

where $dz(t)$ is a Wiener process. The volatility $v(t, T)$ can in the most general form of the model be a function of past and present P's. However, since a bond's price volatility declines to zero at maturity we must have[3]

$$v(t, t) = 0.$$

Define $f(t, T_1, T_2)$ as the forward rate of interest as seen at time t for the period between T_1 and T_2. From equation (14.1),

$$d\log[P(t, T_1)] = [r(t) - \tfrac{1}{2}v(t, T_1)^2]\,dt + v(t, T_1)\,dz(t), \qquad (14.2)$$

$$d\log[P(t, T_2)] = [r(t) - \tfrac{1}{2}v(t, T_2)^2]\,dt + v(t, T_2)\,dz(t). \qquad (14.3)$$

Since

$$f(t, T_1, T_2) = \frac{\log[P(t, T_1)] - \log[P(t, T_2)]}{T_2 - T_1},$$

it follows from equations (14.2) and (14.3) that

$$df(t, T_1, T_2) = \frac{v(t, T_2)^2 - v(t, T_1)^2}{2(T_2 - T_1)}\,dt + \frac{v(t, T_1) - v(t, T_2)}{T_2 - T_1}\,dz(t).$$

$$(14.4)$$

This shows that the process for f depends only on the v's. It depends on r and the P's only to the extent that the v's themselves depend on these variables.

When we put $T_1 = T$ and $T_2 = T + \Delta T$ in equation (14.4) and then take limits as ΔT tends to zero, $f(t, T_1, T_2)$ becomes $F(t, T)$, the coefficient of dz becomes $v_T(t, T)$, and the coefficient of dt becomes $v(t, T)v_T(t, T)$, where subscripts denote partial derivatives. It follows that

$$dF(t, T) = v(t, T)v_T(t, T)\,dt - v_T(t, T)\,dz(t),$$

or, since we can without loss of generality change the sign of $dz(t)$,

$$dF(t, T) = v(t, T)v_T(t, T)\,dt + v_T(t, T)\,dz(t). \qquad (14.5)$$

Once all discount bond price volatilities have been defined at all times, the process for $F(t, T)$ is known. This is analogous to Heath, Jarrow, and Morton's (1992) result, which states that, once all instantaneous forward

---

[3] The $v(t, t) = 0$ condition is equivalent to the assumption that all discount bonds have finite drifts at all times. This is because, if the volatility of the bond does not decline to zero at its maturity, an infinite drift may be necessary to ensure that the bond's price equals its face value at maturity. An early attempt to value bond options from bond prices is Ball and Torous (1983), but as has been pointed out by a number of researchers, their model is not consistent with $v(t, t) = 0$.

rate standard deviations have been defined at all times, the process for $F(t, T)$ is known. Integrating $v_\tau(t, \tau)$ between $\tau = t$ and $\tau = T$, we obtain

$$v(t, T) - v(t, t) = \int_t^T v_\tau(t, \tau) \, d\tau.$$

Since $v(t, t) = 0$, this becomes

$$v(t, T) = \int_t^T v_\tau(t, \tau) \, d\tau.$$

If $m(t, T)$ and $s(t, T)$ are the instantaneous drift and standard deviation of $F(t, T)$, then it follows from equation (14.5) that

$$m(t, T) = s(t, T) \int_t^T s(t, \tau) d\tau.$$

This is the key result in Heath, Jarrow, and Morton (1992).

We now move on to derive a process for $r(t)$. Since

$$F(t, t) = F(0, t) + \int_0^t dF(\tau, t)$$

and $r(t) = F(t, t)$, it follows from equation (14.5) that

$$r(t) = F(0, t) + \int_0^t v(\tau, t)v_t(\tau, t) \, d\tau + \int_0^t v_t(\tau, t) \, dz(\tau). \qquad (14.6)$$

Differentiating with respect to t and using the result that $v(t, t) = 0$,

$$dr(t) = F_t(0, t) \, dt + \left(\int_0^t [v(\tau, t)v_{tt}(\tau, t) + v_t(\tau, t)^2] \, d\tau \right) dt$$

$$+ [v_t(\tau, t)|_{\tau=t}] \, dz(t) + \left(\int_0^t v_{tt}(\tau, t) \, dz(\tau) \right) dt. \qquad (14.7)$$

In general this process for r is non-Markov. There are two reasons for this. First, $v(\tau, t)$ may depend on the values of stochastic variables observed at times earlier than t.[4] Second, the final term in equation (14.7) depends on the history of the Wiener process dz. When $v(\tau, t)$ is dependent only on τ and t, the only possible reason for the process to be non-Markov is the final term in equation (14.7). We will examine this particular case in more detail in Section 14.3.

_____

[4] Note that v does not have to be non-Markov for this to be so. In a Markov model, $v(\tau, t)$ may depend on the term structure at time τ ($\tau < t$).

250

14.2 EUROPEAN OPTION PRICING WHEN BOND PRICE VOLATILITIES ARE FUNCTIONS ONLY OF TIME

When $v(t, T)$ is a function only of t and T, discount bond prices are lognormal. Consider a European call option on a discount bond that matures at time T. Suppose that the strike price is X and the option expiration date is T_X. The option can be treated as the right to exchange one lognormal asset, the discount bond underlying the option, for another lognormal asset, a discount bond that pays off X at time T_X. Merton (1973) showed that the value C of the call option is

$$C = P(t, T)N(d_1) - XP(t, T_X)N(d_2), \qquad (14.8)$$

where

$$
\left.
\begin{aligned}
d_1 &= \frac{\log[P(t, T)/(XP(t, T_X))]}{\sigma_P(t)} + \frac{\sigma_P(t)}{2}, \\
d_2 &= d_1 - \sigma_P(t), \\
\sigma_P(t)^2 &= \int_t^{T_X} [v(\tau, T) - v(\tau, T_X)]^2 \, d\tau.
\end{aligned}
\right\} \qquad (14.9)
$$

The price of the corresponding European put option is

$$XP(t, T_X)N(-d_2) - P(t, T)N(-d_1).$$

For European call options on coupon-bearing bonds, Jamshidian's (1989) approach can be used provided the short rate process is Markov. Suppose that X is the strike price, T_X is the option maturity, and r^* is the value of the short rate at time T_X that makes the coupon-bearing bond price equal to X. Define X_i as the value at time T_X of the ith discount bond underlying the coupon-bearing bond when the short rate is r^*. Let C_i be the value of a European call option on this discount bond when the strike price is X_i and the maturity is T_X. Jamshidian shows that the value of the original option on the coupon-bearing bond is $\sum_i C_i$.

14.3 A CONDITION FOR MARKOV SHORT RATES

When $v(t, T)$ is a function only of t and T, the process for r is Markov when the final term on the right-hand side of equation (14.7) can be expressed in terms of $r(t)$, and non-Markov otherwise. From equation (14.6) a necessary and sufficient condition for the final term on the right-hand side of equation (14.7) to be a function of $r(t)$ is that

$$\int_0^t v_{tt}(\tau, t)\,dz(\tau)$$

be a non-stochastic function of

$$\int_0^t v_t(\tau, t)\,dz(\tau).$$

A necessary and sufficient condition for this is

$$v_{tt}(\tau, t) = \alpha(t)v_t(\tau, t) \quad \text{for } 0 < \tau < t, \tag{14.10}$$

where α is a function only of t.

Integrating (14.10) between time 0 and time t,

$$v_t(\tau, t) = v_s(\tau, s)|_{s=0}\,g(t), \tag{14.11}$$

where

$$g(t) = \exp\left(\int_0^t \alpha(s)\,ds\right).$$

Integrating (14.11) between time τ and time T,

$$v(\tau, T) - v(\tau, \tau) = v_s(\tau, s)|_{s=0} \int_\tau^T g(t)\,dt.$$

Since $v(t, t) = 0$, it follows that $v(\tau, T)$ must have the general form

$$v(\tau, T) = x(\tau)[y(T) - y(\tau)]. \tag{14.12}$$

14.4 SPECIAL CASES

It is of particular interest to examine situations where the volatility structure is stable in the sense that $v(t, T)$ is a function only of $T - t$. It can be shown that there are only two functions of $T - t$ that have the functional form in equation (14.12). These are[5]

$$v(t, T) = k(T - t) \tag{14.13}$$

and

$$v(t, T) = \frac{k[1 - x^{-a(T-t)}]}{a}.$$

Since $x^{-a(T-t)} = e^{-a(T-t)\log x}$, we may without loss of generality write the

[5] The second of these has the functional form $f(t, T) = u(t)[v(T) - v(t)]$, with $u(t) = -kx^{at}$ and $v(t) = x^{-at}$.

second function as

$$v(t, T) = \frac{k[1 - e^{-a(T-t)}]}{a}. \tag{14.14}$$

Note that the model in equation (14.13) is the limit of the model in equation (14.14) as a tends to zero. Also, since $v(t, T) > 0$ when $T > t$, we must have $k > 0$.

The model $v(t, T) = k(T - t)$ ($k > 0$) is similar in spirit to the model in Schaefer and Schwartz (1987), where the volatilities of the prices of bonds are assumed to be proportional to their durations. Since the yield $y(t, T)$ at time t on a bond that matures at time T is given by

$$y(t, T) = -\frac{1}{T - t} \log P(t, T), \tag{14.15}$$

the model has the property that all yields have the same instantaneous standard deviation k. Equation (14.7) becomes

$$dr(t) = [F_t(0, t) + k^2 t] \, dt + k \, dz(t), \tag{14.16}$$

and equation (14.9) becomes

$$\sigma_P = k(T - T_X)\sqrt{T_X - t}.$$

Comparing equation (14.16) with the results in Hull and White (1990a), we see that the model is the continuous-time limit of the Ho and Lee (1986) model. The bond price as a function of the short rate is

$$P(t, T) = A(t, T)e^{-B(t,T)r},$$

where

$$\log A(t, T) = \log \frac{P(0, T)}{P(0, t)} - (T - t)\frac{\partial \log P(0, t)}{\partial t} - \tfrac{1}{2}k^2 t(T - t)^2 \tag{14.17}$$

and

$$B(t, T) = (T - t). \tag{14.18}$$

The main weakness of the $v(t, T) = k(T - t)$ assumption is that it implies that all spot interest rates have the same instantaneous standard deviation. In practice, long-term spot interest rates are generally less volatile than short-term spot interest rates. The function in equation (14.14), $v(t, T) = k[1 - e^{-a(T-t)}]/a$, where a and k are positive constants, reflects this. From equation (14.15) it implies that the instantaneous standard deviation of $y(t, T)$ is

$$\frac{k[1 - e^{-a(T-t)}]}{a(T - t)}.$$

As $T - t$ increases from zero to infinity, this decreases from k to zero. Discount bond price volatilities are an increasing function of the time to maturity. As $T - t$ tends to infinity, $v(t, T)$ tends to k/a.

From equations (14.6) and (14.7),

$$r(t) = F(0, t) + \frac{k^2}{2a^2}[1 - e^{-at}]^2 + \int_0^t ke^{-a(t-\tau)}\, dz(\tau),$$

$$dr(t) = F_t(0, t)\, dt + \left(\frac{k^2}{a}[e^{-at} - e^{-2at}]\right) dt$$

$$+ \left(\int_0^t ake^{-a(t-\tau)}dz(\tau)\right) dt + k\, dz(t).$$

Combining these two equations, we get

$$dr(t) = \left(F_t(0, t) + \frac{k^2}{2a}[1 + e^{-2at}] - ar + aF(0, t)\right) dt + k\, dz(t). \quad (14.19)$$

From (14.9),

$$\sigma_P^2 = \frac{k^2}{2a^3}[1 - e^{-a(T-T_X)}]^2[1 - e^{-2a(T_X-t)}]. \quad (14.20)$$

Comparing equation (14.19) with the results in Hull and White (1990a), we see that the model is the extended Vasicek model with both the reversion rate and the instantaneous standard deviation constant. The bond price as a function of the short rate is

$$P(t, T) = A(t, T)e^{-B(t,T)r},$$

where

$$\log A(t, T) = \log\frac{P(0, T)}{P(0, t)} - B(t, T)\frac{\partial \log P(0, t)}{\partial t}$$

$$- \frac{1}{4a^3}k^2(e^{aT} - e^{at})^2(e^{2at} - 1) \quad (14.21)$$

and

$$B(t, T) = \frac{1}{a}[1 - e^{-a(T-t)}]. \quad (14.22)$$

14.5 COMPARISON

Table 14.1 shows the results of using the $v(t, T) = k(T - t)$ and $v(t, T) = k[1 - e^{-a(T-t)}]/a$ models to value European and American call options on coupon-bearing bonds. The initial term structure of interest

TABLE 14.1. Values of American and European call options on a five-year bond with a face value of $100. The exercise price is $100; the term structure is flat at 10% per annum (compounded semi-annually); the bond pays coupons of $5 every 6 months; $k = 0.15$; $a = 0.1$.

Expiration of option (years)	$v(t, T) = k(T - t)$		$v(t, T) = k[1 - e^{-a(T-t)}]/a$	
	European	American	European	American
0.5	1.45	1.49	1.14	1.19
1.0	1.77	1.94	1.39	1.55
2.0	1.79	2.35	1.39	1.91
3.0	1.39	2.51	1.08	2.06
4.0	0.76	2.54	0.59	2.10
5.0	0.00	2.56	0.00	2.13

rates is assumed to be flat at 10% per annum (with semi-annual compounding). The underlying bond has a face value of $100 and pays a coupon of $5 every 6 months. The strike price of the option is $100. The values of k and a are 0.15 and 0.1, respectively.

The European bond option prices were obtained using equation (14.8) in conjunction with Jamshidian's result that a European option on a coupon-bearing bond is a portfolio of options on discount bonds. The American bond option prices were obtained using the procedure in Hull and White (1990b) for constructing an interest rate tree.

It is interesting to note that the pattern of results in Table 14.1 is quite different from that which would be obtained for stock options. The key difference between the process followed by a bond price and the process followed by a stock price is that the bond price must revert to its face value at maturity. The standard deviation of a bond's future price first increases and then decreases as we look further into the future. At the bond's maturity the standard deviation is zero. The European bond option prices in Table 14.1 reflect this phenomenon. The value of a European bond option first increases and then decreases as its time to maturity increases.

Table 14.1 shows that the difference between the prices of American and European bond options can be quite large when the life of the option is a significant proportion of the life of the bond. For example, the value of a four-year American option on the five-year bond is over three times that of its European counterpart for both volatility functions. The table also shows that the volatility function has a significant effect on the option price. Both of the functions in Table 14.1 give approximately the same volatilities for a short-term bond. However, the $v(t, T) = k(T - t)$

255

function gives significantly higher volatilities for longer-term bonds. This in turn gives rise to significantly higher option prices.

14.6 EXTENSION TO MORE THAN ONE STATE VARIABLE

In this section we indicate how our results can be extended to cover the situation in which bond prices are determined by two (or more) state variables. Suppose that all bond prices $P(t, T)$ obey the following stochastic process:

$$dP(t, T) = rP(t, T)\,dt + u(t, T)P(t, T)\,dz + v(t, T)P(t, T)\,dw,$$

where $E[dz, dw] = \rho\,dt$ and both $u(t, T)$ and $v(t, T)$ are functions only of t and T. Consider a European call option expiring at T_X with strike price X on a discount bond maturing at time T. The option price is as given by equation (14.8) with

$$\sigma_P^2(t) = \int_t^{T_X} \{[v(\tau, T) - v(\tau, T_X)]^2 + [u(\tau, T) - u(\tau, T_X)]^2$$
$$+ 2\rho[v(\tau, T) - v(\tau, T_X)][u(\tau, T) - u(\tau, T_X)]\}\,d\tau.$$

It is not possible to decompose an option on a coupon-bearing bond into a portfolio of options on discount bonds. However, when the short rate is Markov, it is possible to build a tree in three dimensions to represent the short rate process. An analysis analogous to that in Sections 14.1 and 14.3 shows that the short rate is

$$r(t) = F(0, t) + \int_0^t \{v(\tau, t)v_t(\tau, t) + u(\tau, t)u_t(\tau, t)$$
$$+ \rho[v(\tau, t)u_t(\tau, t) + u(\tau, t)v_t(\tau, t)]\}\,d\tau$$
$$+ \int_0^t v_t(\tau, t)\,dz(\tau) + \int_0^t u_t(\tau, t)\,dw(\tau)$$

and

$$dr(t) = F_t(0, t)\,dt + \left(\int_0^t \frac{\partial}{\partial t}[v(\tau, t)v_t(\tau, t)]\,dt + u(\tau, t)u_t(\tau, t) \right.$$
$$\left. + \rho[v(\tau, t)u_t(\tau, t) + u(\tau, t)v_t(\tau, t)]\,d\tau \right)\,dt$$
$$+ [v_t(\tau, t)|_{\tau=t}]\,dz(t) + [u_t(\tau, t)|_{\tau=t}]\,dw(t)$$
$$+ \left(\int_0^t v_{tt}(\tau, t)\,dz(\tau) \right)\,dt + \left(\int_0^t u_{tt}(\tau, t)\,dw(\tau) \right)\,dt.$$

Sufficient (but not necessary) conditions for a Markov interest rate process are

$$v_{tt}(\tau, t) = \alpha(t)v_t(\tau, t) \quad \text{and} \quad u_{tt}(\tau, t) = \alpha(t)u_t(\tau, t).$$

where α is a function of t. This means that v and u have the form

$$v(t, T) = x(t)[y_1(t) - y_1(T)] \quad \text{and} \quad u(t, T) = x(t)[y_2(t) - y_2(T)]$$

for some functions x, y_1, and y_2. More generally, when

$$dP(t, T) = rP(t, T)\,dt + \sum v_i(t, T)P(t, T)\,dz_i$$

and the v_i's are non-stochastic, r is Markov when

$$v_i(t, T) = x(t)[y_i(t) - y_i(T)]$$

for all i.

An inspection of the expressions for r and dr reveals that, in the two-state-variable case, if we are willing to express the interest rate as a sum $r = r_1 + r_2$ of state variables, the necessary and sufficient conditions for the state variables to be Markov are that v and u have the forms

$$v(t, T) = x_1(t)[y_1(t) - y_1(T)] \quad \text{and} \quad u(t, T) = x_2(t)[y_2(t) - y_2(T)]$$

for some functions x_1, x_2, y_1, y_2.[6] More generally, when there are n sources of uncertainty, r can be constructed from a sum of n Markov state variables when

$$v_i(t, T) = x_i(t)[y_i(t) - y_i(T)]$$

for $i = 1, 2, \ldots, n$. This corresponds to the model of Langetieg (1980).

14.7 CONCLUSIONS

This paper has made a number of contributions to our understanding of bond option pricing. It has shown how a yield curve model can be defined in terms of the processes followed by discount bond prices. It has examined in some detail the case where discount bond price volatilities are non-stochastic. This is of particular interest because non-stochastic bond price volatilities allow European bond options to be priced analytically.

For there to be an efficient way of valuing American bond options in a one-factor model, the short rate process underlying the bond price process must be Markov. This paper has produced explicit expressions for those bond price volatility functions that are both non-stochastic and lead

[6] Although r_1 and r_2 are Markov, r itself is in general non-Markov.

to a Markov interest rate process. A subset of these functions that also have the property that they define stationary volatility structures has been identified and the properties of the underlying models examined. The models prove to be those discussed by Ho and Lee (1986) and Hull and White (1990a).

REFERENCES

Ball, C. A., and W. N. Torous. "Bond price dynamics and options." *Journal of Financial and Quantitative Analysis*, 18 (1983), pp. 517–531.

Black, F., E. Derman, and W. Toy. "A one-factor model of interest rates and its application to Treasury bond options," *Financial Analysts Journal*, Jan–Feb 1990, pp. 33–39.

Heath, D., R. Jarrow, and A. Morton. "Bond pricing and the term structure of interest rates: a new methodology for contingent claims evaluation." *Econometrica*, 60, 1 (1992), pp. 77–105.

Ho, T. S., and S. Lee. "Term structure movements and pricing interest rate contingent claims." *Journal of Finance*, 41 (1986), pp. 1011–1028.

Hull, J., and A. White."Pricing interest rate derivative securities." *Review of Financial Studies*, 3 (1990a), pp. 573–592. Also Chapter 13 in this book.

Hull, J., and A. White."Valuing derivative securities using the explicit finite difference method." *Journal of Financial and Quantitative Analysis*, 25 (1990b), pp. 87–100. Also Chapter 6 in this book.

Hull, J., and A. White. "One factor interest rate models and the valuation of interest rate derivative securities." *Journal of Financial and Quantitative Analysis*, 28 (June 1993), pp. 235–254. Also Chapter 17 in this book.

Jamshidian, F. "An exact bond option formula." *Journal of Finance*, 44 (March 1989), pp. 205–209.

Langetieg, T. C. "A multivariate model of the term structure." *Journal of Finance*, 35 (March 1980), pp. 71–96.

Margrabe, W. "The value of an option to exchange one asset for another." *Journal of Finance*, 33 (1978), pp. 177–186.

Merton, R. C. "The theory of rational option pricing." *Bell Journal of Economics and Management Science*, 4 (1973), pp. 141–183.

Nelson, D. B., and K. Ramaswamy, "Simple binomial processes as diffusion approximations in financial models." *The Review of Financial Studies*, 3 (1990), pp. 393–430.

Schaefer, S. M., and E. S. Schwartz. "Time dependent variance and the pricing of bond options." *Journal of Finance*, 42 (1987), pp. 1113–1128.

15. The pricing of options on interest rate caps and floors using the Hull–White model*

In the last several years, a very active market has developed in interest rate caps and floors. In conjunction with this, a number of institutions have offered their customers the option to buy or sell a cap or a floor at a future date. One problem with dealing with these complex securities is that there has been no satisfactory way of determining a reasonable price for them. In this paper we show how these options can be priced using the no-arbitrage Hull–White term structure model.

The basic properties of the Hull–White model are summarized in the first section. The second section describes how interest rate caps and floors are priced under the model as options on discount bonds. In the third section the procedure for valuing a call or a put on an option on a discount bond is developed. This is extended in Section 15.4 to cover the pricing of an call option on a cap which is a call on a portfolio of options.

15.1 THE HULL–WHITE INTEREST RATE MODEL

The Hull and White interest rate model (1990) extends the model of Vasicek (1977) so that it can exactly replicate any term structure of interest rates and volatilities. This model provides analytic solutions for

* This paper was first published as Chapter 4 in *Advanced Strategies in Financial Risk Management*, edited by Robert J. Schwartz and Clifford W. Smith, New York Institute of Finance, 1993. It was later published in *Journal of Financial Engineering*, Vol. 2 (1993), pp. 287–296. It is reprinted here with the permission of both the New York Institute of Finance and the *Journal of Financial Engineering*.

European-style options on discount and coupon bonds. In this section the principal results of the Hull–White model are summarized.

In the most general version of the Hull–White extended Vasicek model, the risk-neutral process for the short-term interest rate is assumed to be

$$dr = [\phi(t) - a(t)r]\,dt + \sigma(t)\,dz,$$

where

$$a(t) = -\frac{\partial^2 B(0, t)/\partial t^2}{\partial B(0, t)/\partial t},$$

$$\phi(t) = -a(t)\frac{\partial \hat{A}(0, t)}{\partial t} - \frac{\partial^2 \hat{A}(0, t)}{\partial t^2} + \left[\frac{\partial B(0, t)}{\partial t}\right]^2 \int_0^t \left[\frac{\sigma(\tau)}{\partial B(0, \tau)/\partial \tau}\right]^2 d\tau.$$

The risk-neutral process for the interest rate is thus defined by the functions $\hat{A}(0, t)$, $B(0, t)$, and $\sigma(t)$. These three functions are the fundamental determinants of all interest rate security prices. The procedure for determining these functions from current term structure and volatility term structure information is outlined below.

Consider the price of a discount bond that pays \$1 at time T. Define

t: The time at which the bond price is to be determined. The current time is 0.

r_t: The short rate prevailing at t. The current short rate is r_0.

$P(r_t, t, T)$: The price at time t of a bond paying \$1 at time T if the short rate is r_t. $P(r_0, 0, T)$ is the current price, also written as $P(T)$.

Under the extended Vasicek model the bond price at time t when the interest rate is r_t is

$$P(r_t, t, T) = e^{[\hat{A}(t, T) - r_t B(t, T)]}, \tag{15.1}$$

where

$$\hat{A}(t, T) = \hat{A}(0, T) - \hat{A}(0, t) - B(t, T)\left[\frac{\partial \hat{A}(0, t)}{\partial t}\right]$$

$$- \tfrac{1}{2}[B(0, T) - B(0, t)]^2 \int_0^t \left[\frac{\sigma(\tau)}{\partial B(0, \tau)/\partial \tau}\right]^2 d\tau,$$

$$B(t, T) = \frac{B(0, T) - B(0, t)}{\partial B(0, t)/\partial t},$$

Now consider a European option on a discount bond. Define

t: The time at which the option price is to be determined.
r_t: The short rate prevailing at t.
T_1: Option maturity time, measured in years.
T_2: Bond maturity time, measured in years.
X: Option exercise price.

The option prices are then

$$\text{Call}(r_t, t, T_1, T_2) = P(r_t, t, T_2)N(d_1) - XP(r_t, t, T_1)N(d_2), \tag{15.2}$$

$$\text{Put}(r_t, t, T_1, T_2) = XP(r_t, t, T_1)N(-d_2) - P(r_t, t, T_2)N(-d_1), \tag{15.3}$$

where

$$d_1 = \frac{\log\left(\frac{P(r_t,t,T_2)}{XP(r_t,t,T_1)}\right)}{\sigma_P} + \frac{\sigma_P}{2}, \qquad d_2 = d_1 - \sigma_P,$$

$$\sigma_P^2 = [B(0, T_2) - B(0, T_1)]^2 \int_t^{T_1} \left[\frac{\sigma(\tau)}{(\partial B(0, \tau)/\partial\tau)}\right]^2 d\tau.$$

Using equations (15.1) to (15.3), the functions $\hat{A}(0, t)$, $B(0, t)$, and $\sigma(t)$ can be inferred from the prices of a variety of options and the current term structure of interest rates. In the rest of this paper it will be assumed that these functions have been determined.

15.2 INTEREST RATE CAPS

An interest rate caplet (one leg of a cap) is equivalent to a put option that matures at the caplet start date on a discount bond which matures at the caplet end date. The strike price for the option is 1 per dollar of principal and the face value of the discount bond is $1 + R_X\tau$ per dollar of principal where τ is the length of the caplet measured in years and R_X is the cap rate. For more details on this, see Hull (1989: pp. 254–55).

Using equation (15.3), the price of the ith caplet in a cap is then

$$\text{Caplet}_i(r_t, t) = [P(r_t, t, T_i)N(-d_{2i}) - \text{Face}_i P(r_t, t, T_{i+1})N(-d_{1i})]\text{Prin}_i, \tag{15.4}$$

where

$$d_{1i} = \frac{\log\left(\frac{\text{Face}_i P(r_t,t,T_{i+1})}{P(r_t,t,T_i)}\right)}{\sigma_{Pi}} + \frac{\sigma_{Pi}}{2}, \qquad d_{2i} = d_{1i} - \sigma_{Pi},$$

$$\sigma_{Pi} = [B(0, T_{i+1}) - B(0, T_i)]^2 \int_t^{T_i} \left[\frac{\sigma(\tau)}{(\partial B(0, \tau)/\partial \tau)} \right]^2 d\tau,$$

$$\text{Face}_i = 1 + R_{Xi} \frac{\text{DAYS}}{\text{YEAR}},$$

and

T_i: Time at which the ith caplet starts, measured in years.
T_{i+1}: Time at which the ith caplet ends, measured in years.
R_{Xi}: Cap rate for ith caplet.
DAYS: Number of days in the period covered by the cap.
YEAR: Number of days in a year.
Prin_i: Principal underlying the ith caplet.

The price of a cap with n elements is

$$\text{Cap Price} = \sum_{i=1}^{n} \text{Caplet}_i.$$

15.3 A CALL OPTION ON A PUT OPTION

In this section we consider a call option which allows the holder to buy a put option on a discount bond. This is equivalent to a call on one element of an interest rate cap.

Consider a European call option expiring at time T_1 on a European put option maturing at T_2 on a discount bond which matures at T_3. The strike price for the put option is X and the exercise price for the call option is K. The current price of the call option on the put option is

$$\hat{E}\left\{ \max[\text{Put}(r_{T_1}, T_1, T_2, T_3) - K, 0] e^{-\int_0^{T_1} r_s \, ds} \right\},$$

where $\hat{E}$ is a risk-neutral expectation over all possible r_t paths for $0 \le t \le T_1$ and the put price is given by equation (15.3). It can be shown that this expectation is equivalent to

$$P(r_0, 0, T_1) \int_{r^*}^{\infty} [\text{Put}(r, T_1, T_2, T_3) - K]\hat{g}'(r)\, dr, \qquad (15.5)$$

where r^* is the rate such that $\text{Put}(r^*, T_1, T_2, T_3) = K$, and $\hat{g}'(r)$ is the risk-neutral forward-adjusted density function for the interest rate. This density function for r_t is a normal density function, with

$$E(r_t) = f(t), \quad \text{the forward rate,}$$

$$\text{Var}(r_t) = \sigma_r^2(t) = \left[\frac{\partial B(0, t)}{\partial t}\right]^2 \int_0^t \left[\frac{\sigma(\tau)}{(\partial B(0, \tau)/\partial \tau)}\right]^2 d\tau.$$

The solution to equation (15.5) is

$$\text{Call on Put} = P(T_2)XM(-d_2, \alpha - \sigma_2, \rho)$$
$$- P(T_3)M(-d_1, \alpha - \sigma_3, \rho) - P(T_1)K\dot{N}(\alpha), \quad (15.6)$$

where

$$d_1 = \frac{\log\left(\frac{P(T_3)}{XP(T_2)}\right)}{\sigma_1} + \frac{\sigma_1}{2}, \qquad d_2 = d_1 - \sigma_1,$$

$$\sigma_1^2 = [B(0, T_3) - B(0, T_2)]^2 \int_0^{T_2} \left[\frac{\sigma(\tau)}{(\partial B(0, \tau)/\partial \tau)}\right]^2 d\tau,$$

$$\sigma_2^2 = [B(0, T_2) - B(0, T_1)]^2 \int_0^{T_1} \left[\frac{\sigma(\tau)}{(\partial B(0, \tau)/\partial \tau)}\right]^2 d\tau,$$

$$\sigma_3^2 = [B(0, T_3) - B(0, T_1)]^2 \int_0^{T_1} \left[\frac{\sigma(\tau)}{(\partial B(0, \tau)/\partial \tau)}\right]^2 d\tau,$$

$$\alpha = \frac{f(T_1) - r^*}{\sigma_r}, \qquad \rho = \sqrt{\frac{\int_0^{T_1} \left[\frac{\sigma(\tau)}{(\partial B(0,\tau)/\partial \tau)}\right]^2 d\tau}{\int_0^{T_2} \left[\frac{\sigma(\tau)}{(\partial B(0,\tau)/\partial \tau)}\right]^2 d\tau}},$$

and $M(\cdot, \cdot, \rho)$ is the cumulative bivariate normal with correlation ρ. Using put–call parity, the value of a put on a put is

$$\text{Put on Put} = \text{Call on Put} - \text{Put}(r_0, 0, T_2, T_3) + P(T_1)K.$$

By analogy, the value of a call on a call is

$$\text{Call on Call} = P(T_3)M(d1, -\alpha + \sigma_3, \rho)$$
$$- P(T_2)XM(d2, -\alpha + \sigma_2, \rho) - P(T_1)KN(-\alpha), \quad (15.7)$$

and a put on a call is

$$\text{Put on Call} = \text{Call on Call} - \text{Call}(r_0, 0, T_2, T_3) + P(T_1)K.$$

15.4 A CALL OPTION ON AN INTEREST RATE CAP

An interest rate cap is a portfolio of put options on a series of discount bonds. Thus, a call on a cap (or caption) is a call on a portfolio of put options. This can be transformed into a portfolio of call options each on a single put option by using the technique developed by Jamshidian (1989) to compute the price of an option on a coupon bond.

Consider a European call option which allows the holder to put the cap described in Section 15.2. Define

T_X: Time at which the option expires.

  X: Option exercise price. The payoff on the option is the greater of the cap price at time T_X less X or zero.

First it is necessary to compute the short rate at time T_X for which the cap price equals the strike price, X. This is called the critical interest rate r^* and is found by solving

$$\sum_{i=1}^{n} \text{Caplet}_i(r^*, T_X) = X,$$

where $\text{Caplet}_i(r^*, t)$ is given by equation (15.4). For all rates greater than r^* the option will be exercised; for all rates less than r^* it will not be exercised.

The critical interest rate is used to allocate the strike price X to each of the elements of the cap underlying the option. Let x_i be the portion of X which is allocated to the ith caplet:

$$x_i = \text{Caplet}_i(r^*, T_X)$$

Note that $\sum_{i=1}^{n} x_i = X$.

From equations (15.4) and (15.6) the value of the call on the ith caplet is then

$$\begin{aligned} \text{Call}_i = \; & P(T_i)M(-d_{2i}, \alpha_i - \sigma_{2i}, \rho_i) \\ & - \text{Face}_i P(T_{i+1})M(-d_{1i}, \alpha_i - \sigma_{3i}, \rho_i) - x_i P(T_X)N(\alpha_i), \quad (15.8) \end{aligned}$$

where

$$d_{1i} = \frac{\log\left(\frac{\text{Face}_i P(T_{i+1})}{P(T_i)}\right)}{\sigma_{1i}} + \frac{\sigma_{1i}}{2}, \qquad d_{2i} = d_{1i} - \sigma_{1i},$$

$$\sigma_{1i}^2 = [B(0, T_{i+1}) - B(0, T_i)]^2 \int_0^{T_i} \left[\frac{\sigma(\tau)}{(\partial B(0, \tau)/\partial \tau)}\right]^2 d\tau,$$

$$\sigma_{2i}^2 = [B(0, T_i) - B(0, T_X)]^2 \int_0^{T_X} \left[\frac{\sigma(\tau)}{(\partial B(0, \tau)/\partial \tau)}\right]^2 d\tau,$$

$$\sigma_{3i}^2 = [B(0, T_{i+1}) - B(0, T_X)]^2 \int_0^{T_X} \left[\frac{\sigma(\tau)}{(\partial B(0, \tau)/\partial \tau)}\right]^2 d\tau,$$

$$\alpha_i = \frac{f(T_X) - r^*}{\sigma_r}, \qquad \rho_i = \sqrt{\frac{\int_0^{T_X} \left[\frac{\sigma(\tau)}{(\partial B(0,\tau)/\partial \tau)}\right]^2 d\tau}{\int_0^{T_i} \left[\frac{\sigma(\tau)}{(\partial B(0,\tau)/\partial \tau)}\right]^2 d\tau}},$$

and the value of the call option on the cap is

$$\text{Call on Cap} = \sum_{i=1}^{n} \text{Call}_i. \tag{15.9}$$

The prices of puts on caps and puts and calls on floors are computed in a similar way.

The prices of a number of captions are given below to give the reader some sense of the value of a call on a cap. The term structure of interest rates is flat at 10% with quarterly compounding. The term structure of volatilities is defined by setting $\sigma(t) = 0.014$ and $a(t) = 0.10$ for all t so that $B(t, T) = \frac{1}{a}\left[1 - e^{-a(T-t)}\right]$. Under this environment, the implied forward rate volatilities (using Black's (1976) model) for quarterly at-the-money caps of varying maturities are as follows:

Term (years):	1	2	3	4	5	7	10
Implied volatility:	13.80	13.43	13.09	12.77	12.48	11.95	11.31

Table 15.1 gives the prices of call options of various terms on 5-year forward start caps which commence at the maturity of the call. In each case the cap rate is 10% and the exercise price on the call is set equal to the forward cap price so that the option is approximately at-the-money.

TABLE 15.1. Call option prices on 5-year forward start caps.

T_X (years)	X = Forward cap price	Call price
0.25	2.76	0.45
0.50	2.85	0.64
0.75	2.90	0.78
1.00	2.94	0.89
2.00	2.97	1.18
3.00	2.90	1.33
4.00	2.77	1.41
5.00	2.60	1.44

REFERENCES

Black, F. "The pricing of commodity contracts." *Journal of Financial Economics*, 3 (1976), pp. 167–179.

Hull, J. *Options Futures and Other Derivative Securities.* Prentice-Hall, Englewood Cliffs, NJ, 1989.

Hull, J., and A. White. "Valuing derivative securities using the explicit finite difference method." *Journal of Financial and Quantitative Analysis*, 25 (1990), pp. 87–100. Also Chapter 6 in this book.

Jamshidian, F. "An exact bond option formula." *Journal of Finance*, 44 (1989), pp. 205–209.

Vasicek, O. A. "An equilibrium characterization of the term structure." *Journal of Financial Economics*, 5 (1977), 177–188.

V

Term Structure Models: Implementation

16. *Introduction: Term structure implementation*

A convenient way of classifying models of the term structure is on the basis of:

(1) whether term structure movements are Markov or non-Markov;
(2) whether they involve one or more than one factor;
(3) whether interest rates are normally distributed or non-normally distributed.

This classification draws attention to some key trade-offs. Non-Markov models give the user complete freedom in the choice of interest rate volatilities, but Markov models are computationally much simpler.[1] Multi-factor models permit a rich pattern of term structure movements, but one-factor models are easier to work with. Models where interest rates are normally distributed generally have some analytic tractability, but lognormal models are arguably more realistic.

The models considered in this section of the book are Markov. Those in Chapters 18 and 20 involve one factor, while those in Chapter 19 involve two factors. Each of the chapters discuss models involving both normally distributed and non-normally distributed interest rates.

Implementation issues are critically important when choices are made between alternative interest rate models. The easiest models to implement are one-factor Markov models where the short rate is normally distributed (that is, Ho–Lee or Hull–White). These models have a great deal of analytic tractability and lead to fast computation. As we move to more than one factor, to non-Markov models, or to non-normally distributed rates, implementation becomes less straightforward.

---

[1] As discussed in Chapters 12 and 20, in a Markov model it is possible to match any pattern of rate volatilities at time zero, but the volatility structure is then non-stationary. Rate volatilities at a future time are liable to be quite different from those at time zero.

The two key implementation issues to consider for any proposed model are:

1. How easy is it to calibrate the model to market data?
2. Once the model has been calibrated to market data, how easy is it to use the model to value derivatives?

It is often calibration considerations that lead practitioners to opt for relatively simple models. An attractive feature of the one-factor/Markov/normal assumption is that calibration is fast and the user has a great deal of flexibility in choosing the interest rate options that are used in the calibration. Our approach to calibrating the Hull–White model is outlined in Section 18.5. We calculate the values of the reversion rate a and the short rate standard deviation σ that minimize

$$\sum_i (P_i - V_i)^2,$$

where P_i is the market price of the ith option and V_i is the price given by the model for the option. The minimization is accomplished using standard "hill-climbing" techniques. The interest rate options used for calibration are normally caps, European swap options, and European bond options, all of which can be valued analytically.

Models such as Hull–White, which involve the normally distributed rates assumption, are sometimes criticized on the grounds that they permit interest rates to become negative. Our experience in implementing the Hull–White model shows that for most currencies negative interest rates have very little chance of occurring and have very little impact on results given by the model. An exception is the Japanese yen. For this currency, the short rate is currently in the 0.5–1% range and the probability of negative interest rates is not insignificant.[2] One procedure that can be followed is to change a negative interest rate to zero for the purposes of calculating the payoff from an interest rate derivative. This is similar in spirit to a suggestion made by Black (1995).

16.1 BUILDING INTEREST RATE TREES

Once a model has been calibrated to market data, it is necessary to build a

---

[2] Interestingly, there has recently been some discussion of the possibility of interest rates actually becoming negative in Japan! This led ISDA to publish a memo discussing the impact of negative interest rates on ISDA Master Agreements in November 1995.

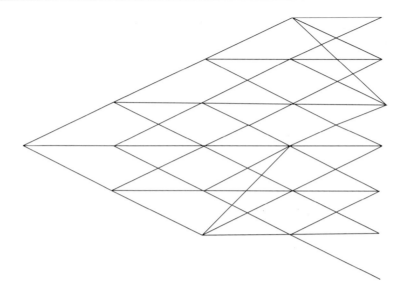

FIGURE 16.1. Tree resulting from our first approach.

tree to value those instruments for which there are no analytic results. Here the difference between a Markov and non-Markov model is significant. For an n-step binomial model, there are $n + 1$ terminal nodes if the model is Markov and 2^n terminal nodes if it is non-Markov.[3]

Our original procedure for building trinomial interest rate trees for Markov models of the short rate is described in Chapter 17. It leads to a tree of the general form shown in Figure 16.1. The branches at each node and their probabilities are chosen so that the mean and standard deviation of the change in the short rate are matched. The procedure is an extension of the explicit finite difference methods described in Chapter 6. The model of the short rate that is considered usually has a function of time, $\theta(t)$, in the drift. As discussed in Chapter 12, this is chosen to ensure that the model is consistent with the initial term structure. The function $\theta(t)$ is determined iteratively as the tree is built. The value of θ applying between time $i\,\Delta t$ and $(i + 1)\,\Delta t$ is chosen so that an $(i + 2)\,\Delta t$ zero-coupon bond is correctly priced at time zero.

Our original procedure worked well for pricing, but required a large tree for accurate computation of delta, gamma, and vega measures. This led us to switch to the new procedure in Chapter 18. This procedure can be

---

[3] For the trinomial tree we favor, there are at most $2n + 1$ terminal nodes. When $n = 20$, $2n + 1 = 41$, whereas 2^n is about one million. When two-factor models are considered, the difference between the number of nodes that have to be considered in Markov and non-Markov models is even more dramatic.

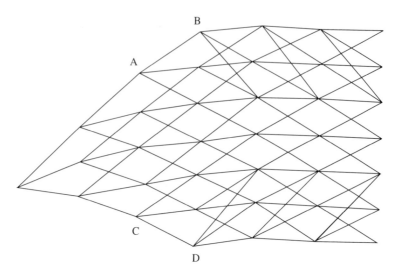

FIGURE 16.2. Tree resulting from our second improved approach.

used for all models of the form[4]

$$df(r) = [\theta(t) - af(r)]\, dt + \sigma\, dz. \qquad (16.1)$$

It is computationally more efficient than the old procedure. A bonus is that it is also easier to implement.

The tree for our new procedure is shown in Figure 16.2. Each node on the tree represents a value for $f(r)$. The tree is totally symmetrical about the central nodes. (For example, the probability on branch AB equals the probability on branch CD.) The position of the central node at time $i\,\Delta t$ corresponds to the expected value of $f(r)$ at that time.

The tree is constructed in two stages. The first stage is to construct a tree for a variable x that is initially zero and follows the process

$$dx = -ax\, dt + \sigma\, dz.$$

This tree has the form shown in Figure 16.3 and is symmetrical about the $x = 0$ line. The second stage is to use a forward induction procedure, displacing each of the nodes on the tree in Figure 16.3 so that the initial term structure is exactly matched. The result of this forward induction procedure is a tree similar to the one shown in Figure 16.2.

In the Hull–White model, $f(r) = r$. As discussed in Chapter 20, the expected value of r, and therefore the position of the central nodes in Figure 16.2, can be determined analytically. Whether analytic results or

---

[4] The parameters a and σ can be functions of time, but, as discussed in Chapters 12 and 20, we do not recommend this.

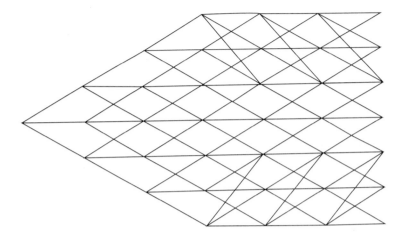

FIGURE 16.3. Tree for variable x following $dx = -ax\,dt + \sigma\,dz$.

forward induction are used to determine Figure 16.2 from 16.3 is largely a matter of taste. Although satisfactory for most purposes, the tree for r that is produced using analytic results is close to, but not exactly consistent with, the initial term structure. This is because the continuous time expected values of r are used in conjunction with a discrete time model.

Since we first proposed the procedure in Chapter 18, we have had many discussions with practitioners on the finer points of implementation. This led to us to write Chapter 20. This chapter expands on Chapter 18 and provides more details on the way we construct and use interest rate trees in our own software. It discusses issues such as how to handle cash flows between nodes, how to change the length of the time step, and how to use analytic results.

The question of how analytic results should be used has led to particular difficulties and has caused some people to claim (incorrectly) that our tree-building procedure does not converge when used in conjunction with a real term structure. It is important to recognize that the r on the tree is the Δt-period r, whereas the r in analytic results is the instantaneous r. The two should not be assumed to be the same. When using analytic results to calculate a bond price or a European option price at a node, it is important to first calculate the instantaneous r from the Δt-period r using equation (20.6). To facilitate implementation of our tree and to illustrate this point, we have provided in Chapter 20 a detailed description of the construction and use of the tree, basing calculations on the DM yield curve on 8 July 1994. Readers can use our results as a check that they have implemented the model correctly.

16.2 TWO-FACTOR MODELS

Chapter 19 shows how the results in Chapter 18 can be extended to two factors. It first considers the case where we wish to model interest rates in two countries simultaneously. For each country we assume a model of the form shown in equation (16.1) and construct trinomial trees for each interest rate separately. It is necessary to ensure that the correct risk-neutral world is considered. Suppose that the interest rates in countries 1 and 2 are r_1 and r_2 respectively. If we are interested in valuing a derivative that will provide cash flows in the currency of country 1, both the r_1 and r_2 trees should be risk-neutral from the viewpoint of an investor in country 1. Normally we construct the r_2 tree so that it is risk-neutral from the perspective of a country 2 investor. To make it risk-neutral from the perspective of a country 1 investor, it is necessary to shift the position of the nodes by a small amount, as described in Section 19.2.

Once the trinomial trees have been correctly constructed, they are combined on the assumption that r_1 and r_2 are uncorrelated. The resulting tree is three-dimensional, with nine branches emanating from each node. The probability on any given branch is the product of the probabilities on the corresponding branches of the original trinomial trees. The probabilities on the branches of the three-dimensional tree are then adjusted to incorporate any correlation that might exist between the two rates. The procedure for doing this is described in Section 19.2.

Chapter 19 also considers the following two-factor model of a single term structure:

$$df(r) = [\theta(t) + u - af(r)] dt + \sigma_1 dz_1, \qquad du = -bu dt + \sigma_2 dz_2.$$

$$(16.2)$$

In this model, a, σ_1, b, σ_2 are constants, and dz_1 and dz_2 are Wiener processes with correlation ρ. This model is similar in spirit to the often-cited Brennan and Schwartz (1979) model. Indeed, it can be characterized as the no-arbitrage version of the Brennan–Schwartz model. In the Brennan–Schwartz model the short rate reverts to a long rate, which itself follows a mean-reverting process. In equation (16.2) the function $f(r)$ is mean-reverting and one component of the reversion level is u, which is itself mean-reverting.

The model in equation (16.2) can be implemented using a three-dimensional Markov tree, provided that a and b are not too close to each other. When $f(r) = r$, the model has some analytic tractability. The price at time t of a discount bond maturing at time T is given by

$$P(t, T) = A(t, T)e^{-B(t,T)r - C(t,T)u},$$

where A, B, and C are known functions. Options on discount bonds can be valued analytically.[5]

With five parameters $(a, b, \sigma_1, \sigma_2, \rho)$ the "best-fit" calibration procedure described for the one-factor model is not necessarily the best approach, since it does not always lead to parameters that make economic sense. It may be better to choose plausible values for some of the five parameters and then estimate the remainder using a best-fit procedure. For example, σ_1 can be interpreted as the standard deviation of the very short rate and can be estimated from the volatilities of short caps. The parameter ρ can be interpreted as the correlation between short and long rates and can be estimated from historical data. Rebonato (1996: Chap. 11) provides a more detailed discussion of the calibration issues involved in the use of the model and shows how he fitted the model to US dollar and DM market data in April 1995.

REFERENCES

Black, F. "Interest rates as options." *Journal of Finance*, 50, 5 (1995), pp. 1371–1376.

Brennan, M., and E. Schwartz. "A continuous time approach to the pricing of bonds." *Journal of Banking and Finance*, 3 (1979), pp. 133–155.

Rebonato, R. *Interest Rate Option Models*. Wiley, New York, 1996.

---

[5] In particular, caps can be valued analytically. Options on coupon-bearing bonds cannot unfortunately be valued analytically since, in a two-factor model, it is not possible to decompose such an option into a portfolio of options on zero-coupon bonds.

17. Single-factor interest rate models and the valuation of interest rate derivative securities *

During the last fifteen years there have been many attempts to describe yield curve movements using a one-factor model. The traditional approach has been to propose a plausible model for the short-term interest rate and deduce from the model the current yield curve and the way it can evolve. The parameters of the model are then chosen so that it reflects market data as closely as possible. Examples of this approach are provided by the work of Vasicek (1977), Dothan (1978), Courtadon (1982), and Cox, Ingersoll, and Ross (1985). Recently some researchers have adopted a different approach. They have taken market data, such as the current term structure of interest rates, as given, and have developed a no-arbitrage yield curve model so that it is perfectly consistent with the data. The main purpose of this paper is to provide some general procedures that can be used when this second approach is adopted.

Ho and Lee (1986) were pioneers in the development of no-arbitrage yield curve models. Their model, which was presented in the form of a binomial tree for discount bond prices, provides an exact fit to the current term structure of interest rates. An alternative to the Ho and Lee model was proposed by Black, Derman, and Toy (1990), who use a binomial tree to construct a one-factor model of the short rate that fits the current volatilities of all discount bond yields as well as the current term structure of interest rates. Hull and White (1990b) suggest two one-factor models of the short rate which are also capable of fitting both current discount bond

* This paper was first published in *Journal of Financial and Quantitative Analysis*, Vol. 28 (1993), pp. 235–254. It is reprinted with the permission of the *Journal of Financial and Quantitative Analysis*.

yield volatilities and the current term structure of interest rates. They show how the parameters of the process followed by the short-term interest rate in the models can be determined from the market data. The continuous-time version of the Ho and Lee model is a particular case of one of the models considered by Hull and White. Heath, Jarrow, and Morton (1990, 1992) consider the process followed by instantaneous forward rates and provide general results that must hold for all arbitrage-free yield curve models.

This brief review of the literature reveals that there have been three main approaches to constructing arbitrage-free models of the term structure. These involve modeling discount bond prices, modeling instantaneous forward rates, and modeling the short rate. In this paper we start by explaining the relationship between the three approaches. We then restrict our attention to one-factor models where the short rate is Markov. We present a general numerical procedure involving the use of trinomial trees for constructing these models so that they are consistent with initial market data.

The procedure proposed in this paper is robust and efficient. It provides a convenient way of implementing models that have already been suggested in the literature such as the extended Vasicek and extended Cox, Ingersoll, and Ross models in Hull and White (1990b), and the lognormal interest rate model in Black and Karasinski (1991). It also enables many other new models to be developed and implemented. The procedure provides an easy way for academics and practitioners to test the effect of a wide range of different assumptions about the interest rate process on the prices of interest rate derivatives. It is important to be able to do this because there is no general agreement on which set of assumptions is best.

The rest of this paper is organized as follows. Section 17.1 compares alternative approaches to constructing arbitrage-free yield curve models and explains the approach used in this paper. Section 17.2 presents our procedure for fitting a one-factor model of the short rate to the initial yield curve using a trinomial interest rate tree. Section 17.3 shows how the procedure can be extended so that the model is fitted to both the initial yield curve and the initial volatilities of all discount bond yields. Section 17.4 compares alternative models that can be implemented using the procedure. Section 17.5 explains how the length of the time step on the tree can be changed. Conclusions are in Section 17.6.

17.1 ALTERNATIVE APPROACHES TO MODELING THE TERM STRUCTURE

There are three broad approaches to constructing arbitrage-free models of the term structure. The first approach, used by Ho and Lee (1986) and Hull and White (1993), involves specifying the process followed by all discount bond prices at all times. The second approach, used by Heath, Jarrow, and Morton (1992), involves specifying the process followed by all instantaneous forward rates at all future times. The third approach used by Black, Derman, and Toy (1990), Hull and White (1990b), and Black and Karasinski (1991) involves specifying the process for the short rate. In this section we explore the relationship between the approaches. We assume that a single factor drives the whole term structure, but the analysis can be extended to the situation where there are several factors.

(a) The Processes for Discount Bond Prices and Forward Rates

We shall adopt the following notation:

$P(t, T)$: price at time t of a discount bond maturing at time T;

$v(t, T)$: volatility of $P(t, T)$;

$F(t, T)$: instantaneous forward rate as seen at time t for a contract maturing at time T;

$r(t)$: short-term risk-free interest rate at time t;

$f(t, T_1, T_2)$: forward rate as seen at time t for the period between time T_1 and time T_2;

$dz(t)$: Wiener process driving term structure movements.

The process that would be followed by $P(t, T)$ in a risk-neutral world is

$$dP(t, T) = r(t)P(t, T)\,dt + v(t, T)P(t, T)\,dz(t). \qquad (17.1)$$

The volatility $v(t, T)$ can in the most general form of the model be any well-behaved function of past and present P's. However, since a bond's price volatility declines to zero at maturity, we must have[1]

$$v(t, t) = 0.$$

The forward rate $f(t, T_1, T_2)$ can be related to discount bond prices as

---

[1] $v(t, t) = 0$ is equivalent to the assumption that all discount bonds have finite drifts at all times. This is because, if the volatility of the bond does not decline to zero at its maturity, an infinite drift may be necessary to ensure that the bond's price equals its face value at maturity.

follows:

$$f(t, T_1, T_2) = \frac{\log[P(t, T_1)] - \log[P(t, T_2)]}{T_2 - T_1}. \qquad (17.2)$$

From (17.1),

$$d \log[P(t, T_1)] = [r(t) - \tfrac{1}{2}v(t, T_1)^2] dt + v(t, T_1) dz(t)$$

and

$$d \log[P(t, T_2)] = [r(t) - \tfrac{1}{2}v(t, T_2)^2] dt + v(t, T_2) dz(t),$$

so that

$$df(t, T_1, T_2) = \frac{v(t, T_2)^2 - v(t, T_1)^2}{2(T_2 - T_1)} dt + \frac{v(t, T_1) - v(t, T_2)}{T_2 - T_1} dz(t).$$
$$(17.3)$$

Equation (17.3) shows that the risk-neutral process for f depends only on the v's. It depends on r and the P's only to the extent that the v's themselves depend on these variables.

When we put $T_1 = T$ and $T_2 = T + \Delta T$ in (17.3) and then take limits as ΔT tends to zero, $f(t, T_1, T_2)$ becomes $F(t, T)$, the coefficient of $dz(t)$ becomes $v_T(t, T)$, and the coefficient of dt becomes $v(t, T)v_T(t, T)$, where subscripts denote partial derivatives. It follows that

$$dF(t, T) = v(t, T)v_T(t, T) dt - v_T(t, T) dz(t),$$

or, since we may without loss of generality change the sign of $dz(t)$,

$$dF(t, T) = v(t, T)v_T(t, T) dt + v_T(t, T) dz(t). \qquad (17.4)$$

Once $v(t, T)$ has been specified for all t and T, the risk-neutral processes for the $F(t, T)$'s are known. The $v(t, T)$'s are therefore sufficient to fully define a one-factor interest rate model.

Integrating $v_T(t, \tau)$ between $\tau = t$ and $\tau = T$, we obtain

$$v(t, T) - v(t, t) = \int_t^T v_T(t, \tau) d\tau.$$

Since $v(t, t) = 0$, this becomes

$$v(t, T) = \int_t^T v_T(t, \tau) d\tau.$$

If $m(t, T)$ and $s(t, T)$ are the instantaneous drift and standard deviation of $F(t, T)$, it follows from (17.4) that

$$m(t, T) = s(t, T) \int_t^T s(t, \tau) d\tau. \qquad (17.5)$$

This is a key result in Heath, Jarrow, and Morton (1992).

(b) The Process for the Short Rate

In this section, we derive the process for $r(t)$ from bond price volatilities and the initial term structure. Since

$$F(t, t) = F(0, t) + \int_0^t dF(\tau, t)$$

and $r(t) = F(t, t)$, it follows from (17.4) that

$$r(t) = F(0, t) + \int_0^t v(\tau, t) v_t(\tau, t) \, d\tau + \int_0^t v_t(\tau, t) \, dz(\tau). \tag{17.6}$$

Differentiating with respect to t and using the result that $v(t, t) = 0$, we obtain

$$dr(t) = F_t(0, t) \, dt + \left(\int_0^t [v(\tau, t) v_{tt}(\tau, t) + v_t(\tau, t)^2] \, d\tau \right) dt$$

$$+ \left(\int_0^t v_{tt}(\tau, t) \, dz(\tau) \right) dt + [v_t(\tau, t)|_{\tau=t}] \, dz(t). \tag{17.7}$$

This is the risk-neutral process for r at time t. It is the process for r that is consistent with the risk-neutral process for bond prices in (17.1). For the purposes of derivative security pricing, we need only concern ourselves with the risk-neutral process for r. This is because derivative securities can be priced by assuming that r follows its risk-neutral process and using the risk-free interest rate for discounting. The procedures that will be described in this paper lead directly to a tree representing the risk-neutral process for r. No assumptions are required about the market price of risk. It is fortunate that, when we move from the real world to a risk-neutral world, the volatilities of all variables remain the same while their drifts change. This means that volatilities observed in the real world can be used to determine the parameters in the risk-neutral process for r.

It is interesting to examine the terms on the right-hand side of (17.7). The first and fourth terms are straightforward. The first term shows that one component of the drift in r is time dependent and equal to the slope of the initial forward rate curve. The fourth term shows that the instantaneous standard deviation of r is $v_t(\tau, t)|_{\tau=t}$. The second and third terms are more complicated, particularly when v is stochastic. The second term depends on the history of v because it involves $v(\tau, t)$ when $\tau < t$. The third term depends on the history of both v and dz. The two terms are therefore liable to cause the process for r to be non-Markov.

Non-Markov models of r are in general less tractable than Markov models. It is computationally feasible to use a non-Markov model when European options are being valued.[2]

However, when American options are valued, it is highly desirable that r be Markov. This is because a Markov process can always be represented by a recombining tree where the number of nodes considered at time $i \Delta t$ grows linearly with i (see Nelson and Ramaswamy 1990 and Hull and White 1990a). For a non-Markov process, the trees that are constructed are in general not recombining and the number of nodes at time $i \Delta t$ grows exponentially with i, so that accurate pricing is computationally extremely time-consuming.

One special case when $r(t)$ is Markov is $v(t, T) = \sigma(T - t)$, where σ is a constant. Equation (17.7) then reduces to

$$dr = [F_t(0, t) + \sigma^2 t] dt + \sigma \, dz(t). \tag{17.8}$$

This is the continuous-time version of the Ho and Lee (1986) model. More generally, Hull and White (1993) show that, when v is non-stochastic, $r(t)$ is Markov if and only if $v(t, T)$ has the functional form

$$v(t, T) = x(t)[y(T) - y(t)]. \tag{17.9}$$

The process for r then has the general form

$$dr = [\theta(t) - \phi(t)r] dt + \sigma(t) \, dz(t).$$

This is the extended Vasicek model considered by Hull and White (1990b).

In this paper we provide a procedure that can be used to construct a wide range of one-factor arbitrage-free models for r. The models are more general than the extended Vasicek model. For example, the standard deviation of r can be a function of r and the drift of r need not be linear in r.

(b) The Approach in this Paper

When v is allowed to be stochastic, it does not seem to be possible to derive a condition similar to (17.9) for a Markov r. It is even difficult to find particular v functions that lead to a Markov r. To expand the range of Markov arbitrage-free models of the short rate available to researchers, we take an alternative approach. We specify a Markov risk-neutral process for r in terms of an unknown function of time, $\theta(t)$, and develop a procedure for choosing this function of time so that the model is consistent with the initial term structure of interest rates. As an extension

---

[2] For example, we can divide the time considered into intervals of length Δt and simulate the Wiener process $\Delta z(t)$, with the values of the $r(t)$'s, $F(t, T)$'s, and $P(t, T)$'s being calculated as necessary from the discrete versions of equations (17.1), (17.4), and (17.7).

to the procedure we show that, if two unknown functions of time are included in the expression assumed for the drift of r, the model can be fitted to both initial term structure and initial volatility data.

Using one state variable and allowing the drift of r to be a function of time provides a relatively simple model that captures the information contained in the initial term structure on expected future trends in r. An alternative approach is to expand the number of state variables. This can be expected to reduce the extent to which the drift must be dependent on time in order to fit the initial term structure, but it does not eliminate the need for time dependence completely. The process for r is in general time dependent in all arbitrage-free models of the term structure that involve a finite number of state variables.[3] Our procedure for determining the functions of time involves using a trinomial tree. As shown by Hull and White (1990a), a trinomial tree is a useful representation of a one-factor model of the short rate. It is capable of duplicating at each node both the expected drift of the short rate and its instantaneous standard deviation. Derivative security prices calculated using the tree converge to the solution of the underlying differential equation for the security price as the length of the time step approaches zero. In a binomial tree with constant time steps, it is not in general possible to match both the expected drift and instantaneous standard deviation at each node without the number of nodes increasing exponentially with the number of time steps.[4]

In this paper we use the trinomial tree in a different way to Hull and White (1990a). Whereas Hull and White (1990a) assume that the short-term interest rate process is known and build a tree to represent that process, this paper assumes that the short-term interest rate process has been specified in terms of unknown functions of time and uses the trinomial tree as a tool to determine these functions.

17.2 FITTING A MODEL TO THE TERM STRUCTURE

In this section we consider models for r where the drift has been specified in terms of a single unknown function of time. We show how to choose this

---

[3] The drift of r in the multifactor version of equation (17.7) always has $F_t(0, t)$ as its leading term. The other terms in the drift are functions of time and the factors. For an arbitrary $F(0, t)$, the drift is a function of time.

[4] Nelson and Ramaswamy (1990) show that, if we require the expected drift and the standard deviation at each node to be correct only in the limit as the length of the time step goes to zero, it is possible to construct a binomial tree where the number of nodes increases linearly with the number of time steps.

function so that the model provides an exact fit to the initial term structure of interest rates.

(a) The Model $dr = \mu(\theta(t), r, t)\, dt + \sigma\, dz(t)$

First we consider a model where the instantaneous standard deviation of r is constant. We assume

$$dr = \mu(\theta(t), r, t)\, dt + \sigma\, dz(t),$$

where σ is a known constant, the functional form for μ is known, and $\theta(t)$ is the unknown function of time. A particular case of the model that is of interest because of its analytic tractability is[5]

$$dr = [\theta(t) - ar]\, dt + \sigma\, dz(t). \tag{17.10}$$

This is a version of the extended Vasicek model discussed by Hull and White (1990b). It has the property that

$$v(t, T) = \frac{\sigma}{a}[1 - e^{-a(T-t)}]. \tag{17.11}$$

We construct a tree whose geometry is similar to that in Hull and White (1990a). The short rate r is defined as the continuously compounded yield on a discount bond maturing in time Δt. The values of r on the tree are equally spaced and have the form $r_0 + j\,\Delta r$ for some Δr, where r_0 is the current value of r and j is a positive or negative integer. The time values considered by the tree are also equally spaced, having the form $i\,\Delta t$ for some Δt, where i is a non-negative integer. The variables Δr and Δt must be chosen so that Δr is between $\frac{1}{2}\sigma\sqrt{3\,\Delta t}$ and $2\sigma\sqrt{\Delta t}$. As pointed out by Hull and White (1990a), there are some theoretical advantages to choosing $\Delta r = \sigma\sqrt{3\,\Delta t}$.

For convenience, the node on the tree where $t = i\,\Delta t$ and $r = r_0 + j\,\Delta r$ ($i \geq 2$) will be referred to as the (i, j) node. We use the following notation:

$R(i)$: yield at time zero on a discount bond maturing at time $i\,\Delta t$;

r_j: $r_0 + j\,\Delta r$;

[5] This particular case of the model has the property that the function $\theta(t)$ can be determined analytically from the term structure. This makes it possible to use the approach in Hull and White (1990a) that is based on a known process for r. We prefer not to do this. Errors are introduced by assuming that the analytic value of θ at time t is correct for the whole time period between t and $t + \Delta t$, and attempts to correct this error by, for example, integrating $\theta(t)$ between t and $t + \Delta t$ are not totally satisfactory. Building a tree in the way that will be described here automatically chooses a value for θ between t and $t + \Delta t$ that matches the current forward bond price. The approach in Hull and White (1990a) is best suited to models where the parameters are not time dependent.

284

$\mu_{i,j}$: the drift rate of r at node (i, j);

$p_1(i, j)$, $p_2(i, j)$, $p_3(i, j)$: probabilities associated with the upper, middle, and lower branches emanating from node (i, j).

We suppose that the tree has already been constructed up to time $n \Delta t$ ($n \geq 0$) so that it is consistent with the $R(i)$, and show how it can be extended one step further. Since the interest rate r at time $i \Delta t$ is assumed to apply to the time period between $i \Delta t$ and $(i + 1) \Delta t$, a tree constructed up to time $n \Delta t$ reflects the values of $R(i)$ for $i \leq n + 1$. In constructing the branches that constitute the tree between times $n \Delta t$ and $(n + 1) \Delta t$, we must choose a value of $\theta(n \Delta t)$ such that the tree is consistent with $R(n + 2)$. The procedure for doing this is explained in Appendix A. Note that, for the purposes of constructing the tree, θ and μ are assumed to be constant within each of the time steps of length Δt.

Once $\theta(n \Delta t)$ has been determined, the drift rates $\mu_{n,j}$ for r at the nodes at time $n \Delta t$ are calculated using

$$\mu_{n,j} = \mu\big(\theta(n \Delta t), r_0 + j \Delta r, n \Delta t\big).$$

The branches emanating from the nodes at time $n \Delta t$ and their associated probabilities are then chosen to be consistent with the $\mu_{n,j}$'s and with σ. The three nodes that can be reached by the branches emanating from node (n, j) are

$$(n + 1, k + 1), \qquad (n + 1, k), \qquad (n + 1, k - 1),$$

with the value of k being chosen so that r_k (the value of r reached by the middle branch) is as close as possible to $r_j + \mu_{n,j} \Delta t$ (the expected value of r). The probabilities are given by

$$p_1(n, j) = \frac{\sigma^2 \Delta t}{2 \Delta r^2} + \frac{\eta^2}{2 \Delta r^2} + \frac{\eta}{2 \Delta r},$$

$$p_2(n, j) = 1 - \frac{\sigma^2 \Delta t}{\Delta r^2} - \frac{\eta^2}{\Delta r^2},$$

$$p_3(n, j) = \frac{\sigma^2 \Delta t}{2 \Delta r^2} + \frac{\eta^2}{2 \Delta r^2} - \frac{\eta}{2 \Delta r},$$

where[6]

$$\eta = \mu_{n,j} \Delta t + (j - k) \Delta r.$$

---

[6] Later in this paper, we will have occasion to use this branching process when the values of r at time $(n + 1) \Delta t$ have the form $r_0 + j \Delta r$, but those at time $n \Delta t$ do not. Suppose that the value of an r at time $n \Delta t$ is r^* and its drift is μ^*. The value of k is chosen so that r_k is as close as possible to $r^* + \mu^* \Delta t$, and the expressions for the probabilities are still correct with

$$\eta = r^* + \mu^* \Delta t - (r_0 + k \Delta r).$$

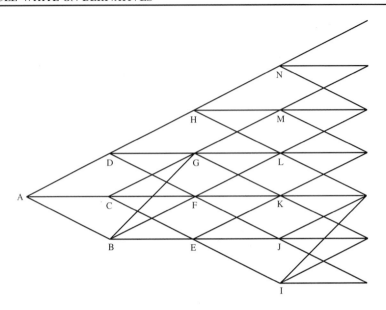

Table of rates and probabilities

Node	A	B	C	D	E	F	G
Rate	10.00	7.58	10.00	12.42	7.58	10.00	12.42
p_1	0.462	0.044	0.507	0.415	0.286	0.221	0.166
p_2	0.493	0.477	0.451	0.534	0.627	0.657	0.667
p_3	0.045	0.479	0.042	0.051	0.087	0.122	0.167

Node	H	I	J	K	L	M	N
Rate	14.85	5.15	7.58	10.00	12.42	14.85	17.27
p_1	0.121	0.042	0.455	0.370	0.293	0.228	0.171
p_2	0.657	0.426	0.499	0.570	0.623	0.654	0.667
p_3	0.222	0.532	0.046	0.060	0.084	0.118	0.162

FIGURE 17.1. Tree constructed for the model $dr = [\theta(t) - ar]\,dt + \sigma\,dz(t)$ when $\sigma = 0.014$, $a = 0.1$, and $\Delta t = 1$ year. The zero-coupon interest rates for maturities of 1, 2, 3, 4, and 5 years are 10%, 10.5%, 11%, 11.25%, and 11.5%. The values calculated for θ are: $\theta(0) = 0.0201$, $\theta(1) = 0.0213$, $\theta(2) = 0.0124$, $\theta(3) = 0.0175$.

Provided that Δr is chosen within the range $\frac{1}{2}\sigma\sqrt{3\,\Delta t}$ to $2\sigma\sqrt{\Delta t}$ mentioned above, the probabilities are always between 0 and 1.

Figure 17.1 illustrates the procedure by showing the tree that is constructed for the model in (17.10) when $a = 0.1$, $\sigma = 0.014$, and $\Delta t = 1$. The term structure is assumed to be upward sloping with the yields on 1-, 2-, 3-, 4-, and 5-year discount bonds being 10%, 10.5%, 11.0%, 11.25%,

TABLE 17.1. Convergence of the proposed procedure for a one-year call option on a five-year discount bond when the model $dr = [\theta(t) - ar]\,dt + \sigma\,dz(t)$ is used with $a = 0.1$ and $\sigma = 0.014$. The term structure increases linearly from 9.5% to 11% over the first three years and then increases linearly from 11% to 11.5% over the next two years.

Total no. of time steps	Exercise price[a]				
	0.96	0.98	1.00	1.02	1.04
5	2.30	1.31	1.00	0.69	0.37
25	2.47	1.68	0.95	0.58	0.25
50	2.48	1.64	1.00	0.55	0.26
100	2.48	1.64	0.99	0.54	0.26
Analytic value	2.48	1.64	0.99	0.53	0.26

a The exercise price is expressed as a proportion of the forward bond price.

11.5%, respectively. Table 17.1 shows the results of using the same model with progressively smaller values of Δt to calculate the prices of one-year European call options on five-year discount bonds. Since these option prices are known analytically, the results provide a test of the speed of convergence of the procedure. The table illustrates that convergence is reasonably fast.

(b) Other Models

We now consider an extension of the above approach to the general class of models

$$dr = \mu\big(\theta(t), r, t\big)\,dt + \sigma(r, t)\,dz(t). \tag{17.12}$$

Here the instantaneous standard deviation of r is a general function of r and t. One particular case of (17.12) that is of interest is

$$dr = [\theta(t) - ar]\,dt + \sigma\sqrt{r}\,dz(t). \tag{17.13}$$

This is a version of the extended Cox–Ingersoll–Ross model that is considered by Cox, Ingersoll, and Ross (1985) and Hull and White (1990b). It has the property that

$$v(t, T) = \sigma\sqrt{r}\,\frac{2(e^{\gamma(T-t)} - 1)}{(\gamma + a)(e^{\gamma(T-t)} - 1) + 2\gamma},$$

where

$$\gamma = \sqrt{a^2 + 2\sigma^2}.$$

A more general family of models corresponding to (17.12) is

$$dr = [\theta(t) - ar]\,dt + \sigma r^\beta\,dz(t). \tag{17.14}$$

where β is a constant. When $\beta = 0$, (17.14) reduces to the model in (17.10); when $\beta = 0.5$, it reduces to the model in (17.13). When $\beta = 0$, the model is capable of fitting any initial term structure. When $\beta > 0$, r must be non-negative for the standard deviation of r to be well defined. This means that, as r tends to zero, the drift of r must be non-negative. One consequence of this is that the condition $\theta(t) \geq 0$ must be satisfied. It can be shown that it is impossible for a $\beta > 0$ model to satisfy this condition and to fit all initial term structures. In particular, term structures where $F(0, t)$ is positive, but $F_t(0, t)$ is highly negative for some values of t, cannot be fitted.[7]

Analogously to Hull and White (1990a), we deal with (17.12) by defining a function $x(r)$ of r that has a constant instantaneous standard deviation. This function is

$$x(r) = \sigma(r_0, 0) \int \frac{dr}{\sigma(r, t)} \,.$$

It follows the process

$$dx = \left[\mu\big(\theta(t), r, t\big) u(r, t) + w(r, t) \right] dt + \sigma(r_0, 0) \, dz(t), \qquad (17.15)$$

where

$$u(r, t) = \frac{\sigma(r_0, 0)}{\sigma(r, t)}, \qquad w(r, t) = -\tfrac{1}{2}\sigma(r_0, 0) \frac{\partial \sigma(r, t)}{\partial r} + \frac{\partial x}{\partial t} \,.$$

We construct a tree for x where the spacing Δx between the x-values is constant and equal to $\sigma(r_0, 0)\sqrt{3 \, \Delta t}$. Assume that a tree has been constructed up to time $n \, \Delta t$. The value of $\theta(n \, \Delta t)$ is calculated as described in Appendix A with r_j now being defined as the value of r at the (i, j) node for x. The branching process for x between times $n \, \Delta t$ and $(n + 1) \, \Delta t$ is then calculated to represent (17.15) using the same procedure as that described for r in Section 17.2(a).

17.3 FITTING A MODEL TO TERM STRUCTURE AND VOLATILITY DATA

In this section we move on to consider models for r that involve two

---

[7] A lognormal model that does not have this problem is a version of Black and Karasinski (1991):
$$d\log r = [\theta(t) - a\log r] dt + \sigma \, dz.$$
An alternative to the extended Cox–Ingersoll–Ross model ($\beta = 0.5$) that does not have the problem is
$$dr = r[\theta(t) - ar] dt + \sigma\sqrt{r}\, dz.$$
It appears that both of these models can be fitted to any initial term structure where $F(0, t) > 0$. They can be implemented using the procedure described in this paper.

functions of time, $\theta(t)$ and $\phi(t)$, and can be fitted to both the initial term structure of interest rates and initial volatility data. We assume that the volatility data consists of discount bond yield volatilities estimated from historical data.

It is important to emphasize that the models developed in this section match the volatilities of the yields on discount bonds only at time zero. There is no guarantee that the pattern of discount bond yield volatilities at later times will be similar to the pattern at time zero.[8] In practice, we find that they are sometimes quite different. Models such as (17.14) in Section 17.2 are more robust. Although they do not match the volatilities at time zero exactly, they have the advantage that they tend to give rise to reasonably stationary volatility structures.[9] They may be more appropriate than the models in this section for valuing long-lived options because the price of a long-lived option can be quite sensitive to the way bond yield volatilities evolve.

One model involving two functions of time is

$$dr = [\theta(t) - \phi(t)r]\,dt + \sigma r^{\beta}\,dz(t). \tag{17.16}$$

This has the same general flavor as (17.14). Another is

$$d\log r = [\theta(t) - \phi(t)\log r]\,dt + \sigma\,dz(t).$$

This is considered by Black and Karasinski (1991).

For the sake of generality, we assume

$$dr = \mu\big(\theta(t),\,\phi(t),\,r,\,t\big)\,dt + \sigma(r,\,t)\,dz(t). \tag{17.17}$$

As in Section 17.2(b), we work in terms of a transformed variable x whose instantaneous standard deviation is constant. For computational convenience, we make one change to the geometry of the tree. We make the tree binomial during the first time step and trinomial thereafter. During the first time interval there is a probability of 0.5 of moving up a new node U and a probability 0.5 of moving down to a new node D. Define

r_u, r_d: values of r at nodes U and D, respectively;

x_u, x_d: values of x at nodes U and D, respectively;

$R_u(i), R_d(i)$: yields at nodes U and D, respectively, on a discount bond maturing at time $i\,\Delta t$;

[8] In general, a non-Markov model is necessary if we require the volatilities of the yields on discount bonds to have some particular pattern at all times.

[9] When $\beta = 0$ or $\beta = 0.5$ in (17.14), $v(t, T)$ is a known function of $T - t$ and r. In general, for models similar to those in equation (17.14) and footnote 7, the volatility structure is stationary in the sense that $v(t, T)$ can depend only on $T - t$ and the term structure at time t.

μ_u, μ_d: the drift rates of r at nodes U and D, respectively;

$V(i)$: volatility at time zero of the yield on a discount bond maturing at time $i\,\Delta t$.

Unlike the values of x considered in Section 17.2(b), the values of x_u and x_d are not necessarily equal to $x(r_0) + j\,\Delta x$ for any integer j. However, the values of x considered at time $n\,\Delta t$ when $n > 1$ do have this form.

The first step in the construction of the tree is to determine $R_u(i)$ and $R_d(i)$ for all $i \geq 1$. These must be consistent with the known values of $R(i)$ so that

$$e^{-r_0\Delta t}[0.5e^{-(i-1)R_u(i)\Delta t} + 0.5e^{-(i-1)R_d(i)\Delta t}] = e^{-iR(i)\Delta t}. \qquad (17.18)$$

They must also be consistent with the known values of $V(i)$. Since $V(i)\sqrt{\Delta t}$ is the standard deviation of the distribution of the natural logarithm of the yield on a discount bond maturing at time $i\,\Delta t$,

$$V(i)\sqrt{\Delta t} = 0.5\log\frac{R_u(i)}{R_d(i)}. \qquad (17.19)$$

Equations (17.18) and (17.19) can be solved for $R_u(i)$ and $R_d(i)$ using the Newton–Raphson procedure. Since $R_u(2)$ and $R_d(2)$ are r_u and r_d, respectively, the solution to (17.18) and (17.19) when $i = 2$ determines the two nodes at time Δt.

The tree is constructed from time Δt onwards using an approach similar to that in Section 17.2. There are two functions of time, $\theta(t)$ and $\phi(t)$. These are chosen to be consistent with $R_u(i)$'s and $R_d(i)$'s using the procedure explained in Appendix B. The branching process is determined as described in Section 17.2. Footnote 6 describes a minor modification necessary for the segment of the tree between Δt and $2\,\Delta t$.

Figure 17.2 illustrates the procedure by showing the tree that is produced for the model

$$dr = [\theta(t) - \phi(t)r]\,dt + \sigma r^\beta\,dz(t). \qquad (17.20)$$

when $\sigma = 0.14$, $\beta = 1$, and $\Delta t = 1$ year. The term structure of interest rates is assumed to be flat at 10% per annum. The volatilities of 1-, 2-, 3-, 4-, and 5-year rates are assumed to be 13%, 12%, 11%, 10%, and 9% per annum, respectively.

17.4 COMPARISON OF MODELS

The procedures in Section 17.3 allow two different models to be fitted to

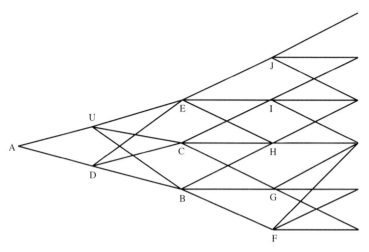

Table of rates and probabilities

Node	A	D	U	B	C	E	F	G	H	I	J
Rate	10.00	8.81	11.20	7.85	10.00	12.74	6.16	7.85	10.00	12.74	16.24
p_1	0.500	0.042	0.411	0.282	0.154	0.088	0.047	0.321	0.153	0.074	0.045
p_2	0.500	0.450	0.537	0.629	0.666	0.627	0.506	0.605	0.665	0.606	0.494
p_3		0.508	0.052	0.089	0.180	0.285	0.447	0.074	0.182	0.320	0.461

FIGURE 17.2. Tree constructed for the model $dr = [\theta(t) - \phi(t)r] dt + \sigma r\, dz(t)$ when $\sigma = 0.14$ and the time step is one year. The term structure of interest rates is flat at 10% per annum. The current volatilities of 1-, 2-, 3-, 4-, and 5-year discount bond yields are 13%, 12%, 11%, 10%, and 9% per annum respectively. The values calculated for θ and ϕ are: $\theta(1) = 0.0165$, $\theta(2) = 0.0193$, $\theta(3) = 0.0244$, $\phi(1) = 0.164$, $\phi(2) = 0.190$, $\phi(3) = 0.241$.

the same term structure of interest rates and volatility data. This makes it possible to assess the impact of different model assumptions on option prices. For bond options and bond futures options lasting less than nine months we find very little difference between the option prices produced by different models. This means that most exchange-traded options can be expected to be relatively insensitive to the model chosen once the term structure of interest rates and discount bond yield volatilities have been determined.

Over-the-counter bond options and swap options frequently last considerably longer than exchange-traded options.[10] It is therefore important to investigate the impact of the model chosen on longer-dated

---

[10] A swap option is an option to exchange a fixed rate bond for a floating rate bond and can be regarded as a type of bond option.

bond options. As the life of the option is increased beyond nine months, we continue to find very little difference between the prices produced by different models for at-the-money options.[11] But for deep-in-the-money and deep-out-of-the-money options, the absolute differences are significant. This is illustrated by Table 17.2, which shows the prices for 1-, 2-, 3-, and 4-year call options on 5-year discount bonds using the model in (17.20) with $\beta = 0, 0.5$, and 1.0. The term structure and initial volatility data are the same as in Figure 17.2 and σ is chosen so that the initial instantaneous standard deviation of r is the same for all models and equal to 0.014. All results are based on 100 time steps. The pattern of results in Table 17.2 can be explained by the effect of β on the skewness of the distributions of future interest rates.[12] In proportional terms, the differences between the prices produced by the models are quite high for deep-out-of-the-money options.

One particularly popular over-the-counter interest rate option is a cap. This is designed to provide insurance against the rate of interest paid on a floating-rate loan rising above a predetermined level (the cap rate). As explained in Hull and White (1990b), a cap can be regarded as a portfolio of put options on bonds. Table 17.3 compares cap prices when $\beta=0, 0.5$, and 1.0 and the models are fitted to the same yield curve and volatility data. The results are generally similar to those for bond options in Table 17.2. The model chosen makes very little difference for at-the-money caps, but can have a significant effect on the prices of out-of-the-money and in-the-money caps.[13]

The correct value for β is an issue that is difficult to resolve by analyzing interest rate data. Dybvig (1988) provides evidence supporting a one-factor model as a parsimonious but reasonable representation of the term structure. Chan et al. (1990) have considered the model in (17.16) with the two functions of time being constants. Using monthly data on 1-month Treasury bill yields between June 1964 and December 1989, they conclude that $\beta = 1.36$ provides the best fit. Our own empirical research shows that maximum-likelihood estimates of β are greatly influenced by

[11] We define an at-the-money European bond option as one where the strike price equals the forward bond price.

[12] As β increases, low interest rates (high bond prices) become less likely and high interest rates (low bond prices) become more likely. This means that the prices of out-of-the-money calls increase. The prices of out-of-the-money puts decrease and, from put–call parity, the prices of in-the-money calls must therefore also decrease.

[13] Since caps pay off when interest rates are high (bond prices low), the impact of changing beta on the prices of in-the-money and out-of-the-money caps is the reverse of that for in-the-money and out-of-the-money call options on bonds (see footnote 12).

TABLE 17.2. Prices of European call options on a five-year discount bond with a face value of $100 when the interest rate model $dr = [\theta(t) - \phi(t)r] dt + \sigma r^\beta dz(t)$ is fitted to the term structure of interest rates and initial discount bond yield volatilities using a trinomial tree. The term structure of interest rates is flat at 10% per annum. The volatility of the yield on a t-year discount bond is assumed to be $(14 - t)\%$ per annum. The parameter σ is chosen so that σr^β equals 0.014 when $r = 0.1$.

Option maturity (years)	β	Exercise price[a]				
		0.96	0.98	1.00	1.02	1.04
	0.0	2.55	1.58	0.84	0.38	0.14
1.0	0.5	2.57	1.60	0.84	0.37	0.12
	1.0	2.59	1.61	0.84	0.36	0.10
	0.0	2.56	1.59	0.85	0.39	0.15
2.0	0.5	2.58	1.61	0.86	0.37	0.13
	1.0	2.61	1.63	0.86	0.35	0.10
	0.0	2.48	1.44	0.67	0.24	0.06
3.0	0.5	2.50	1.46	0.67	0.22	0.04
	1.0	2.52	1.48	0.67	0.20	0.03
	0.0	2.43	1.26	0.37	0.05	0.00
4.0	0.5	2.43	1.27	0.37	0.03	0.00
	1.0	2.44	1.28	0.37	0.02	0.00

a The exercise price is expressed as a proportion of the forward bond price.

TABLE 17.3. Prices, as a percent of principal, of instruments designed to cap an interest rate that is reset every three months. The term structure is flat at 10% per annum with quarterly compounding. The yield volatilities are those for the $\beta = 0$ model with $\sigma = 0.015$ and $a = 0.1$.

Cap maturity (years)	β	Cap rate (%)				
		9.0	9.5	10.0	10.5	11.0
	0.0	0.76	0.49	0.27	0.14	0.07
1.0	0.5	0.76	0.48	0.27	0.14	0.07
	1.0	0.75	0.48	0.27	0.15	0.08
	0.0	1.85	1.30	0.81	0.52	0.30
2.0	0.5	1.83	1.29	0.81	0.53	0.32
	1.0	1.82	1.28	0.81	0.54	0.34
	0.0	2.96	2.16	1.43	1.00	0.64
3.0	0.5	2.92	2.14	1.43	1.02	0.67
	1.0	2.89	2.12	1.44	1.04	0.71
	0.0	4.03	3.02	2.08	1.51	1.02
4.0	0.5	3.98	2.99	2.08	1.54	1.07
	1.0	3.93	2.97	2.08	1.57	1.12
	0.0	5.06	3.86	2.73	2.03	1.41
5.0	0.5	4.98	3.82	2.73	2.07	1.48
	1.0	4.91	3.78	2.73	2.10	1.54

the few observations in a sample where large interest rate movements take place.

An alternative approach to choosing between the models in equation (17.14) is to use the market prices of options. The test of a model's quality is how little the volatility parameters must be varied in order to price correctly a wide range of interest rate options. This is similar to the approach suggested by MacBeth and Merville (1979) and Rubinstein (1985) for evaluating equity option pricing models. The difference is that there are two volatility parameters, a and σ, rather than one.

17.5 CHANGING THE LENGTH OF THE TIME STEP

For many one-factor interest rate models, bond prices are not known analytically as a function of the short rate.[14] When bond options are valued, the interest rate tree must therefore have the same life as the bond. This presents a problem when a short-dated option on a long-dated bond is being valued. The Δt required during the life of the option is generally much smaller than that required for the period of time between the end of the life of the option and the end of the life of the bond. For example, when a 3-month option on a 10-year bond is being valued, it might be appropriate to use 50 time steps each of length 0.005 years during the first 3 months and 39 steps each of length 0.25 years during the remaining 9.75 years. In this section we show how this type of variation in Δt can be achieved.

Suppose that at time τ we require the length of time steps to change from Δt_1 to Δt_2. The new time step length Δt_2 is, we assume, an integral multiple of the old one, Δt_1. The tree is constructed using time steps of length Δt_1 until time $\tau + \Delta t_2$ as described in Sections 17.2 and 17.3. The tree is then used to calculate the value of the Δt_2-maturity interest rate at each of the nodes at time τ. This calculation is necessary because up to time τ the short rate on the tree is the Δt_1-maturity rate. From time τ onwards, it is the Δt_2-maturity rate. Once the calculation has been carried out, the tree constructed between time τ and time $\tau + \Delta t_2$ can be dispensed with.

[14] The extended Vasicek model is the only model where bond prices are known analytically. For the extended Cox–Ingersoll–Ross model in (17.13), Cox, Ingersoll, and Ross (1985) provide an expression for bond prices in terms of an analytically intractable integral. We find that it is computationally more efficient to construct a trinomial tree for calculating bond prices in the extended Cox–Ingersoll–Ross model than to evaluate the integral numerically.

From time τ onwards, the tree is constructed in time steps of length Δt_2. The new Δx is chosen to be equal to the old Δx times $\sqrt{\Delta t_2/\Delta t_1}$. At time $\tau + \Delta t_2$, one of the short rates to be considered can be chosen arbitrarily. The rest are determined by the new Δx. Footnote 6 describes the modifications to the standard calculations necessary to define the branching process between times τ and $\tau + \Delta t_2$.

The geometry of a tree where the size of the time step increases by a factor of three after two steps is illustrated in Figure 17.3.

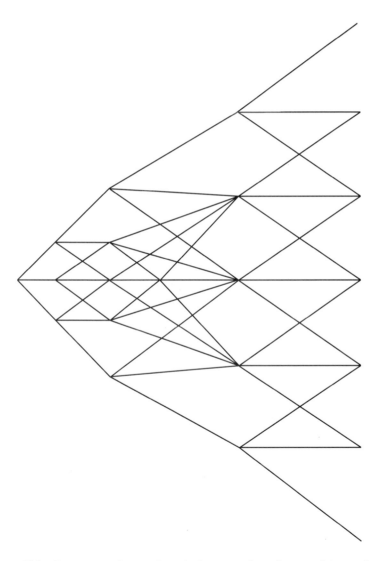

FIGURE 17.3. Geometry of tree when Δt increases by a factor of three after the second step.

295

17.6 CONCLUSIONS

From a computational perspective, there are compelling arguments in favor of using a yield-curve model that is Markov when valuing interest rate derivative securities. It is also desirable that the model fit the initial term structure so that it prices at least one well-known class of securities correctly. One approach to developing a Markov model of the short rate that fits the term structure is to specify a process for the short rate that has one or two unknown functions of time in the drift and then estimate these functions so that the process is consistent with the initial term structure and other market data. Examples of models that are developed using this approach are the extended Vasicek and extended Cox–Ingersoll–Ross models in Hull and White (1990b), and the lognormal interest rate model in Black and Karasinski (1991).

This paper has developed a general procedure, involving the construction of a trinomial tree for the short rate, that implements the approach. The procedure is robust and numerically efficient. It provides an alternative to the model-specific procedures for constructing trees that are suggested by authors such as Ho and Lee (1986) and Black and Karasinski (1991). It provides a way in which the extended Vasicek, the extended Cox–Ingersoll–Ross model, and a wide range of other one-factor models can be implemented.

Once the tree has been constructed, bond options and other non-path-dependent interest rate derivative securities can be valued in the usual way by working back through the tree from the end of the life of the security to time zero. Path-dependent derivative securities can be valued by using Monte Carlo simulation to randomly sample paths through the tree. If required, the length of the time step can be changed during the life of the tree.

APPENDIX A

In this appendix we assume that the tree has been constructed up to time $n \Delta t$ and show how $\theta(n \Delta t)$ is obtained. Define $Q(i, j)$ as the value of a security that pays off \$1 if node (i, j) is reached, and zero otherwise. We assume that the $Q(i, j)$'s are calculated as the tree is being constructed using the relationship

$$Q(i,j) = \sum_{j^*} Q(i-1,j^*)q(j^*,j)e^{-r_{j^*} \Delta t},$$

where $q(j^*, j)$ is the probability of moving from node $(i - 1, j^*)$ to node (i, j).[15] (For any given j^*, this is zero for all except three of the j's.) This means that, when $\theta(n \, \Delta t)$ is being estimated, the $Q(i, j)$'s are known for all $i \leq n$.

The value as seen at node (n, j) of a bond maturing at time $(n + 2) \, \Delta t$ is

$$e^{-r_j \Delta t} E[e^{-r(n+1)\Delta t} \mid r(n) = r_j],$$

where E the risk-neutral expectations operator and $r(i)$ is the value of r at time $i \, \Delta t$. The value at time zero of a discount bond maturing at time $(n + 2) \, \Delta t$ is therefore given by

$$e^{-(n+2)R(n+2)\Delta t} = \sum_j Q(n, j)e^{-r_j \Delta t} E[e^{-r(n+1)\Delta t} \mid r(n) = r_j]. \tag{A1}$$

If we write $\epsilon(n, j)$ as the value of $\{r(n + 1) - r(n) \mid r(n) = r_j\}$, then

$$E[e^{-r(n+1)\,\Delta t} \mid r(n) = r_j] = e^{-r_j \Delta t} E[e^{-\epsilon(n,j)\Delta t}]. \tag{A2}$$

Expanding $e^{-\epsilon(n,j)\Delta t}$ as a Taylor series, taking expectations, and ignoring terms of higher order than Δt^2, we obtain

$$E[e^{-r(n+1)\Delta t} \mid r(n) = r_j] = e^{-r_j \Delta t}[1 - \mu_{n,j}\Delta t^2]. \tag{A3}$$

Since the drift $\mu_{n,j}$ of the short rate is a known function of $\theta(n \, \Delta t)$, we can determine $\theta(n \, \Delta t)$ from (A1) and (A2). For example, in the models in (17.10) and (17.14),

$$\mu_{n,j} = \theta(n \, \Delta t) - ar_j,$$

so that

$$\theta(n \, \Delta t) = \frac{\sum_j Q(n, j)e^{-2r_j \Delta t}(1 + ar_j\Delta t^2) - e^{-(n+2)R(n+2)\Delta t}}{\sum_j Q(n, j)e^{-2r_j \Delta t} \, \Delta t^2}. \tag{A4}$$

The estimates of $\theta(n \, \Delta t)$ given by this equation are found to be satisfactory for most purposes. They lead to a tree where discount bond prices calculated from the tree at time zero replicate those in the market to a least four significant figures. Any errors in the estimates tend to be self-correcting. For example, if the estimate for $\theta(n \, \Delta t)$ is slightly low, the estimate for $\theta((n + 1) \, \Delta t)$ tends to compensate for this by being slightly too high. If an even better fit to the initial yield curve is required, more terms in the Taylor series expansion can be used or an iterative procedure can be developed.

In the case of the extended Vasicek model in (17.10), the expectation in

---

[15] A useful byproduct of storing the Q's is that all discount bond prices and European-style derivative securities can be valued immediately as $\sum_j Q(N, j)U(N, j)$ where $N \, \Delta t$ is the time when the security matures and $U(N, j)$ is the payoff at node (N, j).

(A2) is known analytically:

$$E[e^{-r(n+1)\Delta t} \mid r(n) = r_j] = e^{-r_j\Delta t}e^{[-\theta(n\Delta t)+ar_j+\sigma^2\Delta t/2]\Delta t^2}.$$

Using (A1), this leads to

$$\theta(n\,\Delta t) = \frac{1}{\Delta t}(n+2)R(n+2) + \tfrac{1}{2}\sigma^2\,\Delta t + \frac{1}{\Delta t^2}\log\sum_j Q(n,j)e^{-2r_j\Delta t+ar_j\Delta t^2}.$$

(A5)

This is an improvement over the estimate in (A4) and leads to a tree that replicates discount bond prices at time zero with an accuracy of about eight significant figures.[16]

APPENDIX B

In this appendix we describe how $\theta(n\,\Delta t)$ and $\phi(n\,\Delta t)$ are calculated when a model is being fitted to both the term structure of interest rates and the current volatility structure. We assume that the tree has been constructed up to time $n\,\Delta t$. Define

$Q_u(i,j)$: the value as seen at node U of a security that pays off \$1 if node (i,j) is reached, and zero otherwise;

$Q_d(i,j)$: the value as seen at node D of a security that pays off \$1 if node (i,j) is reached, and zero otherwise;

We assume that the $Q_u(i,j)$'s and $Q_d(i,j)$'s are known for $i \leq n$. As with the Q's in Appendix A, it is possible to calculate them as the tree is being constructed.

Analogously to (A1), when $n \geq 2$, the values as seen at nodes U and D of bonds maturing at time $(n+2)\,\Delta t$ are given by

$$e^{-(n+1)R_u(n+2)\Delta t} = \sum_j Q_u(n,j)e^{-r_j\Delta t}E[e^{-r(n+1)\Delta t} \mid r(n) = r_j] \qquad (\mathrm{B1})$$

and

$$e^{-(n+1)R_d(n+2)\Delta t} = \sum_j Q_d(n,j)e^{-r_j\Delta t}E[e^{-r(n+1)\Delta t} \mid r(n) = r_j], \qquad (\mathrm{B2})$$

respectively.

Equation (A3) is still true. In this case, $\mu_{n,j}$ is a known function of both

---

[16] The tree does not replicate the discount bond prices exactly even though equation (A5) is exact. This is because the trinomial distribution for interest rates in the tree is not a perfect representation of the normal distribution being assumed.

$\theta(n\,\Delta t)$ and $\phi(n\,\Delta t)$. Using (A3) in conjunction with (B1) and (B2), therefore, provides a pair of simultaneous equations for determining $\theta(n\,\Delta t)$ and $\phi(n\,\Delta t)$. In the case of (17.16), the equations are linear in these unknowns:

$$\theta(n\,\Delta t) \sum_j Q_u(n,j)e^{-2r_j\Delta t}\,\Delta t^2 - \phi(n\,\Delta t) \sum_j Q_u(n,j)e^{-2r_j\Delta t}r_j\,\Delta t^2$$
$$= \sum_j Q_u(n,j)e^{-2r_j\Delta t} - e^{-(n+1)R_u(n+2)\Delta t}$$

and

$$\theta(n\,\Delta t) \sum_j Q_d(n,j)e^{-2r_j\Delta t}\,\Delta t^2 - \phi(n\,\Delta t) \sum_j Q_d(n,j)e^{-2r_j\Delta t}r_j\,\Delta t^2$$
$$= \sum_j Q_d(n,j)e^{-2r_j\Delta t} - e^{-(n+1)R_d(n+2)\Delta t}.$$

REFERENCES

Black, F., E. Derman, and W. Toy. "A one-factor model of interest rates and its application to Treasury bond options." *Financial Analysts Journal*, January–February 1990, pp. 33–39.

Black, F., and P. Karasinski. "Bond and option pricing when short rates are lognormal." *Financial Analysts Journal*, July–August 1991, pp. 52–59.

Chan, K. C., G. A. Karolyi, F. A. Longstaff, and A. B. Sanders. "Alternative models of the term structure: an empirical comparison." Working Paper, Ohio State University, 1990.

Courtadon, G. "The pricing of options on default-free bonds." *Journal of Financial and Quantitative Analysis*, 17 (March 1982), pp. 75–100.

Cox, J. C., J. E. Ingersoll, and S. A. Ross. "A theory of the term structure of interest rates." *Econometrica*, 53 (1985), pp. 385–467.

Dothan, L. U. "On the term structure of interest rates." *Journal of Financial Economics*, 6 (1978), pp. 59–69.

Dybvig, P. H., "Bond and bond option pricing based on the current term structure." Working Paper, Olin School of Business, University of Washington, 1988.

Heath, D., R. Jarrow, and A. Morton. "Bond pricing and the term structure of interest rates: a discrete time approximation." *Journal of Financial and Quantitative Analysis*, 25 (December 1990), pp. 419–440.

Heath, D., R. Jarrow, and A. Morton. "Bond pricing and the term structure of interest rates: a new methodology for contingent claims evaluation." *Econometrica*, 60, 1 (1992), pp. 77–105.

Ho, T. S. Y., and S.-B. Lee. "Term structure movements and pricing of interest rate claims." *Journal of Finance*, 41 (December 1986), pp. 1011–1029.

Hull, J., and A. White. "Valuing derivative securities using the explicit finite difference method." *Journal of Financial and Quantitative Analysis*, 25 (March 1990a), pp. 87–100. Also Chapter 6 in this book.

Hull, J., and A. White. "Pricing interest-rate derivative securities." *The Review of Financial Studies*, 3 (1990b), pp. 573–592. Also Chapter 13 in this book.

Hull, J., and A. White. "Bond option pricing based on a model for the evolution of bond prices." *Advances in Futures and Options Research*, 6 (1993), pp. 1–13. Also Chapter 14 in this book.

MacBeth, J. D., and L. J. Merville. "An empirical examination of the Black–Scholes call option pricing model." *Journal of Finance*, 34 (1979), pp. 1173–1186.

Nelson, D. B., and K. Ramaswamy. "Simple binomial processes as diffusion approximations in financial models." *The Review of Financial Studies*, 3 (1990), pp. 393–430.

Rubinstein, M. "Non-parametric tests of alternative options pricing models using all reported trades and quotes on the 30 most active CBOE options classes from August 23, 1976, through August 31, 1978." *Journal of Finance*, 40 (June 1985), pp. 455–480.

Vasicek, O. A. "An equilibrium characterization of the term structure." *Journal of Financial Economics*, 5 (1977), pp. 177–188.

18. Numerical procedures for implementing term structure models I: Single-factor models *

In recent years there has been a trend toward developing models of the term structure where the initial term structure is an input rather than an output. These models are often referred to as no-arbitrage models. The first no-arbitrage model was proposed by Ho and Lee (1986) in the form of a tree of discount bond prices. This model involved one underlying factor and assumed an arithmetic process for the short rate. The Ho–Lee model was later extended to include mean reversion by Hull and White (1990). (Hull and White refer to this as the extended Vasicek model.) One-factor no-arbitrage models where the short rate follows a lognormal process have been proposed by Black, Derman, and Toy (1990) and Black and Karasinski (1991). Heath, Jarrow, and Morton (1992) develop a model of the term structure in terms of the processes followed by forward rates. Hull and White (1993) show how a range of different one-factor no-arbitrage models can be developed using trinomial trees.

Choosing between the different no-arbitrage models of the term structure that have been suggested in the literature involves some difficult trade-offs. A two- or three-factor Heath–Jarrow–Morton model probably provides the most realistic description of term structure movements, but it has the disadvantage that it is non-Markov. This means that it must be implemented using either Monte Carlo simulation or a non-recombining tree. Computations are very time consuming and American-style derivatives are difficult, if not impossible, to value

Of the one-factor Markov models, those where the interest
ıys non-negative are the most attractive. However, the only
une-tactor model that is both capable of fitting an arbitrary initial term
structure and analytically tractable is the Hull–White extended Vasicek
model. In this model negative interest rates can occur.

The main purpose of this paper is to discuss numerical procedures that
can be used to implement a variety of different term structure models
including the Ho–Lee, Hull–White, and Black–Karasinski models. The
paper provides a significant improvement over the trinomial tree
procedure suggested in Hull and White (1993). In a subsequent paper we
will show how the procedures here can be extended to model two term
structures simultaneously and to represent a family of two-factor models.

The rest of this paper is organized as follows. Section 18.1 reviews the
approaches which have been suggested for developing one-factor models
of the term structure. Section 18.2 describes how the new procedure can
be used for the Hull–White model. Section 18.3 extends the procedure the
other models. Section 18.4 discusses the calculation of hedge parameters.
Section 18.5 considers calibration issues. Conclusions are in Section 18.6.

18.1 ONE-FACTOR INTEREST RATE MODELS

Heath, Jarrow, and Morton (1992) provide the most general approach to
constructing a one-factor no-arbitrage model of the term structure. Their
approach involves specifying the volatilities of all forward rates at all
times. The expected drifts of forward rates in a risk-neutral world are
calculated from their volatilities and the initial values of the forward rates
are chosen to be consistent with the initial term structure. Unfortunately
the model that results from the Heath–Jarrow–Morton approach is
usually non-Markov. There are only a small number of known forward
rate volatility functions that give rise to Markov models.[1] To develop
additional Markov one-factor models, an alternative to the Heath–
Jarrow–Morton approach has become popular. This involves specifying a
Markov process for the short-term interest rate, r, in terms of a function
of time, $\theta(t)$. The function of time is chosen so that the model exactly fits
the current term structure.

The Ho and Lee (1986) model can be used to provide an example of the

---

[1] These are the Ho and Lee (1986) and Hull and White (1990).

alternative approach. The continuous time limit of the Ho and Lee (1986) model is[2]

$$dr = \theta(t)\,dt + \sigma\,dz.$$

In this model all zero-coupon interest rates at all times are normally distributed and have the same variance rate, σ^2. The value of $\theta(t)$ is chosen to make the model consistent with the initial term structure. As a rough approximation, $\theta(t)$ is the slope of the forward curve at time zero.[3]

Since Ho and Lee published their paper, it has been shown that their model has a great deal of analytic tractability (see, for example, Hull and White, 1990). Define $F(t, T)$ as the instantaneous forward rate at time t for a contract maturing at T. The parameter $\theta(t)$ is given by

$$\theta(t) = F_t(0, t) + \sigma^2 t,$$

where the subscript denotes the derivative. The price $P(t, T)$ at time t of a discount bond maturing at time T can be expressed in terms of the value of r at time t:

$$P(t, T) = A(t, T)e^{-r(T-t)},$$

where

$$\log A(t, T) = \log\frac{P(0, T)}{P(0, t)} + (T - t)F(0, t) - \tfrac{1}{2}\sigma^2 t(T - t)^2.$$

Since zero-coupon interest rates are normally distributed, discount bond prices are lognormally distributed. This means that it is possible to use a variant of Black–Scholes to value options on discount bonds. The price c at time t of a European call option on discount bond is given by

$$c = P(t, s)N(h) - XP(t, T)N(h - \sigma_P), \tag{18.1}$$

where T is the maturity of the option, s is the maturity of the bond underlying the option, X is the strike price,

$$h = \frac{1}{\sigma_P}\log\frac{P(t, s)}{P(t, T)X} + \frac{\sigma_P}{2},$$

and

$$\sigma_P^2 = \sigma^2(s - T)^2(T - t).$$

The variable σ_P is the product of the forward bond price volatility and the

---

[2] Note that all the processes for r in this paper are those in a risk-neutral world rather than in the real world.

[3] A more precise statement is that $\theta(t)$ is the partial derivative with respect to t of instantaneous futures rate for a contract with maturity t. When interest rates are stochastic, forward and futures rates are not exactly the same.

square root of the life of the option.

European options on coupon-bearing bonds can be valued analytically using the approach in Jamshidian (1989). This approach uses the fact that all bonds are instantaneously perfectly correlated to express an option on a coupon-bearing bond as the sum of options on the discount bonds that make up the coupon-bearing bond.

The Hull–White (extended Vasicek) model can be regarded as an extension of Ho–Lee that incorporates mean reversion. The short rate r follows the process

$$dr = [\theta(t) - ar]\,dt + \sigma\,dz$$

in a risk-neutral world. The short rate is pulled towards its expected value at rate a. There are two volatility parameters, a and σ. The parameter σ determines the overall level of volatility; the reversion rate parameter, a, determines the relative volatilities of long and short rates. As in the Ho–Lee model, the probability distribution of all rates at all times is normal.

Like Ho–Lee, the Hull–White model has a great deal of analytic tractability. The parameter $\theta(t)$ is given by

$$\theta(t) = F_t(0, t) + aF(0, t) + \frac{\sigma^2}{2a}(1 - e^{-2at}). \qquad (18.2)$$

The price at time t of a discount bond maturing at time T is given by

$$P(t, T) = A(t, T)e^{-B(t,T)r},$$

where

$$B(t, T) = \frac{1}{a}[1 - e^{-a(T-t)}]$$

and

$$\log A(t, T) = \log \frac{P(0, T)}{P(0, t)} + B(t, T)F(0, t) - \frac{\sigma^2}{4a}(1 - e^{-2at})B(t, T)^2.$$

The price c at time t of a European call option on discount bond is given by equation (18.1) with

$$\sigma_P^2 = \frac{\sigma^2}{2a}(1 - e^{-2a(T-t)})B(T, s)^2.$$

As in the case of Ho–Lee, European options on coupon-bearing bonds can be valued analytically using the decomposition approach in Jamshidian (1989).

Another model of the short rate was suggested by Black, Derman, and

Toy (1990). The continuous time limit of their model is:

$$d \log r = \left[\theta(t) + \frac{\sigma'(t)}{\sigma(t)} \log r \right] dt + \sigma(t) \, dz.$$

This model has no analytic tractability. The probability distribution of the short rate at all times is lognormal and the reversion rate $-\sigma'(t)/\sigma(t)$ is a function of the short rate volatility $\sigma(t)$. In practice the Black–Derman–Toy model is often implemented with $\sigma(t)$ constant. It then reduces to a lognormal version of Ho–Lee:

$$d \log r = \theta(t) \, dt + \sigma \, dz.$$

Black and Karasinski (1991) decoupled the reversion rate and the volatility in the Black–Derman–Toy model to get

$$d \log r = [\theta(t) - a(t) \log r] \, dt + \sigma(t) \, dz.$$

Black and Karasinski provide a procedure involving a binomial tree and time steps of varying lengths for implementing their model.

One issue that arises in both the Hull–White and Black–Karasinski models is whether a and σ should be functions of time.[4] The advantage of making these parameters functions of time is that it is possible to fit the volatility structure at time zero exactly. The disadvantage is that the volatility structure at future times is liable to be quite different from the volatility structure today. We first noticed this when trying to fit the "hump" in cap volatilities by making a a function of time. The resulting volatility structure as seen at a time immediately after the hump proves to be steeply downward sloping—quite different from the initial volatility structure.

A reasonable approach may be to introduce a small amount of time dependence into the a and σ parameters without trying to match initial volatilities exactly. For example, we might choose to set the reversion rate a to zero beyond year 7 to reflect the fact that the volatility curve appears to "level out" at about this time. This type of modification to the basic model can be easily accommodated by the tree-building technology that we describe here.

18.2 BUILDING TREES FOR THE HULL–WHITE MODEL

In this section we present a procedure for building trees for the

---

[4] Like Black and Karasinski, Hull and White provide results for the general case where a and σ are functions of time in their original 1990 paper.

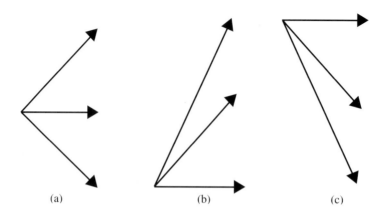

(a)   (b)   (c)

FIGURE 18.1. Alternative branching processes.

Hull–White model

$$dr = [\theta(t) - ar]\, dt + \sigma\, dz. \qquad (18.3)$$

Although this model has many analytic properties, a tree is necessary to value instruments such as American-style swap options and indexed amortizing rate swaps. In the next section we will extend the tree-building procedure to accommodate a range of models.

Hull and White (1993) construct a trinomial tree to represent movements in r by using time steps of length Δt and considering at the end of each time step r-values of the form $r_0 + k\, \Delta r$, where k is a positive or negative integer and r_0 is the initial value of r. The tree-branching can take any of the forms shown in Figure 18.1. Here we improve upon Hull and White (1993) by arranging the geometry of the tree so that the central node always corresponds to the expected value of r. We find that this leads to faster tree construction, more accurate pricing, and much more accurate values for hedge parameters.

The first stage is to build a tree for r on the assumption that $\theta(t) = 0$ and the initial value of r is zero. The process assumed for r during the first stage is therefore

$$dr = -ar\, dt + \sigma\, dz.$$

For this process, $r(t + \Delta t) - r(t)$ is normally distributed. For the purpose of tree construction we define r as the continuously compounded Δt-period rate. We denote the expected value of $r(t + \Delta t) - r(t)$ as $r(t)M$ and the variance of $r(t + \Delta t) - r(t)$ as V. We first choose the size of the time step, Δt. We then set the size of the interest rate step in the tree, Δr, as

$$\Delta r = \sqrt{3V}.$$

Theoretical work in numerical procedures suggests that this is a good choice of Δr from the viewpoint of error minimization.

Our objective is to build a tree similar to that shown in Figure 18.2, where the nodes are evenly spaced in r and t. To do this we must resolve which of the three branching methods shown in Figure 18.1 will apply at each node. This will determine the overall shape of the tree. Once this is done, the branching probabilities must also be calculated.

Define (i, j) as the node for which $t = i\,\Delta t$ and $r = j\,\Delta r$. Define p_u, p_m, and p_d as the probabilities of the highest, middle, and lowest branches emanating from a node. The probabilities are chosen to match the expected change and variance of the change in r over the next time interval Δt. The probabilities must also sum to unity. This leads to three equations in the three probabilities. When r is at node (i, j) the expected change during the next time step of length Δt is $j\,\Delta r\, M$ and the variance of the change is V. If the branching from node (i, j) is as in Figure 18.1(a), the solution to the equations is

$$p_u = \tfrac{1}{6} + \tfrac{1}{2}(j^2 M^2 + jM),$$
$$p_m = \tfrac{2}{3} - j^2 M^2,$$
$$p_d = \tfrac{1}{6} + \tfrac{1}{2}(j^2 M^2 - jM),$$

respectively. If the branching has the form shown in Figure 18.1(b), the solution is

$$p_u = \tfrac{1}{6} + \tfrac{1}{2}(j^2 M^2 - jM),$$
$$p_m = -\tfrac{1}{3} - j^2 M^2 + 2jM,$$
$$p_d = \tfrac{7}{6} + \tfrac{1}{2}(j^2 M^2 - 3jM).$$

Finally, if it has the form shown in Figure 18.1(c), the solution is

$$p_u = \tfrac{7}{6} + \tfrac{1}{2}(j^2 M^2 + 3jM),$$
$$p_m = -\tfrac{1}{3} - j^2 M^2 - 2jM,$$
$$p_d = \tfrac{1}{6} + \tfrac{1}{2}(j^2 M^2 + jM).$$

Most of the time the branching in Figure 18.1(a) is appropriate. When $a > 0$, it is necessary to switch from the branching in Figure 18.1(a) to the branching in Figure 18.1(c) when j is large. This is to ensure that the probabilities p_u, p_m, and p_d are all positive. Similarly it is necessary to switch from the branching in Figure 18.1(a) to the branching in Figure 18.1(b) when j is small. Define $j_{\max}$ as the value of j where we switch from the Figure 18.1(a) branching to the Figure 18.1(c) branching and $j_{\min}$ as the value of j where we switch from the Figure 18.1(a)

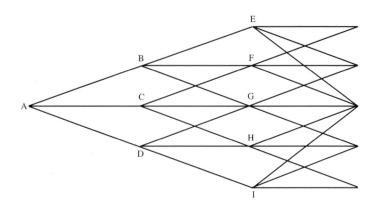

Node	A	B	C	D	E	F	G	H	I
r (%)	0.00	1.73	0.00	−1.73	3.46	1.73	0.00	−1.73	−3.46
p_u	0.167	0.122	0.167	0.222	0.887	0.122	0.167	0.222	0.087
p_m	0.666	0.656	0.666	0.656	0.026	0.656	0.666	0.656	0.026
p_d	0.167	0.222	0.167	0.122	0.087	0.222	0.167	0.122	0.887

FIGURE 18.2. The tree with $\theta(t) = 0$ when $f(r) = r$, $a = 0.1$, $\sigma = 0.01$, and $\Delta t = 1$ year.

branching to the Figure 18.1(b) branching. It can be shown from the above equations that p_u, p_m, and p_d are always positive providing j_{max} is chosen to be an integer between $-0.184/M$ and $-0.816/M$ and j_{min} is chosen to be an integer between $0.184/M$ and $0.816/M$. (Note that when $a > 0$, $M > 0$.) In practice we find that it is most efficient to set j_{max} equal to the smallest integer greater than $-0.184/M$ and j_{min} equal to $-j_{max}$.

We illustrate the first stage of the tree construction by showing how the tree in Figure 18.2 is constructed for $\sigma = 0.01$, $a = 0.1$, and $\Delta t = 1$ year. In this example we set $M = -a \Delta t$ and $V = \sigma^2 \Delta t$. This is accurate to the order of Δt.[5] The first step in the construction of the tree is to calculate Δr from Δt. In this case $\Delta r = 0.01\sqrt{3} = 0.0173$. The next step is to calculate the bounds for j_{max}. These are $0.184/0.1$ and $0.816/0.1$ or 1.84 and 8.16. We set $j_{max} = 2$. Similarly we set $j_{min} = -2$. The probabilities on the branches emanating from each node are calculated using the above equations for p_u, p_m, and p_d.

Note that the probabilities at each node depend only on j. For example, the probabilities at node B are the same as the probabilities at

---

[5] For slightly faster convergence we can set M and V equal to their exact values:

$$M = e^{-a\Delta t} - 1, \qquad V = \sigma^2(1 - e^{-2a\Delta t})/2a.$$

node F. Furthermore the tree is symmetrical. The probabilities at node D are the mirror image of the probabilities at node B.

The next stage in the tree construction is to displace the nodes at time $i \, \Delta t$ by an amount α_i to produce a new tree, Figure 18.3. The value of r at node (i, j) in the new tree equals the value of r at node (i, j) in the old tree plus α_i. The probabilities on the tree are unchanged. The values of the α_i's are chosen so that the tree prices all discount bonds consistently with the initial term structure.

The effect moving from the tree in Figure 18.2 to the tree in Figure 18.3 is to change the process being modeled from

$$dr = -ar \, dt + \sigma \, dz$$

to

$$dr = [\theta(t) - ar] \, dt + \sigma \, dz.$$

If we define $\hat{\theta}(t)$ as the estimate of θ given by the tree between times t and $t + \Delta t$, the drift in r at time $i \, \Delta t$ at the midpoint of the tree is $\hat{\theta}(t) - a\alpha_i$ so that[6]

$$[\hat{\theta}(t) - a\alpha_i] \, \Delta t = \alpha_i - \alpha_{i-1},$$

or

$$\hat{\theta}(t) = \frac{\alpha_i - \alpha_{i-1}}{\Delta t} + a\alpha_i.$$

This equation relates the $\hat{\theta}$'s to the α's. In the limit as $\Delta t \to 0$, $\hat{\theta}(t) \to \theta(t)$.[7]

To facilitate computations, we define $Q_{i,j}$ as the present value of a security that pays off \$1 if node (i, j) is reached and zero otherwise. The α_i and $Q_{i,j}$ are calculated using forward induction. We will illustrate the procedure by showing how the tree in Figure 18.3 is calculated from the tree in Figure 18.2 when the t-year zero rate is $0.08 - 0.05e^{-0.18t}$. (This corresponds approximately to the term structure at the beginning of 1994.)

The value of $Q_{0,0}$ is 1. The value of α_0 is chosen to give the right price for a zero-coupon bond maturing at time Δt. That is, α_0 is set equal to the initial Δt period interest rate. Since $\Delta t = 1$ in this example, $\alpha_0 = 0.0382$.

---

[6] Equation (18.2) provides an analytic expression for $\theta(t)$. We prefer not to use this and to construct the tree using the iterative approach described here. This is because it leads to a tree where the initial term structure is matched exactly. If the value of θ at time t is assumed to apply to the time interval between t and $t + \Delta t$, the initial term structure is matched exactly only in the limit as Δt tends to zero.

[7] It is not necessary to calculate θ or $\hat{\theta}$ in order to construct or use the tree.

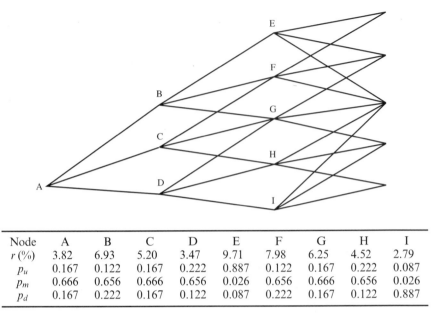

Node	A	B	C	D	E	F	G	H	I
r (%)	3.82	6.93	5.20	3.47	9.71	7.98	6.25	4.52	2.79
p_u	0.167	0.122	0.167	0.222	0.887	0.122	0.167	0.222	0.087
p_m	0.666	0.656	0.666	0.656	0.026	0.656	0.666	0.656	0.026
p_d	0.167	0.222	0.167	0.122	0.087	0.222	0.167	0.122	0.887

FIGURE 18.3. The final tree when $f(r) = r$, $a = 0.1$, $\sigma = 0.01$, $\Delta t = 1$ year, and the t-year zero rate is $0.08 - 0.05e^{-0.18t}$.

The next step is to calculate the values of $Q_{1,1}$, $Q_{1,0}$, and $Q_{1,-1}$. There is a probability of 0.1667 that the (1, 1) node is reached and the discount rate for the first time step is 3.82%. The value of $Q_{1,1}$ is therefore $0.1667e^{-0.0382} = 0.1604$. Similarly $Q_{1,0} = 0.6417$ and $Q_{1,-1} = 0.1604$.

Once $Q_{1,1}$, $Q_{1,0}$, and $Q_{1,-1}$ have been calculated, we are in a position to determine α_1. This is chosen to give the right price for a zero-coupon bond maturing at time $2\,\Delta t$. Since $\Delta r = 0.0173$ and $\Delta t = 1$, the price of this bond as seen at node B is $e^{-(\alpha_1 + 0.0173)}$. Similarly the price as seen at node C is $e^{-\alpha_1}$ and the price as seen at node D is $e^{-(\alpha_1 - 0.0173)}$. The price as seen at the initial node A is therefore

$$Q_{1,1}e^{-(\alpha_1 + 0.0173)} + Q_{1,0}e^{-\alpha_1} + Q_{1,-1}e^{-(\alpha_1 - 0.0173)}. \qquad (18.4)$$

From the initial term structure this bond price should be $e^{-0.04512 \times 2} = 0.9137$. Substituting for the Q's in equation (18.3), we obtain

$$0.1604e^{-(\alpha_1 + 0.0173)} + 0.6417e^{-\alpha_1} + 0.1604e^{-(\alpha_1 - 0.0173)} = 0.9137.$$

This can be solved to give $\alpha_1 = 0.0520$.

The next step is to calculate $Q_{2,2}$, $Q_{2,1}$, $Q_{2,0}$, $Q_{2,-1}$, and $Q_{2,-2}$. These are found by discounting the value of a single $1 payment at one of nodes E–I back through the tree. This can be simplified by using previously determined Q values. Consider as an example $Q_{2,1}$. This is the value of a security that pays off \$1 if node F is reached and zero otherwise. Node F can be reached only from nodes B and C. The interest rates at these nodes are 6.93% and 5.20% respectively. The probabilities associated with the B–F and C–F branches are 0.656 and 0.167. The value at node B of \$1 received at node F is therefore $0.656e^{-0.0693}$. The value at node C is $0.167e^{-0.0520}$ and the present value is the sum of each of these weighted by the present value of \$1 received at the corresponding node. This is

$$0.656e^{-0.0693} \times 0.1604 + 0.167e^{-0.0520} \times 0.6417 = 0.1997.$$

Similarly, $Q_{2,2} = 0.0183$, $Q_{2,0} = 0.4737$, $Q_{2,-1} = 0.2032$, and $Q_{2,-2} = 0.0189$.

The next step is to calculate α_2. After that, the $Q_{3,j}$'s can then be computed. We can then calculate α_3; and so on.

To express the approach more formally, we suppose the $Q_{i,j}$'s have been determined for $i \leq m$ ($m \geq 0$). The next step is to determine α_m so that the tree correctly prices a discount bond maturing at $(m+1)\Delta t$. The interest rate at node (m, j) is $\alpha_m + j\Delta r$ so that the price of a discount bond maturing at time $(m+1)\Delta t$ is given by

$$P_{m+1} = \sum_{j=-n_m}^{n_m} Q_{m,j} \exp[-(\alpha_m + j\Delta r)\Delta t], \qquad (18.5)$$

where n_m is the number of nodes on each side of the central node at time $m\Delta t$. The solution of this equation is

$$\alpha_m = \frac{\log \sum_{j=-n_m}^{n_m} Q_{m,j} e^{-j\Delta r\Delta t} - \log P_{m+1}}{\Delta t}.$$

Once α_m has been determined, the $Q_{i,j}$ for $i = m+1$ can be calculated using

$$Q_{m+1,j} = \sum_{k} Q_{m,k} q(k, j) \exp[-(\alpha_m + k\Delta r)\Delta t],$$

where $q(k, j)$ is the probability of moving from node (m, k) to node $(m+1, j)$ and the summation is taken over all values of k for which this is non-zero.

18.3 EXTENSION TO OTHER MODELS

We now show how the procedure in the previous section can be extended to more general models of the form

$$df(r) = [\theta(t) - af(r)] \, dt + \sigma \, dz.$$

These models have the advantage that they can fit any term structure.[8] When $f(r) = \log r$, the model is a version of the Black and Karasinski (1991) model.

We start by setting $x = f(r)$ so that

$$dx = [\theta(t) - ax] \, dt + \sigma \, dz.$$

The first stage is to build a tree for x on the assumption that $\theta(t) = 0$ and the initial value of x is zero. The procedure here is identical to the procedure for building the tree in Figure 18.2 outlined in the previous section.

Similarly to the previous section we then displace the nodes at time $i \, \Delta t$ by an amount α_i to provide an exact fit to the initial term structure. The equations for determining α_i and $Q_{i,j}$ inductively are slightly different from those in the previous section. $Q_{0,0} = 1$. Suppose the $Q_{i,j}$'s have been determined for $i \leq m$ $(m \geq 0)$. The next step is to determine α_m so that the tree correctly prices an $(m+1) \, \Delta t$ discount bond.

Define g as the inverse function of f, so that the Δt-period interest rate at the jth node at time t_m is

$$g(\alpha_m + j \, \Delta x).$$

The period 0 price of a discount bond maturing at time t_{m+1} is given by

$$P_{m+1} = \sum_{j=-n_m}^{n_m} Q_{m,j} \exp[-g(\alpha_m + j \, \Delta x) \, \Delta t]. \qquad (18.6)$$

This equation can usually be solved with a small number of iterations using the Newton–Raphson procedure. When $m = 0$, equation (18.4) can be solved to give $\alpha_0 = f(r_0)$, where r_0 is the continuously compounded yield on the Δt maturity discount bond.

Once α_m has been determined, the $Q_{i,j}$ for $i = m+1$ can be calculated using

$$Q_{m+1,j} = \sum_k Q_{m,k} q(k,j) \exp[-g(\alpha_m + k \, \Delta x) \, \Delta t],$$

[8] Not all no-arbitrage models have this property. For example, the extended Cox–Ingersoll–Ross model, considered by Cox, Ingersoll, and Ross (1985) and Hull and White (1990), which has the form

$$dr = [\theta(t) - ar] \, dt + \sigma \sqrt{r} \, dz,$$

cannot fit steeply downward-sloping yield curves. This is because the process is not well defined when $\theta(t)$ is negative. When r is small, the negative drift makes r become negative resulting in imaginary volatilities.

where $q(k, j)$ is the probability of moving from node (m, k) to node $(m + 1, j)$ and the summation is taken over all values of k for which this is non-zero.

Figure 18.4 shows the results of applying the procedure to the model

$$d \log r = [\theta(t) - a \log r] \, dt + \sigma \, dz$$

when $a = 0.22$, $\sigma = 0.25$, $\Delta t = 0.5$, and the t-year zero-coupon yield is $0.08 - 0.05e^{-0.18t}$.

The procedures that have been described here can be extended in a number of ways. First, the parameter a can be a function of time. This does not affect the positions of the central nodes or Δx. It leads to the probabilities, and possibly the rules for branching, being different at each time step. Second, the parameter σ can be made a function of time. The easiest approach here is to make the time step on the tree inversely proportional to σ^2. Third, iterative procedures can be devised to choose functions of time for a and σ so that aspects of the initial term structure are matched. (As explained earlier we do not recommend this.) Finally, the length of time step can be changed using a procedure analogous to that outlined in Hull and White (1993).

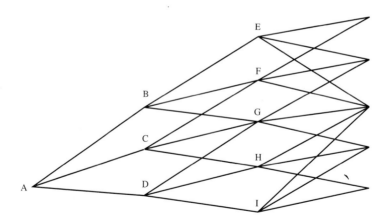

Node	A	B	C	D	E	F	G	H	I
x	−3.3725	−2.8751	−3.1813	−3.4875	−2.4300	−2.7362	−3.0424	−3.3486	−3.6548
r (%)	3.43	5.64	4.15	3.06	8.80	6.48	4.77	3.51	2.59
p_u	0.167	0.118	0.167	0.228	0.861	0.118	0.167	0.228	0.081
p_m	0.666	0.654	0.666	0.654	0.058	0.654	0.666	0.654	0.058
p_d	0.167	0.228	0.167	0.118	0.081	0.228	0.167	0.118	0.861

FIGURE 18.4. The tree when $f(r) = \log(r)$, $a = 0.22$, $\sigma = 0.25$, $\Delta t = 0.5$ year, and the t-year zero rate is $0.08 - 0.05e^{-0.18t}$.

18.4 CALCULATION OF HEDGE STATISTICS

Delta, in this case the partial derivative of the price of a security with respect to the short rate r, can be calculated directly from the tree in the usual way. In practice, practitioners are usually interested in calculating the partial derivative of a security price with respect to a number of different shifts in the term structure. A popular approach is to divide the zero curve or the forward curve into a number of sections or "buckets" and consider changes in the zero curve where there is a small shift in one bucket and where the rest of the zero curve is unchanged.

To calculate a delta with respect to a shift in the term structure, we compute the value of the security in the usual way. We then make the shift in the term structure, reconstruct the tree, and observe the change in the security price.

A key feature of our tree-building procedure is that the position of the branches on the tree relative to the central branch and the probabilities associated with the branches do not depend on the term structure. A small change in the term structure affects only the α_i. The result of all this is a control variate effect where the delta is estimated very accurately.[9]

We favor calculating two vega measures: the partial derivative with respect to the parameters a and σ. In each case we make a small change to the parameter, reconstruct the tree and observe the effect on the security price. In the case of σ, a small change affects only the spacing of the nodes; it does not alter the probabilities. In the case of a, a small change affects the probabilities in a symmetrical way; it does not affect the positions of nodes. In both cases there is a control variate effect that leads to the partial derivatives being calculated with a high degree of accuracy.

There are many different gamma measures that can be calculated. We favor a single overall measure of curvature: the second partial derivative of the security price with respect to r. This can be calculated directly from the tree.

18.5 CALIBRATION

The Black–Scholes stock option model has the simplifying feature that it

---

[9] In Hull and White (1993) a small change in the term structure is liable to lead to a change in all the branching probabilities. This introduces "noise" and results in the effect of small changes in the term structure on the price of a derivative being estimated with much less precision.

involves only one volatility parameter. The usual procedure for calibrating the model to the market is to imply this parameter from the market prices of actively traded stock options. The models presented here are more complicated than Black–Scholes in that they involve two volatility parameters, a and σ. The parameter σ determines the overall volatility of the short rate. The parameter a determines the relative volatilities of long and short rates. In practice both parameters are liable to change over time.

We favor inferring both parameters from broker quotes or other market data on the prices of interest rate options. Our procedure is to choose the values of a and σ that minimize

$$\sum_i (P_i - V_i)^2,$$

where P_i is the market price of the ith interest rate option and V_i is the price given by the model for the ith interest rate option. The minimization is accomplished using an iterative search "hill-climbing" technique. When calibrating the Hull–White model to the prices of seven at-the-money swap options we find that the best fit values of a and σ give a root mean square pricing error of about 1% of the option price.

18.6 CONCLUSIONS

This paper has proposed a new numerical procedure for one-factor term structure models. The approach can be used for the Hull–White extended Vasicek model and for lognormal models similar to those proposed by Black, Derman, and Toy (1990) and Black and Karasinski (1991). The new approach is simpler and faster than previously suggested approaches. What is more, it gives greater accuracy for both the pricing of interest rate derivatives and hedge parameters.

REFERENCES

Black, F., E. Derman, and W. Toy. "A one-factor model of interest rates and its application to Treasury bond options." *Financial Analysts Journal*, January–February 1990, pp. 33–39.

Black, F. and P. Karasinski. "Bond and option pricing when short rates are lognormal." *Financial Analysts Journal*, July–August, 1991, pp. 52–59.

Heath, D., R. Jarrow, and A. Morton. "Bond pricing and the term structure of interest rates: a new methodology." *Econometrica*, 60, 1 (1992), pp. 77–105.

Ho, T.S.Y. and S.-B. Lee. "Term structure movements and the pricing interest rate contingent claims." *Journal of Finance*, 41 (December 1986), pp. 1011–1029.

Hull, J. and A. White. "Pricing interest rate derivative securities." *Review of Financial Studies*, 3, 4 (1990), pp. 573–592. Also Chapter 13 in this book.

Hull, J. and A. White, "One-factor interest rate models and the valuation of interest rate derivative securities." *Journal of Financial and Quantitative Analysis*, 28 (1993), pp. 235–254. Also Chapter 17 in this book.

Jamshidian, F., "An exact bond option pricing formula." *Journal of Finance*, 44 (March 1989), pp. 205-209.

19. Numerical procedures for implementing term structure models II: Two-factor models*

The most general approach to constructing models of the term structure is the one suggested by Heath, Jarrow, and Morton (1992). This involves specifying the volatilities of all forward rates at all times. The expected drifts of forward rates in a risk-neutral world are calculated from their volatilities and the initial values of the forward rates are chosen to be consistent with the initial term structure.

Unfortunately the models that result from the Heath–Jarrow–Morton approach are usually non-Markov, meaning that the parameters of the process for the evolution of interest rates at a future date depend on the history of interest rates as well as on the term structure at that date. To develop Markov one-factor models, an alternative approach has become popular. This involves specifying a Markov process for the short-term interest rate, r, in terms of a function of time, $\theta(t)$. The function of time is chosen so that the model exactly fits the current term structure.

Hull and White (1994) considered models of the short rate r of the form

$$dx = [\theta(t) - ax] \, dt + \sigma \, dz, \tag{19.1}$$

where $x = f(r)$ for some function f, a and σ are constants, and $\theta(t)$ is a function of time chosen so that the model provides an exact fit to the initial term structure. This general family contains many of the common one-factor term structure models as special cases. When $f(r) = r$ and

$a = 0$, the model reduces to

$$dr = \theta(t)\,dt + \sigma\,dz.$$

This is the continuous time limit of the Ho and Lee (1986) model. When $f(r) = r$ and $a \neq 0$, the model becomes

$$dr = [\theta(t) - ar]\,dt + \sigma\,dz$$

and is a version of the Hull and White (1990) extended Vasicek model. When $f(r) = \log r$, the model is

$$d\log(r) = [\theta(t) - a\log(r)]\,dt + \sigma\,dz,$$

which is a version of Black and Karasinski (1991).

In this paper we extend the ideas in Chapter 18 to show how the yield curves in two different countries can be modeled simultaneously. We also show how the Hull–White approach can be used to develop a variety of different Markov two-factor models of the term structure.

19.1 THE HULL–WHITE ONE-FACTOR TREE-BUILDING PROCEDURE

In this section we summarize the procedure in Chapter 18 for building a tree for the model in equation (19.1).

The first step is to set $\theta(t) = 0$, so that the model becomes

$$dx = -ax\,dt + \sigma\,dz. \tag{19.2}$$

A time step Δt is chosen and a trinomial tree is constructed for the model in equation (19.2) on the assumption that the initial value of x is zero. The spacing between the x-values on the tree, Δx, is set equal to $\sigma\sqrt{3\,\Delta t}$. The probabilities on the tree are chosen to match the mean and the standard deviation of changes in x in time Δt.

The standard branching process on a trinomial tree is "one up, no change, or one down". This means that a value $x = j\,\Delta x$ at time t leads to a value of x equal to one of $(j + 1)\,\Delta x$, $j\,\Delta x$, or $(j - 1)\,\Delta x$ at time $t + \Delta t$. Due to mean reversion, for sufficiently large positive and negative values of j when this branching process is used, it is not possible to match the mean and standard deviation of changes in x with positive probabilities on all three branches. To overcome this problem, a non-standard branching process is used in which the values for x at time $t + \Delta t$ are either $(j + 2)\,\Delta x$, $(j + 1)\,\Delta x$, and $j\,\Delta x$, or $j\,\Delta x$, $(j - 1)\,\Delta x$, and $(j - 2)\,\Delta x$.

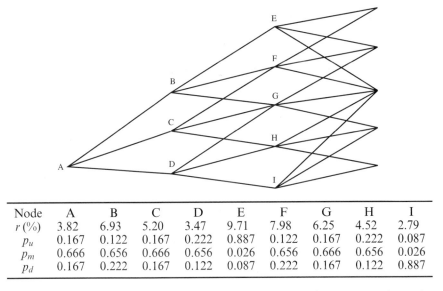

Node	A	B	C	D	E	F	G	H	I
r (%)	3.82	6.93	5.20	3.47	9.71	7.98	6.25	4.52	2.79
p_u	0.167	0.122	0.167	0.222	0.887	0.122	0.167	0.222	0.087
p_m	0.666	0.656	0.666	0.656	0.026	0.656	0.666	0.656	0.026
p_d	0.167	0.222	0.167	0.122	0.087	0.222	0.167	0.122	0.887

FIGURE 19.1. The tree assumed for both r_1 and r_2. This corresponds to the process $dr = [\theta(t) - ar] \, dt + \sigma \, dz$, where $a = 0.1$, $\sigma = 0.01$, $\Delta t = 1$ year, and the t-year zero rate is $0.08 - 0.05e^{-0.18t}$.

Once the tree has been constructed so that it corresponds to equation (19.2), it is modified by increasing the values of x for nodes at time $i \, \Delta t$ by an amount α_i. The α_i's are chosen inductively so the tree is consistent with the initial term structure. This produces a tree corresponding to equation (19.1). When the Ho–Lee or Hull–White model is used, so that $x = r$, the values of α_i can be calculated analytically. In other cases an iterative procedure is necessary.

This procedure provides a relatively simple and numerically efficient way of constructing a trinomial tree for x and implicitly determining $\theta(t)$. The tree has the property that the central node at each time is the expected value of x at that time. Figure 19.1 shows the tree that is produced when $x = r$, $a = 0.1$, $\sigma = 0.01$, $\Delta t = 1$ year, and the function $0.08 - 0.05e^{-0.18t}$ defines the t-year zero rate.[1] Note that the branching is non-standard at nodes E (where j is positive and large) and I (where j is large and negative).

19.2 MODELING TWO INTEREST RATES SIMULTANEOUSLY

Certain types of interest rate derivatives require the yield curves in two

---

[1] Figure 19.1 is the same as Figure 18.3 in Chapter 18. Fuller details of how it is developed are given in that chapter.

different countries to be modeled simultaneously. Examples are diff swaps and options on diff swaps. In this section we explain how the procedure in Chapter 18 can be extended to accommodate two correlated interest rates.

For ease of exposition, we suppose the two countries are the USA and Germany, and that cash flows from the derivative under consideration are to be realized in US dollars (USD). We first build a tree for the USD short rate and a tree for the Deutschmark (DM) short rate using the procedure outlined above and described in more detail in Hull and White (1994). As a result of the construction procedure, the USD tree describes the evolution of USD interest rates from the viewpoint of a risk-neutral USD investor and the DM tree describes the evolution of DM rates from the viewpoint of a risk-neutral DM investor.

Adjusting the Deutschmark Tree

Since cash flows are realized in USD, the DM tree must be adjusted so that it reflects the evolution of rates from the viewpoint of a risk-neutral USD investor rather than a risk-neutral DM investor. Define

r_1: USD short rate from the viewpoint of a risk-neutral US investor;
r_2: DM short rate from the viewpoint of a risk-neutral DM investor;
r_2^*: DM short rate from the viewpoint of a risk-neutral US investor;
X: the exchange rate (number of USD per DM);
σ_X: volatility of exchange rate, X;
ρ_X: instantaneous coefficient of correlation between the exchange rate, X, and the DM interest rate, r_2;
ρ: instantaneous coefficient of correlation between the interest rates, r_1 and r_2.

Suppose that the processes for r_1 and r_2 are

$$dx_1 = [\theta_1(t) - a_1 x_1]\, dt + \sigma_1\, dz_1, \qquad dx_2 = [\theta_2(t) - a_2 x_2]\, dt + \sigma_2\, dz_2,$$

where $x_1 = f_1(r_1)$ and $x_2 = f_2(r_2)$ for some functions f_1 and f_2, and dz_1 and dz_2 are Wiener processes with correlation ρ. The reversion rate parameters a_1 and a_2 and the standard deviations σ_1 and σ_2 are constant. The drift parameters θ_1 and θ_2 are functions of time.

We show in Appendix A the process for r_2^* is

$$dx_2^* = [\theta_2(t) - \rho_X \sigma_2 \sigma_X - a_2 x_2^*]\, dt + \sigma_2\, dz_2,$$

where $x_2^* = f_2(r_2^*)$. The effect of moving from a DM risk-neutral world to a USD risk-neutral world is to reduce the drift of x_2 by $\rho_X \sigma_2 \sigma_X$. The expected value of x_2 at time t is reduced by

$$\int_0^t \rho_X \sigma_X \sigma_2 e^{-a_2(t-\tau)} \, d\tau = \frac{\rho_X \sigma_2 \sigma_X}{a_2} (1 - e^{-a_2 t}).$$

To adjust the DM tree so that it reflects the viewpoint of a risk-neutral US investor the value of x_2 at nodes at time $i \, \Delta t$ (i.e., after i time steps) should therefore be reduced by[2]

$$\frac{\rho_X \sigma_2 \sigma_X}{a_2} (1 - e^{-a_2 i \Delta t}).$$

Note that this is true for all functions f_2, not just $f_2(r) = r$.

To give an example, we suppose that $f_1(r_1) = r_1$, $f_2(r_2) = r_2$, $a_1 = a_2 = 0.1$, and $\sigma_1 = \sigma_2 = 0.01$. We also suppose that the t-year zero rate in both USD and DM is $0.08 - 0.05e^{-0.18t}$ initially. (This resembles the US yield curve at the beginning of 1994.)

The tree initially constructed for both r_1 and r_2 when $\Delta t = 1$ is shown in Figure 19.1. Suppose the correlation ρ_X between r_2 and the exchange rate is 0.5, and the exchange rate volatility σ_X is 0.15. To create the tree for r_2^* from the r_2 tree, the interest rates represented by nodes on the tree at the one-year point are reduced by $0.5 \times 0.01 \times 0.15(1 - e^{-0.1})/0.1 = 0.00071$ (0.071%). Similarly interest rates at the two- and three-year points are reduced by 0.00136 and 0.00194, respectively.

Constructing the Tree Assuming Zero Correlation

We next combine the trees for USD and DM interest rates on the assumption of zero correlation. The result is a three-dimensional tree where nine branches emanate from each node. The probability associated with any one of the nine branches is the product of the unconditional probabilities associated with corresponding movements in two short rates.

In the three-dimensional tree, there is one node at time 0, nine nodes at time Δt, twenty-five nodes at time $2 \, \Delta t$, twenty-five nodes at time $3 \, \Delta t$, and so on. (Note that the effect of mean reversion is to curtail the rate at which the number of nodes on the tree increases.) Each node at time $i \, \Delta t$ on the combined tree corresponds to one node at time $i \, \Delta t$ on the first tree and one node at time $i \, \Delta t$ on the second tree. We will use a notation where

---

[2] Using the notation in Chapter 18, this is the amount by which α_i should be adjusted once the tree has been constructed. Since the r on the tree is the Δt period rate rather than the instantaneous rate, the adjustment is exact only in the limit as Δt tends to zero.

node XY on the combined tree corresponds to node X on the first tree and node Y on the second tree.

The nine nodes at time Δt and the probability of reaching each of the nodes from the initial node AA are:

BD	BC	BB
0.0278	0.1111	0.0278

CD	CC	CB
0.1111	0.4444	0.1111

DB	DC	DB
0.0278	0.1111	0.0278

For example, the probability of reaching node BC from node AA is $0.1667 \times 0.6666 = 0.1111$. To illustrate how probabilities are calculated over the second time step, consider node BD, where $r_1 = 6.93\%$, $r_2 = 3.47\%$, and $r_2^* = 3.40\%$. From B we branch to E, F, G, and from D to G, H, I. So from BD we branch to the 9 combinations of E, F, G and G, H, I. The nine nodes that can be reached from node BD, together with their probabilities, are:

EI	EH	EG
0.0149	0.0800	0.0271

FI	FH	FG
0.0800	0.4303	0.1456

GI	GH	GG
0.0271	0.1456	0.0493

For example, the probability of reaching node EG from node BD is $0.122 \times 0.222 = 0.0271$, the product of the probability of branching from B to E and from D to G.

To express the calculations more formally, we define node (i, j) as the node on the r_1 tree at time period $i \, \Delta t$ at which the number of prior up-moves in the interest rate minus the number of prior down-moves is j. Similarly node (i, k) is the node on the r_2^* tree at time period $i \, \Delta t$ at which the number of prior up-moves in the interest rate minus the number of prior down-moves is k. Let $r_1(i, j)$ be the value of the r_1 at node (i, j), and $r_2^*(i, k)$ be the value or r_2^* at node (i, k) on the r_2^* tree.

The three-dimensional tree is a combination of the two two-dimensional trees. At time $i \, \Delta t$ the nodes are denoted (i, j, k), where

$r_1 = r_1(i, j)$ and $r_2^* = r_2^*(i, k)$ for all j and k. Assume the probabilities associated with the upper, middle, and lower branches emanating from node (i, j) in the r_1 tree are p_u, p_m, and p_d. Similarly, assume that the upper, middle, and lower branches emanating from node (i, k) in the r_2^* tree are q_u, q_m, and q_d. In the three-dimensional tree there are nine branches emanating from the (i, j, k) node. The probabilities associated with the nine branches are:

		r_1-move		
		Lower	Middle	Upper
	Upper	$p_d q_u$	$p_m q_u$	$p_u q_u$
r_2^*-move	Middle	$p_d q_m$	$p_m q_m$	$p_u q_m$
	Lower	$p_d q_d$	$p_m q_d$	$p_u q_d$

Building in Correlation

We now move on to consider the situation where the correlation ρ between r_1 and r_2^* is non-zero. Suppose first that the correlation is positive. The geometry of the tree is exactly the same, but the probabilities are adjusted to be:

		r_1-move		
		Lower	Middle	Upper
	Upper	$p_d q_u - \epsilon$	$p_m q_u - 4\epsilon$	$p_u q_u + 5\epsilon$
r_2^*-move	Middle	$p_d q_m - 4\epsilon$	$p_m q_m + 8\epsilon$	$p_u q_m - 4\epsilon$
	Lower	$p_d q_d + 5\epsilon$	$p_m q_d - 4\epsilon$	$p_u q_d - \epsilon$

Note that the sum of the adjustments in each row and column is zero. As a result, the adjustments do not change the mean and standard deviations of the unconditional movements in r_1 and r_2^*. The adjustments have the effect of inducing a correlation between r_1 and r_2^* of 36ϵ. The appropriate value of ϵ is therefore $\frac{1}{36}\rho$.

The choice of the probability adjustments is motivated by the fact that in the limit as Δt tends to zero the probabilities tend to $p_u = q_u = \frac{1}{6}$, $p_m = q_m = \frac{2}{3}$, and $p_d = q_d = \frac{1}{6}$. When the correlation is 1.0, the adjusted probability matrix is in the limit:

		r_1-move		
		Lower	Middle	Upper
	Upper	0	0	1/6
r_2^*-move	Middle	0	2/3	0
	Lower	1/6	0	0

For correlations between 0 and 1, the correlation matrix is the result of interpolating between the matrix for a correlation of 0 and the matrix for a correlation of 1.[3]

Suppose $\rho = 0.2$, so that $\epsilon = 0.00556$. The probabilities on the branches emanating from node AA become

BD	BC	BB
0.0222	0.0889	0.0556

CD	CC	CB
0.0889	0.4889	0.0889

DD	DC	DB
0.0556	0.0889	0.0222

while the probabilities on branches emanating from node BD become

EI	EH	EG
0.0093	0.0578	0.0549

FI	FH	FG
0.0578	0.4747	0.1234

GI	GH	GG
0.0549	0.1234	0.0437

For example, the probability of moving from node AA to node BC is $0.1111 - 4 \times 0.00556 = 0.0889$; the probability of moving from node BD to node EG is $0.0271 + 5 \times 0.00556 = 0.0549$.

For negative correlations, the procedure is the same as for positive correlations except that the probabilities are:

		r_1-move		
		Lower	Middle	Upper
	Upper	$p_d q_u + 5\epsilon$	$p_m q_u - 4\epsilon$	$p_u q_u - \epsilon$
r_2^*-move	Middle	$p_d q_m - 4\epsilon$	$p_m q_m + 8\epsilon$	$p_u q_m - 4\epsilon$
	Lower	$p_d q_d - \epsilon$	$p_m q_d - 4\epsilon$	$p_u q_d + 5\epsilon$

In this case $\epsilon = -\frac{1}{36}\rho$. For a correlation of -0.2, the probability on the branch from AA to BC is as before $0.1111 - 4 \times 0.00556 = 0.0889$; the probability of moving from node BD to node EG is $0.0271 - 0.00556 = 0.0215$.

[3] The procedure described here can with appropriate modifications be used to construct a three-dimensional tree for any two correlated variables from two trees that describe the movements of each variable separately. The two trees can be binomial or trinomial.

The only difficulty with this procedure is that some probabilities are liable to become negative at some nodes. We deal with this as follows. At any node where $\epsilon = \frac{1}{36}\rho$ leads to negative probabilities, we use the maximum value of ϵ for which probabilities are non-negative.

To illustrate this rule, suppose that $\rho = 0.8$ instead of 0.2 in our earlier example, so that the calculated value of ϵ is 0.02222. Using this value of ϵ at node BD would cause the probabilities on the branches to EH, EI, and FI to become negative. The maximum values of ϵ for which the three probabilities are non-negative are 0.0200, 0.0149, and 0.0200, respectively. We would therefore use a value of ϵ of 0.0149, which corresponds to $\rho = 0.5364$, for all branches emanating from BD.

As Δt approaches zero, p_u, p_m, and p_d approach $\frac{1}{6}$, $\frac{2}{3}$, and $\frac{1}{6}$. Also q_u, q_m, and q_d approach $\frac{1}{6}$, $\frac{2}{3}$, and $\frac{1}{6}$. The proportion of the probability space over which it is necessary to adjust ϵ reduces to zero. Although the procedure we have outlined does induce a small bias in the correlation, this bias disappears in the limit as Δt approaches zero. As a result the procedure converges.

An Example

We illustrate the procedure by using it to price a security whose payoff is calculated by observing the three-month DM rate in three years' time and applying it to a USD principal of 100. This is one component of a diff swap in which the swap payment in dollars is determined by the difference between the German and US interest rates.

As before, we suppose that the process for both short rates is

$$dr = [\theta(t) - ar]\,dt + \sigma\,dz,$$

with $a = 0.1$ and $\sigma = 0.01$.

The t-year zero-coupon bond rate in each country is assumed to be $0.08 - 0.05e^{-0.18t}$ and the volatility of the exchange rate is assumed to be 15% per annum. This example enables us to test the convergence of the tree-building procedure, since the security can be valued analytically using the formulas in Wei (1994).

Recall that ρ_X is defined as the correlation between the exchange rate and the DM rate and ρ is the correlation between the two interest rates. Table 19.1 shows results for a number of combinations of ρ and ρ_X. It illustrates that prices calculated by the tree do converge rapidly to the analytic price in a variety of different correlation environments.

TABLE 19.1. Value of a security whose payoff is calculated by observing the three-month DM rate in three years' time and applying it to a USD principal of 100.

No. of time steps	$\rho = 0.5$ $\rho_X = 0.5$	$\rho = 0.5$ $\rho_X = -0.5$	$\rho = -0.5$ $\rho_X = 0.5$	$\rho = -0.5$ $\rho_X = -0.5$
5	1.3971	1.4834	1.4045	1.4909
10	1.3976	1.4839	1.4055	1.4918
20	1.3978	1.4842	1.4059	1.4923
40	1.3980	1.4844	1.4062	1.4926
60	1.3981	1.4845	1.4063	1.4927
80	1.3981	1.4845	1.4063	1.4927
100	1.3981	1.4845	1.4064	1.4928
Analytic	1.3981	1.4845	1.4064	1.4928

Note: Both the USD and DM rates are assumed to follow the process $dr = [\theta(t) - ar]\,dt + \sigma\,dz$, where $a = 0.1$, $\sigma = 0.01$, and the t-year zero rate is $0.08 - 0.05e^{-0.18t}$.

19.3 TWO-FACTOR MODELS OF A SINGLE TERM STRUCTURE

In this section we consider two factor models of the form

$$df(r) = [\theta(t) + u - af(r)]\,dt + \sigma_1\,dz_1, \qquad (19.3)$$

where the drift parameter u has an initial value of zero, is stochastic, and follows the process

$$du = -bu\,dt + \sigma_2\,dz_2.$$

As in the one-factor models considered in Hull and White (1994), the parameter $\theta(t)$ is chosen to make the model consistent with the initial term structure. The stochastic variable u is a component of the reversion level of r and itself reverts to a level of zero at rate b.[4] The parameters a, b, σ_1, and σ_2 are constants and dz_1 and dz_2 are Wiener processes with instantaneous correlation ρ.

This model provides a richer pattern of term structure movements and a richer pattern of volatility structures than the one-factor models considered in Section 19.1. Figure 19.2 gives an example of forward rate standard deviations and spot rate standard deviations that are produced using the model when $f(r) = r$, $a = 3$, $b = 0.1$, $\sigma_1 = 0.01$, $\sigma_2 = 0.0145$, $\rho = 0.6$.[5] The volatilities that are observed in the cap market often have the "humped" shape shown in this figure.

---

[4] There is no loss of generality in assuming that the reversion level of u is zero and that its initial value is zero. For example, if u reverts to some level c, $u^* = u - ct$ reverts to 0. We can define u^* as the second factor and absorb the difference between u and u^* in $\theta(t)$.

[5] These parameters were chosen to produce the desired pattern. Many other different volatility patterns can be achieved.

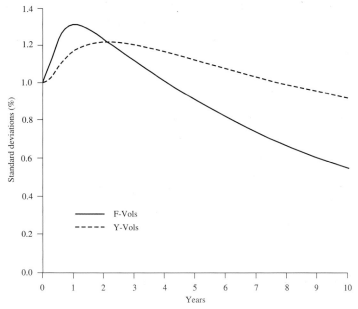

FIGURE 19.2. Forward rate volatilities (F-Vols) and spot rate volatilities (Y-Vols) in a two-factor model when $f(r) = r$, $a = 3$, $b = 0.1$, $\sigma_1 = 0.01$, $\sigma_2 = 0.0145$, and $\rho = 0.6$.

When $f(r) = r$, the model is analytically tractable. As shown in Appendix B, the bond price in that case has the form

$$P(t, T) = A(t, T)\exp[-B(t, T)r - C(t, T)u].$$

The price c at time t of a European call option on a discount bond is given by

$$c = P(t, s)N(h) - XP(t, T)N(h - \sigma_P),$$

where T is the maturity of the option, s is the maturity of the bond, X is the strike price,

$$h = \frac{1}{\sigma_P}\log\frac{P(t, s)}{P(t, T)X} + \frac{\sigma_P}{2},$$

and σ_P is as given in Appendix B. Since this is a two-factor model, the decomposition approach in Jamshidian (1989) cannot be used to price options on coupon-bearing bonds.

Constructing the Tree

To construct a tree for the model in (19.3), we simplify the notation by defining $x = f(r)$, so that

$$dx = [\theta(t) + u - ax]\, dt + \sigma_1\, dz_1,$$

with

$$du = -bu\, dt + \sigma_2\, dz_2.$$

Assuming $a \neq b$, we can eliminate the dependence of the first stochastic variable on the second by defining

$$y = x + \frac{u}{b - a}, \tag{19.4}$$

so that

$$dy = [\theta(t) - ay]\, dt + \sigma_3\, dz_3, \qquad du = -bu\, dt + \sigma_2\, dz_2,$$

where

$$\sigma_3^2 = \sigma_1^2 + \frac{\sigma_2^2}{(b - a)^2} + \frac{2\rho\sigma_1\sigma_2}{b - a},$$

and dz_3 is a Wiener process. The correlation between dz_2 and dz_3 is

$$\frac{\rho\sigma_1 + \sigma_2/(b - a)}{\sigma_3},$$

The approach described in Section 19.2 can be used to construct a tree for y and u on the assumption that $\theta(t) = 0$ and the initial values of y and u are zero. Using a similar approach to that described in Chapter 18, we can then construct a new tree by increasing the values of y at time $i \, \Delta t$ by α_i. The α_i's are calculated using a forward induction technique similar to that described in Chapter 18, so that the initial term structure is matched. The details are given in Appendix C.

An Example

Table 19.2 shows the results of using the tree to price three-month options on a ten-year discount bond. The parameters used are those that give rise to the humped volatility curve in Figure 19.2. The initial t-year zero rate is assumed to be $0.08 - 0.05e^{-0.18t}$. Five different strike prices are considered.

The table illustrates that prices calculated from the tree converge rapidly to the analytic price. The numbers here and in other similar tests we have carried out provide support for the correctness of the somewhat complicated formulas for $A(t, T)$ and σ_P in Appendix B.

TABLE 19.2. Value of three-month option on a ten-year discount bond with a principal of 100 for the model in Figure 19.2.

No. of time steps	Strike price[a]				
	0.96	0.98	1.00	1.02	1.04
5	1.9464	1.0077	0.2890	0.0397	0.0012
10	1.9499	1.0077	0.2968	0.0370	0.0016
20	1.9512	1.0085	0.3000	0.0366	0.0015
40	1.9536	1.0107	0.3022	0.0369	0.0014
60	1.9529	1.0099	0.3020	0.0367	0.0014
Analytic	1.9532	1.0101	0.3023	0.0367	0.0014

a The strike price is expressed as a proportion of the forward bond price.
Note: The t-year zero rate is $0.08 - 0.05e^{-0.18t}$.

19.4 CONCLUSIONS

This paper shows that the approach in Chapter 18 can be extended in two ways. It can be used to model two correlated interest rates when each follows a process chosen from the family of one-factor models considered in our previous paper. It can also be used to implement a range of different two-factor models.

An interesting by-product of the research described in this paper is a method for combining trinomial trees for two correlated variables into a single three-dimensional tree describing the joint evolution of the variables. This method can be extended so that it accommodates a range of binomial as well as trinomial trees.

APPENDIX A

In this appendix we show how to calculate the process for the DM interest rate from the viewpoint of a USD investor. Our approach is an alternative to that in Wei (1994).

Define Z as the value of a variable seen from the perspective of a risk-neutral DM investor and Z^* as the value of the same variable seen from the perspective of a risk-neutral USD investor. Suppose that Z depends only on the DM risk-free rate, so that

$$dZ = \mu(Z)Z \, dt + \sigma(Z)Z \, dz_2,$$

where dz_2 is the Wiener process driving the DM risk-free rate and μ and σ are functions of Z. The work of Cox, Ingersoll, and Ross (1985), and

329

others, shows that the process for Z^* has the form

$$dZ^* = [\mu(Z^*) - \lambda\sigma(Z^*)]Z^* \, dt + \sigma(Z^*)Z^* \, dz_2,$$

where the risk premium λ is a function of Z^*.[6]

We first apply this result to the case where the variable under consideration is the DM price of a DM discount bond. Define P as the value of this variable from the viewpoint of a risk-neutral DM investor and P^* as its value from the viewpoint of a risk-neutral USD investor. From the perspective of a risk-neutral DM investor, the variable is the price of a traded security, so that

$$dP = r_2 P \, dt + \sigma_P P \, dz_2, \tag{A1}$$

where σ_P is the volatility of P and other variables are as defined in the main part of the paper. Hence[7]

$$dP^* = [r_2^* - \lambda\sigma_P]P^* \, dt + \sigma_P P^* \, dz_2. \tag{A2}$$

The risk-neutral process for the exchange rate X from the viewpoint of a risk-neutral USD investor is

$$dX = (r_1 - r_2^*)X \, dt + \sigma_X X \, dz_X, \tag{A3}$$

where dz_X is a Wiener process.

The variable XP^* is the price in USD of the DM bond. The drift of XP^* in a risk-neutral USD world must therefore be $r_1 XP^*$. From equations (A2) and (A3) this drift can also be written as

$$XP^*(r_1 - \lambda\sigma_P + \rho_X\sigma_X\sigma_P).$$

It follows that

$$\lambda = \rho_X\sigma_X.$$

When moving from a risk-neutral DM investor to a risk-neutral USD investor, there is a market price of risk adjustment of $\rho_X\sigma_X$.

We can now apply the general result given for Z at the beginning of this appendix to the variable $f(r_2)$. We are assuming that

$$df_2(r_2) = [\theta_2(t) - af_2(r_2)] \, dt + \sigma_2 \, dz_2.$$

Hence

$$df_2(r_2^*) = [\theta_2(t) - \rho_X\sigma_X\sigma_2 - af_2(r_2^*)] \, dt + \sigma_2 \, dz_2.$$

---

[6] Here λ is the difference between the market price of the DM interest rate risk from the perspective of a risk-neutral DM investor and the market price of DM interest rate risk from the perspective of a risk-neutral USD investor.

[7] Note that r_2 in equation (A1) becomes r_2^* in equation (A2). This is because the r_2 in (A2) is, strictly speaking, $r_2(P)$. The Cox–Ingersoll–Ross result outlined at the beginning of this appendix shows that this becomes $r_2(P^*)$ or r_2^* in equation (A2).

APPENDIX B

In this appendix we show that the complete yield curve can be calculated from r and u in the model considered in Section 19.3 when $f(r) = r$.

The differential equation satisfied by a discount bond price f is

$$f_t + [\theta(t) + u - ar]f_r - buf_u + \tfrac{1}{2}\sigma_1^2 f_{rr} + \tfrac{1}{2}\sigma_2^2 f_{uu} + \rho\sigma_1\sigma_2 f_{ru} - rf = 0.$$

By direct substitution, a solution to this equation is

$$f = A(t, T)e^{-B(t,T)r - C(t,T)u},$$

provided that

$$B_t - aB + 1 = 0, \tag{B1}$$

$$C_t - bC + B = 0, \tag{B2}$$

$$A_t - \theta(t)AB + \tfrac{1}{2}\sigma_1^2 AB^2 + \tfrac{1}{2}\sigma_2^2 AC^2 + \rho\sigma_1\sigma_2 ABC = 0. \tag{B3}$$

The solution to equation (B1) that satisfies the boundary condition $B(t, t) = 0$ is

$$B(t, T) = \frac{1}{a}[1 - e^{-a(T-t)}].$$

The solution to equation (B2) that is consistent with this and satisfies the boundary condition $C(t, t) = 0$ is

$$C(t, T) = \frac{1}{a(a - b)}e^{-a(T-t)} - \frac{1}{b(a - b)}e^{-b(T-t)} + \frac{1}{ab}.$$

By direct substitution, the solution to equation (B3) for A and θ that satisfies the boundary conditions $A(t, T) = A(0, T)$ when $t = 0$ and $A(t, T) = 1$ when $t = T$ is

$$\log A(t, T) = \log \frac{P(0, T)}{P(0, t)} + B(t, T)F(0, t)$$

$$+ \phi(0, t)B(t, T) + \int_0^t \phi(0, \tau)\, d\tau - \int_0^t \phi(\tau, T)\, d\tau,$$

$$\theta(t) = F_t(0, t) + aF(0, t) + \phi_t(0, t) + a\phi(0, t),$$

where $F(t, T)$ is the instantaneous forward rate for time T as seen at time t, and

$$\phi(t, T) = \tfrac{1}{2}\sigma_1^2 B(t, T)^2 + \tfrac{1}{2}\sigma_2^2 C(t, T)^2 + \rho\sigma_1\sigma_2 B(t, T)C(t, T).$$

This reduces to

$$\log A(t, T) = \log \frac{P(0, T)}{P(0, t)} + B(t, T)F(0, t) - \eta,$$

where

$$\eta = \frac{\sigma_1^2}{4a}(1 - e^{-2at})B(t, T)^2 - \rho\sigma_1\sigma_2[B(0, t)C(0, t)B(t, T) + \gamma_4 - \gamma_2]$$
$$- \tfrac{1}{2}\sigma_2^2[C(0, t)^2 B(t, T) + \gamma_6 - \gamma_5],$$

$$\gamma_1 = \frac{e^{-(a+b)T}[e^{(a+b)t} - 1]}{(a + b)(a - b)} - \frac{e^{-2aT}(e^{2at} - 1)}{2a(a - b)},$$

$$\gamma_2 = \frac{1}{ab}\left[\gamma_1 + C(t, T) - C(0, T) + \tfrac{1}{2}B(t, T)^2\right.$$
$$\left. - \tfrac{1}{2}B(0, T)^2 + \frac{t}{a} - \frac{e^{-a(T-t)} - e^{-aT}}{a^2}\right],$$

$$\gamma_3 = -\frac{e^{-(a+b)t} - 1}{(a - b)(a + b)} + \frac{e^{-2at} - 1}{2a(a - b)},$$

$$\gamma_4 = \frac{1}{ab}\left[\gamma_3 - C(0, t) - \tfrac{1}{2}B(0, t)^2 + \frac{t}{a} + \frac{e^{-at} - 1}{a^2}\right],$$

$$\gamma_5 = \frac{1}{b}\left[\tfrac{1}{2}C(t, T)^2 - \tfrac{1}{2}C(0, T)^2 + \gamma_2\right],$$

$$\gamma_6 = \frac{1}{b}\left[\gamma_4 - \tfrac{1}{2}C(0, t)^2\right],$$

The volatility function σ_P at time 0 for an option lasting between t and T is given by

$$\sigma_P^2 = \int_0^t \{\sigma_1^2[B(\tau, T) - B(\tau, t)]^2 + \sigma_2^2[C(\tau, T) - C(\tau, t)]^2$$
$$+ 2\rho\sigma_1\sigma_2[B(\tau, T) - B(\tau, t)][C(\tau, T) - C(\tau, t)]\} \, d\tau.$$

This shows that σ_P^2 has three components. Define

$$U = \frac{1}{a(a - b)}[e^{-aT} - e^{-at}], \qquad V = \frac{1}{b(a - b)}[e^{-bT} - e^{-bt}].$$

The first component of σ_P^2 is

$$\frac{\sigma_1^2}{2a}B(t, T)^2(1 - e^{-2at}).$$

The second is

$$\sigma_2^2 \left[\frac{U^2}{2a} (e^{2at} - 1) + \frac{V^2}{2b} (e^{2bt} - 1) - 2\frac{UV}{a+b} (e^{(a+b)t} - 1) \right].$$

The third is

$$\frac{2\rho\sigma_1\sigma_2}{a} (e^{-at} - e^{-aT}) \left[\frac{U}{2a} (e^{2at} - 1) - \frac{V}{a+b} (e^{(a+b)t} - 1) \right].$$

APPENDIX C

In this appendix we explain how the tree for the two-factor model discussed in Section 19.3 is fitted to the initial term structure. We assume that a three-dimensional tree for y and u has been constructed on the assumption that $\theta(t) = 0$ using the procedure in Section 19.2, that the spacing between y-values on the tree is Δy, and that the spacing between the u-values on the tree is Δu. From equation (19.4) when $y = j \Delta y$ and $u = k \Delta u$, the short rate r is given by the initial tree to be

$$r = g \left[j \Delta y - \frac{k \Delta u}{b - a} \right],$$

where g is the inverse function of f.

As in Chapter 18, we work forward through the tree, calculating the α's that must be added to the y's so that the tree is perfectly consistent with the initial term structure. Once α_i, the appropriate α for time $i \Delta t$, has been calculated, it is used to calculate Arrow–Debreu prices for the nodes at time $i \Delta t$. (The Arrow–Debreu price for a node is the present value of a security that pays off \$1 if the node is reached and zero otherwise.) These are then used to calculate α_{i+1}, and so on.

Define $Q_{i,j,k}$ as the present value of a security that pays off \$1 if $y = \alpha_i + j \Delta y$ and $u = k \Delta u$ at time $i \Delta t$, and zero otherwise. $Q_{0,0,0} = 1$. Similarly to equation (18.6) in Chapter 18,

$$P_{m+1} = \sum_{j,k} Q_{m,j,k} \exp\{-g[\alpha_m + j \Delta y - k \Delta u/(b - a)]\Delta t\},$$

where the summation is taken over all values of j and k at time $m \Delta t$. When $f(r) = r$, so that $g(r) = r$, this can be solved analytically for α_m:

$$\alpha_m = \frac{\log \sum_{j,k} Q_{m,j,k} \exp\{[-j \Delta y + k \Delta u/(b - a)] \Delta t\} - \log P_{m+1}}{\Delta t}.$$

In other situations, a one-dimensional Newton–Raphson search is required.

The Q's are updated as the tree is constructed using

$$Q_{m+1,j,k} = \sum_{j^*,k^*} Q_{m,j^*,k^*} q(j, k, j^*, k^*) \exp\{-g[\alpha_m + j^* \Delta y - k^* \Delta u/(b - a)] \Delta t\},$$

where in the summation j^* and k^* are set equal to all possible pairs of values of j and k at time $m \Delta t$. The variable $q(j, k, j^*, k^*)$ is the probability of a transition from node (m, j^*, k^*) to $(m + 1, j, k)$.

REFERENCES

Black, F., and P. Karasinski. "Bond and option pricing when short rates are lognormal." *Financial Analysts Journal*, July–August, 1991, pp. 52–59.

Cox, J. C., J. E. Ingersoll, and S. A. Ross. "An intertemporal general equilibrium model of asset prices." *Econometrica*, 53 (1985), pp. 363–384.

Heath, D., R. Jarrow, and A. Morton. "Bond pricing and the term structure of interest rates: a new methodology." *Econometrica*, 60, 1 (1992), pp. 77–105.

Ho, T. S. Y., and S.-B. Lee. "Term structure movements and the pricing interest rate contingent claims." *Journal of Finance*, 41 (December 1986), pp. 1011–1029.

Hull, J., and A. White. "Pricing interest rate derivative securities," *Review of Financial Studies*, 3, 4 (1990), pp. 573–592. Also Chapter 13 in this book.

Hull, J., and A. White. "Numerical procedures for implementing term structure models I: Single-factor models." *Journal of Derivatives*, 2, 1 (Fall 1994), pp. 7–16. Also Chapter 18 in this book.

Jamshidian, F. "An exact bond option pricing formula." *Journal of Finance*, 44 (March 1989), pp. 205–209.

Wei, J. "Valuing differential swaps." *Journal of Derivatives*, 1, 3 (Spring 1994), pp. 64–76.

20. Using Hull–White interest rate trees*

In Chapter 18, the authors describe a procedure for constructing
trinomial trees for one-factor yield curve models of the form

$$dx = \theta(t) - ax\,dt + \sigma\,dz, \tag{20.1}$$

where r is the short rate, $x = f(r)$ is some function of r, a and σ are
constants, and $\theta(t)$ is a function of time chosen so that the model provides
an exact fit to the initial term structure of interest rates. The model can be
written

$$dx = a\left[\frac{\theta(t)}{a} - x\right]dt + \sigma\,dz.$$

This shows that, at any given time, x reverts toward $\theta(t)/a$ at rate a. Its
variance rate per unit time is σ^2.

When $f(r) = r$, the model reduces to the Hull–White (1990) model:

$$dr = a[\theta(t) - x]\,dt + \sigma\,dz. \tag{20.1a}$$

The attraction of the Hull–White model is its analytic tractability. As
shown in Hull and White (1990, 1994a), bonds and European options at
some future time t can be valued analytically in terms of the initial
term structure and the value of r at time t. When $f(r) = \log r$ and a and
σ are allowed to be functions of time, the model becomes that of Black
and Karasinski (1991). When $f(r) = \log r$ and $a(t) = \sigma'(t)/\sigma(t)$, and
$\sigma'(t) = \partial\sigma/\partial t$, the model becomes the Black, Derman, and Toy (1990)
model. In Section 20.3 below, we describe how to extend the basic tree-
building procedure to accommodate time-varying mean reversion and
volatility.

The construction of the Hull–White tree involves two stages. The first
stage involves defining a new variable x^* obtained from x by setting both

* Copyright © 1996 by Institutional Investor. This paper was first published in *Journal of
Derivatives*, Vol. 3 (Spring 1996), pp. 26–36. It is reprinted with the permission of
Institutional Investor.

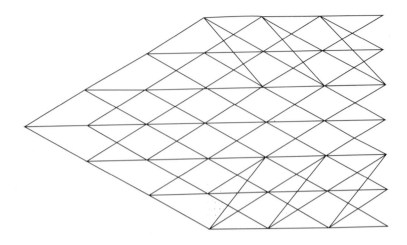

FIGURE 20.1. The initial tree (setting $\theta(t) = 0$ and $x(0) = 0$).

$\theta(t)$ and the initial value of x equal to zero. The process for x^* is

$$dx^* = -ax^* \, dt + \sigma \, dz. \tag{20.2}$$

We construct a tree for x^* that has the form shown in Figure 20.1. The central node at each time step has $x^* = 0$. The vertical distance between the nodes on the tree is set equal to $\Delta x^* = \sqrt{3V}$, where V is the variance of the change in x in time Δt, the length of each time step. The probabilities at each node are chosen to match the mean and standard deviation[1] of the change in x^* for the process in equation (20.2). Defining the expected change in x^* as Mx^*, at node $j \, \Delta x^*$ the up-, middle-, and down-branching probabilities are

$$p_u = \tfrac{1}{6} + \tfrac{1}{2}(j^2 M^2 + jM),$$

$$p_m = \tfrac{2}{3} - j^2 M^2, \tag{20.3a}$$

$$p_d = \tfrac{1}{6} + \tfrac{1}{2}(j^2 M^2 - jM).$$

As indicated in Figure 20.1, we cope with mean reversion by allowing the branching to be non-standard at the edge of the tree. At the top edge of the tree where the branching is non-standard, the modified probabilities

---

[1] The expected value and variance of the change in x^* over some time Δt are

$$E[dx^*] = Mx^* = (e^{-a\Delta t} - 1)x^*, \quad \mathrm{Var}[dx^*] = V = \sigma^2(1 - e^{-2a\Delta t})/2a.$$

336

become

$$p_u = \tfrac{7}{6} + \tfrac{1}{2}(j^2 M^2 + 3jM),$$
$$p_m = -\tfrac{1}{3} - j^2 M^2 - 2jM, \qquad (20.3b)$$
$$p_d = \tfrac{1}{6} + \tfrac{1}{2}(j^2 M^2 + jM);$$

and at the bottom edge of the tree where the branching is non-standard the modified probabilities become

$$p_u = \tfrac{1}{6} + \tfrac{1}{2}(j^2 M^2 - jM),$$
$$p_m = -\tfrac{1}{3} - j^2 M^2 + 2jM, \qquad (20.3c)$$
$$p_d = \tfrac{7}{6} + \tfrac{1}{2}(j^2 M^2 - 3jM).$$

The second stage in the construction of the tree involves forward induction. We work forward from time zero to the end of the tree, adjusting the location of the nodes at each time step in such a way that the initial term structure is matched. This produces a tree of the form shown in Figure 20.2. The size of the displacement is the same for all nodes at a particular time t, but is not usually the same for nodes at two different times. The effect of this second stage is to convert a tree for x^* into a tree for x.

The full details of the tree-building procedure are given in Chapter 18. In Chapter 19, we describe extensions where two interest rates are

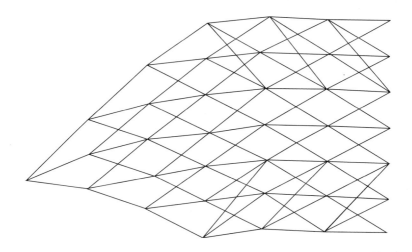

FIGURE 20.2. The final tree for x.

modeled simultaneously and where the tree-building technology is used to construct two-factor models of a single term structure.

The purpose of this article is to provide more details on the basic Hull–White tree-building procedure. We discuss how to use analytic results when $f(r) = r$. We provide sample results based on a real yield curve that the reader can use to test his or her own implementation of the model. We show how the tree-building procedure can be used for models such as that of Black and Karasinski (1991), where a and σ are functions of time, but point out some pitfalls of these models. We also discuss issues such as how the length of the time step can be changed, how cash flows that occur between time steps can be handled, and so on.

20.1 ANALYTIC RESULTS

Bond Prices

When $f(r) = r$, the model in equation (20.1) is analytically very tractable. For example, as shown in Hull and White (1990, 1994a),

$$P(t, T) = A(t, T)e^{-B(t,T)r}, \tag{20.4}$$

where $P(t, T)$ is the price at some time t of a zero-coupon bond maturing at time T, r is the short-term rate of interest at time t, and A and B are functions only of t and T. The function A is determined from the initial values $P(0, T)$ of the discount bonds:

$$\left. \begin{aligned} A(t, T) &= \frac{P(0, T)}{P(0, t)} \exp[B(t, T)F(0, t) - \sigma^2 B^2(t, T)(1 - e^{-2at})/4a], \\ B(t, T) &= (1 - e^{-a(T-t)})/a. \end{aligned} \right\} \tag{20.5}$$

$F(0, t)$ is the instantaneous forward rate that applies to time t as observed at time zero. It can be computed from the initial price of a discount bond as $F(0, t) = -\partial \log[P(0, t)]/\partial t$.

The variable r in equation (20.4) is the instantaneous short rate, while the interest rates on the Hull–White tree are Δt-period rates. The two should not be assumed to be interchangeable. Let R be the Δt-period rate at time t, and r be the instantaneous rate at time t. Using equation (20.4),

$$e^{-R\Delta t} = A(t, t + \Delta t)e^{-B(t,t+\Delta t)r},$$

so that

$$r = \frac{R\Delta t + A(t, t + \Delta t)}{B(t, t + \Delta t)}. \tag{20.6}$$

To calculate points on the term structure given the Δt-period rate R at a node of the Hull–White tree, it is first necessary to use equation (20.6) to get the instantaneous short rate r. Equation (20.4) can then be used to determine rates for longer maturities. When this procedure is followed, it can be shown that the prices of discount bonds computed are independent of the forward rate $F(0, t)$.[2]

Expected Future Rates

Inspection of equations (20.1) and (20.2) shows that $x(t)$ and $x^*(t)$ differ only by some function of time. Define this difference as

$$\alpha(t) = x(t) - x^*(t). \tag{20.7}$$

This is the difference between the location of comparable nodes in the x and x^* trees at time t. In particular, it is the difference between the central or expected values of x and x^* at time t, and, since the expected value of x^* is zero, $\alpha(t)$ can be interpreted as the expected value of $x(t)$. As has been pointed out by Kijima and Nagayama (1994) and Pelsser (1994), $\alpha(t)$ can be calculated analytically for the model where $f(r) = r$. Differentiating equation (20.7), we find from equations (20.1) and (20.2) that

$$\frac{\partial \alpha(t)}{\partial t} = \theta(t) - a\alpha(t),$$

or

$$\alpha(t) = \exp\left\{-at\left[r(0) + \int_0^t \theta(q)e^{aq}\, dq\right]\right\}.$$

Substituting the analytic expression for $\theta(t)$ given in Hull and White (1990, 1994a) this reduces to

$$\alpha(t) = F(0, t) + \frac{\sigma^2}{2a^2}(1 - e^{-at})^2. \tag{20.8}$$

The use of the analytic expression for α to determine the location of the

---

[2] Since the forward rate is computed from the first derivative of the yield curve, it is very sensitive to the exact shape of the yield curve. Slight variations in the yield curve create large changes in the computed forward rate. If the computed bond price had depended on the forward rate, the results would be very sensitive to exactly how one computed the yield curve.

central nodes in the tree avoids the need to obtain them from forward induction.[3] However, the resulting tree does not provide an exact fit to the initial term structure. This is because the tree is a discrete representation of the underlying continuous stochastic process. The advantage of the forward induction procedure is that the initial term structure is always matched exactly by the tree itself.

20.2 AN EXAMPLE

As an example of the implementation of the model, we use the data in Table 20.1. This data, which is for the DM yield curve on 8 July 1994 was kindly provided to us by Antoon Pelsser of ABN Amro Bank.

Data points for maturities between those indicated are generated using linear interpolation.

The zero curve was used to price a 3-year[4] (= 3 × 365 day) put option on a zero-coupon bond that will pay $100 in 9 years (= 9 × 365 days).

TABLE 20.1. The DM zero-coupon yield curve, 8 July 1994.

Maturity	Days	Rate
3 days	3	5.01772
1 month	31	4.98284
2 month	62	4.97234
3 month	94	4.96157
6 month	185	4.99058
1 year	367	5.09389
2 years	731	5.79733
3 years	1096	6.30595
4 years	1461	6.73464
5 years	1826	6.94816
6 years	2194	7.08807
7 years	2558	7.27527
8 years	2922	7.30852
9 years	3287	7.39790
10 years	3653	7.49015

[3] Forward induction is always necessary when $f(r) \neq r$ since there are no analytic results in that case.

[4] The fundamental unit of time in this example is 1 day. For convenience we define 1 year as 365 days, which is approximately the length of a real year, and quote rates and volatilities per year. The data in Table 20.1 is quoted on this basis. Thus the 10-year rate of 7.49015% is actually a rate of 0.0205210% per day. This rate applies for 3,653 days, or about 10.0082 years. This convention may seem cumbersome but is necessary to avoid the ambiguity associated with the variable length of a calendar year.

Interest rates were assumed to follow the Hull–White (equation (20.1a)) model. The strike price was $63, and the parameters a and σ were chosen to be $a = 0.1$ and $\sigma = 0.01$. These two parameters determine the volatility of the discount bond for option pricing purposes. The values chosen were roughly representative of the values that are observed in the market. The tree was constructed out to the end of the life of the option. The zero-coupon bond prices at the final nodes were calculated analytically as described in the previous section.

To illustrate the process, consider the construction of a three-step tree. First, we must determine the time and rate step sizes, and where non-standard branching (if any) takes place. The size of the time step is $\Delta t = 1.0$ years. As shown in Chapter 18, the expected change in r^* and the variance of the change in r^* in time Δt are given by

$$E[dr^*] = Mr^* = (e^{-a\Delta t} - 1)r^*, \quad \text{Var}[dr^*] = V = \sigma^2(1 - e^{-2a\Delta t})/2a.$$

For the given parameter values, $M = 0.095162582$ and $\sqrt{V} = 0.009520222$. Since the step size $\Delta r = \sqrt{3V}$, we have $\Delta r = 0.016489508$. Finally, as shown in Chapter 18, non-standard branching

TABLE 20.2. Data defining a three-step tree in r^*.

j	Rate $= j\,\Delta r$	p_u	p_m	p_d	Eqn.
2	0.032979	0.899291	0.011093	0.089616	(20.3b)
1	0.016490	0.123613	0.657611	0.218776	(20.3a)
0	0.0	0.166667	0.666667	0.166667	(20.3a)
−1	0.016490	0.218776	0.657611	0.123613	(20.3a)
−2	0.032979	0.089616	0.011093	0.899291	(20.3c)

TABLE 20.3. The amount α by which the interest rates at each time step must be raised in order to replicate the bond prices computed from the zero-coupon discount rates.

Time step, i	$t = i\,\Delta t$ (years)	Zero rate (%)	Discount bond price	α (%)	Forward rate (%)	$\alpha(t)$: eqn. (20.8) (%)
0	0.0	5.017720	1.000000	5.092750	5.01772	5.017720
1	1.0	5.092755	0.950348	6.502572	5.29994	5.304470
2	2.0	5.795397	0.890557	7.339323	7.20614	7.222572
3	3.0	6.304557	0.827673	8.053817	7.83041	7.864004
4	4.0	6.733466	0.763885			
	9.0	7.397410	0.513879			

TABLE 20.4. The four time steps in the interest rate tree. The probability of transiting from node (i, j) to nodes $(i + 1, j + 1)$, $(i + 1, j)$, and $(i + 1, j - 1)$ are normally $p_u(j)$, $p_m(j)$, and $p_d(j)$ respectively. When $j = \pm 2$, the alternative branching schemes are used.

j	Transition probabilities			Node rates, R (%)			
	p_u	p_m	p_d	$i = 0$	$i = 1$	$i = 2$	$i = 3$
2	0.8993	0.0111	0.0896			10.637	11.352
1	0.1236	0.6576	0.2188		8.1515	8.9883	9.7028
0	0.1667	0.6667	0.1667	5.0928	6.5026	7.3393	8.0538
−1	0.2188	0.6576	0.1236		4.8536	5.6904	6.4049
−2	0.0896	0.0111	0.8993			4.0414	4.7559

TABLE 20.5. Computing the price of a bond that pays $1 at time $2 \, \Delta t$ (2 years). Each value is calculated as
$$v_{i,j} = (p_u v_{i+1,j+1} + p_m v_{i+1,j} + p_d v_{i+1,j-1}) \exp(-R_{i,j} \Delta t).$$

j	Transition probabilities			Bond price		
	p_u	p_m	p_d	$i = 0$	$i = 1$	$i = 2$
2	0.8993	0.0111	0.0896			1.0
1	0.1236	0.6576	0.2188		0.9217	1.0
0	0.1667	0.6667	0.1667	0.8906	0.9370	1.0
−1	0.2188	0.6576	0.1236		0.9526	1.0
−2	0.0896	0.0111	0.8993			1.0

TABLE 20.6. Computing the option payoff at each terminal node $(i = 3)$ on the tree. The Δt-period rate R is the rate that applies from 3 to 4 years. The instantaneous rate r is computed using equation (20.6). The forward rate at time 3 years was computed to be 0.078304. On the basis of this, equation (20.5) gives
$$A(3, 4) = 0.994229, \qquad A(3, 9) = 0.881944,$$
$$B(3, 4) = 0.951626, \qquad B(3, 9) = 4.511884.$$
The bond price $P(3, 9)$, is computed with equation (20.4) and the option payoff is $100 \max[0.63 - P(3, 9), 0]$.

j	Δt-period rate, R	Instantaneous rate, r	Bond price	Option payoff
2	0.113517	0.113206	0.529196	10.080445
1	0.097028	0.095878	0.572229	5.777133
0	0.080538	0.078550	0.618761	1.123884
−1	0.064049	0.061222	0.669078	0.0
−2	0.047559	0.043895	0.723486	0.0

takes place at nodes $\pm j^*$, where j^* is the smallest integer greater than $-0.184/M$. In this case, j^* is 2. The data defining the initial tree is shown in Table 20.2.

The rates at each node in the tree at each time step are now shifted up by some amount α, chosen so that the revised tree correctly prices discount bonds. Since there are nodes at the 1-, 2-, and 3-year points, we need the discount bond prices corresponding to these dates as well as the 4-year price, one time step beyond the option maturity. When the option price is calculated, the 9-year bond price will be required as well. This data, interpolated from the data in Table 20.1, is shown in Table 20.3. Table 20.3 also shows the value of α required to fit the bond prices at each time step. An efficient procedure for implying the value of α is given in Chapter 18. For reference purposes, the instantaneous forward rate and the instantaneous values of α (based on equation (20.8)) are also shown.

Combining the α's from Table 20.3 with the rates and probabilities in Table 20.2 produces the complete tree. The tree is presented in Table 20.4, which gives the Δt-period rates at each node of the tree and the probabilities of branching from one node to the next. Table 20.5 shows how this tree can be used to compute the price of a 2-year discount bond. At each step the bond price is computed as the discounted value of the

TABLE 20.7. Discounting the option price back through the tree. At the third step, the option value is as given in Table 20.6. The computed value at earlier steps is

$$v_{i,j} = (p_u v_{i+1,j+1} + p_m v_{i+1,j} + p_d v_{i+1,j-1}) \exp(-R_{i,j}\,\Delta t),$$

where $R_{i,j}$, the rate at node j and time step i, is $\alpha_i + j\,\Delta r$. Note that, when $j = \pm 2$, non-standard branching applies. When $j = 2$ the computed value is

$$v_{i,j} = (p_u v_{i+1,j} + p_m v_{i+1,j-1} + p_d v_{i+1,j-2}) \exp(-R_{i,j}\,\Delta t),$$

and when $j = -2$ the computed value is

$$v_{i,j} = (p_u v_{i+1,j+2} + p_m v_{i+1,j+1} + p_d v_{i+1,j}) \exp(-R_{i,j}\Delta t).$$

				Time step, i			
j	p_u	p_m	p_d	0	1	2	3
2	0.8993	0.0111	0.0896			8.2987	10.0804
1	0.1236	0.6576	0.2188		4.1977	4.8362	5.7771
0	0.1667	0.6667	0.1667	1.8734	1.7854	1.5910	1.1239
−1	0.2188	0.6576	0.1236		0.4885	0.2323	0.0000
−2	0.0896	0.0111	0.8993			0.0967	0.0000
			α (%)	5.0928	6.5026	7.3393	8.0538

TABLE 20.8. Value of a 3-year put option on a 9-year, $100, zero-coupon bond. The strike price is $63. The volatility parameters are $a = 0.1$ and $\sigma = 0.01$.

Steps	Tree-based value	Analytic value
10	1.8491	1.8093
30	1.8179	1.8093
50	1.8060	1.8093
100	1.8128	1.8093
200	1.8089	1.8093
500	1.8090	1.8093

expected value at the next time step. Calculations of the type shown in Table 20.5 are used to determine what value of α is needed at each time step in order to replicate the discount bond prices. Table 20.6 shows the calculations required to compute the discount bond prices at the option maturity, 3 years. Finally, Table 20.7 shows the discounting of the option value back through the tree.

The results of pricing this put option for trees of different sizes are shown in Table 20.8. This example provides a good test of one's implementation of the model, because the gradient of the zero curve changes sharply immediately after the expiration of the option. Small errors in the construction and use of the tree are liable to have a big effect on the option values obtained. For example, when 100 time steps are used, the value of the option is reduced by about $0.25 if the Δt-period rate is assumed to be the instantaneous rate.

20.3 MAKING VOLATILITY PARAMETERS TIME-DEPENDENT

When a and σ are functions of time, the model in equation (20.1) becomes

$$dx = [\theta(t) - a(t)x] \, dt + \sigma(t) \, dz. \qquad (20.9)$$

The three functions of time in this diffusion equation each play a separate role. The function $\theta(t)$ is chosen so that the prices of all discount bonds are matched at the initial time. The other two functions provide two extra degrees of freedom that allow us to match the initial volatility of all zero-coupon rates and the volatility of the short rate at all future times. The tree can then be tuned to price not only the zero-coupon bonds but also a set of interest rate derivatives at their current market prices. The initial volatility of all rates depends on $\sigma(0)$ and $a(t)$. The volatility of the short rate at future times is determined by $\sigma(t)$. Unless $\sigma(t)$ and $a(t)$ are constants, the volatility term structure is non-stationary.

Our tree-building procedure can be extended to accommodate the model in equation (20.9). Analogously to the constant a and σ case, we begin by building a tree for x^*, where

$$dx^* = -a(t)x^* \, dt + \sigma(t) \, dz.$$

We first choose the times $t_0, t_1, \ldots, t_n$ at which nodes will be placed, where $t_0 = 0$ and $t_i = i\,\Delta t$ for $i = 0, \ldots, n$. The vertical (x^* dimension) spacing between adjacent nodes at time t_{i+1} is then set equal to $\sqrt{3V_i}$, where

$$V_i = \sigma^2(t_i)(1 - e^{-2a(t_i)\Delta t})/2a(t_i).$$

Suppose that the value of x^* at the jth node at time t_i is $x^*_{i,j}$. The mean and standard deviation of x^* at time t_{i+1} conditional on $x^* = x^*_{i,j}$ at time t_i are approximately $x^*_{i,j} + M_i x^*_{i,j}$ and $\sqrt{V_i}$, where

$$M_i = (e^{-a(t_i)\Delta t} - 1).$$

We match these by branching from $x^*_{i,j}$ to one of $x^*_{i+1,k-1}$, $x^*_{i+1,k}$, or $x^*_{i+1,k+1}$, where k is chosen so that $x^*_{i+1,k}$ is as close as possible to $x^*_{i,j} + M_i x^*_{i,j}\Delta t$. We then calculate the displacements $\alpha(t)$ necessary for the tree to match the initial term structure.

The $a(t)$ and $\sigma(t)$ can be set in advance of the numerical procedure. Alternatively, it is not difficult to devise a numerical procedure that chooses $a(t)$ and $\sigma(t)$ so that the initial prices of caps or swap options (or both) are matched. When used for $x = \log r$, this type of tree-building procedure has the advantage over Black and Karasinski (1991) that the length of the time step is under the control of the user.

It seems appealing to take advantage of all the degrees of freedom in a model to exactly fit initial market data. However, the resulting non-stationarity in the volatility term structure may have many untoward and unexpected effects. To illustrate this, we use the $x = r$ model,

$$dr = [\theta(t) - a(t)r] \, dt + \sigma(t) \, dz,$$

and show the effect of matching cap prices.

Caps are usually priced using Black's model, under which the price at time zero of a caplet expiring at T on a rate that applies from T to $T + \tau$ is

$$C = \tau P e^{-R(T+\tau)}[F(T, T + \tau)N(d_1) - XN(d_2)],$$

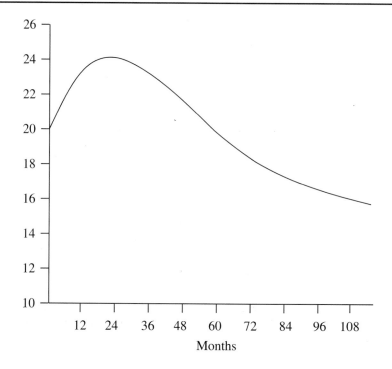

FIGURE 20.3. Black's volatility for at-the-money caplets reset monthly.

where P is the notional principal, R is the zero-coupon rate with a maturity $T + \tau$, $F(T, T + \tau)$ is the forward rate for the period T to $T + \tau$, X is the cap rate, and

$$d_1 = \frac{\log[F(T, T + \tau)/X]}{v(T)\sqrt{T}} + \frac{v(T)\sqrt{T}}{2}, \qquad d_2 = d_1 - v(T)\sqrt{T},$$

where $v(T)$ is the volatility for the caplet expiring at T.

The data set that we will use for calibration consists of the market prices of at-the-money caps that are reset monthly ($\tau = 1$ month). The particular $v(T)$ function we assume for illustration purposes is shown in Figure 20.3.[5] This has a similar shape to the $v(T)$ function commonly observed in the market. We assume the term structure is flat at 7% continuously compounded.

In order to match the Black volatilities, we first used them in conjunction with Black's model to calculate caplet prices. We then match the caplet prices in two ways:

[5] This volatility curve is $v(T) = [1 + bT + c(1 - e^{-dT})]v(0)$ for $T \leq 5$, $b = 0.1$, $c = 0.5$, $d = 0.8$, and $v(0) = 0.2$. The curve was extended beyond $T = 5$ by assuming that the gradient of $v(T)T$ when $T > 5$ equals its gradient when $T = 5$.

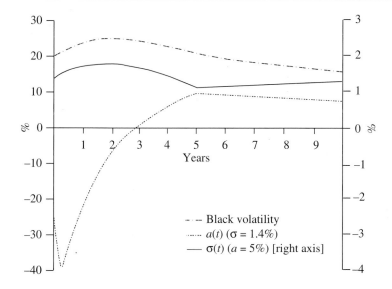

FIGURE 20.4. Value of $a(t)$ when $\sigma = 1.4\%$ (left-hand scale) and value of $\sigma(t)$ when $a = 5\%$ (right-hand scale) required to replicate caplet prices computed from Black volatilities in Figure 20.3.

1. We fix the short rate standard deviation σ and allow the reversion rate a to be a function of time.
2. We fix a and allow σ to be a function of time.

Figure 20.4 shows the value of $a(t)$ required to fit the market data when σ is fixed[6] at 1.4% and the value of $\sigma(t)$ required to fit the market data when a is fixed at 5%. It can be seen that the implied $a(t)$ and $\sigma(t)$ exhibit severe non-stationarity. Although by construction this non-stationarity leads to caplets being priced correctly, it is liable to lead to unacceptable results when used to price other instruments.

Any instrument whose price depends on the future volatility structure, rather than today's volatility structure, is liable to be mispriced by a model with time-dependent volatility parameters. One example of such a security is an American-style call option, where the decision to exercise at some future date depends on the volatility structure at that date. Another example is a caption, an option to buy a cap, where the decision to exercise the option at expiration depends on the value of the cap at that time.

[6] The choices of the fixed value for σ and the fixed value for a are arbitrary, although the implied values of $a(t)$ and $\sigma(t)$ are representative of the type of non-stationarity that results from the given volatility structure. The best fixed value of σ (or a) to use might be the one that minimizes the variance of the implied $a(t)$ (or $\sigma(t)$).

This example illustrates the types of problems that can arise when a model is implemented in such a way that the volatility structure is not stationary. It is a problem that afflicts all Markov interest rate models including the Black–Derman–Toy and Black–Karasinski models. By fitting a one-factor Markov interest rate model to today's option prices, we make it exactly reflect the initial volatility structure. However, we are also unwittingly making a statement about how the volatility term structure will evolve in the future. Using all the degrees of freedom in the model to fit the volatility exactly constitutes an over-parametrization of the model. It is our opinion that there should be no more than one time-varying parameter used in Markov models of the term structure evolution and that this should be used to fit the initial term structure.

20.4 OTHER ISSUES

There are a number of other practical issues to consider when implementing Hull–White trees for valuing interest rate derivatives. In this section we review a number of these and indicate how they can be handled.

In our description of the tree-building procedure in Chapter 18, it was assumed that the length of the time step is constant. In practice, it is sometimes desirable to change the length of the time step.[7] Changing the length of the time step is straightforward. When drawing the tree for x^*, we first choose the times $t_0, t_1, \ldots, t_n$ at which nodes will be placed, where $t_0 = 0$. Defining $\Delta t_i = t_{i+1} - t_i$ for $i = 0, \ldots, n - 1$, we then set the vertical (x^* dimension) spacing between adjacent nodes at time t_{i+1} equal to $\sqrt{3V_i}$, where

$$V_i = \sigma^2(1 - e^{-2a\Delta t_i})/2a.$$

From this point, the construction is similar to the procedure followed when the volatility parameters are a function of time. Suppose that the value of x^* at the jth node at time t_i is $x^*_{i,j}$. The mean and standard deviation of x^* at time t_{i+1} conditional on $x^* = x^*_{i,j}$ at time t_i are approximately $x^*_{i,j} + M_i x^*_{i,j}$ and $\sqrt{V_i}$, where

$$M_i = (e^{-a\Delta t_i} - 1).$$

We match these by branching from $x^*_{i,j}$ to one of $x^*_{i+1,k-1}$, $x^*_{i+1,k}$, or

[7] Suppose the lognormal model is used to value a European 6-month option on a 5-year bond. It might be appropriate to use a longer Δt between 6 months and 5 years than during the first six months. This is because the part of the tree between 6 months and 5 years is used only to value the underlying bond.

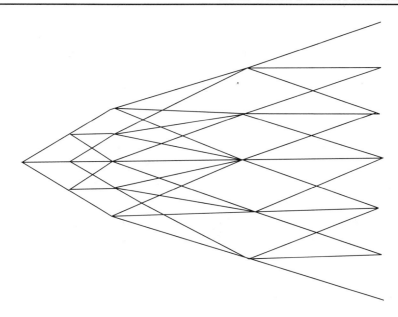

FIGURE 20.5. The tree for x^* when the length of the time step changes.

$x^*_{i+1,k+1}$, where k is chosen so that $x^*_{i+1,k}$ is as close as possible to $x^*_{i,j} + M_i x^*_{i,j} \Delta t_i$. Note that, whenever the size of the time step changes, $t_i \neq t_{i+1}$, the vertical (x^* dimension) spacing between nodes increases by $\sqrt{\Delta t_{i+1}/\Delta t_i}$. This means that the branching is non-standard at points when the length of the time step changes. Figure 20.5 illustrates the tree that is constructed when the time step increases by a factor of 3 after two time steps.

The tree for x is constructed from the tree for x^* to match the initial zero-coupon yield curve as described in Chapter 18. Note that, when the length of the time step changes from t_i to t_{i+1}, the interest rates considered at the nodes automatically change from the t_i-period rates to the t_{i+1} rates.

Another issue in the construction of the tree concerns cash flows that occur between nodal dates. Suppose a cash flow occurs at time τ when the immediately preceding nodal date is t_i and the immediately following nodal date is t_{i+1}. One approach is to discount the cash flow from time τ to the nodes at time t_i using estimates of the $\tau - t_i$ rates prevailing at the nodes at time t_i.[8] Another approach is to assume that a proportion $(\tau - t_i)/(t_{i+1} - t_i)$ of the cash flow occurs at time t_{i+1} while the remainder

[8] In the case of the Hull–White $x = r$ model, these rates can be calculated analytically.

occurs at time t_i.[9] A final approach is to avoid the problem altogether by changing the length of the time step so that every payment date is also a nodal date.

Barrier options present a further problem in the use of the tree because convergence tends to be slow when nodes do not lie exactly on barriers. In the case of an interest rate option, the barrier is typically expressed in terms of a bond price or a particular rate. When $x = r$, analytic results can be used to express the barrier as a function of the Δt-period rate. Non-standard branching can then be used to ensure that nodes always lie on the barrier. Ritchken (1995) describes such an approach, and shows that a substantial improvement in performance is possible with it. An alternative approach that has more general applicability is to extend the idea suggested by Derman *et al.* (1995) to interest rate trees. This approach involves using a procedure to correct values of the derivative calculated at nodes close to a barrier. A final problem in the use of interest rate trees is path dependence. This can sometimes be handled in the way described by Hull and White (1993). The requirements for the Hull–White method to work are:

1. The value of the derivative at each node must depend on just one function of the path for the short rate r (e.g., the maximum, minimum, or average value).
2. In order to update the path function as we move forward through the tree, we need to know only the previous value of the function and the new value of r.

Hull and White show how their approach can be used for index-amortizing swaps and mortgage-backed securities. The relevant path function in each case is the remaining principal.

20.5 SUMMARY

The Hull–White tree-building procedure is a flexible approach to constructing trees for a wide range of different one-factor models of the term structure. The tree is constructed in such a way that it is exactly consistent with the initial term structure. In this paper we have shown how the basic procedure presented in our earlier paper can be extended. Some of these extensions involve the use of analytic results and some

---

[9] This approach has the effect of apportioning the cash flow to nodal dates, while ensuring that the expected time when the cash flow occurs is correct.

involve changing the geometry of the tree to reflect special features of the derivative under consideration. We have devoted some time in this paper to a discussion of what happens when the volatility parameters are made time-dependent. It not difficult to extend the Hull–White tree to incorporate time-dependent parameters so that the prices of caps or swap options (or both) are matched. However, this is liable to result in unacceptable assumptions about the evolution of volatilities.

REFERENCES

Black, F., E. Derman, and W. Toy. "A one-factor model of interest rates and its application to Treasury bond options." *Financial Analysts Journal*, January–February 1990, pp. 33–39.

Black, F. and P. Karasinski. "Bond and option pricing when short rates are lognormal." *Financial Analysts Journal*, July–August, 1991, pp. 52–59.

Ho, T. S. Y., and S.-B. Lee. "Term structure movements and the pricing interest rate contingent claims." *Journal of Finance*, 41 (December 1986), pp. 1011–1029.

Hull, J., and A. White. "Pricing interest rate derivative securities." *Review of Financial Studies*, 3, 4 (1990), pp. 573–592.

Hull, J., and A. White. "Efficient procedures for valuing European and American path-dependent derivatives." *Journal of Derivatives*, 1, 1 (Fall 1993), pp. 21–31. Also Chapter 8 in this book.

Hull, J., and A. White. "Numerical procedures for implementing term structure models I: Single-factor models." *Journal of Derivatives*, 2, 1 (Fall 1994a), pp. 7–16. Also Chapter 18 in this book.

Hull, J., and A. White. "Numerical procedures for implementing term structure models II: Two-factor models." *Journal of Derivatives*, 2, 1 (Winter 1994b), pp. 37–48. Also Chapter 19 in this book.

Kijima, M., and I. Nagayama. "Efficient numerical procedures for the Hull–White extended Vasicek model." *The Journal of Financial Engineering*, 3, 4 (September–December 1994), pp. 275–292.

Pelsser, A. "An efficient algorithm for calculating prices in the Hull–White model." Derivative Product Research and Development Working Paper, ABN Amro Bank, 1994.

Ritchken, P. "On pricing barrier options." *Journal of Derivatives*, 3, 2 (Winter 1995), pp. 19–28.

Index